ILLINOIS STUDIES IN LANGUAGE AND LITERATURE

Vol. XXX Nos. 2–3

THE LANGUAGE OF THE LATIN TEXT OF CODEX BEZAE

With an Index Verborum

BY
ROBERT C. STONE

WIPF & STOCK · Eugene, Oregon

Wipf and Stock Publishers
199 W 8th Ave, Suite 3
Eugene, OR 97401

The Language of the Latin Text of Codex Bezae
With an Index Verborum
By Stone, Robert C.
ISBN 13: 978-1-60608-750-3
Publication date 6/9/2009
Previously published by University of Illinois Press, 1946

PREFACE

In spite of several attempts to determine the provenience of Codex Bezae, no study of the linguistic characteristics of either the Latin or the Greek text has been undertaken expressly to see what light might thus be thrown on the problem. This study is intended to supply that lack so far as the Latin text is concerned.

The transcript used as a basis for my work is that of Scrivener, 1864, which I have collated carefully with the facsimile of the MS. itself, published at Cambridge, 1899, and have corrected upon one or two minor points in a few places (p. 10). Since this study aims to discover, through an analysis of the original linguistic phenomena presented by the MS., any possible clue as to its provenience, only the readings of the original hand have been considered, and all corrections inserted by later hands have been ignored. Similarly, the several leaves added in the ninth century to replace lost portions of the codex (p. 10, note 11) have also been omitted from consideration.

It is inevitable in Latin versions of the Bible that there should remain traces of the influence of the Greek from which they were ultimately derived. This is especially true of bilingual codices, in which greater conformity between the two texts is desirable. Therefore it has been necessary throughout this study to indicate the constructions which seem to be mere imitations of Greek usage, and to distinguish them from those which are peculiar to the Latin.

In the quotations of illustrative examples from the text, I have given the Latin exactly as it appears in Scrivener, without punctuation or capital letters, except in the case of proper nouns, where it seemed best to use capitals. The erroneous spellings have also been retained; but in cases where any obscurity arises on this account, the correct form appears in parenthesis after the incorrect, e.g. *berua* (*uerba*), except in the Index.

The word "scribe" is used in the singular throughout the text merely for convenience. It is meant to include the person who originally made the translation, and any subsequent copyist, or copyists, if there were more than one.

This work is an outgrowth of my doctoral dissertation, written in 1936, and has been revised extensively for the present purpose. I am greatly indebted to the late Professor W. A. Oldfather, of the University of Illinois, for his guidance and advice since the inception of this work. I must also express my gratitude to Professor W. P. Hatch, of the Episcopal Theological School at Cambridge, Massachusetts, who read the typescript of the book, for his useful criticisms and suggestions, many of which have found their way into the following pages. Grateful appreciation is also extended to Dr. K. M. Abbott, of Ohio State University, for his help with certain matters in the section on phonology, and for suggestions concerning bibliography.

R. C. S.

CONTENTS

CHAPTER I

INTRODUCTION

THE RIDDLE of the origin and history of the Graeco-Latin Codex Bezae (Greek D; Latin d) has resisted efforts of scholars to solve it for more than a century. The problem is still veiled in obscurity, particularly in relation to the origin of the MS., but its history at least has begun to yield to inquiry.

Codex Bezae was supposedly obtained by Theodore Beza, the Genevan reformer, from the monastery of St. Irenaeus at Lyons in 1562, the year in which the Huguenot troops sacked the city. The MS. had been taken some years earlier (1546) to the council of Trent by William a Prato, Bishop of Clermont, and was there used to support certain Greek readings then under debate.[1] While in Italy it was collated, and many readings were sent to R. Stephanus by a friend of his for inclusion in the apparatus of his 1550 edition of the Greek Testament.[2] Following its employment at the council of Trent it was doubtless returned to the monastery of St. Irenaeus, whence it had been borrowed. Beza himself made slight use of the MS. in his editions, and in 1581 presented it to the University of Cambridge, where it has remained ever since.

The history of Codex Bezae prior to the sixteenth century is more obscure, although some portions of it have been established with considerable certitude. That it was in France in the tenth century is contended by Harris.[3] While the fact is true, as we shall see below, Harris' argument does not hold, because the "Bezan annotator" to whom he refers belongs not to the tenth century but before 800.[4] Even as early as the ninth century Codex Bezae seems almost certainly to have been in Lyons. That the scholarly Bishop of Lyons, Florus (†ca. 860), may have brought the codex there is suggested by Quentin,[5] who has based his contention on the agreement of certain scriptural quotations in the Martyrology of Ado (written at Lyons in 850–860) with the text of d. The theory is well elaborated, and receives confirmation from some interesting facts noted by E. A. Lowe.[6] In the colophon to Mark, which is among the added pages written in the ninth century, a blue ink is used (folio 348). Blue ink is rare in Latin manuscripts, and Lowe finds it in but two others, both from Lyons, one of the ninth, the other of the eighth century. A peculiar interrogation mark is also noted in these added pages, and this is found in but five other manuscripts, all connected with Lyons and perhaps written or annotated

[1] Cf. the references given by J. H. Ropes, *The Text of Acts*, in Jackson and Lake, *Beginnings of Christianity*, pt. I, vol. III, p. lvi, note 4.

[2] Stephanus refers to the MS. as β'; for its identification with our Codex Bezae, see Scrivener, *Bezae Codex Cantabrigiensis*, pp. ix–x.

[3] This contention is based on the fact that the Sortes Sanctorum in D are from the same original as those in g', the St. Germain Latin Bible. Harris says (*Codex Bezae*, p. 11): "Moreover, the two series of annotations belong to nearly the same period of time; the S. Germain MS. being of the ninth century, and the Bezan annotator being referred by Scrivener to the tenth. And since the two Codices in question are both found in modern times in French abbeys, we may perhaps be allowed to assume that the Codex Bezae was in France in the tenth century."

[4] *Infra*, p. 10, note 9.

[5] "Le Codex Bezae à Lyon au IXᵉ siècle?" *Rev. Ben.*, 23(1906), 1–23.

[6] "The Codex Bezae and Lyons," *JTS*, 25(1924), 270–74. Cf. also the same author's *Codices Lugdunenses Antiquissimi*, Lyons, 1924.

by Florus himself. Thus Codex Bezae was doubtless at Lyons when the added pages were written.[7]

Of the history of the MS. before the ninth century nothing certain is known. Some general conclusions have been reached by Lowe.[8] All the annotators (except one) and all liturgical marks and sortes are concerned with the Greek portion of the MS. None of these annotators is later than the year 800.[9] Therefore, Lowe concludes that until about that year the MS. lay in a centre where Greek was the literary and ecclesiastical language; but that after 800 it lay in some Latin centre. This accounts for the lack of later annotators, and agrees well with Quentin's theory.[10]

Codex Bezae is written in a rather large uncial hand, and there is a striking resemblance between the shape of the Greek and the Latin letters. Each page of the MS. contains only one column, the Greek being on the left-hand page and the Latin on the right when the book lies open. It is written in short sense-lines or *στίχοι*. As the MS. now stands it contains, with some omissions,[11] Matthew, John, Luke, Mark, 3 John 11–15 (in Latin only), and Acts. There has been much speculation as to what the MS. originally contained. To judge by the numbering of the quires, sixty-six leaves are missing between the Gospels and Acts. The Apocalypse and the three Epistles of John would about fill these missing sheets.[12]

The scribe of Codex Bezae was frequently careless in the technical execution of his work. There are at least one hundred and fifty-seven palaeographical errors, such as dittography, haplography, and transposition of lines.[13] Of the many passages confused in meaning we shall speak in a later chapter. At this point mention should also be made of the extremely short list of mostly trivial errors noted in Scrivener's edition. The following table will show them:[14]

Reference	*Scrivener*	*MS.*
Mt 1.16	ihm	ihm
Mt 1.21	vocavis	uocauis
Mt 4.7	temptavis	temptauis
Mt 5.16	videant	uideant
Mt 17.14	eum	cum
Mt 18.3	convertamini	conuertamini
Mt 18.16	verbum	uerbum
Mt 23.23	crauiora	grauiora

[7] Harris, *op. cit.*, p. 13, comes to the conclusion that D was "not far away from France" in the ninth century, on grounds of the lectionary system, which agrees closely with the readings of the seventh century lectionary of Luxeuil.

[8] "The Codex Bezae," *JTS*, 14(1912–13), 385–88.

[9] A. S. Hunt, as quoted by Lowe, *loc. cit.*, p. 388. Clark, *Acts of the Apostles*, p. lvii, says he asked Hunt to re-examine the marginal notes, and that his opinion remained the same.

[10] This position is accepted as sound by Clark, *Acts*, p. 177.

[11] These are, in Greek: Mt 1.1–20; 6.20–9.2; 27.2–12; J 1.16–3.26; A8.29–10.14; 21.2–10, 15–18; 22.10–20; 22.29–28.31; in Latin: Mt 1.1–11; 6.8–8.27, 26.65–27.1; J 1.1–3.16; A 8.20–10.4; 20.31–21.2; 21.7–10; 22.2–10; 22.20–28.31. Nine of the leaves are of later date (*saec. ix*, Lowe) and comprise the following, in Greek: Mt 3.8–16; J 18.4–20.13; Mk 16.16–20; in Latin: Mt 2.21–3.7; J 18.2–20.1; Mk 16.6–20.

[12] See Ropes, *op. cit.*, p. lxviii, and references; also Scrivener, *op. cit.*, pp. xiv–xv.

[13] Some of these errors seem to be due to phonology; the scribe would repeat the phrase to himself as he wrote, and write as it sounded. Cf. Mt 23.17, *autemplum = aut templum;* J 16.30, *hocredimus = hoc credimus;* L 4.7, *eruntua = erunt tua;* and others. Cf. the theory held by Resch, and based on this very phenomenon, that Codex Bezae was written from dictation: Harris, *Four Lectures on the Western Text*, pp. 3, 11. Harris' conclusion is just: such errors may or may not be due to dictation; all can be explained by haplography.

[14] Cf. also L 24.5, where the MS. looks like *faetae;* and Acts 21.18, where *omnes* is omitted by Scrivener because it was written *secunda manu*. These errors, and those noted above, concern only the Latin text of the MS.

Mt 23.29	justorum	iustorum
Mt 28.6	locu	locū
J 6.12	sui	suis
J 16.29	inullum	nullum
L 21.25	slo	salo
Mk 1.14	galileam	galilaeam
Mk 3.31,34	ejus	eius
A 12.19	invenisse	inuenisset
A 14.13	ciuitate	ciuitatē
A 14.15	dm	$\overline{dm}$

Codex Bezae has commonly been assigned to the sixth century, but there is no reason for denying it an earlier date. F. G. Kenyon[15] states that there would be no palaeographical difficulty in a fifth-century date if other evidence seemed to point in that direction, and E. A. Lowe[16] definitely puts the MS. in the fifth century. There are two other bits of evidence which point to the same conclusion. F. C. Burkitt[17] argues from the work of corrector G, who occupied himself with the Latin side of the MS. throughout Matthew and the early chapters of Acts. He dates G in the fifth century and says he is contemporary with the MS. itself, that he examined it and made his corrections before it was put into public use. It is pointed out that G makes his corrections on his own authority, not on that of any other Latin version, and this signifies to Burkitt that he must have worked in the fifth century, because after about A.D. 500 no one "would dare to have an opinion of his own as to what was the appropriate way to render the Greek of the Gospels into Latin."[18] Scrivener's objection to the fifth century, "the debased dialect of the Latin version,"[19] is dismissed with the comment that the Latin was meant merely to be a "crib," and would in this capacity have no need to maintain any great dignity of language.

J. Chapman arrives at the same conclusion as to date from a different line of reasoning.[20] He states that the parent of Codex Bezae had the Western order of the Gospels, i.e. Mt, Mk, J, L, and that in D this had been changed to the Old Latin order, i.e. Mt, J, L, Mk.[21] He then concludes that the MS. was "written in a Latin country where the Old Latin order was considered a matter of course, and before the Greek order introduced by St. Jerome had become well known. Such conditions are most unlikely in South Italy, Sardinia, or Gaul after ca. 450, one might say after 420. The beginning of the fifth century seems the most probable date."[22] This conclusion, of course, breaks down if we accept the opinion of Lowe that before 800 the MS. lay in a centre where Greek was the literary and ecclesiastical language, and where all evidence points to almost exclusive Greek interest in the MS.

[15] "Review of Codex Bezae," *JTS*, 1(1899–1900), 293–99.
[16] *Codices Lugd. Antiq.*, p. 49.
[17] "The Date of Codex Bezae," *JTS*, 3(1901–02), 501–13.
[18] Kenyon, in the article referred to above, assigns G to the seventh century; and in his *Handbook to Textual Criticism of the New Testament*, p. 91, he points out that Burkitt's argument, based on such fine distinction of hands and individual peculiarities of correctors, is insecure. We agree, but the possibility nevertheless remains.
[19] *Op. cit.*, p. xvi.
[20] *ZNTW*, 6 (1905), 339 ff.
[21] His position is based on the use of the dots between the words in some of the books and the absence of this practice in others; also on the spelling of John (*iohanes* or *iohannes*).
[22] *Loc. cit.*, p. 346.

The problem of the provenience of Codex Bezae is of great interest, and has given rise to many conflicting views. As long ago as 1793, Dr. Thomas Kipling, who first brought out an edition of the MS., ventured the suggestion that it was written in Egypt. He based his opinion on four points, the rudeness of the Latin version, the large number of Alexandrian forms, errors in transcription in the Greek text, and certain liturgical notes peculiar to Egypt. These points were all rejected, and rightly so, as invalid by Scrivener.[23] Kipling was followed by David Schulz, in his *Disputatio de Codice D*, 1827; but from that time onward no one has favored the Egyptian origin of our MS. until A. C. Clark[24] recently declared himself inclined to accept it. That Codex Bezae is a provincial product, i.e. non-Italian, has been set forth repeatedly by Lowe,[25] and Clark follows this opinion on grounds of the extraordinary Graecisms found in the Latin version, which point to a locality where Greek was more familiar than Latin. Some of the errors of rendering Greek words into Latin, however, would not have been made by a real Greek. The person who composed the Latin version, then, was neither Latin nor Greek, but someone who knew Greek imperfectly and Latin even less well. So Clark looks for a trilingual locality where Greek and Latin were known beside the native tongue, and his choice narrows down to Palestine and Egypt. That knowledge of Greek and Latin was widespread in these localities, we know both from inscriptions and papyri, as well as from literary sources.[26]

With these preliminaries Clark proceeds to set forth his reasons for preferring Egypt. First, Egypt has been the home of many bilingual manuscripts; second, the use of *στίχοι*, such as appear in D, is also found in a number of Egyptian bilinguals; third, and most important, is the fact that the Michigan papyrus, a third-century fragment of Acts,[27] shows that a text nearly identical with D existed at an early date in Egypt, and the MS. of Thomas[28] indicates by its quotations that a similar text existed near Alexandria in the seventh century. Clark supposes, accordingly, that D was written in Egypt some time in the fifth century; but he somewhat weakens the force of his argument by adding that, due to the wide diffusion of this text throughout the Roman world at an early date, other explanations are possible.[29]

[23] *Op. cit.*, p. xxix.

[24] *Op. cit.*, pp. lv–lxiv.

[25] *JTS*, 14(1913), 385, and *ibid.*, 25(1924), 271.

[26] The *Passio Perpetuae* (202–03) and the *Peregrinatio Aetheriae* (end of saec. iv) are interesting in this connection for certain passages which illustrate the use of bilingual or trilingual MSS. in the service of the church.

[27] H. A. Sanders, "A Papyrus Fragment of Acts in the Michigan Collection," *HTR*, 20 (1927) 1 ff.

[28] The MS. of Thomas is the revision of the version made for Philoxenus by Polycarp, and was done by Thomas of Heraclea in 616–617. This faithful Syriac translation was prepared at Alexandria from a Greek MS. many of whose "readings . . . agree closely with D" (Clark, *op. cit.*, p. xvi).

[29] Clark, *op. cit.*, p. lxiv, also adds a few points which he says do not prove, but are consistent with, his theory: the b-d type of uncial, found only in one other uncial manuscript, that of the Pauline Epistles, which Tischendorf refers to Egypt; the order of the Gospels, which agrees with that of the Freer MS., fifth century, the only Greek uncial manuscript of the Gospels positively known to be Egyptian; certain abbreviations of *nomina sacra*. For others who are favorable toward an Egyptian provenience, see Chantrain's review of Clark's *Acts*, in *Rev. Phil.*, 61(1935), 215, and Lietzmann, in *Ant.*, 11(1935), 147. Professor Kirsopp Lake (*Journal of Biblical Literature*, LIII(1934), p. 45) writes of this theory, "At present . . . I am enchanted with Professor Clark's view that codex Bezae comes from the Greco-Roman world of Alexandria. Whether this enchantment will endure, time—and perhaps thought—must settle, but the theory is provocative and stimulating." Professor W. H. P. Hatch, in *The "Western" Text of the Gospels* (Seabury-Western Theological Seminary, Evanston, 1937), p. 6, note, says, "The

We must admit, however, that the conditions in Egypt during the period in question (third to fifth century) were favorable for the production of such a MS. as Codex Bezae.

Another piece of corroborating evidence may be mentioned here. Professor H. A. Sanders, after a careful examination of the Washington Manuscript of the four Gospels,[30] has made some interesting observations. The Washington Manuscript was written in the fourth century, and its home is Egypt. It closely corresponds to D in method of punctuation and paragraphing, and has a similar text. This may add some weight to the probability that D also was written in Egypt, at a slightly later date.

F. H. Chase[31] has argued that Antioch, in Syria, was the birthplace of the Bezan Text, at least of Acts, because of certain peculiarities in Greek readings which can best be explained by reference to an underlying Syriac text. That such an Old Syriac version existed at an early date Chase[32] assumes from the use of a text closely allied with Codex Bezae, and based on a Syriac version, at Carthage by Tertullian (160–240), in South Gaul by St. Irenaeus (†202), and at Antioch by Theophilus (ca. 180). The Syriac text must have been very early, then, to allow time for the formation of the Syriacised Greek which these writers used.[33] Furthermore, Antioch was the kind of a city in which such a Syriacised Greek text would naturally arise, Greeks and Syrians dwelling there in large numbers, and even intermarrying until the races were well mixed. These observations open up a possibility that D might have originated there. The further fact that we have another text of the same Syriacising tendency, and one which is definitely connected with Antioch (the fragment of the Gospel of Peter), adds a measure of support to Chase's argument, but certainly does not raise probability to a point "little short of certainty." For that Codex Bezae was written at Antioch, or anywhere else in the East for that matter, does not necessarily follow from the above statement of the possibilities of the case. Harris has shown that Oriental and Greek influence was prevalent even as far west as Gaul at an early date,[34] and Chase himself, as we have seen, refers to the use of a Syriacised text by Irenaeus. Codex Bezae, then, may easily have been influenced by the Syriac even in such a remote locality as Gaul. The arguments propounded by Sanday to support his statement that the Latin version may have been made at Antioch[35] have been justly condemned as inadequate by Ropes.[36]

Southern Italy has often been suggested as the home of Codex Bezae. F. E.

---

present writer also inclines to the view that the Bezan Manuscript orignated in Egypt." In personal correspondence with the author, Professor Hatch says he bases his belief on certain errors which could have been made only by a Copt. For instance, the scribe often confuses *τ* and *δ*, writing *τε* for *δέ*. *δ* occurs in Greek loanwords in Coptic, but not in native words; *τ* is very frequent in Coptic words. There is also some confusion of *l* and *r*, which were both represented by the same sign in hieroglyphic, and a Copt might naturally make this blunder.

[30] *The New Testament MSS. in the Freer Collection, Part I,* "The Washington Manuscript of the Four Gospels," Macmillan, 1912.

[31] *The Old Syriac Element in Codex Bezae,* 1893.

[32] *Ibid.*, pp. 103 ff.

[33] Harris, *Four Lectures*, pp. 14–34, has shown that an Old Syriac text of Acts actually did exist, and thus Chase's hypothesis becomes a fact.

[34] *Codex Bezae,* p. 179; he quotes Salvian of Marseilles (saec. v), *De Gubern. Dei*, iv.14; Greg. of Tours, Bk. x, p. 438 (ed. Arndt and Krusch); and refers to Duchesne in *Revue Critique* for July 15, 1890.

[35] *The Guardian*, May 18 and 25, 1892; quoted by Chase, *op. cit.*, pp. 143 ff.

[36] *Op. cit.*, p. ccxliii, note 2.

Brightman suggests this locality on the basis of a careful study of the lectionary system which has been indicated in the margins of the MS. by various scribes and correctors.[37] He shows that the system is Byzantine, and that no conditions existed in Gaul or in any other far western province to which the Byzantine lectionary could have any practical relations. In Southern Italy, however, such conditions did exist from the seventh century onward, because of the influx of Greeks resulting from the Moslem conquests in the East. Southern Italy presented "a mixed population, in which the Greek element was of the Byzantine rite," an atmosphere in which Codex Bezae might meet a practical need. The objection to this view is that during the fifth and sixth centuries (the time in which the writing of D falls) Southern Italy was almost entirely Latin, for there was a great gap between the ancient and medieval periods of Greek life in Italy. Is it likely that Codex Bezae would have been written at a time when there was so little of the background of church life as seems to be implied by the very numerous annotators and correctors?[38]

Kirsopp Lake has suggested the possibility of Italian origin for Codex Bezae because of its relationship with Codex 1071 (Laurae A. 104).[39] D and Codex 1071 have eight readings from the *Pericope Adulterae* (John 8.1–11) in common against all other MSS. Codex 1071 is almost certainly Italian in origin, and by a curious set of circumstances was brought from Amalfi to the Laura on Mt. Athos sometime in the twelfth century. It belongs to a well-marked group, and is the only member of its family which has the *Pericope*. The inference is that the *Pericope* was incorporated into Codex 1071 from D, because of their striking similarity in this passage, and that therefore D must have been in Italy before the twelfth century, and may have been there all the time.

Ropes has objected to Southern Italy because of historical difficulties, and these are not the only ones. Kenyon withholds assent on the ground that Greek was so well known there that the Greek side of the MS. ought to have been better written than it is; whereas all indications point to a scribe whose native tongue was Latin. "We want a locality where Latin was the prevalent tongue, but where Greek was still in use for ecclesiastical purposes, for the liturgical notes are all on the Greek side."[40] Lowe objects to Southern Italy on palaeographical grounds.[41] There are two main points: first, that a style of uncial writing is used which is foreign to Italian literary manuscripts but is common in the provinces; second, that the scribe was accustomed to Greek rather than Latin methods, for he conforms the shape of the Latin letters to the Greek, signs the quires in Greek letters, etc. The first point has been referred to above and carries considerable weight.[42]

In preference to Southern Italy, Ropes believes that Sicily best satisfies the requirements for Codex Bezae.[43] Latin was the official language of the island under

[37] "The Marginal Notes of Lections," *JTS*, 1(1899–1900), 446–54.

[38] Cf. Ropes, *op. cit.*, pp. lxiv–lxvi. The fact that all the Greek annotators and correctors were active before 800 would add weight to these other objections.

[39] "On the Italian Origin of Codex Bezae," *JTS*, 1(1899–1900), 441–45.

[40] Kenyon, *Handbook*, p. 92.

[41] *JTS*, 14(1912–13), 385–88.

[42] *Supra*, p. 12, note 29. Against the second point G. Mercati, "On the Non-Greek Origin of the Codex Bezae," *JTS*, 15(1913–14), 448–51, has directed some remarks which tend to show that the scribe was very familiar with Latin methods. Lowe himself, *ibid.*, 25(1924), 270–71, admits Mercati is right, but he is not ready to grant that Codex Bezae was written in a Latin centre, such as South Italy, for this "would be to ignore all the non-Latin features of the manuscript."

[43] *Op. cit.*, pp. lxvii–lxviii.

the Roman Empire, but the mass of the people continued to speak Greek. Starting with the end of the sixth century there was a considerable influx of Greeks from the East, and by the eighth century the church was firmly attached to the Eastern tradition. Early in the ninth century the country was violently disturbed by Arab invasions. Ropes concludes, "All this would well account for the origin of Codex Bezae and for its use for centuries in a locality or localities where the Greek language and Greek customs were continuously in vogue, but where Latin was also known. The disturbed condition of the country early in the ninth century would likewise explain the acquisition of the manuscript by scholars of Lyons at about that date." This view has much to commend it.

That Sardinia may have been the original home of Codex Bezae has been suggested by Alexander Souter.[44] He shows that Codex Claromontanus in all probability was written in Sardinia, because its peculiar Latin text of the Pauline Epistles is the same as that used by Lucifer of Cagliari. The fact that in 533 the Byzantine Empire took control of the island and brought with it the Greek language, thus necessitating a bilingual bible for the service of the church, also fits in well with the sixth-century date of the Claromontanus MS. which, according to Souter, was prepared to meet that particular situation. He says in conclusion, "It is remarkable that our three great bilingual codices, Claromontanus . . . , Codex Bezae . . . , and Laudianus . . . , are all attributed to the sixth century. Laudianus is known to be a Sardinian book. May not all these have been prepared in Sardinia to meet the historical situation to which I have referred?" Ropes states that there are many points of contact between Claromontanus and Codex Bezae, and that they are very likely to be associated in origin,[45] but he believes that Sicily is where that origin is to be sought.

We come finally to a view strongly advocated at one time, but now generally abandoned, namely that Codex Bezae was written in Southern France about the sixth century, and remained during its whole history in France (with the exception of its trip to the council of Trent in 1546) until acquired by Beza in the sixteenth century. Scrivener in his edition of 1864 advocated Gaul as the place of origin of the MS., and his evidence, briefly stated, is as follows. He first says that "all outward appearances point to Gaul as the native country of Codex Bezae,"[46] namely the order of the Gospels, which is peculiarly Western; the intrusion of Latin letters on the Greek side (the opposite phenomenon being ascribed to the "mere strangeness of the task"); the Latin forms and terminations existent in the Greek text; and the orthography of the liturgical notes, which is supposedly Celtic. His internal evidence consists mainly of two points, that the Latin is an independent translation made from the Greek of D, and that the rustic character of this Latin shows forms and constructions which look "more like French than Latin." Scarcely one of these arguments has escaped criticism, and we will here merely mention the objections which have been raised. The intrusion of Latin letters on the Greek side and vice versa proves nothing; in a bilingual manuscript such errors are perfectly natural. The same may be said for the Latin forms and terminations which appear in the Greek, for in this case, too, there are examples of the opposite tendency. That the

[44] "The Original Home of Codex Claromontanus (D^PAUL)," *JTS*(1904–05), 240–43.
[45] *Op. cit.*, p. lviii, note 2.
[46] *Bezae Codex Cantabrigiensis*, p. xxxi.

orthography of the liturgical notes is Celtic cannot be supported, and that they were written in Gaul at all has been shown to be impossible, for it is highly improbable that Greek was the common language of the people or of the churches in any part of Gaul during the fifth and sixth centuries,[47] and certainly the seventh and eighth centuries in that area produced no scholars with the capacity and interests of the early annotators of the MS. The fatal blow to the whole argument is the fact that the lectionary system itself is Byzantine and was never used in Gaul.[48]

The Greek and Latin sides of the MS. have no doubt affected each other greatly, but to say that the Latin is a mere translation of the Greek[49] is to ignore the many differences between the two, and also the relation of the Latin to other Latin renderings.[50] Concerning the character of the Latin and its relation to Gaul we will say more when we come to examine the text for ourselves.

J. Rendel Harris[51] also conjectured that the MS. was probably written in Gaul. His book consists largely of a study of the so-called "sixth-century transition forms," from which he concludes that the Vulgar Latin of the scribe was well on its way to becoming one or another of the Romance tongues; and in his judgment it approaches closest to the French, wherefore "we should hardly expect that in the sixth century it [the MS.] was very far from the place where Beza said it was found; i.e. Lyons."[52] Since Harris' evidence is so largely linguistic we shall discuss it fully in our chapter on the linguistic phenomena.

The only other scholar who has favorably mentioned Gaul as the home of Codex Bezae is F. G. Kenyon, and he considers it as only a bare possibility, concluding that the problem "of the place of origin of D must remain for the present unsolved."[53]

The aim of the foregoing discussion has been to present briefly the various views which have been held concerning the origin of Codex Bezae and to give a conspectus of the problem with all its conflicting evidence and the many possibilities for speculation which it offers. The evidence for the various theories has been set forth along with the criticisms which have been directed against each. Some of the positions have already been shown to be untenable; others are still possibilities. It is the purpose of the following linguistic study of the Latin text to discover the precise character of the language, and to see if any light can thus be shed on the problem of provenience. Can a linguistic analysis give us any clue as to where Codex Bezae was written? If not, it may at least enable us definitely to eliminate certain localities, and thus to strengthen the arguments for others.

[47] With the possible exception of Massalia. For a thorough discussion of this point, see H. G. Wackernagel in *RE*, XIV, 2146.

[48] Brightman, "Marginal Notes of Lections," *JTS*, 1(1899–1900), 448–54; cf. also Ropes, *op. cit.*, pp. lxiii–lxiv.

[49] Scrivener, *op. cit.*, pp. xxxi–xxxii.

[50] Ropes, *op. cit.*, pp. lxxviii, cxi.

[51] *Codex Bezae*, 1891.

[52] *Op. cit.*, p. 26.

[53] *Handbook*, p. 92.

Chapter II

LINGUISTIC PHENOMENA

A. PHONOLOGY

1. Vowels

The vowel changes in Codex Bezae are relatively few, and are regular; there are no unusual departures from classical phonology. The frequency of the interchange of *i* and *e* and of *o* and *u* is not great enough to be called an outstanding feature of vowel change in the MS., which fact might add somewhat to the probability that the codex was not written in Gaul, where these changes were especially characteristic; but we can base no definite conclusion on this point.

a: remains constant throughout the MS. Note that this sound regularly remained unchanged in most localities (Grandgent, 82; Bonnet, 95).[1]

e>a

long, unaccented: *iaiuno*, Mt 4.2; 9.15; and frequently.

short, accented: *talanta*, Mt 25.15, and twelve times in the remainder of the chapter. The Greek *τάλαντα* may have been a contributing factor in this, as Professor Hatch suggests.

short, unaccented: *carcare*, L 3.20; 21.12. This is a case of progressive assimilation (Leumann-Hofmann, 96).

e>ae

long, accented: *caene*, Mt 20.28.

long, unaccented: *occultae*, Mt 2.7.

short, accented: *aeo*, J 6.56; *aeum*, J 9.13.[2]

short, unaccented: *saecuti*, Mt 9.27; *saecutae*, Mt 12.15; *saecundum*, Mt 9.29; *usquae*, Mt 11.23; A 1.22; in the imperative form *uadae*, Mt 13.14; in the ablative ending *regae*, A 7.10; sometimes in the vocative, *phariseae cecae*, Mt 23.26; *plenae* and *inimicae*, A 13.10; and very common in the syllable *pre* throughout, e.g. *interpraetatum*, Mt 1.23; *praetiosam*, Mt 13.46; *praesbyteris*, L 20.1; A 21.18 (Väänänen, 39).

e>i

long, accented: *habitat*, L 6.8; *tris*, L 13.21; *mi*, A 20.23.

long, unaccented: *possideritis*, Mt 10.9; *disponsatam*, L 1.27.

short, accented: *uindedit*, Mt 13.46.

short, unaccented: *hordiacios*,[3] J 6.9; *lentium*,[3] J 13.4; *dilictionem*, J 13.35; and

[1] References put thus in the text are uniformly to page number. The names of the works referred to may be found in the bibliography, pp. 69 ff. There is much in the inscriptions which bears on practically every point treated in the section on language. It does not seem to me necessary to include references to this material in the present work. Anyone who is interested in looking further into the matter will find abundant examples in the indices to *Inscriptiones Latinae Christianae Veteres*, Diehl, Berlin, 1925–31, and *Inscriptiones Latinae Selectae*, Dessau, Berlin, 1892–1916.

[2] As Dr. Abbott has pointed out, this really represents a change in the sound of *ae*. It is listed here because of its spelling. Cf. Leumann-Hofmann, 75.

[3] This change first occurs in hiatus. Cf. Väänänen, 60–61.

hisitaueritis, Mt 21.21, where a double change has taken place, *haes->hes->his-* (Baehrens, 41).

es>is: quite common in nominative and accusative plural: *omnis*, Mt 11.13; *canis*, Mt 15.27; *obis*, J 10.3; *praesis* as nominative singular, Mt 27.11; and *diligis* for second person singular of the future, Mt 22.37.

is>es: this is even more marked: *omnes* as nom. sing., Mt 5.22,28; J 3.16; and throughout; *panes*, J 6.35; and *uites*, J 15.1 are nom. sing.; *dicentes*, Mt 13.14, is gen. sing., as are *homines*, Mt 10.36; and *consummationes*, Mt 24.3. *Potestes* appears twice as second pers. plu. of the present, Mt 12.34; J 7.34.

e>o: one time only does this appear, *nosciebat*, Mk 9.6. This may be meant for *non sciebat*,[4] however, as the nasal before *s* was often omitted (p. 21).

We see that Codex Bezae presents no irregularities in the changes of the vowel *e*. The use of *ae* for *e* occurs frequently in all writers of the Late Latin period (Bonnet, 97–101; Taylor, 23; Schuchardt, I, 469–70). In the substitution of *i* for *e* we note a decided conservatism, however, in contrast to the general tendency, especially in Gaul (Grandgent, 83; Bonnet, 106 ff.) *Es* and *is* were always confused (Grandgent, 104).

i>e

long, unaccented: *demittere*, Mk 2.7; *inredebant*, Mk 5.40 (Baehrens, 53).
short, accented: *lentium*, J 13.4; *sinestra*, Mt 6.3.
short, unaccented: *osteum*, Mt 6.6; *teloneum*, Mt 9.9; *habetent*, Mt 13.32; *splendede*, L 16.19; *besteis*, Mk 1.13; *pontefex*, A 4.6; 5.24.

The change *i>e* is not very common in Codex Bezae, but occurs with greater frequency in the case of short *i* than of long (Bonnet, 117–26; Grandgent, 84–85; Taylor, 26).

i>ei: occurs once in Codex Bezae, *feidelis*, Mt 24.45. For a few similar instances from inscriptions, see Sommer, 74, and the discussion in Leumann-Hoffmann, 77.

is>es: (*supra*).

o>ae: in one instance, *praepalare*, Mt 1.19.

o>u

long, unaccented: *consulari*, Mt 2.18; *lucustas*, Mk 1.6.
short, unaccented: *urnatis*, Mt 23.29; *agricula*, J 15.1.
The changes are all regular. Their infrequency alone is noteworthy.

u>e: one instance occurs: *pleres*, A 17.12.

u>i: only in short, unaccented syllables: *scoriscatio*, Mt 24.27; *monimentis*, L 8.27.

u>o

long, accented: *prodocere*, A 12.6.
short, accented: *norum*, L 12.53; *hoc*, Mt 17.17; 22.12; J 4.16; 6.25; 20.27; A 19.37.
short, unaccented: *confondaris*, Mt 20.28; *baiolare*, J 16.12; *paruolis*, L 10.21;

[4] Dr. Abbott suggests the possibility of mere scribal error for this, *no(n) sciebat* being unlikely here because of the frequent occurrence of *nescio* in the text.

proconsolem, A 13.8; 19.38; *docenta,* A 19.19; and the nom. sing. *infructuos,* Mt 13.22; *populos,* A 5.13.

Here again the only noteworthy feature is the small number of changes, in view of the fact that confusion of *o* and *u* is especially characteristic of Gallic writing (Grandgent, 85).

u>y: *illym,* Mt 15.22; *cyminum,* Mt 23.23. This is merely the Greek upsilon.

2. Diphthongs

ae>a: *damonia,* L 13.22.

ae>e: *Iudeae,* Mt 19.1, and common throughout; *cecae,* Mt 23.26; *crecus,* A 16.3; *querere,* Mt 2.13, and common throughout. The nom. plu. ending is affected: *tenebre,* Mt 27.45; *pauce,* A 17.4; gen. sing.: *aque,* Mt 10.42; *caene,* Mt 20.28; *terre,* Mt 27.54; the demon. pron. *ille,* J 5.39, and *iste,* Mk 6.2, are fem. nom. plu.; the relative *que* is fem. nom. plu. in Mt 21.9, and neu. ac. plu. in J 14.10; 17.7.

The relative frequency of this change in Codex Bezae is in accordance with the general tendency in Late Latin (Grandgent, 88; Taylor, 22; Bonnet, 97 ff.; Seelmann, 225; Leumann-Hofmann, 75; Väänänen, 37).

oe>oi: *coipit,* Mk 10.28; *coiperunt,* A 2.4 (Sommer, 74 ff.).

3. Syncope

Only three instances occur in Codex Bezae: *socram* (*soceram*), Mt 10.35; *stablario* (*stabulario*), L 10.35; *consoldauit* (*consolidauit*), A 3.16. Cf. Leumann-Hofmann, 91 ff.; Väänänen, 73 ff.

4. Added Vowels

There are a few instances where a vowel has been incorrectly inserted: *confortians,* L 22.43; *serpiat* (*serpo*), A 4.17; *audiebat* (*audeo*), A 7.32. In Acts 16.19 we have a solitary instance of prothetic *i: ispes* (*spes*) (Leumann-Hofmann, 98).

5. Consonants[5]

b>p: *optulunt,* Mt 9.32; *piscipus,* J 6.11; *suptus,* L 8.16; *exproprari,* L 9.22. There are no cases of the change *p>b.*

b>u:[6] *lauoratis,* Mt 11.28; *beruum,* Mt 12.36; *ueati,* Mt 13.16; *parauolam,* Mt 13.36; *uiuit* (*bibit*), J 4.12; *dociuiles,* J 6.45; *liuerabat,* J 8.32; *diauolo,* J 8.44; *uethleem,* L 2.4; *pleue,* L 11.27; *uases,* A 3.7. The future tense of verbs is often made with *u* instead of *b* (examples are given for Matthew only): *uocauis* and *saluauit,* 1.21; *temptauis,* 4.7; *moechaueris,* 5.27; *consummauitis,* 10.23; *praeparauit,* 11.10; *stauit,* 12.25; *iustificaueris* and *condemnaueris,* 12.37; *locauit,* 21.41.

u>b: *nobissimum,* Mt 5.26; *nobi,* Mt 9.16; *nobellum,* Mt 9.17; *parbulis,* Mt 11.25; *bellere,* Mt 12.1; *beruum,* Mt 12.36; *berba,* Mt 24.35; *pabor,* L 4.36; *trabaricator,* L 6.4; *fobeam,* L 6.39; *perseberantes,* A 1.14. *Obes* is very common for *oues:* e.g.,

[5] For a discussion of consonants in Late Latin, see Grandgent, 104–37; Bonnet, 150 ff.; Taylor, 33–40.

[6] This permutation and its opposite are very common, and it is unnecessary to list all examples; only a few typical ones are given.

Mt 10.6; 12.11; J 10.3, etc. The perfect tense looks like the future: *habitabit* Mt 4.13; *introibit*, Mt 12.4; *exultabit*, J 8.56. *Habe* (for *aue*) is regular: *habe*, Mt 26.49; 27.29; L 1.28; Mk 15.18; *habete*, Mt 28.9 (Leumann-Hofmann, 130; Baehrens, 79 ff.; Väänänen, 86 ff.).

c>g: *gogitare*, Mt 10.19; *golligit* Mt 12.30; *ingrassatum*, Mt 13.15; *gubitum*, L 12.25; *digimus*, A 21.23; *obsegro*, A 21.39.

g>c: *interrocauerunt*, Mt 16.1; *dicitum*, J 20.25; *cladium*, L 22.36; *fracmentorum*, Mk 8.20; *cratia*, A 14.26; *craecos*, A 11.20; *crecus*, A 16.3; *craeci*, A 19.10. Cf. Leumann-Hofmann, 122–26; Baehrens, 87–88.

c>q: in one case, *qui*, A 2.45.

c>t: *dit*, Mt 13.14; *sartofagum*, L 7.14; *hunt*, A 21.28.

t>c: *mittunc*, Mt 9.17. This change is rare. For examples, see Schuchardt, I, 159–62.

ct>t: *amitibus*, A 2.24 (Seelmann, 348; Baehrens, 85).

c final, omitted: *hae*, Mt 13.56; 22.36; *illi*, L 17.21.

c incorrectly added: *hic*, J 12.21; *sic*, A 5.38; 7.1 (Grandgent, 112; Seelmann, 368).

c intervocalic, omitted: *amie*, L 11.5 (Pirson, 97–99).

d>c: *ciscipulorum*, L 7.19; and **d>ct:** *uinctictae*, L 21.22. These changes seem to be irregular, since I have not found them attested elsewhere. It is not likely that the error is palaeographical, for *c* or *ct* and *d* do not look much alike in uncials. They can possibly be explained as mere scribal errors, or perhaps on the analogy of *t>c* and *d>g*, both of which are noted by Schuchardt, I, 158 ff.

d>g: *quagringentorum*, A 5.36; *progregientibus*, A 13.42.

d>p: *ponec*, Mt 22.44. This is probably to be explained through the influence of the following *ponam*, since I have not found such a change recorded in other texts.

d>t: only at the end of words in Codex Bezae: *aput*, Mt 6.1; J 8.38; *illut*, Mt 15.11; 26.42; J 7.4; *aliut*, Mk 4.4; A 19.32; also a few proper nouns: *Heliut*, Mt 1.14,15; *Dauit* L 1.70 (Väänänen, 122).

t>d: at the end of words: *capud*, J 20.7; A 4.11; 16.12. *Quod* occurs regularly for *quot*, Mt 15.34; 16.9,10; etc.; similarly *quodquod* for *quotquot*, Mt 14.36; 22.9; etc. The verb form *reliquid* is frequent: Mt 19.20; J 4.3; 8.29; and *dereliquid* in L 10.40. *Ad* is practically universal for *at*, as in *ad ille dixit*, J 4.32; *ad illa dixit*, J 8.11, etc. Changes not at the end of words are *quando*, Mt 12.12; *constitudo*, L 14.32; *dendibus*, A 7.54. In one instance *th>d: Bedsaida*, J 12.21.

The proportionately large number of cases of uncertainty between *d* and *t* at the end of words is regular (Grandgent, 119; cf. Leumann-Hofmann, 176). The omission of final *d* occurs but once, *qui*, A 1.11. The omission of *d* after *n* also occurs once, *desponentes*, A 15.11. Double *d* becomes single twice, *quodam* for *quoddam*, A 11.5; 18.23. There is one case of incorrect insertion of *d*, *admare*, L 22.62.[7]

[7] This may have been an unconscious scribal error, since the phrase *ad mare* occurs not infrequently throughout the Gospels.

g>c: (p. 20)

g>q: only in the word *sanguis: sanquis,* L 11.50; *sanquinem* A 20.28.

gn>ngn: *ingnorabant,* Mk 14.40.

m>b: in the proper noun *Eliezib,* Mt 1.13; and in *dixeribus,* Mt 21.26.

m>f: *fanu,* Mk 14.58; possibly due to the following *factum.*

m>p: *portuis,* A 13.34.

m>n:[8] occurs very frequently before labials: *inpleretur,* Mt 1.22 and regularly throughout; *conpleretur,* 2.15 and regularly; *conburet,* 3.12; *inpetum,* 8.32; *synphoniacos,* 9.23; *pronptus,* 26.41. There was also irregularity before dentals: *quandiu,* 5.25. The change **n>m** is noted only in the adverb *forsitam,* L 11.20; 20.13; and regularly throughout Acts (Leumann-Hofmann, 120).

m>nt: only final *m* is affected: *Barnabant,* A 11.22; *eunt,* A 12.16. Cf. p. 64.

m final, omitted: in uninflexional endings: *septe,* Mt 16.10; A 13.19; *aute,* Mt 23.3; *duodeci,* J 6.70; *pala* J 16.25 (Leumann-Hofmann, 174). The frequent dropping of *m* in case endings will be taken up in the section on syntax. See also the discussion in Väänänen, 124 ff. Before *p, m* is often omitted: *teptantes,* Mt 19.3; 22.18; A 5.9; *adsuptis,* A 17.5. Cf. also *circuiri,* L 21.20, which is found repeatedly (Seelmann, 274).

m inserted: in two instances we find *m* inserted before *s: manums,* J 7.44; *ualetudinems,* Mk 3.15.

n>m: see under **m>n** (*supra*).

n superfluous (Grandgent, 131): *thensauros,* Mt 2.11, and so throughout; *praesens,* Mt 27.21; *forans,* L 1.10; *locuplens,* L 19.2, *nonuum,* Mk 2.21; *hanc,* A 2.40; *requens* (=*requies*), A 7.49; *trens,* A 19.8. The second person singular of verbs is often made to look like a participle: e.g., *exiens,* Mt 5.26; *sciens,* J 13.7; *concipiens,* L 1.31; *docens,* A 21.21 (Bonnet, 152–53). The third person singular is confused with the plural by the insertion of an *n* before final *t.* These cases will be discussed in the section on syntax.

n dropped: *hic,* Mt 17.20; *speluccm,* Mt 21.13; *tras,* J 6.25; *speratis,* J 8.49; *adnutiare,* L 4.18; *abscodisti,* L 10.21; *trasire,* L 18.25; *no,* L 23.40; *defuctus,* A 7.15; *istigassent,* A 14.19; *ascedisset,* A 18.22. A participle is made to appear as a second person singular: *cludes,* Mt 6.6; *uides,* J 11.32; *impones,* L 4.40; *dices,* L 12.16; *audies,* A 5.5 (Baehrens, 95). In one instance *ns* drops out: *trabaricator,* L 6.4.

nc>n: *santus* frequently: Mk 1.24; A 1.8; 4.30; 15.29; *inextintibili,* L 3.17 (cf. Seelman, 278).

p>b: see under **b>p** (p. 19).

[8] All references given are found in Matthew. The change is so common that a complete list for all the books would be useless.

p>f: *froferet*, L 6.45.

ph>f: very frequent in some words, as *profetam*, Mt 2.5, etc.; *farisaei*, Mt 16.6,11; J 4.1; etc.: *Cafarnaum*, Mt 4.13; 11.23; and in some other words: *Alfei*, Mt 10.3; *cofinos*, Mt 14.20; *sartofagum*, L 7.14; *Frygiam*, A 2.10 (Bonnet, 163–65; Grandgent, 139; Mørland, 61).

p omitted or added: there is one case where *p* is omitted before *t: promtus*, Mk 14.38 (Grandgent, 132). The addition of *p* in *pexiuit*, A 18.23, may be due to the following *per*.

qu>c: *persecuntur*, Mt 10.23; *locuntur*, Mt 12.36; A 2.7; *secuntur*, J 10.4; *coniam*, J 16.26; *anticus*, L 9.8; *inicus*, L 16.10. Cf. Baehrens, 65 ff.; Väänänen, 94–95.

qu>q: *qem*, J 5.38; *aliqod*, L 18.4 (Grandgent, 107).

r dropped before *s: susu*, Mt 27.51; *desusum*, J 3.31; *diosum*, L 4.9; *susum*, A 2.19 (Grandgent, 123). One other case of omitted *r: Phygiam*, A 16.6.

s added to the beginning of a word: *scoriscatio*, Mt 24.27; *scoruscantia*, L 9.29; *scoruscus* and *scoruscat*, L 17.24; *scoruscanti*, L 24.4; *sconspectu*, A 7.46.[9] Incorrect insertion of *s* is noted in *hominusm*, Mt 17.22; *spsem*, A 2.26.

t>c: (p. 20).

t>d: (p. 20).

t inserted between *s* and *r:* this is regular throughout in *Istrahel*, *Istrahelitae*, for *Israhel*, which is found but ten times. A similar case is *etrit*, Mt 16.19.

t final, dropped: this does not occur very frequently in Codex Bezae: *dixerin*, Mt 5.11; *trade*, Mt 26.46; *scripsi*, J 5.46; *posse*, L 5.14; *es*, L 9.50; *sedere*. Mk 4.1; *esse*, Mk 9.34; *potes*, Mk 15.31; *manen*, A 20.23 (Grandgent, 120).

u>b: (p. 19).

u>m: *mermis*, Mk 9.44.

u dropped after *b: obiauit*, J 11.20.

x>s: *destera*, Mt 6.3, possibly on the analogy of *sinestra* in the line above. This, however, was a very common change in Vulgar Latin (Seelmann, 353).

x>xs: *iuxsta*, J 6.4; *sexs*, Mk 9.2 (Väänänen, 111–12). The opposite, **xs>x,** is found twice, both in the same word: *exurrexit*, Mk 5.42; *exurrexerit*, A 7.18 (Seelmann, 352).

6. Aspiration[10]

The aspirate, *h*, is somewhat indiscriminately used in Vulgar Latin, and we find many instances of this uncertainty in Codex Bezae. Cf. Leumann-Hofmann, 138–39; Baehrens, 100.

h added: *thus*, Mt 2.11; *exhorta*, Mt 13.5, and *exhortum*, Mk 4.5,6; *haruit*, Mt 21.19; *hostendite*, Mt 22.19; *habundabit*, Mt 25.29; *hosteis*, J 20.19; *hieris*, L 9.57;

[9] G. Loewe, *Prodromus Corporis Glossariorum Latinorum*, 1876, p. 355, and Baehrens, p. 59.
[10] Grandgent, 106–07.

honeratis and *honera*, L 11.46; *hebrii*, A 2.15; *habire*, A 4.15; *hopus*, A 5.38; *horabit*, A 10.9; *hemulatores*, A 21.20. In proper nouns: *Heliacib*, Mt 1.13; *Heleazer*, Mt 1.15; *Hiericho*, Mk 10.46; *Hiconio*, A 13.51; and *Helias*, Mt 11.14 and throughout.

h omitted: *arundinem*, Mt 11.7; *ypocritae*, Mt 23.29; L 11.39; *clamydem*, Mt 27.31; *sepulcrum*, Mt 27.66; *ebraeice*, J 5.2; 20.16; *ora*, J 5.35; Mk 6.35; 14.35,41; 15.33; *abeo*, L 12.50; 19.26; *ac*, L 12.20; and many others.

7. Assimilation and Metathesis

Most forms throughout Codex Bezae remain unassimilated. In a few cases prepositions are assimilated to the following word: *an nos*, Mt 27.4; *at turbam*, Mt 17.14; *at te*, A 21.37; *im mare*, Mt 8.32; *suc caelo*, A 4.12.

Only one instance of metathesis is noted, *inosp*, A 4.34.

8. Remarks

In concluding this section we must say a few words about the claims which Harris has made for the Gallic origin of d from considerations of phonetic peculiarities.[11] He mentions the weakening of certain intervocalic consonants and calls attention to the same phenomenon in early French. The forms cited are *hante* for *habente* in Mt 18.25; *neglentes* for *negligentes* in Mt 22.5; *accentes* for *accedentes* in L 20.27; *nessitas* for *necessitas* in L 21.23; and *fate* for *facite* in Mk 1.3. In the first place, these are isolated examples, and in a MS. which shows numerous instances of haplography they may just as well be due to this latter cause;[12] in the second place, where such weakenings occur they are not necessarily to be connected with Gaul, but were doubtless common in all parts of the Empire (Grandgent, 112); and finally, the instances are too few to justify any definite conclusion as to locality.

In the same connection, Harris cites *amie*, L 11.5, and *ame*, Mt 26.50, which are closer to the French *ami* than to the Italian *amico*. The criticisms just recorded may be applied to arguments based upon these forms also. Such cases as *hoernum*, Mt 28.15; *cottie*, A 2.47; and *nustertiana*, A 10.30, where *di* has dropped out, Harris compares to the French *aujourd'hui*, where *hui* = *hodie*. These are again markedly isolated instances, for *cottie* appears once against *cottidie* ten times; the form *hodierno* appears (A 20.26) as well as *hoernum*; and *hodie* always appears in its regular form.

Harris also comments on a peculiar pronunciation of *iu* (chap. xii), which gives a consonantal sound to the initial letter, i.e. *dy*. He cites *ad Iudaeis*, A 20.19, and *ad iuuentate*, Mk 10.20, and explains them as being pronounced *a diudaeis* and *a diuuentate*. This is probably correct, but the same peculiarity is noted in several Old Latin Biblical texts[13] as well as in writings from various parts of the Empire

[11] *Codex Bezae*, chaps. iv, xii.

[12] For the frequent occurrence of haplography, cf. the following instances which occur within the small compass of 15 folios: *sama* for *samariam*, J 4.4; *hierosomis* for *hierosolymis*, 4.20; *honis* for *hominis*, 5.27; *aum* for *autem*, 6.16; *irasmini* for *irascimini*, 7.23; *murantes* for *murmurantes*, 7.32; *dentre* for *de uentre*, 7.38.

[13] Harris gives a few forms from the Lyons Pentateuch. I have found *zabulus* for *diabulus* (which Harris cites as evidence of the same tendency) in several MSS. cited in the apparatus of Wordsworth and White, *Novum Test. Lat.*, pt. 1, 1899 (on Mt 4.5,8,11; L 4.3,5; J 8.44). These are all of the seventh century or later and are Insular MSS. Cf. also Dessau, *Inscriptiones Latinae*, Nos. 8254 (*zaconus* for *diaconus*), 2415 (*azutoribus* for *adiutoribus*), 2089 (*Zonysius* for *Dionysius*).

(Seelmann, 239), so can have no weight in proving that Codex Bezae comes from Gaul.

B. MORPHOLOGY

1. Declension

During the Vulgar Latin period the tendency was to decrease the number of declensions, the fourth and fifth being gradually absorbed into the others (Grandgent, 148). In Codex Bezae this process has not advanced very far, the declensions for the most part being well preserved. The fourth declension, however, shows a decided tendency to change into the second.

1>3

eius puelles[14] (*puellae*), A 16.19.

2>3

homo austeris (*austerus*), L 19.21.
omnis scriba doctis (*doctus*), Mt 13.52.
dare intellectum salutis populi eius (*populo*), L 1.77.
sps patris uestris (*uestri*), Mt 10.20.

2>4

de sub caelu (*caelo*), L 17.24.
plenae omnis dolus (*doli*), A 13.10.
de dormitione somnus (*somni*), J 11.13.

3>1

lampadae[15] (*lampades*), Mt 25.8.
retiam (*rete*), Mt 4.18,20; J 21.6,8,11; Mk 1.19; *retiae* (*retia* nom.plu.), L 5.6; *retias* (*retia* acc.plu.), Mt 4.21; L 5.2,4,6; Mk 1.16.

3>2

a dextris altari[16] (*altaris*), L 1.11.
ex circumcisio (*circumcisione*), A 10.45.
fratrorum (*fratrum*), Mt 25.40.
hominorum (*hominum*), L 14.24.
in praesepio[17] (*praesepe*), L 2.7,12,16.
regioni illius (*regionis*), L 15.15.
coperit eam uaso[18] (*uase*), L 8.16.

4>2

actos suos (*actus*), A 19.18.
concurso (*concursu*), A 19.40.
conspecto (*conspectu*), L 4.7; 13.26; 15.18,21; 19.27; 21.36; A 10.30.
cornum (*cornu*), L 1.69.
ficui (*ficus*), Mk 11.21.
fructos (*fructus*), Mt 21.34,43; L 6.43; 12.17,18; *fructo* (*fructu*), Mt 12.33; L 6.44; 20.10.

[14] *Puelles* is for *puellis;* cf. p. 18.
[15] This is a collateral form of the regular declension, however, and is found occasionally elsewhere. Cf. Neue-Wagener, I, 497, and Georges, *Lex.*
[16] Cf. Neue-Wagener, I, 832, and Georges, *Lex.*
[17] Neue-Wagener, I, 827, and Georges, *Lex.*
[18] Neue-Wagener, I, 854, and Georges, *Lex.*

grados (*gradus*), A 12.10.
habito regno (*habitu*), A 12.21.
in intellecto (*intellectu*), L 2.47.
magistrati (*magistratus*), A 16.22,35; *magistratos*, A 16.19.
porticos (*porticus*), J 5.2.
sensui (*sensus*), A 20.19.
tonitrum (*tonitrus*, gen.), J 12.29; *tonitrui*, Mk 3.17.
uultos (*uultus*), L 24.5.
spirito (*spiritu*), very common, and regular throughout Acts: Mt 1.20; (*see* Index Verborum for other examples); *nescitis cuius spiritui estis* (*spiritus*), L 9.55; *spirite* (voc. for *spiritu*), Mk 1.25; 5.8; 9.25.

5>2

post tertium dieum (*diem*), A 10.40.

Miscellaneous Variations

Some unusual case forms appear in Codex Bezae.[19] We find the ante-classical nominative singular *trabis* for the regular *trabs* in L 6.42; and *nubs* as nominative singular instead of *nubes* in Mt 17.5; L 9.34; Mk 9.7. The accusative *sanguem* occurs for *sanguinem* in J 6.54–56. The letter *i* is incorrectly inserted in the nominative plural *ueteria*, Mt 13.52; and in the genitive plural *ciuitatium*, L 5.12; 6.17.

Syncopation of endings occurs also, although it is relatively infrequent. The following genitive plural forms are syncopated: *regnum*, Mt 11.8; *pharisaeum*, L 11.37; *ficum*, Mk 11.13; *manum*, A 8.18. There was also a tendency to shorten endings in *ii* to *i*: *ali*, J 7.12,41; 12.29; but full form elsewhere; *euangeli*, Mk 1.1. In the word *filius* this shortening seems to have been regular. *Fili* is found as nominative plural twenty-five times, while *filii* occurs but four times; as genitive singular, *fili* eighteen times, and *filii* not at all (see Index Verborum for references). The vocative plural is *fili*: Mk 10.24; A 13.26. *Filis* is dative plural in L 11.13 and ablative plural in L 7.35. Cf. also *is* for *eis*, Mt 26.51. On the other hand, we find some forms lengthened: *hii* in Mt 25.46; Mk 12.44; A 2.15; 15.13; *hiis* in Acts 5.32; 15.23; 16.2; 17.17.

Declension of Proper Nouns[20]

Codex Bezae shows almost complete adherence to classical tradition in names of persons which are Latin or Greek (*Cornelius*, *Paulus*, *Philippus*, *Petrus*, etc.), and in the names of towns and countries throughout the Roman world (*Syria*, *Achaia*, *Bithynia*, *Athenae*, *Corinthus*, *Ephesus*, etc.). The names which show most irregularity are those of "Hebrew" origin.[21]

Most Hebrew proper nouns are uninflected, as *Abel*, Mt 23.35; *Adam*, L 3.38; *Belzebul*, Mt 10.25, etc.; *Bethleem*, Mt 2.1, etc.; *Betphage*, Mt 21.1; *Cafarnaum*, Mt 4.13, etc.; *Chorazain*, Mt 11.21; *Dauid*, Mt 1.17; *Elisabet*, L 1.5; *Gennesared*, L 5.1; *Getsamini*, Mt 26.36; *Isac* Mt 22.32; *Istrahel*, Mt 9.34; *Iacob*, Mt 22.32; *Iericho*, Mt 20.29; Mk 10.46; *Ioseph*, Mt 1.18, etc.; *Lot*, L 17.28; *Leui*, L 5.27,29; *Nazareth*, Mt 4.13, etc.; *Noe*, Mt 24.37,38; *Pharao*, A 7.10,13,21; *Saul*, A 13.21; *Samuel*, A

[19] For irregularities due to the confusion of *es* and *is*, see the section on phonology.
[20] To list all the names that are regularly declined is unnecessary; only the cases which are unusual are given. I have also omitted the names in the genealogical lists in Matthew 1 and Luke 3.
[21] This term is loosely used; all names quoted from the O.T., names of ancient towns in Palestine, and names of persons neither Latin nor Greek are meant.

3.24;13.20; *Magadan*, Mt 15.39; Mk 8.10. There are some exceptions to this general rule. *Abraam*, while usually uninflected, has a genitive and dative form in *ae:* Mt 3.9; L 3.8; *Danielum* as accusative of *Daniel* is found in Mt 24.15; *Sodoma* is declined as a neuter plural of the second declension: genitive (syncopated) *Sodomum*, Mt 10.15; dative and ablative *Sodomis*, L 10.12; 17.29; *Solomon* has a genitive in *is*, Mt 12.42, and an ablative in *e*, Mt 12.42. The name *Jerusalem* is variable: *Hierusalem* is used throughout as an indeclinable form; *Hierosolymis* is also found, generally used as an ablative, but also as an accusative in J 5.1; A 13.13; the form *Hierosolyma* is most frequently accusative, but appears as a nominative in Mt 2.3, and as an ablative in Mt 4.25.

Names ending in *-as* are regularly put into the first declension. E.g.:

N. Helias, Mt 11.14
G. Heliae, L 1.17
D. Heliae, Mt 17.4
A. Heliam, Mt 17.10; Helian, L 9.19[22]

Other names following the same paradigm are *Ananias*, *Andreas*, *Barnabas*, *Barabbas*, *Caiphas*, *Esaias*, *Hieremias*, *Ionas*, *Iudas*, *Matthias*, *Satanas*, *Silas*, *Thomas*, *Zacharias*. One exception is *Herodias*, which follows the third declension, *Herodiadis*, etc.

Names in *-es* go into the third declension. E.g.:

N. Herodes,	Mt 2.3	Iohannes,	Mt	3.14
G. Herodis,	Mt 2.1	Iohannis,	Mt	11.12
D. Herodi,	Mk 6.18	Iohanni,	Mt	11.4
A. Heroden,	Mt 2.12	Iohannen (-em),	Mt	3.13
A. Herode,	Mt 2.19	Iohanne,	Mt	11.7

The name *Moyses* is slightly exceptional, following the third declension except in the genitive, where it follows the second: *Moysi*, Mt 23.2; *Moysei*, L 24.44.

Iesus is declined as follows:

N. Iesus,	Mt	3.15
G. Iesu,	J	13.23
D. Iesu,	Mt	8.34
A. Iesum,	Mt	1.25 (Iesun, J 12.9; L 5.12; A 2.32)
A. Iesu,	Mt	9.27
V. Iesu,	Mt	8.29

There are a few miscellaneous irregularities in declension of names. *Lazar* is found as nominative for *Lazarus* in J 11.4. The ablative of *Tyrus*, which regularly follows the second declension, is *Tyru* in L 10.13. The name *Sidon* is markedly irregular:

N. . . .		
G. . . .		
D. Sidoni,	Mt	11.22
A. Sidonem,	Mk	3.8
A. { Sidona,	Mt	11.21
Sidoni,	L	10.13

[22] The accusative varies between *m* and *n* in all names.

2. Gender

There was much confusion of gender throughout the Vulgar Latin period, the neuter finally disappearing entirely (Grandgent, 146; Väänänen, 143; Mørland, 63 ff.). Codex Bezae shows several instances of change in gender, and gives evidence, from the many errors in agreement, that the feeling for gender was rapidly being lost. In accordance with the general tendency, the neuter suffers most.

neuter > masculine

castellum: in alium castellum, L 9.56; *in quendam castellum,* L 17.12; *castellus,* L 19.30.
donum: aequalem donum, A 11.17.
faenum: uiridem faenum, Mk 6.39.
forum: in foros, Mt 23.7.
mare: maris (nom. sing.), Mt 8.27; *ad marem,* Mk 3.7.
signum: signum contradicentem, L 2.34.
templum: hunc templum, Mk 14.58.
uerbum: hic uerbus, J 21.23; *uerbus eius,* L 4.32; *quendam uerbum,* A 19.38.

neuter plural > feminine singular

testimonium: erat conueniens testimonia illorum, Mk 14.59.[23]
a dmo facta est haec, Mt 21.42, is a Hebraism (Plater-White, 18).

masculine > neuter

filius: mortuum filius, L 7.12.
puer: puer meum, L 7.7.
umerus: super umera hominum, Mt 23.4.

masculine > feminine

apex: unam apicem, L 16.17.

feminine > masculine

domus: in quemcumque domum, L 9.4; *superiorem domum stratum,* L 22.12.

The numerous errors in agreement indicate the scribe's lack of feeling for gender. Cf.: *facti sunt plurimae uirtutes,* Mt 11.20; *turbae secuti sunt eum,* Mt 14.13; *cum sua omnia eiecerit ante eas uadet,*[24] J 10.4; *peccata . . . detentae sunt,*[25] J 20.23; *factum est timor magnus,* L 1.65; *reuertar in domum meum . . . mundatum adornatum,* L 11.24,25; *capilli . . . numeratae sunt,* L 12.7; *habet centum oues et perdiderit unum,*[26] L 15.4; *daemonia dicentes,* Mk 5.12; *diuidi linguae,* A 2.3; *cui adsensum est numeri,* A 5.36; *factum est . . . tumultus,* A 19.23.

3. Pronouns: Relative

While much confusion exists in the agreement of relative pronouns in Codex Bezae, we are not justified in concluding that distinction of gender, number, and case has entirely vanished, although there was a general tendency in that direction.

qua > quam: *caritas quam dilexisti me,* J 17.26.

[23] Perhaps this is due to the *μαρτυρία* of D, as Professor Hatch suggests.
[24] The Greek may be responsible here: *τὰ ἴδια* refers to the neuter *πρόβατα*. Our scribe writes *sua omnia* after the Greek, but lapses into the Latin gender of *oues* in *ante eas*.
[25] Perhaps *ae* is for *a*; see the section on phonology.
[26] *Unum* for the Greek *ἕν*.

quae (fem. and neut.)>**qui:** *qui . . . exeunt de ore . . . illa communicant,* Mt 15.18; *uerbis meis qui conplebuntur,* L 1.20; *mirabantur in uerbis . . . qui exiebant de ore,* L 4.22; *manus qui tradet me,* L 22.21; *in porticum qui uocatur Solomonis,* A 3.11; *intendebant . . . his qui dicebantur,* A 8.6.

quae>quod: *da mihi quod me tanget partem,* L 15.12; *rememoratus est . . . uerborum quod dixerat,* Mk 14.72.

quam>quem: *in uitam aeternam quem . . . dat,* J 6.27; *omnem ualetudinem quem habebant,* A 5.15; *aput quem erat ecclesiam,*[27] A 13.1.

quam>quod: *substantiam suam quod habuit misit,* L 21.4.

quas>quos: *gentes super quos,* A 15.17.

quem>quod: *in igne aeternam quod praeparauit pater,* Mt 25.41; *iuxta agrum quod dedit Iacob,* J 4.5.

qui>quae: *uteri quae non genuerunt,* L 23.29; *quae ex Graecis erant aduersus Aebraeos,* A 6.1; *sermonibus quae a Paulo dicebantur,* A 13.45.

qui>quod: *calicem bibere quod ego uiuiturus sum,* Mt 20.22; *sanguis . . . quod effunditur,* L 11.50.

quo>quem: *in eum diem quem susceptus est,* A 1.2.

quo>quod: *de lentio quod erat cinctus,* J 13.5; *quod . . . tempore misit . . . seruum,* L 20.10.

quod>quae: *gaudium magnum quae erit,* L 2.10; *a fermento . . . quae est hypocrisis,* L 12.1.

quod>qui: *templum qui sanctificauit aurum,* Mt 23.17; *faenum agri hodie qui est,* L 12.28.

quos>quod: *serbabam eos . . . quod dedisti mihi,* J 17.11; *quod mihi dedis uelo ut . . . illi sint,* J 17.24.

4. Pronouns: Demonstrative

eam>eum: *in sede . . . sedet supra eum,* Mt 23.22.

eas>ea (neut.plu.): *gnosco eas (oues) . . . non rapiet . . . ea*[28] *de manu mea,* J 10.27,28.

eos>ea (neut.plu.): *ihs . . . ad se uocabat ea*[29] *(infantes),* L 18.16.

hic>hoc: *hoc est . . . sanguis meus,* Mt 26.28; Mk 14.24.

hunc>hoc: *in diem hoc,* L 19.42; *accipiens calicem . . . dixit accipite hoc,* L 22.17.

id>eam: *regnum . . . omnes in eam conatur,* L 16.16.

[27] The relative is incorrectly in the accusative by attraction. Professor Hatch suggests that the word order has probably been influenced by that of D.

[28] This is due to the Greek gender of πρόβατα, the scribe constantly confusing the genders in Latin; cf. J 10.4,14; L 15.4.

[29] Again due to the Greek, παιδία.

id>eum: *uerbum audit . . . accipit eum*, Mt 13.20; *in altare . . . super eum*, Mt 23.18; *dissoluere templum . . . et . . . aedificare eum*, Mt 26.61; (*daemonium*) *nōn potuerunt eicere eum*, Mk 9.18.

illam>illud: (*ouem*) *usque dum inueniat illud*, L 15.4; *ex generatione uitis usque . . . cum illud bibam*, Mk 14.25.

illam>illum: *ab hac creatura uitis . . . cum illum bibam*, Mt 26.29.

illud>illum: *regnum di . . . non intrauit in illum*, Mk 10.15.

illum>illud: *non potest calix iste transire nisi illut bibam*, Mt 26.42; (*spiritum*) *ut eicerunt illut*, Mk 9.18.

ipsum>ipse: *rumpet uinum nouum utres ueteres et ipse effundetur*, L 5.37.

5. Verbs: Conjugation

Confusion of conjugations is not as noticeable in Codex Bezae as one might expect. In the majority of cases which do occur the third tends to go into the second, which is contrary to the general tendency in other texts (Grandgent, 166), but in accordance with the usage in the *Peregrinatio* (Bechtel, 88).

1>3: this seems to occur only in the future tense: *rememoreris*, Mt 5.23; *operemur*, J 6.28; *honoret*, J 12.26; *reprobent*, L 6.22.

2>1: *miserabuntur*, Mt 5.7.

2>3: *lugunt*, Mt 5.5; *lugetis* (fut.), L 6.25; *respondetis* (fut.), L 22.68; *respondite*, Mk 11.29; *suademus* (fut.), Mt 28.14.

3>1: *prendederunt*, J 21.3 (as though compound of *do*); *relinquat* (pres.), Mk 13.34; *speratis* (*spernatis*, pres.), J 8.49; *bibetis* (subj.), L 12.29; *tollet, emet* (subj.), L 22.36; *tradet* (subj.), L 12.58.

3>2: in the present tense: *agent*, L 7.25; A 20.21; *cadent*, Mt 15.27; *dices*, L 20.21; *dicet*, Mt 22.36; J 4.10; *dicent*, J 4.33; *dimittentur*, L 5.20; *edet*, J 6.54; *edent*, Mt 15.27; *eicient*, L 11.19; *metet*, J 4.36; *metent*, L 12.24; *mittent*, L 5.38; *pendet*, Mt 22.40; *pluet*, Mt 5.45; *ponent*, Mt 5.15; *quaeret*, Mk 8.12; *recedet*, L 9.39; *recumbet*, L 7.37; *serent*, L 12.24; *soluet*, L 13.15; *spernent*, L 18.9; *tanget*, L 15.12; *tolles*, L 19.21; *tollet*, L 6.30; *uibet* (*bibet*), J 6.54. One future form goes into the second, *plangebunt*, Mt 24.30, as does one perfect, *linuit* (*leuit*), J 9.6,11.

3>4: present subj., *serpiat*, A 4.17.

4>1: present ind., *exentiat*, Mk 3.21.

Irregularities in Tense Forms

Present: *neunt* for *nent*, L 12.27.

Perfect: *dedis*, J 17.24; *salibit*, J 21.7; *adiubauit*, L 1.54; *crepauit*, A 1.18; *referit*, A 7.46; *sileuit*, A 15.12; *colleximus*, Mt 25.38; *collexistis*, Mt 25.35,43.

Syncope in the perfect indicative: *dubitasti*, Mt 14.31; *enauigarunt*, A 14.26; *ex-*

clamasse, Mk 15.39; *expirasse*, Mk 15.39; *exquisierat*, Mt 2.16; *glorificasti*, J 17.10; *grabastis*, A 3.14; *inplestis*, Mt 23.32; A 5.28; *inplerunt*, A 13.27; *iudicastis*, A 13.46; 16.15; *lamentastis*, Mt 11.17; *lapidastis*, J 10.32; *lauarastis*, J 4.38; *manducastis*, J 6.26; A 11.3; *manducarunt*, Mt 14.21; J 6.13,23; *nauigarunt*, L 8.22; *negastis*, A 3.13; *nostis*, J 7.28; 8.19; *parasti*, L 12.20; *plorastis*, L 7.32; *postulatis*, A 3.14; *potastis*, Mt 25.35,42; *praeparasti*, Mt 21.16; *prophetarunt*, Mt 11.13; L 16.16; *renuntiarunt*, Mt 28.11; *reuelasti*, Mt 11.25; L 10.21; *saltastis*, Mt 11.17; L 7.32; *seminasti*, Mt 13.27; 25.24; L 19.21; *silerunt*, A 15.13; *sollicitasti*, A 21.38; *uetastis*, L 11.52; *uisitastis*, Mt 25.36,43.

Syncope in the pluperfect subjunctive: *adpropiassent*, Mt 21.1; *adpropinquasset*, Mt 21.34; A 21.33; *breuiasset*, Mk 13.20; *condemnassetis*, Mt 12.7; *considerasset*, A 12.12; *consummasset*, Mt 13.53; 26.1; *dimisset*, Mt 14.23; *enauigassemus*, A 20.15; *erogasset*, L 15.14; *germinasset*, Mt 13.26; *gustasset*, A 20.11; *ingratiasset*, A 12.21; *istigassent*, A 14.19; *iudicasset*, A 3.13; *iudicassent*, A 13.27; *iaiunassent*, A 13.3; *lapidassent*, A 14.19; *nossetis*, J 8.19; *obsecrassent*, A 4.31; *orassent*, A 13.3; *ordinassent*, A 14.23; *postulasset*, A 13.16; *praedicasset*, A 13.24; *pulsasset*, A 12.13; *remigassent*, J 6.19; *salutasset*, A 18.21,22; 21.19; *salutassemus*, A 21.6; *significasset*, A 12.17.

Imperative: the passive imperative has the incorrect form *mundari*, L 5.13.

Irregular verbs show many departures from classical form. Compounds of *eo* form an imperfect in *-iebam*, etc.: *exiebat*, L 6.19; *exiebant*, J 8.9; L 4.22,41; A 8.7; *pertransiebat*, L 19.1; *pertransiebant*, A 16.6; *rediebant*, Mk 6.31; *transiebat*, L 5.15; *transiebant*, Mk 9.30. The future is formed irregularly: *exies*, Mt 5.26; L 12.59; *exiet*, Mt 2.6; J 10.9; Mk 10.12; *exient*, Mt 13.49; *periet*, J 10.28; 11.50; L 21.18; *pertransiet*, L 2.35; *transiet*, Mt 5.18; Mk 13.30; *transient*, Mt 24.35. An irregular participial form is found: *abientes*, L 8.14; 22.13; *exientes*, L 5.2; Mk 6.34.

Forms of *fero* and its compounds which depart from the regular are: *differitis*, L 12.7,24, and *conferitis*, L 24.17 in the present indicative; *adferi* is passive infinitive in Mk 6.27. The imperative has a tendency to end in *s: adfers*, J 20.27; L 13.7; *offers*, L 5.14; Mk 1.44. *Transferre* seems to be imperative: L 22.42; Mk 14.36.[30]

Possum shows the following irregularities: *potebat*, L 19.3; *posuisti*, L 19.21; *poterint*, L 21.15.

The defective verb *odi* is conjugated on the analogy of the fourth conjugation: future, *odies*, Mt 5.43; *odiet*, L 16.13; *odient*, Mt 24.10; perfect, *odiuit*, J 15.18; *odierunt*, J 15.24,25; and the participle *odientibus*, Mt 5.44; L 6.27.

6. Verbs: Voice

The passive forms are still flourishing in Codex Bezae. The breakdown of the synthetic into analytic forms, while foreshadowed,[31] has not yet reached any appreciable dimensions. In spite of the general regularity, however, cases of the confusion of active forms with passive, and deponent forms with passive and active are not lacking. These are recorded in the following lists.

[30] In the first reference it is possible that the form is an infinitive, but in the second it is clearly meant to be imperative. Since they occur, however, in relating the same episode, perhaps both are imperative.
[31] See the section on participles, p. 57.

Verbs that have become deponent:

certo:[32] *certamini introire,* L 13.24; *alius quis certabatur,* L 22.59.

confundo:[33] *qui enim confusus fuerit me et meos hunc filius hominis confundetur,* L 9.26; the same in Mk 8.38.

conuerto: *non conuertatur retro,* Mt 24.18.

egeo: *coepit egeri,* L 15.14.

nuncupo: *nuncupati sunt . . . discipulos christianos,*[34] A 11.26.

paeniteo:[32] *paeniteor,* L 17.4; *paenitemini,* Mt 4.17; Mk 1.15; *paenitebuntur,* L 16.30.

pareo: *monumentum paretur decorum,* Mt 23.27.

seduco: *ut seducantur . . . electos,*[34] Mt 24.24.

trepido: *non . . . uestrum cor . . . trepidetur,* J 14.27.

Deponents with active forms:

calumnior: *si cuius aliquid calumniaui restituo,* L 19.8.

iniurior: *seruos eius iniuriauerunt,* Mt 22.6; *iniuriauerunt eos,* A 14.5.

lamentor:[35] *non lamentastis,* Mt 11.17.

scrutor: *scrutate scripturas,* J 5.39.

Deponents with passive meanings:

consolor:[36] *noluit consolari,* Mt 2.18; *beati qui lugunt quoniam ipsi consolabuntur,* Mt 5.4; *hic consolatur tu autem adfligeris,* L 16.25; *consolati sunt non mediocriter,* A 20.12.

demolior: *quae demolita sunt eius raeaedificabo,* A 15.16.

iniurior: *tradetur . . . et iniuriabitur,* L 18.32.

loquor: *loquetur et quod haec fecit in memoriam,* Mt 26.13.

misereor: *beati misericordes quia ipsi miserebuntur,* Mt 5.7.

obliuiscor: *unum non est oblitum,* L 12.6.

operor: *manifestetur opera eius quoniam deo sunt operata,* J 3.21.

Active forms with passive meanings:

in signum contradicentem, L 2.34.

a quo regnum dei euangelizat, L 16.16.

in quo beneplacui, Mt 3.17; *in quo conplacui,* Mt 17.5; *in quem conplacui,* Mk 1.11; *in quo conplacuit anima mea,* Mt 12.18, are formed on the analogy of the Greek εὐδοκέω.

C. SYNTAX

1. Number[37]

The collective nouns *ciuitas, generatio, grex, multitudo, plebs, populus,* and *turba*

[32] The deponent forms of these words are common enough in Biblical texts to be cited as collateral forms to the active in *Thes. Ling. Lat.* (for *paeniteo* see Georges, *Lex.*). They are included here, however, because they depart from classical usage.

[33] Georges, *Lex.*, and Rönsch, 354.

[34] The use of the accusative case here with the passive form might be merely a barbarous error; cf., however, Mt 24.24, cited below, where the same kind of error appears, but where the mistake seems clearly to be in the voice of the verb.

[35] This word has a collateral form *lamento,* but that is not found in classical Latin.

[36] A rare and ante-classical form exists, *consolo.* This usage may be a survival of that early form. Cf. *Thes. Ling. Lat.*, IV, 481,2.

[37] On the question of congruence and number, see the discussions in Synt., chaps. I–III; and Svennung, 155–72.

appear in Codex Bezae sometimes with a singular verb and sometimes with a plural. Often the singular verb is used, but a following modifier (such as a participle) or a pronoun referring to the collective is in the plural. The following examples will illustrate these various usages.

ciuitas: *ciuitas exiit . . . et uidentes eum rogauerunt*, Mt 8.34.

generatio: *generatio uiperarum quomodo potestes bona loqui*, Mt 12.34; *o generatio incredula . . . quousque uobiscum ero*, Mt 17.17; *o generatio incredula . . . usque quo ero ad uos*, L 9.41.

grex: *fecit impetum totus grex . . . et mortui sunt*, Mt 8.32; *nolite timere pusillum gregem*,[38] L 12.32. Elsewhere always with a singular verb.

multitudo: *facta est multitudo . . . laudantes*, L 2.13; *coepit omnis multitudo . . . gaudentes laudare*, L 19.37; *multitudo magna audientes . . . uenerunt*, Mk 3.8; *conuenit multitudo et consaesae sunt*, A 2.6; *ita ut crederent . . . copiosa multitudo*, A 14.1; *sileuitque omnis multitudo et audiebant*, A 15.12.

plebs: *erat plebs expectans . . . et mirabantur*, L 1.21.

populus: *populus qui sedebat in tenebris uiderunt lumen*, Mt 4.16; *propter populum . . . ut credant*, J 11.42; *testificabantur ergo populus qui erat cum eo*, J 12.17; *stabat populus uidens subsannabant autem eum*, L 23.35; *populus uero adclamabant*, A 12.22. In ten other instances, however, where the word is used it is found with a singular verb.

turba: *conuocans turbam dixit eis*, Mt 15.10; *plurima . . . turba strauerunt uestimenta sua*, Mt 21.8; *sequebantur illum turba multa*, J 6.2; *turba haec . . . maledicti sunt*, J 7.49; and J 12.9; 12.34; Mk 2.13; 4.1; 5.24; 9.15; A 6.7; 16.22.

Turba, of all the collective nouns, seems to have caused the most confusion in number. Beside the examples given above of its use in the singular with plural verbs or modifiers, the word is found in three cases followed by the singular. Very frequently it is used in the plural followed by a plural. Nowhere, however, is it found in the plural followed by a singular verb.

There are a few instances where other nouns or pronouns are in the wrong number. Singular instead of plural occurs in the following: *duo minus*, L 21.2; *filius*, Mk 3.17, where it refers to two men who are mentioned in the preceding verse; *doctores in quo*, A 13.1; *quidam* (plu.) . . . *in quo*, A 19.13,14. The plural is used incorrectly for the singular as follows: *dixit . . . illis diabolus si filius es dei . . .*, L 4.3; *permitte . . . mihi . . . Ihs dixit illis* (referring to the same person as *mihi*), L 9.62; *in sinus Abrahae*, L 16.22; *inposuit eis nomina*[39] *Boanges*, Mk 3.17; *fiat habitatio eorum* (referring to the same person as *illius* below) *deserta . . . et episcopatus illius sumat alius*, A 1.20; *uiri . . . quidam nomine Simon*, A 8.9; *uidentes . . . Cyprum et relinquentes eas a sinistra*, A 21.3.

A few abstract nouns are used in the plural in a concrete sense. This is not entirely an un-Latin usage, but its origin in connection with Biblical texts has been

[38] See p. 38, *infra*.

[39] Perhaps the scribe followed the Greek ὄνομα, mistaking it for the plural because of a similar ending.

ascribed to the influence of the Hebrew (Plater-White, 18).[40] The following instances occur in Codex Bezae: *propter incredulitates eorum*, Mt 13.58; *ambulantes in . . . iustitiis dmi*, L 1.6; and *qui faciet omnes uoluntates meas*, A 13.22.

Verbs in Codex Bezae are very frequently out of concord with reference to number. The following list gives the references where verbs are in the plural but should be in the singular: Mt 26.49; J 7.37; 10.1; 20.13; L 5.36; 8.9, 29; 24.13; Mk 6.14,34; A 2.5; 4.3; 5.2; 11.26,27; 15.38,39; 18.23; 19.1,31. A few of these changes may be explained by the scribe's tendency to regard the subject of the verb and an intervening subordinate clause as a double subject: e.g., *Barnabas uero adsumpto Marco nauigauerunt*, A 15.39. Some cases may be due to phonology, the nasal *n* being incorrectly inserted before final *t*: e.g., *intrant* for *intrat*.[41] Others, however, must be attributed to ignorance or carelessness on the part of the scribe.

Verbs in the singular, but which belong in the plural, occur in the following references: Mt 2.9; 28.6; J 10.28; L 6.3; Mk 3.11; 6.53; 11.8; A 3.25; 4.7; 5.32,40; 7.57; 12.16; 13.27; 15.15,36; 17.4; 19.6; 20.25; 21.21. Here, again, we may attribute some cases to incorrect omission of the nasal,[41] but on the whole they are due to ignorance or carelessness.

Singular verbs with double subjects are not very numerous, and occur for the most part when the verb comes first in the sentence: Mk 3.31, *et uenit mater eius et fratres eius;* also Mk 1.5; 8.27; A 5.17; 7.15; 10.23; 13.11; 14.14; 17.14. Two instances occur where the verb does not come first: *sollicitudo saeculi et seductio diuitiarum simul suffocat*, Mt 13.22; and *quaecumq·manus tua et uoluntas tua praedestinauit*, A 4.28.

In some cases a singular verb with plural subject is clearly due to the influence of the Greek: *paruit zizania* (ἐφάνη τὰ ζιζάνια), Mt 13.26; *si fuerit alicui homini centum oues* (γένηται . . . ἑκατὸν πρόβατα), Mt 18.12; and *in parabolis omnia dicitur* (πάντα λέγεται), Mk 4.11.

2. Case

Nominative

The only departure from classical usage is the employment of the nominative as an absolute, alongside the ablative and accusative absolutes. This construction, common in all Vulgar Latin (Grandgent, 47; Bonnet, 565–68), is found but once in Codex Bezae: *circueuntes . . . discipuli eius cum surrexisset introibit in Lystram ciuitatem*, A 14.20.

Genitive

The genitive absolute, in place of the ablative absolute, is not uncommonly employed in the Old Latin versions of the Bible (Plater-White, 35). It is clearly an imitation of the Greek construction, and seems to be limited to Ecclesiastical texts.[42] The occurrences of this construction in Codex Bezae are: *cogitantium omnium . . . de Iohane . . . dixit*, L 3.15; *omnium mirantium in omnibus quae faciebat*

[40] This must be stated with caution. Greek often uses abstract nouns in the plural in a concrete sense, and it may be that we are here dealing with imitation of the Greek, since in the three instances cited D has plural forms, *i.e.*, ἀπιστείας, δικαιώμασιν, θελήματα.

[41] See p. 21, *supra*.

[42] Bonnet reports no instances in Gregory of Tours; it is lacking in the *Peregrinatio* (Bechtel, Löfstedt), and the *Liber Historiae Francorum* (Taylor), and no mention of it is made in the other commentaries on Late Latin works, or in the handbooks on Vulgar Latin which I have examined. Cf. Leumann-Hofmann, 449.

dixit, L 9.43; *audientium . . . eorum haec . . . dixit parabolam*, L 19.11; *quorundam dicentium de templo . . . dixit*, L 21.5; *deficientium hominum a timore*, L 21.26; *incipientium . . . horum fieri erigite uos*, L 21.28; *accipientium . . . eorum panem ab eo aperti sunt oculi eorum*, L 24.31; *haec . . . eorum loquentium ipse stetit in medio*, L 24.36; *adpraehendi*[43] *manum caeci eduxit eum*, Mk 8.23.

The genitive of quality is used in Vulgar Latin almost to the exclusion of the ablative of quality (Löfstedt, 160; Bonnet, 548 ff.; *Synt.*, 128). In our MS. the ablative appears once: *prospicite . . . uiros testimonio bono ·vii·*, A 6.3. The following examples illustrate the use of the genitive: *modice fidei*, Mt 14.31; 16.8; *in hominibus consolationis*, L 2.14; *uos pusillae fidei*, L 12.28; *uident illum . . . sedentem . . . sane mentis*, Mk 5.15; *nescitis cuius spiritui estis*, L 9.55 (cf. p. 25).

The definitive genitive, which was originally a possessive genitive of the "*Ortsgotthei*" (i.e., giving the name of the deity who presided over a certain locality, as *Silari ad flumen*) and gradually came to be used in expressions of place, was extended in Late Latin to abstract terms also, possibly under the influence of Hebrew, at least in Ecclesiastical writers.[44] It is very common in Codex Bezae, and the following are typical examples: *in Bethleem Iudaeae*, Mt 2.1,5,6; *tolerabilius erit terrae Sodomum et Gomorrae*, Mt 10.15; *panes propositionis*, Mt 12.4; *secus mare Galilaeae*, Mt 15.29; J 6.1; *trans torrentem Cedri*, J 18.1; *super mare Tiberiadis*, J 21.1.

In the use of the genitive after certain adjectives we approach the usage of early Latin, e.g., *retiam plenam . . . magnorum piscium*, J 21.11; *nihil dignum mortis*, L 23.15 (Lindsay, Pl. 17). Also in one instance it occurs after an adverb, *in obuiam eius*, J 12.13.

The employment of the genitive as the direct object of verbs is extensive in Biblical texts, and is presumably due to Greek influence.[45] The following list shows the verbs which take the genitive in Codex Bezae, the Greek of D being indicated in parentheses.

accipio (λαμβάνω): *quaerentes occasionem . . . accipere eius*, L 11.54.

adpraehendo (ἐπιλαμβάνω): *ut adpraehenderent uerborum eius*, L 20.20.

audio (ἀκούω): *audientes eius uerborum horum*, J 7.40; *ds peccatorum non audit*, J 9.29,31; *obis (oues) uocis eius audiunt*, J 10.3; *non audierunt eorum*, J 10.8; *uocis meae audient*, J 10.16 (*audiunt*, 10.27); *si quis audierit meorum berborum (uerborum)*, J 12.47; *audiuit synfoniae et chori*, L 15.25; *ei iustum est . . . uestri audire . . . iudicate*, A 4.19.

curo (θεραπεύω ἀπό): *curabit multos . . . iniquorum spirituum*, L 7.21.[46]

deficio (ὑστερέω): *ne cuius defecistis*, L 22.35.

[43] This example is extremely strange, however, and it might be a mere blunder for *adpraehendit . . . [et]*.

[44] For a full account of this development, see Leumann-Hofmann, 394 and 395, remark b.

[45] The genitive with verbs also occurs occasionally in those Latin poets who were conscious imitators of Greek models; cf. Süss, 40–41.

[46] A rare usage in place of the ablative with *ab*. In this case, however, I do not believe it is a genuine Grecism, but due to the scribe copying exactly the Greek of the corresponding στίχος without giving thought to what he had written above, thus mixing the construction. The passage reads: *curabit multos ab infirmitatibus et plagis et iniquorum spirituum;* D has ἀπό with the genitive. For other errors to be thus explained, see pp. 37, 38.

dominor (κατακυριεύω): *reges gentium dominantur eorum*, Mt 20.25; L 22.25; Mk 10.42.

obtineo (τυγχάνω): *digni fuerint . . . obtinere et resurrectionis ex mortuis*, L 20.35.

principor (κατεξουσιάζω): *magni principantur eorum*, Mt 20.25.

tango (ἅπτω): *si tetigero tantum uestimenti eius*, Mt 9.21; *omnis populus quaerebat tangere eius*, L 6.19.

Sometimes the genitive follows verbs of filling: *repletae sunt nuptiae discumbentium*, Mt 22.10; *esurientes inpleuit bonorum*, L 1.53 (see p. 37).

Another usage, found extensively in Late Latin, is that of the genitive after comparatives.[47] The following instances are to be noted in our MS.: *maiora horum ostendit ei opera*, J 5.20; *plura signa faciet quorum hic faciet*, J 7.31; *pater . . . omnium maior est*, J 10.29; *maior eius qui misit*, J 13.16; *maiora horum faciet*, J 14.12; *maiorem huius dilectionem nemo habet*, J 15.13; *maius horum praeceptorum aliud non est*, Mk 12.31.

The partitive genitive is regularly replaced by the ablative with *de* or *ex* in Codex Bezae (p. 47), a phenomenon so common in all Vulgar Latin (Bonnet, 610; Draeger, I, 628; Grandgent, 43) that only an instance or so will suffice by way of illustration: *unum de prophetis*, Mt 16.14; *nemo ex uobis*, J 7.19. The classical construction, however, may still be found occasionally: *quidam scribarum et pharisaeorum*, Mt 12.38; *quidam . . . stantium*, Mt 27.47; *propter quod eorum opus lapidastis me*, J 10.32; *multi Iudaeorum*, J 12.11; *quod a foris est calicis et catilli*, L 11.39; *unum mercennariorum tuorum*, L 15.21.

Dative

There are fewer irregularities in the dative case than in the others, and these are found for the most part in connection with its adverbial use.

Adorare, which in classical Latin is construed with the accusative, is followed usually by the dative in Codex Bezae: *adorare ei*, Mt 2.2,8,11; 9.18; 15.25; 28.9; *adorare patri*, J 4.21,23. In all these instances D has προσκυνέω + dat. The accusative, however, occurs in Mt 4.9,10; 18.26; A 10.25.[48]

Contingere is followed by the dative in L 8.19, imitating the Greek συντυχεῖν: *contingere ei*.

The dative follows *misereri*, but only pronouns seem to be used in this manner: *tibi*, Mt 16.22; *nobis*, L 17.13; *mihi*, L 16.24; 18.13,39; Mk 10.47.

There was some confusion of case with *benedicere* and *maledicere* in Ecclesiastical literature. They govern both the accusative and dative with no difference in sense. Both cases are about equally popular, but *benedicere* seems to prefer the accusative and *maledicere* the dative.[49] In Codex Bezae, *benedicere* usually takes the accusative: *benedixit d̅m̅*, L 2.28; *benedixit eos*, L 2.34; *benedicite maledicentes uos*, L 6.28; but it takes the dative in Mt 5.44: *benedicite maledicentibus uos*. *Maledicere* also generally

[47] Ed. Wölfflin, *AR*, 7(1892), 115–31, *Der Genitivus comparationis und die präpositionalen Umschreibungen*; also Draeger, I, 492 ff. Löfstedt (*Synt.*, 118–19) finds the beginnings of this construction in Old Latin rather than in Greek influence, and Mørland follows this view (111), as do Leumann-Hofmann (428).

[48] D also has the accusative in Mt 4.10 and A 10.25; in Mt 4.9 and 18.26 the dative.

[49] This was the general tendency in Ecclesiastical Latin; Salonius, 144; Löfstedt, 218.

appears with the accusative, contrary to the tendency elsewhere: *maledicentes uos*, L 6.28; Mt 5.44.

The dative of the possessor is employed often. This construction seems to have been used more frequently in some authors (Bonnet, 544) than it was in classical times. This is not true, however, in Codex Bezae, although the construction is common, e.g., *unde huic omnis sapientia haec*, Mt 13.54; *unde . . . nobis . . . panes tanti*, Mt 15.33; *fuerit alicui homini centum oues*, Mt 18.12; *quid igitur erit nobis*, Mt 19.27; *cura ei non est de ouibus*, J 10.13; *non erat illis filius*, L 1.7; *duo debitores erant cuidam faeneratori*, L 7.41; *argentum et aurum non est mihi*, A 3.6.

Other constructions with the dative are regular and need no comment.

Accusative

The accusative absolute is a construction which arose out of the confusion between the ablative and accusative cases (Leumann-Hofmann, 449; Mørland, 106). It was used by some authors frequently, by others more sparingly (Bonnet, 561; Löfstedt, 158). In Codex Bezae it is employed very often: cf. *tanta . . . ab illo signa facta . . . non credebant*,[50] J 12.37; *continuo surgentem eam ministraret eis*, L 4.39; *saepius eum ligatum . . . disrumpebat*, Mk 5.4; *moras facientes et docentes superuenerunt Iudaei*, A 14.19; *desponentes sic . . . presbyteros quae . . . dicebantur*, A 15.11; *oportet me sollemnem diem aduenientem facere Hierosolymis iter*, A 18.21;[51] *salutantes aute [m e]os*[52] *adduxerunt iubenem*, A 20.12.

Some verbs are incorrectly construed with the accusative, although the number is insignificantly small:

abutor: regularly with the ablative, but once with the accusative: *consilium dei abusi sunt*, L 7.30.

confundo: twice followed by the accusative where *confundor* is clearly used as a deponent: *hunc filius hominis confundetur*, L 9.26; Mk 8.38.[53]

noceo: usually with the dative, but with the accusative twice: *non te nocui*, Mt 20.13; *exibit ab eo nihil nocens eum*, L 4.35.

Verbs of filling regularly take the accusative in the active voice, to designate the thing filled. In Codex Bezae the passive is twice found with the accusative designating that with which something is filled: *inpleti sunt aepulationem*, A 5.17; *repleta est tota ciuitas confusionem* A 19.29.

The adjective *dignus*, regularly followed by the ablative, is once used with the accusative: *dignus est . . . operarius mercedem suam*, L 10.7.

Other uses of the accusative are regular and need no special comment.

Ablative

The ablative absolute, as one would naturally expect, is employed most frequently of all the absolute constructions. To list examples of this familiar construction

[50] This may be nominative, neut. plu.

[51] Professor Hatch looks upon this as an unhappy attempt to render D: τὴν ἑορτὴν ἡμέραν ἐρχομένην ποιῆσαι; *iter* represents nothing at all in the Greek MSS., and may be due to the scribe's misunderstanding. On the whole passage, see Ropes's note (*op. cit.*, p. 177).

[52] The bracketed letters restore the sense to *aute os* of the MS.

[53] Cf. the mention of these two instances above, p. 31.

would serve no purpose. Mention should be made, however, of mixed absolute constructions. Taylor (71–72) has cited examples of the accusative and ablative used together in an absolute construction, and the explanation offered, namely, that it is due to the confusion of the ablative and accusative cases by reason of the weakness of final *m*, is probably correct. Cases of this kind which occur in Codex Bezae are: *Ihm . . . nato*, Mt 2.1; *consummata omnem temptationem*, L 4.13; *exeunte . . . Petrum et Iohannen*, A 3.11; *pollicitationem sps sancti accepta*, A 2.33; *uocatis duobus famulorum . . . et militem fidelem*, A 10.7; *adsupto* (*adsumpto*) *Iohannen*, A 12.25.

Ablative and nominative were likewise confused: *audientes . . . omni populo*, L 20.45; *cognito Ihs . . . dixit*, Mk 2.8.

There is another type of mixed absolute in which genitive and ablative are used together. The explanation in some instances seems to be that the scribe started to write an ablative absolute, but looking at the Greek copied the genitive of the corresponding στἰχος in the latter part of his construction: *incendentibus . . . ignem . . . et circumsedentium*, L 22.55; *non credentibus eis a gaudio et mirantium*, L 24.41. In the following cases, however, the genitive and ablative are confused in the same στἰχος: *multis . . . turbis adstantium*, L 12.1; *eo longe iter habentes* (*habentis*), L 15.20.

The ablative is found after adjectives and verbs of filling. There was confusion between the ablative and genitive with these words even in early Latin (Lindsay, Pl., 17): *pleni hypocrisi et iniquitate*, Mt 23.28; *sicut ira plenus*, J 11.33; *plenum est rapina et iniquitate*, L 11.39; *inpletus spo sancto*, A 4.8; *inplens aceto*, Mt 27.48; *spiritu sancto replebitur*, L 1.15.

The Hebrew cognate accusative is expressed in Biblical texts by an ablative (Plater-White, 20). This is naturally most frequent in the O.T., but appears in Codex Bezae in a quotation from the O.T.: *morti* (*sic*) *morietur*, Mk 7.10. Similar instances, but not in quotations, are *timuerunt timore magno*, Mk 4.41, and *obstipuerunt . . . stupore magno*, Mk 5.42, which are due possibly to the influence of the construction in question.

In expressions of time the ablative and accusative alternate with no apparent differentiation of meaning, e.g., *statis toto die otiosi*, Mt 20.6, and *mansit . . . duo dies*, J 11.6.

The function of the partitive genitive is taken over by the ablative with *de* or *ex* (p. 47).

Unclassified Confusions in Case

Codex Bezae is full of errors in agreement of cases. To mention them all would take more space than the subject merits, but a few select examples and possible explanations of the confusion are in order.

In some instances a relative pronoun attracts its antecedent into its own case: *qui ascenderit primum piscis tolle*, Mt 17.27; *nec ipsum facile puto mundum capere qui scribuntur libri*, J 21.25; *qui autem sequebatur eum populus docebat*, L 5.27; *curate qui sunt in ea* (*ciuitate*) *infirmi*, L 10.9; *nos ipsi testes sumus . . . et spm sanctum quem dedit ds*, A 5.32; and many similar cases.

There are also instances where the relative pronoun is attracted to the case of its antecedent: *narrationem de his quibus completa sunt*, L 1.1; *de omnibus quibus fecit malis*, L 3.19; *laudare dm de omnibus quibus uiderunt*, L 19.37; *euertere uias domini quas sunt rectas*, A 13.10.

The nominative appears where there should be a genitive in A 6.15; and vice versa in L 6.17; A 5.36.

The nominative occurs where an accusative is needed in Mt 24.15; J 11.52; 14.16,17; 17.3; Mk 6.11; 7.4; 9.2,14; A 1.23; 13.44; 15.22; 16.16; and vice versa in L 1.9; 8.22; 11.1; 17.2; 18.17; 22.41; Mk 4.19; 5.25; A 2.17; 4.10; 5.32; 13.28 14.9; 18.6; 20.23.

The nominative appears for the vocative in L 18.39, *filius Dauid.*

The genitive is used where an accusative is needed in Mk 14.13; A 5.36; 7.33; and vice versa in A 1.17; 2.38; 4.9,34.

The genitive also appears where an ablative should be, mostly after prepositions, and due, in many instances, to a slavish following of the Greek: L 12.4; 24.27; Mk 9.42; A 3.24; 19.13; and vice versa in L 11.30; 22.50; A 3.15; 4.25; 13.36; 16.25.

The dative is incorrectly used for the accusative in A 15.2; and in A 8.12 the accusative modifies a dative: *crederent Philippo euangelizantem.*

The accusative and ablative cases are very frequently confused. A large number of instances can be explained, however, because final *m* was unstable and easily dropped out (p. 37), readily causing confusion. The following passages may be explained in this manner: Mt 2.14; 5.10; 14.35; 25.34,41; 27.62; J 13.26; L 5.29; 8.37; 11.42; 15.10; 21.4; Mk 2.25; 5.40; 8.37; 11.13; 14.47; 15.21; A 3.14; 5.1; 19.21,36. The addition of the nasal *n* or *m* has caused confusion in L 13.29; A 2.40; 15.2,20; 18.15; 19.25. Other examples, however, can not be thus explained, and must have been due to sheer carelessness or ignorance: *in mundo hunc,* J 9.39; *in diem hoc,* L 19.42; *timore . . . magnum conpraehensi erant,* L 8.37; and also J 8.31; L 10.4; Mk 5.4; 10.10; 12.33; A 13.22; 17.30; 19.29.

The accusative takes the place of the vocative in L 12.32; *nolite timere pusillum gregem.*

The ablative appears incorrectly for the nominative: *multisque numeris . . . reuersi sunt,* A 11.21; and *disputante* for *disputans,* A 18.28.

The following mixtures of case are perhaps caused by the scribe taking a look at the Greek side, after he had begun his phrase in a normal Latin construction: *ex his pusillis fidem habentium,* Mk 9.42; *uestri audire magis quam* $\overline{dm}$, A 4.19; *plenus* $\overline{spo}$ *sancto et fidei,* A 11.24.

Conclusions

From the character of the errors listed above in the use of cases it must be concluded that the largest fraction of them are due to gross carelessness or else to ingorance. Kenyon (*Handbook,* 92) has remarked that the Greek "has the appearance of having been written by a scribe whose native tongue was Latin." And yet, after examining the examples adduced one would, to my mind, rather agree with the view of Clark (*Acts,* lviii), that "the translator was neither a Latin nor a Greek, but someone whose Greek was not perfect and whose Latin was much worse." That any scribe whose native tongue was Latin, unless he were very poorly trained indeed, could have made so many and such barbarous errors, is almost incredible.

3. Pronouns

Demonstrative

The demonstrative pronouns of most frequent occurrence in Codex Bezae are the following: *is*, 2,550 times; *ille*, 1,113; *hic*, 826; *ipse*, 304.[54] The frequency in the various cases is as follows:

Case	*is*	*ille*	*hic*	*ipse*
Nom. sing.	1	175	247	95
Nom. plu.	—	86	53	45
Gen. sing.	461	26	28	13
Gen. plu.	125	15	14	8
Dat. sing.	290	243	25	7
Dat. plu.	196	210	18	2
Acc. sing.	850	168	182	49
Acc. plu.	318	49	153	26
Abl. sing.	202	89	69	40
Abl. plu.	107	52	37	19

From these figures the following general conclusions may be drawn. In the nominative case *ille* and *hic* are preferred, the latter being largely confined to the neuter gender, the former to the masculine and feminine. In the oblique cases, forms of *is* are distinctly predominant, with the exception of the dative, where *illi* and *illis* are nearly as frequent as *ei* and *eis*. The comparatively large number of cases where *hic* appears in the accusative is due to the fact that it is used almost exclusively as the neuter pronoun.

The exchange of one pronoun for another is common throughout the MS., *is* and *ille* being practically interchangeable, as the following instances show, where *ille* and *is* are used in the same context to refer to the same person with no distinction in meaning: Mt 12.2,10, *dixerunt illi . . . interrogauerunt eum;* Mt 12.46,47, *querentes loqui ei . . . dixit quidam illi. Ipse* retains for the most parts its intensive significance, but is sometimes substituted for *ille*.

The relative frequency of the various pronouns and their use in the different cases agree in general with the results of other studies of Late Latin works, although these are of somewhat later date (saec. vii–viii) than Codex Bezae.[55]

The Reflexive Pronoun

The reflexive pronoun *suus* appears 436 times in the MS. There are some instances of the substitution of *eius* for reflexive forms, although they are comparatively few; the substitution of the reflexive for *eius* is still rarer.[56]

eius for **suus**: *ipse uos baptizabit . . . cuius uentilabrum in manu eius*, Mt 3.12; L 3.17; *sufficit discipulo ut fiat sicut magister eius et seruus sicut dominus eius*,

[54] The other pronouns, *iste, idem, alter*, etc., are infrequent, and do not affect our general statistics. *Ille* and *hic*, in a large percentage of the cases listed, are used as adjectives; *is* very rarely.

The following table shows how the scribe of d translates the Greek pronouns of most frequent occurrence:

	is	*ille*	*ipse*	*hic*	*iste*	*suus*
αὐτός	1969	619	127	17	3	70
ἐκεῖνος . .	—	151	1	1	—	1
οὗτος	4	1	3	604	62	—

[55] Cf. Taylor, 116–18, and the references there cited. See also Salonius, 229 ff., for conditions in the late sixth century.

[56] This confusion was not general before the seventh century (Pei, 205), and classical usage still obtains almost entirely in Gregory of Tours (Bonnet, 695–97). We should expect, however, to find the misuse of these forms in Codex Bezae, in keeping with the general character of the scribe, as already noted above.

Mt 10.25; *inimici homines domestici eius,* Mt 10.36; *locutus est per os sanctorum profetarum eius,* L 1.70; *de abundantia cordis loquitur os eius,* L 6.45; *quando . . . custodit aulam suam in pace est substantia eius,* L 11.21; *educatus est in domo patris eius,* A 7.20; *ascendit in cor eius uisitare fratres suos,* A 7.23; *accesserunt ad eum discipuli eius,* Mt 5.2; 9.19; 13.36; etc. The confusion of *suus* and demonstrative forms, especially when used with the word *discipuli,* is frequent.

illius for **suus**: *discipuli autem illius dicunt,* Mk 5.31.

ipsius for **suus**: *notum a saeculo est dno opus ipsius,* A 15.18.

suus for **eius**: *uidentes . . . pharisaei dixerunt discipulis suis (Iesu),* Mt 9.11; *cum uidissent quosdam discipulorum suorum (Iesu) . . . uituperauerunt,* Mk 7.2.

eum for **se**: *uidit spiritum . . . descendentem . . . super eum,* Mt 3.16, seems to require the reflexive, although the subject of *uidit* is somewhat ambiguous; *coepit Ihs ostendere . . . quia oportet eum,* Mt 16.21.

suis for **illis**: *propter Iudaeos qui erant in locis suis* (D, ἐκείνοις), A 16.3.

Homo *and* unus

The substantive *homo* during the Late Latin period gradually was reduced to the function of an indefinite pronoun, and survives in French in the indefinite *on* (Grandgent, 8, 37; Salonius, 246). There are a few cases in Codex Bezae which seem to indicate this tendency, although some are doubtful, and in all of them *homo* merely translates the Greek ἄνθρωπος: *non potest homo accipere quidquam,* J 3.27; *in sabbato circumciditis hominem,* J 7.22; *circumcisionem accipit homo in sabbato,* J 7.23; *simile est . . . grano sinapis quod accipiens homo seminauit,* Mt 13.31.[57] There is also a peculiar usage of *homo* in Codex Bezae, examples of which I have not found elsewhere, i.e., the habit of connecting *homo* with another substantive (or with an adjective which is used substantively) almost in the sense of *quidam.* This peculiarity, too, seems to be due to literal translation from the Greek: *inimicus homo hoc fecit,* Mt 13.28; *simile est . . . homini negotianti,* Mt 13.45; *simile est . . . homini patrifamilias,* Mt 20.1; *homo fuit patrifamilias,* Mt 21.33; *uenit homo diues,* Mt 27.57; *uidit hominem caecum,* J 9.1; note *homines pastores* L 2.15, where *pastores* seems to be used as an adjective equivalent to *pastorales.*

Unus loses its numerical sense and becomes equivalent to the indefinite *quidam* in the following; the Greek has εἷς in each case: *unus princeps ueniens adorabat ei,*[58] Mt 9.18; *unus accedens ait illi,* Mt 19.16; *adcurrit unus et . . . rogabat eum,* Mk 10.17 (Grandgent, 37).

Relative Pronoun qui

The relative pronoun *qui* is used with great frequency throughout the MS. as a

[57] Although this usage very closely resembles the French, we can not take it as evidence that the MS. is of Gallic origin, for "*hic autem usus uocis 'homo' non unius Galliae proprius est, sed etiam Hispaniae et dialectorum Italicarum.*" K. Meister in *Rh. Mus.*, New Series, 64 (1909), 389.

[58] In this case the εἰς- of the Greek εἰσελθών was perhaps mistaken for εἷς, but Professor Hatch calls my attention to the fact that *unus* (or the equivalent) appears also in the Vulgate, the Peshîttâ, and the Bohairic, which fact suggests that there very likely was some early Greek MS. that read εἷς at this point; and, besides, it is pretty clear that d in any event is not a direct translation of D.

connecting link between sentences, with the force of "and he did" or "but he did":[59] cf. *angelus Dei apparuit in uisu Ioseph dicens . . . suscipe puerum . . . qui autem exsurgens accepit puerum*, Mt 2.13,14; *scribas interrogabat populi . . . qui autem dixerunt*, Mt 2.4,5; *dicit eis uenite post me . . . qui autem . . . secuti sunt eum*, Mt 4.19,20; *comminatus est eis . . . qui autem exeuntes diuulgabant eum*, Mt 9.30,31 (Plater-White, 127).

Articular Use of Pronouns[60]

This is a characteristic development of Late Latin. The demonstrative pronouns gradually weakened, being often confused with one another, as we have seen, and some of them came to have no more force than that of the definite article. In translations of the Bible, and in other Ecclesiastical works, where the influence of Greek was strong, this tendency seems to be even more marked than in secular writings, for the Greek article bothered the Latin translators, who used various methods of rendering this somewhat intractable form.

The pronouns which appear in Codex Bezae in the function of the article are *hic*, *ille*, *ipse*, and *is*. Since the shade of difference between these words used as demonstratives or as articles is sometimes slight, and there is often doubt as to which use is intended, I have limited myself in the following examples to cases where the demonstrative does not appear in D, but does so in the Latin, an indication that the scribe was evidently attempting to translate the Greek article.

hic as article: *destruam hunc templum*, Mk 14.58; *nobis . . . est haec repromissio*, A 2.39; *principes huius populi*, A 4.8; *factum erat hoc signum sanitatis*, A 4.22; *adtulit hanc pecuniam*, A 4.37; *auditus est . . . hic sermo*, A 11.22; *de hac uia Dni*, A 19.23; *aedituam esse magnae Dianae et huius Iouis*, A 19.35. *In hoc mundo*, J 8.26, should be noted, for the phrase is peculiar to John and appears with articular *hic* seventeen times in that Gospel (Rönsch, 421).

ille as article: *nuntiauerunt omnia haec illis undecim*, L 24.9; *inuenerunt congregatos illos xi*, L 24.33; *in porta illa pulchra templi*, A 3.10; *conspicientes . . . illum que curatum* (τὸν τεθεραπευμένον), A 4.14; *in illas partes Babylonis*, A 7.43; *praedicans illud regnum Ihu*, A 20.25.

ipse as article:[61] (all the examples occur in Acts): *uos . . . ipsum sanctum et iustum grabastis*, 3.14; *praetorque templi et ipsi pontefices* (*sic*) *haesitabant*, 5.24; *cum abisset ipse praetor*, 5.26; *ipsum Iacob* (τὸν Ἰακώβ), 7.8; *ipsi Pharao* (τῷ), 7.13; *ipsi Abraham* (τῷ), 7.17; *Ipsius Ioseph* (τοῦ), 7.18; *hunc ipsum Moysen* (τοῦτον τὸν), 7.35; *ipsius Moloch* (τοῦ), 7.43; *ipse altissimus inhabitauit*, 7.48; *ipsi testes deposuerunt uestimenta sua*, 7.58; *erat in ipsa ciuitate magika faciens*, 8.9; *adsumptum est ipsum uas in caelum*, 10.16; *descendens . . . ad ipsos uiros dixit*, 10.21; *introibimus in domum ipsius uiri*, 11.12; *adorabantur omnes ipso proposito cordis permanere*, 11.23; *resurrexit ipsi Istrahel salbatorem Ihm*, 13.23;

[59] The point is not that such a usage was not recognized even by good stylists, but I doubt if there are many Latin authors earlier than the time of d who employ this locution so frequently.

[60] Clark, *Acts*, p. 200; Salonius, 235; Löfstedt, 64; Rönsch, 419.

[61] The use of *ipse* as an article exclusively in Acts seems to indicate that a different person had translated the book. Clark, *Acts*, pp. 205 ff., has listed a few other stylistic peculiarities which point to the same conclusion, namely, the use of the *nomina sacra*, and some differences in vocabulary.

ad ipsos (τοὺς) *qui miserunt eos*, 15.33; *audiebant . . . eos ipsi uincti*, 16.25; *non solum ipsius Ephesi sed . . . omnis Asiae*, 19.26; *ipso . . . uolente Paulo*, 19.30; *de ipsa turba*, 19.33; *habeo ipsam animam caram mihi*, 20.24.

is as article: *usque in eum diem*, Mt 24.38; *uos estis filii . . . eius dispositionis quam Ds disputatauit*, A 3.25; *domini eius puelles*, A 16.19.

iste appears to be articular in but a single instance: *ista uerba haec* (οἱ λόγοι οὗτοι), L 24.17.

unus as indefinite article: *aduocans Ihs puerum unum*, Mt 18.2; *uidens ficum unam*, Mt 21.19; *unus . . . quidam ex illis*, J 11.49. D has εἷς in the first two instances, and εἷς δέ τις in the last (so that here *unus* may still retain most of its original force, as Professor Hatch has suggested).

A relative clause was often the solution which the scribe used for the problem of the Greek article, e.g., *interfecit omnes pueros qui erant in Bethleem* (πάντας τοὺς παῖδας τοὺς), Mt 2.16; *persecuti sunt prophetas qui ante uos fuerunt* (τοὺς προφήτας τοὺς), Mt 5.12; *patrem uestrum qui in caelis est* (πατέρα ὑμῶν τὸν ἐν τοῖς οὐρανοῖς), Mt 5.16; *mittens legatos rogat quae* (τὰ) *ad pacem*, L 14.32. This is so common that to multiply examples is unnecessary. For the difficulties into which this usage led the Latin scribe, cf. Clark, *Acts*, p. 201.

4. Comparison of Adjectives and Adverbs[62]

The general loss of feeling for the different degrees of comparison, which was manifest in popular speech even of an early period, but which greatly increased in the centuries following the Golden Age, is well illustrated by the use of these forms in Codex Bezae. There is no regularity; the scribe uses the different degrees with no thought of their original force. Typical examples are given.

Positive

The positive degree is used in the following examples where the comparative should be used, translating the Greek, however, where the same lack of distinction seems to be common: *bonum tibi est introire . . . quam . . . mitti*, Mt 18.8,9; Mk 9.43; *neque habeo ipsam animam caram mihi quam consummere cursum meum*, A 20.24. The superlative would be natural in *hoc est primum et magnum mandatum*, Mt 22.38; *gloria in altis Deo*, L 2.14; *qui . . . minor est . . . hic erit magnus*, L 9.48.

Commonly the positive degree, joined with an adverb, was used to represent the superlative: *gaudio magno ualde*, Mt 2.10; *in montem altum nimis*, Mt 4.8; *in montem excelsum nimis*, Mt 17.1; *in montem altum ualde*, L 4.5; *erat enim diues ualde*, L 18.23; *uestimenta . . . facta sunt . . . candida nimis*, Mk 9.3; *erat enim magnus ualde*, Mk 16.3. All these instances are translations of the Greek; but the phenomenon was very common in popular speech from Cicero's time on (Löfstedt, 35–36), even where there was seemingly no Greek influence.

[62] For a thorough discussion of the problem of comparison, see Ed. Wölfflin, *Lateinische und Romanische Komparation*, Erlangen, 1879 (also published in Ed. Wölfflin, *Ausgewählte Schriften*, Leipzig, 1933, pp. 126–92). A brief discussion and citation of literature is given in Salonius, 185–203. See also Mørland, 173–75; Hunger, *Die Syntax des spätlateinischen Oribasius*, 1933, pp. 22–33; and Svennung, 277 ff.

Comparative

In the following cases the positive degree would be correct: *colligerunt meliora* (τὰ κάλλιστα) *in uasis mala autem foris miserunt*, Mt 13.48; *cadit in igne saepius* (ἐνίοτε) *in aqua*, Mt 17.15; *ego . . . sum senior* (πρεσβύτης), L 1.18; *exi celerius* (ταχέως) *in plateas*, L 14.21; *animequior esto* (θάρσει), L 23.43; Mk 10.49; *quoniam saepius* (πολλάκις) *eum ligatus . . . disrumpebat*, Mk 5.4; *quicumque uoluerit maior* (μέγας) *inter uos esse*, Mk 10.43; *surge celerius* (ἐν τάχει), A 12.7; *discipulos fecissent plures* (πολλούς), A 14.21; *et uiri et mulieres pleres* (*plures*, D, ἱκανοί) *crediderunt*, A 17.12. In the following instances D also has the comparative: *quod facis citius fac*, J 13.27; *uos melius scitis ut nefas sit*, A 10.28; *dicere aliquid aut audire nouius*, A 17.21.

The comparative is used for the superlative in *quod mandatum in lege maius* (μεγάλη), Mt 22.36; *quis est sine peccato . . . prior* (πρῶτος) *. . . mittat lapidem*, J 8.7. Here again some cases are mere translation: *minor . . . qui est in regno caelorum maior illo est*, Mt 11.11; *quis maior est in regno caelorum*, Mt 18.1; *maior uestrum erit uester minister*, Mt 23.11; *qui minor est . . . in regno*, L 7.28; *qui maior in uobis est fiat sicut minus*, L 22.26.

One of the clearest evidences that there was no strong feeling for the degrees of comparison is that comparative forms were often accompanied by *magis*, *plus*, or *amplius*, thus showing that these forms in themselves were looked upon as having no markedly different force from that of the positive. One such case is noted in Codex Bezae: *nec quicquam proficiebat sed magis deterius*[63] *habebat*, Mk 5.26, an attempt at translating μᾶλλον ἐπὶ τὸ χεῖρον.

There is a similar usage of the superlative followed by an intensifying adverb: *duo daemoniaci . . . pessimi ualde* (D lacking), Mt 8.28.

Superlative

In addition to the misuse of the superlative already noted, we find superlative forms which are used with positive force: *ita erit et generationi huic pessimae* (πονηρᾷ), Mt 12.45; *ne contemnatis unum horum minimorum* (μικρῶν), Mt 18.10; *plurimo* (ἱκανῷ) *tempore . . . mentem abstulisset eis*, A 8.11. The scribe simply translates the Greek in *facti sunt plurimae uirtutes*, Mt 11.20; *plurima . . . turba strauerunt uestimenta sua*, Mt 21.8; *committere illi de plurimis*, L 11.53.

The superlative misused for the comparative is found in Acts 4.22: *annorum . . . erat plurimum ·xl· . . . homo* (πλειόνων).

5. Prepositions

The use of prepositions was greatly extended in the popular speech of the Late Latin period, and prepositional phrases were frequently employed where in classical times an oblique case would have been used. This encroachment of prepositional phrases, however, upon the functions of the oblique cases was gradual, and even by the sixth century and later the prepositional phrases had by no means superseded the oblique cases (Bonnet, 581; Taylor, 104). We find this condition existing in Codex Bezae.

[63] Comparative form from an obsolete positive *deter;* cf. Walde-Hofmann, *Lateinisches Etymologisches Wörterbuch*, s.v. *deterior*.

One of the most striking phenomena of popular Latin is the confusion of the ablative and accusative cases after prepositions. This was doubtless caused by the dropping of final *m*, which made the distinction between the two cases in many instances impossible. The occurrence of the ablative instead of the accusative can not always be thus explained, but the confusion resulting in such cases gradually led to the breakdown of case distinction to such an extent that ablatives generally were used as accusatives. A further, and entirely natural, consequence of this confusion was that the opposite tendency became manifest, i.e., the accusative was substituted for the ablative after certain prepositions (Svennung, 382–85).

The following table shows the cases governed by the various prepositions, as well as their frequency.

Prep.	*Acc.*	*Abl.*	*Other Cases and Indecl. Nouns*	*Total*
a, ab	15	462	22	499
ad	579	5	10	594
cum	15	246	4	265
de	5	470	11	495
ex	3	150	6	159
in[64]	852	1308	78	2238
per	146	6	3	155
propter	121	2	1	124
super	239	19	1	259
Totals[65]	2413	2782	123	53[illegible]8

Prepositions of less frequent occurrence are:

With accusative: *aduersum* (32); *ana* (1); *contra* (15); *inter* (34); *penes* (3); *praeter* (5); *retro* (3); *secus* (9); *trans* (11); *ultra* (6).

With ablative: *coram* (16); *foras* (2); *pro* (41).

With accusative and ablative or indecl. noun: *ante* (46, acc. 44, indecl. 2); *apud* (42, acc. 41, abl. 1); *circa* (28, acc. 26, abl. 2); *extra* (14, acc. 13, indecl. 1); *intra* (15, acc. 12, abl. 3); *iuxta* (11, acc. 9, indecl. 2); *post* (73, acc. 72, abl. 1); *prae* (4, acc. 2, abl. 2); *propre* (3, acc. 2, indecl. 1); *secundum* (45, acc. 44, abl. 1); *sine* (23, acc. 1, abl. 22); *sub* (21, acc. 12, abl. 9); *subtus* (3, acc. 2, abl. 1); *supra* (12, acc. 11, abl. 1); *usque* (7, acc. 4, abl. 3); *usque ad* (39, acc. 36, abl. 1, indecl. 1); *usque in* (17, acc. 16, abl. 1).

The proportionate frequency of the ablative and the accusative after prepositions in Codex Bezae is about the same as that noted in studies of other works; neither case seems to be especially preferred (Taylor, 106; Pei, 235).

Usage[66]

a, ab

The ablative with *a* is employed to show cause, where the classical usage does not

[64] Of course with the preposition *in*, either case is correct, depending on the meaning. In general, the classical usage is followed, but not invariably. The extremely large number of instances involved has made it seem hardly worth while to draw up statistics on the point. For a few sample illustrations, see the special paragraph on this preposition.

[65] Figures include the prepositions of less frequent occurrence listed immediately below the table.

[66] Not all the expressions and usages here included are novel; those are also included which, while occurring occasionally in classical Latin, are especially common in Vulgar Latin. See the discussion in Väänänen, 204–06, 211–13.

ordinarily employ a preposition, or else uses *ob*, *per*, or *propter: a timore exclamauerunt*, Mt 14.26; *uae mundo a scandalis*, Mt 18.7; *a timore . . . eius commoti sunt custodes*, Mt 28.4; *quaerebat uidere . . . et non potebat a turba*, L 19.3; *a gaudio non aperuit ianuam*, A 12.14.

A, *ab* with the ablative is used in expressing temporal relationship, where classical Latin generally uses *ex* (Leumann-Hofmann, 529): *ab hora illa*, Mt 15.28, and frequently throughout; cf. *a iuuentute*, Mt 19.20.

Local relation is likewise expressed in the same manner, but is confined to expressions like the following: *dic ut sedeant . . . unus a dextris . . . unus a sinistris*, Mt 20.21; *sede a dextris meis*, Mt 22.44; *stans a dextris*, L 1.11; *a dextera mea est*, A 2.25; cf. *a dexteram meam*, L 20.42, which may be a mistake for the ablative, but is more likely meant for *ad dext.m.* (by haplography).

A characteristic of Late Latin which is found but once in Codex Bezae is the use of a periphrastic prepositional phrase for the ablative of comparison (Salonius, 113; Leumann-Hofmann, 427). It appears with the preposition *a: a templo maior est hic*, Mt 12.6.[67]

The peculiar expression in J 11.18, *proximum Hierosolymis a stadiis quindecim*, is perhaps to be explained as an attempt at using *a* with *proximum* to express spatial relationship (Leumann-Hofmann, 422), but even so the preposition has been misplaced. Cf., however, the Greek, ἀπὸ σταδίων.

In Ecclesiastical Latin the ablative with *ab* follows certain verbs which mean "beware of" or "be afraid of." This is probably a usage imitated from the Greek. The verbs thus treated in Codex Bezae are: *attendere*[68] (προσέχειν ἀπό): *attendite ab hominibus*, Mt 10.17; *adtendite a fermento farisaeorum*, Mt 16.6, and frequently; *obseruare* (φυλάσσειν ἀπό): *obseruate ab omni cupiditate*, L 12.15 (Löfstedt, *Verm. Stud.*, 111–12); *timere* (φοβεῖσθαι ἀπό): *ne timueritis ab his*, Mt 10.28; *dico . . . non timere ab his*, L 12.4; *uidere* (βλέπειν ἀπό): *uidete a fermento pharisaeorum*, Mk 8.15.

ad

Instead of the usual dative, *ad* and the accusative are used after verbs such as *ait*, *dicere*, *respondere*, although not very frequently in Codex Bezae. Some instances are *Andreas et Philippus dicunt ad Ihm*, J 12.22; *quidam . . . dixerunt ad eum*, L 19.39; *dixerunt ad eos*, A 4.19; *respondit ad eos*, A 5.29. The Greek in these cases has πρός+acc., except in the first, where the dative appears.

Ad is used with a noun or pronoun to express purpose:[69] *ad quod uenisti ame (amice)*, Mt 26.50; *regiones . . . albae sunt ad messem*, J 4.35; *ad* (εἰς) *hoc . . . ueni*, Mk 1.38; similar phrases occur very frequently.

The expression of cause by *ad* and the accusative is another striking feature to be noted:[70] *ad durum cor uestrum dimisit . . . Moyses*, Mt 19.8; *nemo sciuit . . . ad quid dixit*, J 13.28; *ad duritiam cordis uestri scripsit Moyses praeceptum*, Mk 10.5.

The regular classical constructions of *ad* need no comment. The expression in J 5.35, *uoluistis exultare ad oram (horam) in lumine eius*, is an extension of the classical *ad tempus*, "for a season." *Obes (oues) suas uocat ad nomen*, J 10.3, is also

[67] Also a Semitic idiom, as Professor Hatch reminds me. This is also the view of Löfstedt (*Synt.*, 257).

[68] Also followed by *de:* Mt 16.11,12; etc.

[69] For the gerund and gerundive with *ad* in expressions of purpose, cf. p. 58.

[70] Also in the Vulgate, as Professor Hatch observes.

derived from the classical meaning of "according to" with words denoting rule, measure, and the like.

The ablative after *ad* is very infrequent. For the expressions *ad iuuentute mea*, Mk 10.20, and *ad iudaeis*, A 20.19, which seemingly are instances of this error, see the comment on page 23.

A common phenomenon in Late Latin is the extension in meaning of prepositions (Grandgent, 39–41). *Ad* approaches the meaning of *apud* in such expressions as the following: *accusaturus sum uos ad patrem*, J 5.45; *ad eum habitaculum faciam*, J 14.23; *usque quo ero ad uos*, L 9.41; also J 17.5; 20.10; L 2.52; A 15.22. In *conuertere corda patrum ad filios*, L 1.17, and similar expressions, the meaning of *contra* is approached.

ana

This preposition is borrowed from the Greek ἀνά. It is found once in Codex Bezae[71] as a distributive preposition with a numeral: *nequae ana duos tunicas habere*, L 9.3.

ante (incorrectly *anti* in A 16.9)

Used in expressions of place and time, this preposition adheres strictly to the classical tradition. It is found once, however, in a usage which became common in the post-classical period and in poetry, i.e., following the comparative: *praecucurrit citius ante Petrum*, J 20.4 (Leumann-Hofmann, 500).

circa

We find no departures from standard usage, except in a few extensions of meaning. *Circa* clearly means *in* in Mk 4.1: *in naui ascendens sedere circa mare;* and it has the sense of *iuxta* in expressions like the following: *dum seminat aliut cecidit circa uiam*, Mk 4.4; *caecus saedebat circa uiam*, Mk 10.46.

cum

There is one peculiarity to be noted here. An adverbial meaning was sometimes given to *cum* and a noun (Taylor, 110), and in Codex Bezae this usage seems to occur for the most part when *cum* is followed by an accusative: *abiit in montanam cum festinationem*, L 1.39; *deducebant eos cum uim*, A 5.26; *tradebant eis cum omnem fiduciam $\overline{Dnm}$ $\overline{Ihm}$ $\overline{Xpm}$*, A 16.4. *Cum* is on the whole regularly used, and is followed by the accusative only rarely.

de

The use of this word was so greatly extended that it became almost the favorite preposition of Vulgar Latin (Löfstedt, 103 ff.). It is frequent in our MS., being third only to *in* and *ad*. Its uses are manifold.

De often replaces *ex* and *ab* with names of places, and in other expressions indicating separation, although the classical usage still prevails: *congregabunt de regno eius*, Mt 13.41; *segregabunt malos de medio iustorum*, Mt 13.49; *turbae secutae sunt eum . . . de ciuitatibus*, Mt 14.13; *uenit mulier de Samaria*, J 4.7; *$\overline{Ihs}$ uenit de Iudaea in Galilaeam*, J 4.47; *eice primum trauem* (*trabem*) *de oculo tuo*, L 6.42; and elsewhere.

The ablative of means or instrument is expressed with *de* and a noun: *de fructo*

[71] For its use elsewhere, cf. *Thes. Ling. Lat.*, II, 12, 38 ff.

. . . *arbor adgnoscitur*, Mt 12.33; *ut non arguantur operas eius de luce*, J 3.20; *lauare pedes . . . et tergere de lentio*, J 13.5; *arbor de fructo suo cognoscitur*, L 6.44; *tange eam de manibus tuis*, Mk 5.23; *cumque significasset eis de manu ut silerunt*, A 12.17.

Agent, usually expressed by *ab*, is also expressed by *de*: *inuenta est in utero habens de spiritu sancto*, Mt 1.18; *quod . . . in ea natum est de spo sancto est*, Mt 1.20. The Greek has ἐκ, but source and agency are frequently expressed in exactly the same manner in that language.

Cause is sometimes expressed by *de* and the ablative: *fatigatus de itinere*, J 4.6; *de opere bono non lapidamus te*, J 10.33.

The ablative with *de* is used to express origin: *qui . . . de terra est . . . de terra loquitur*, J 3.31; *salus de Iudaeis est*, J 4.22; *uos de hoc mundo estis, ego non sum de hoc mundo*, J 8.23; *nos de fornicatione non sumus nati*, J 8.41.

De replaces the classical *ex* with the ablative of material: *coronam de spinis*, Mt 27.29.

The partitive genitive is often replaced by *de* and a noun (see also under *ex*). Cf. the following: *unum de prophetis*, Mt 16.14; *quidam de stantibus hic*, Mt 16.28; *unum de minimis istis*, Mt 18.6; *quis de duobus*, Mt 21.31; *aliquis de principibus . . . de pharisaeis*, L 6.2; etc.

Other genitive constructions are replaced by prepositional phrases with *de*:[72] *excusationem non habent de peccato*, J 15.22; *de fructum de praecordia eius . . . suscitare xpm*, A 2.30; *transmisit presbyteros de ecclesiam*, A 20.17.

Besides being followed occasionally by the accusative, *de* is once found with the nominative: *audiens de Ihs*, L 7.3.

ex

This preposition was also employed in place of the partitive genitive, a usage not uncommon in classical Latin, but very widely found in the Late Latin period (p. 35; see also under *de*): *unum ex his*, Mt 10.29; *quinque . . . ex his*, Mt 25.2; *unus ex discipulis*, J 6.8; *nemo ex uobis*, J 7.19; *unum ex profetis*, L 9.19; and frequently elsewhere.

The ablative of instrument is once expressed by *ex* and a noun: *diligis Dmn . . . ex toto corde tuo*, Mk 12.30. The Greek has ἐξ with the genitive.

Note the peculiar use of *ex* in Mt 20.2: *conueniens . . . cum operariis ex denario diem* (ἐκ δηναρίου).

Ex appears very rarely with the accusative, e.g., *possidit praedium ex mercedem*, A 1.18; *discedere omnes Iudaeos ex urbem*, A 18.2; and once with the genitive: *sum Iudaeus Tarsesis ex Ciliciae non ignotae ciuitatis*, A 21.39.

foras

Found but twice as a preposition in Codex Bezae, both times with the ablative; in each case it takes the place of *extra*: *exeuntes foras ciuitate*, Mt 10.14; *exiit foras*

[72] The use of a *de* phrase for the genitive is one of Scrivener's main reasons for assigning the MS. to Gaul (*Bezae Cod. Cant.*, pp. xl, xliv). He states that the construction looks "more like French than Latin." His point is not well taken, however, for this phenomenon appears in documents from all over the Empire, as a glance at the list of examples given by Grandgent (p. 43) will show, as well as the inscriptional evidence; one needs but to look at the indices in the volumes of *CIL*, as also some of the handy shorter collections and studies, e.g., H. Martin, *Notes on the Syntax of the Latin Inscriptions Found in Spain*, 1909, pp. 41–42; and Ernst Diehl, *Vulgärlateinische Inschriften*, 1910, index. It is precarious to attempt to localize one or two such usages definitely enough to base a theory upon them.

ciuitate, Mt 21.17. *Foras* with the accusative was used to some extent in this manner in Late Latin, but with the ablative very seldom (Leumann-Hofmann, 510).

in

Cause is sometimes expressed by *in* with either the ablative or the accusative: *in hoc . . . scient omnes quoniam mei discipuli estis*, J 13.35; *in hoc credimus quoniam a Deo existi*, J 16.30; *exultauit in laetitia infans*, L 1.44; *laudantes Dm in omnibus quibus audierunt*, L 2.20; *Martha . . . abalienabatur in multum ministerium*, L 10.40.

Means or instrument, and sometimes agent, is expressed by *in* and the ablative:[73] *ipse uos baptizabit in spu sancto et igni*, Mt 3.11; *hoc . . . genus non exit nisi in oratione et iaiuno* (*ieiunio*), Mt 17.21; *operatus est in eis* (*talenta*), Mt 25.16; *glorifica tuum nomen in gloria quam habebam aput te*, J 12.28; *non in pane solo uiuet homo sed in omni uerbo Dei*, L 4.4; *dicebant . . . quia in principem*[74] *daemoniorum eicit daemonia*, Mk 3.22; *redemptorem misit in manu angeli*, A 7.35.

Expressions of purpose are occasionally made with *in: in iudicium ueni in mundo hunc*, J 9.39; *mittite retias uestras in capturam*, L 5.4; *nihil tuleritis in uiam*, L 9.3; *unguere corpus meum in sepulturam*, Mk 14.8. This usage was known as early as Plautus, but was rare until the Late Latin period (Leumann-Hofmann, 537).

Time expressions constantly use *in:* e.g., *qui . . . sustinuerit in finem hic liberabitur*, Mt 24.13; *in crastinum . . . conuenerunt*, Mt 27.62; *non sitiet in aeternum*, J 4.14; *in finem dilexit eos*, J 13.1. With the ablative such phrases as *in illo tempore*, *in illo die*, etc., are very common.

The unclassical usage of *in* with the names of towns and cities is quite common: *magi . . . uenerunt in Hierosolyma*, Mt 2.2; *uenit . . . in Bethaniam*, J 11.17; 12.1; *adduxerunt eum in Hierosolyma*, L 2.22; *fugerunt . . . in Lystra et Derben*, A 14.6; *ueni in Damascum*, A 22.11. The classical usage is still found, however: L 17.1; A 11.26; 13.14; 14.21; 16.1.

A common usage of *in* with the accusative is the factitive, an imitation of the Hebrew, where *in* means "as," "for," "to be" (Plater-White, 20; Leumann-Hofmann, 537): *ante praesides stabitis . . . in testimonium illis*, Mt 10.18; Mk 13.9; *hic factus est in caput anguli*, Mt 21.42; L 20.17; A 4.11; *praedicabitur euangelium . . . in testimonium . . . gentibus*, Mt 24.14; *loquetur . . . in memoriam eius*, Mt 26.13; *effunditur in remissionem peccatorum*, Mt 26.28; *mittere eam in corbam*, Mt 27.6; *lumen in reuelationem et gloriam populi tui*, L 2.32; *offers . . . in testimonium illis*, Mk 1.44; (*Ds*) *excitauit Dauit* (*David*) *eis in regem*, A 13.22; and once with the ablative: *orationis tuae . . . ascenderunt in recordatione*, A 10.4.

In is frequently followed by the ablative where the accusative should be used. In the following passages *in* and the ablative appear where the Greek has εἰς and the accusative: *intra in cubiculo tuo*, Mt 6.6; *ueniens in patria sua*, Mt 13.54; and Mt 2.13,15; 10.11,17,23; 12.9; 13.41; 14.32; 17.15; 19.1; 24.9; 26.18,30,41; J 5.29; 6.21; L 1.39; and frequently elsewhere.

Just as often the accusative appears where the ablative is correct: *sicut scriptum est in Esaiam prophetam*, Mk 1.2; *amant . . . salutationes in foros*, Mt 23.7; *mansit*

[73] This is a Hebraism (Plater-White, 20), and it comes into Latin through the Greek, where ἐν with the dative was used; cf. Salonius, 98; Süss, 79. Deissmann, *Bible Studies*, pp. 118 ff., admits that this is a Hebraism in the O.T., and possibly in the Gospels, but not in the Pauline Epistles.

[74] The accusative in this usage is exceptional.

in Galilaeam, J 7.9; and other typical cases in Mt 14.10; 16.27; 21.19; 25.43,44; J 7.39; 10.23; 11.30; 13.23; L 8.32; 18.30; 19.42; 23.19; Mk 6.2; 8.14; 14.3.

The preposition *in* is sometimes extended in meaning. In such cases as *in alias ciuitates euangelizare regnum Dei,* L 4.43, it approaches the meaning of *ad* after verbs of saying (p. 45). *Contra* would be expected in *tres diuisi in duobus et duo in tribus,* L 12.52; *inter* would be natural in *quid sunt in tam multos,* J 6.9; and the meaning of *intra* is approached in *Petrus in se conuersus dixit,* A 12.11. In oaths *in* sometimes has the meaning of *per: non iurare . . . in caelum . . . in terram . . . in Hierosolyma . . . in caput,* Mt 5.34,35; *qui iurauerit in templo . . . in auro templi . . . in altare . . . in dono,* Mt 23.16–19. *Super* would be more natural in L 10.6: *requiescit in eum pax uestra*; and A 7.10: *constituit eum in Aegyptum et omnem domum suam.*

A few other uncommon uses of *in* may be noted. With the reflexive it means "together" in J 20.4: *currebant . . . ambo in se.* After *abscondo* we find *in* and the accusative:[75] *abscondit in farinae mensuras tres,* Mt 13.33; L 13.21.

iuxta

Usually this word signifies proximity, as *ciuitatem . . . iuxta agrum,* J 4.5; and *a monte . . . qui est iuxta Hierusalem,* A 1.12; but it signifies conformity to a pattern or standard (like *secundum*) in *facere illud iuxta figuram quam uiderat,* A 7.44; and it approaches the meaning of *ante* in *posuit iuxta pedes apostolorum,* A 4.37.

per

A few departures from classical usage are found. Agent or instrument is frequently expressed by *per* and the accusative:[76] *mittens per discipulos suos dixit ei,* Mt 11.2; *dictum est per Esaiam prophetam,* Mt 12.17, and frequently in this expression; *discipuli per nauiculum uenerunt,* J 21.8; *signa per apostolas fiebant,* A 2.43; etc.

Cause is expressed with *per: per iniudiam tradiderunt eum,* Mt 27.18.

The use of *per* in expressions of time is somewhat extended in our MS. Duration of time with *per* is classical but infrequent: *per omne tempore seruiens Dno,* A 20.19. The following temporal phrases are frequent and seem to express mostly time at which, a function of the ablative usually: *per diem . . . festum consueuerat praesis (praeses) dimittere unum,* Mt 27.15; Mk 15.6; *per nocte uenientes furati sunt eum,* Mt 28.13; *per nocte . . . angelus Dni aperuit ianuas,* A 5.19.

prae

Used classically to show cause only with negation, expressed or implied, as *non possent accedere prae turba,* Mk 2.4, it is also found with an affirmative expression in Codex Bezae: *prae gaudio eius . . . uendit omnia,* Mt 13.44.

Prae occurs once with the accusative in an expression of comparison: *isti Galilaei prae omnes Galilaeos fuerunt peccatores,* L 13.2.

propter

Only one irregularity is noted, namely that *propter* is used for *pro: [non]*[77] *propter istos rogo solum sed et pro his,* J 17.20.

[75] Georges, *Ausf.*, s.v. *abscondo,* I; *Thes. Ling. Lat.*, I, 153, 62 ff.
[76] This is found occasionally in classical Latin, however.
[77] Must be supplied from the Greek to give correct sense to the sentence.

retro

This word was employed widely as a preposition from the time of the Old Latin versions of the Bible (Leumann-Hofmann, 501), but is found in Codex Bezae only three times in this capacity: *uenit retro me,* L 14.27; *inposuerunt ei crucem ut adferret retro Ihm,* L 23.26; *uade retro me Satana,* Mk 8.33.

secundum

The meaning *apud* is clearly needed in A 17.28: *in ipso . . . uiuimus et mouemur et simus in diurnum sicut qui secundum uos sunt quidam dixerunt.*

secus

In common speech from the third century on *secus* was employed with local meaning (Leumann-Hofmann, 517). In Codex Bezae it has almost the sense of *iuxta,* and its use is limited to the following expressions: *secus mare,* Mt 13.1 15.29; Mk 1.16; *secus uiam,* Mt 13.4; L 18.35; *secus flumen,* A 7.21.

sub and subtus

Sub with the ablative in expressions of time was common in the Late Latin period (Leumann-Hofmann, 539), and we have two examples in Codex Bezae: *multi leprosi . . . sub Eliseo profeta,* L 4.27; *dispersi a conflictatione quae facta est sub Stephano,* A 11.19.

Subtus was first used as a preposition by Vitruvius, and enjoyed great popularity later (Leumann-Hofmann, 540). Three instances occur in Codex Bezae: *ponam . . . suptus pedes tuos,* Mt 22.44; *suptus lectum ponit,* L 8.16; *catelli subtus mensa manducant,* Mk 7.28.

super

This was a widely used preposition and took on several new functions. It is found as an expression of location equivalent to *iuxta, circum,* and the like: *ut suspendatur mola asinaria super collum eius,* Mt 18.6; *uidens ficum unam super uiam,* Mt 21.19; *super cathedra Moysi sederunt scribae,* Mt 23.2; *manifestauit se ipsum . . . super mare Tiberiadis,* J 21.1; *super terra pax,* L 2.14; *dum populus super eum esset,* L 5.1.

Super followed by the ablative sometimes expresses cause:[78] *multi super natiuitate eius gaudebunt,* L 1.14; *omnis turba admirabatur super doctrina eius,* Mk 11.18; *stupens super doctrina dni,* A 13.12; and Mt 22.33; L 1.29; Mk 1.22; 3.5; A 3.12.

Hostile intention is frequently expressed with *super* in the sense of *contra: exsurget . . . gens super gentem,* Mt 24.7; *leuabit super me calcaneum suum,* J 13.18; *suscitauerunt . . . persecutionem super Paulum,* A 13.50; also L 9.5; 11.17; 12.53; Mk 3.25; A 4.27; 8.1.

Super in the sense of "concerning" is noted rarely:[79] *qui confidens super se quoniam sunt iusti,* L 18.9; *adtendite uobis super istis hominibus quidnam incipiatis agere,* A 5.35.

After an adjective *super* is found once in the sense of "unto": *ipse suabis est super ingratos et iniquos,* L 6.35.

[78] This may be due to imitation of D, where ἐπί+dat. occurs in all these instances, as Professor Hatch notes. The causal use of ἐπί is not uncommon in Greek.

[79] Found in popular speech as early as Plautus (Leumann-Hofmann, 540).

Misereri followed by *super* is probably due to Semitic influence (Plater-White, 89): *misereor super turbam hanc*, Mt 15.32.

Super is found once after the comparative: *fili saeculi huius sapientores super filios lucis . . . sunt*, L 16.8.

usque[80]

Usque is seldom used alone as a preposition, but is found occasionally: *usque Bethleem*, L 2.15; *usque decima (hora)*, A 19.9. It is found more frequently followed by adverbs: *usque nunc*, Mt 24.21; J 16.24; *usque septies*, Mt 18.21; *usque deorsum*, Mt 27.51.

Usque ad expresses location: *usquae ad caelum exaltaueris*, Mt 11.23; *adduxerunt eum usque ad supercilium montis*, L 4.29; and L 10.15; Mk 2.2; A 1.8. This is also classical.

It is found in expressions of time, which is also classical: *erat ibi usque ad mortem Herodes*, Mt 2.15; *sinite . . . crescere usque ad messem*, Mt 13.30; and Mt 26.38; A 1.5; 3.21. The expression *similiter et secundus . . . usque ad septem*, Mt 22.26, is closely allied to the above usage.

In sentences denoting "from one point to another" we find *usque ad*: *incipiens a nouissimis usque ad primos*, Mt 20.8; *a constitutione mundi usque ad generationem hanc*, L 11.50; and Mt 23.35; 24.31; A 7.45; 8.10.

Usque in is found in the same usage in Mt 24.27; A 10.30; also in temporal expressions: *usque in eum diem quo introiit Noe in arcam*, Mt 24.38; *ego sum uobiscum . . . usque in consummationem saeculi*, Mt 28.20; and Mt 11.23; 27.8; Mk 14.25; 15.33; A 1.2; 2.29; 20.7. This appears occasionally in classical Latin.

Double Prepositions and Prepositions Combined with Adverbs[81]

ab ante

This combination occurs but once in Codex Bezae and is used adverbially: *antecedens ab ante*[82] *ascendit in murum*, L 19.4.

ab intus

This is also an adverbial expression and is used to translate the Greek ἔσωθεν: *ab intus . . . estis pleni hypocrisi*, Mt 23.28; *ab intus . . . de corde . . . praecedunt*, and *haec mala ab intus procedunt*, Mk 7.21,23.

ab inuicem

Used for the Greek ἀπ' ἀλλήλων: *segregat eos ab inuicem*, Mt 25.32; *ita ut separarentur ab inuicem*, A 15.39. In A 12.20, *ab inuice ciuitates uenerunt*, translates the Greek ἐξ ἀμφοτέρων τῶν πόλεων παρῆσαν.

ad inuicem

This expression replaced the reciprocal *inter se* (Salonius, 238 ff.): *dicunt discipuli*

[80] Leumann-Hofmann, 498.
[81] Cf. Skutsch, in *Fleckeis. Jahr.*, Suppl.-Bd. 27(1902) 95 ff.; Hamp, *AR*, 5(1888), 321–68; Salonius, 218 ff.
[82] Some would write this and similar expressions as one word, *abante*, etc.; but, as Löfstedt (269) remarks, the question is unimportant.

ad inuicem, J 4.33; *litagabant . . . Iudaei ad inuicem,* J 6.52; and J 16.17; L 4.36; 20.14; Mk 4.41; 12.7; A 4.15; 21.14.

a foris

As an adverb we find *a foris* in Mt 23.27,28: *a foris monumentum paretur decorum . . . a foris . . . paretis hominibus iusti;* also in L 11.39: *quod a foris est calicis . . . mundatis.*[83]

a longe

This expression is used in Biblical Latin for the Greek μακρόθεν or ἀπὸ μακρόθεν: *uidet Abraham a longe,* L 16.23; *publicanus a longe stans,* L 18.13; and L 22.54; Mk 5.6; 11.13; 14.54; 15.40.

a modo

The Greek ἀπ' ἄρτι is thus translated: *non uidebitis me a modo,* Mt 23.39; and Mt 26.29,64; J 13.19; 14.7. In Luke ἀπὸ τοῦ νῦν is thus rendered: 1.48; 12.52; 22.18,69.

a susu (*sursum*)

This is found but once: Mt 27.51, *a susu usque deorsum.*

de intus (cf. *ab intus*)

One instance occurs: *ille de intus respondens,* L 11.7.

de longe (cf. *a longe*)

This occurs in Mt 26.58: *Petrus sequebatur eum de longe;* and Mt 27.55; L 17.12; Mk 8.3.

de retro

In answer to the question "whence": *uenit de retro et tetigit uestimentum eius,* Mk 5.27.

de sub

This occurs but once in Codex Bezae, although it was a common expression (Hamp, 361): *scoruscus . . . de sub caelo scoruscat,* L 17.24.

in contra

As an adverb this expression is found in L 19.30: *ite in contra qui est castellus.*[84] It is prepositional in L 8.22: *pertranseamus in contra stagnum.*

in inuicem (cf. *ad inuicem*)

This is found twice: *si dilictionem habeatis in inuicem,* J 13.35; *de hoc queritis in inuicem,* J 16.19.

in obuiam

Two instances of this expression are found: *exierunt in obuiam sponsi,* Mt 25.1; *exierunt in obuiam eius,* J 12.13.

[83] Hamp (*loc. cit.,* p. 345) says that in this latter case *a foris* is used as a preposition with the genitive, following the Greek ἔξωθεν τοῦ. But the genitive is clearly partitive after *quod,* and *a foris* is adverbial.

[84] The Greek for this barbarous Latin is εἰς τὴν κατέναντι κώμην.

in occulto

This expression translates the Greek ἐν τῷ κρυπτῷ: *ut elemosyna tua sit in occulto,* Mt 6.4; and Mt 6.6; J 7.4. Cicero uses the expression.

in palam

There are two usages of this expression. In the first it translates the Greek εἰς φανερόν, ἐν φανερῷ: *non est . . . absconsum quod non in palam uenit,* L 8.17; *nec factum est occultum sed ut ueniat in palam,* Mk 4.22; in the second it translates the Greek ἐν παρρησίᾳ: *querit illut in palam esse,* J 7.4; *non in prouerbiis loquar uobis sed in pala,* J 16.25; *nun in palam loqueris,* J 16.29.

in quantum

Bonnet (620, note 1) notes this expression, and says it is an old one, going back to Tacitus.[85] It occurs in Mt 9.15: *possunt ieiunare (ieiunare) in quantum cum ipsis est sponsus;* and Mt 25.40: *in quantum fecistis uni horum . . . mihi fecistis.*

intus in

This expression is used as a preposition in Mk 15.16: *duxerunt eum intus in atrium.*

per ter

This combination of preposition and adverb occurs twice in Acts (Rönsch, 234): *hoc factum est per ter,* 10.16; 11.10.

sub ante

This appears but once, as a preposition: *introierunt sub ante lucem in templum,* A 5.21.

usque ad (and *usque in*): see under *usque*, p. 51.

6. Verbs

Tenses

Present for past

The substitution of the present tense for the past is general throughout Codex Bezae. Folk Latin was characterized by this confusion, and the situation has been frequently commented upon (Taylor, 128; Bonnet, 637). Even in classical authors the historical present is very frequently found. The majority of cases in our MS., however, can not be called historical present; they are more likely due to the tendency, which prevailed in popular writing generally, to use the present for the past. A few examples of so common a phenomenon are sufficient: *tunc surgunt*[86] *. . . et aptauerunt lampadas suas,* Mt 25.7; *cum remigassent stadia uigintiquinque . . . uident Ihm . . . et timuerunt,* J 6.19; and among others Mt 4.6,18,19; 19.22*; J 4.28; 6.5–10; 8.27; 13.4; L 5.26; Mk 1.21*; 5.15; A 7.23*; 19.12; 21.5.

[85] Gerber and Greef, *Lexicon Taciteum*, Leipzig, 1903, p. 1254, cite four instances.

[86] This confusion is also common in the Greek text, and d follows the Greek except in this case and the others marked by an asterisk (*). It will be noted that the cases where d differs from the Greek are more numerous in the substitution of the present for the future.

Present for future

This substitution is characteristic of popular speech in the ante-classical as well as the Late Latin period (Löfstedt, 212, and the references there cited). Some references in Codex Bezae where the present has the force of the future are: *uiri Nineuitae resurgunt* in iudicio . . . et condemnabunt eam,* Mt 12.41; *congregabunt . . . omnis . . . et mittunt,* Mt 13.41; *ibit ad eum . . . et dicit*,*[87] L 11.5; and Mt 21.3*; 22.37*; 25.32*; J 7.36*; 12.48; 14.3; L 13.9*; 18.5*, 20*; Mk 12.30*; 16.3*; A 1.5*; 11.16*; 18.10*.

Imperfect

Regular uses of the imperfect abound. Thus we have it used to express customary or continued action in past time: *docebat eos in synagogas eorum,* Mt 13.54; and Mt 14.4,5; 20.31; 21.46; J 7.40–44; L 2.19,41; 16.14; Mk 6.20; etc. It is employed as a descriptive tense in Mt 14.24; 21.8; 26.58; J 3.19; 6.17; L 19.1–3; 23.9–11; A 17.5; etc.

The imperfect sometimes denotes a single occurrence in past time and stands for the perfect. That the distinction between these two tenses is not entirely clear in Codex Bezae also appears from the fact that they are often used side by side in the same sentence. The following passages illustrate: *interrogabat . . . dixerunt,* Mt 2.4; *daemones . . . rogabant eum,* Mt 8.31*; *accesserunt ad Philippum . . . et rogabant eum,* J 12.21; and Mt 3.14*; 15.36; 17.5; 18.28–33; L 6.20; 9.16; 12.54; Mk 1.34; A 8.17. Here there is general agreement with the Greek.

In one passage the imperfect has very strangely taken the place of the future: *mitte in Ioppen et accersi Simonem . . . qui loquebatur* (λαλήσει) *uerba ad te,* A 11.13,14.

Future (*see also* Periphrasis for the future tenses, p. 55).

The common employment of the present for the future would naturally result in some cases of the opposite phenomenon. These are infrequent, however, and are due in large measure, no doubt, to the phonological difficulty with *i* and *e* (p. 18): *omne sarmentum quod . . . non adferet fructum tollit illud,* J 15.2,5*; *adferent ei surdum,* Mk 7.32*; *dicitis nimbus uenit et fiet sic,* L 12.54,55*; and Mt 22.36*; L 6.45*; 8.14; 17.8; Mk 4.15*; 9.44*; A 6.13*. This is infrequent in the Greek for only two of the references cited have the future in D.

The future tense is sometimes given the force of an imperative (Leumann-Hofmann, 555), a usage common in the Greek text also. The following instances occur in Matthew: *scriptum est non temptauis (temptabis) $\overline{Dnm}$ $\overline{Dm}$ tuum,* 4.7; *$\overline{Dnm}$ $\overline{Dm}$ tuum adorabis . . . seruies,* 4.10; and 5.21,24,33,36,40,43; 6.5; 18.17; 19.18; 27.24.

Prohibition and strong negation are likewise expressed occasionally by the future (Plater-White, 104; Kühner, II, 111): *non erunt haec tibi,* Mt 16.22; *non ex te fructus erit in aeternum,* Mt 21.19. D has the imperative in these two instances.

Perfect

In the following passages the perfect takes the place of the present: *quis est qui*

[87] This and other cases may be due to the frequent interchange of *u* and *e* (p. 18); but cf. Löfstedt, *loc. cit.*

tradidit[88] *te* (ὁ παραδιδῶν, i.e., παραδιδούς), J 21.20; *hunc quem uidistis et scitis*, A 3.16; *uos semper spo sancto obstitistis*, A 7.51; *et audistis et uidetis*, A 19.26. The Greek has the correct present in all these cases.

Likewise the perfect is incorrectly used for the future: *uenit hora . . . cum . . . adorauerunt patri*, J 4.23.

The rendering of the perfect tenses of the passive voice and of deponents by *fui* instead of *sum*, *fueram* instead of *eram*, etc., is frequent (40 instances) in Codex Bezae. This substitution was known as far back as Plautus, is found in Cicero and Caesar, and is extensive in Livy (Draeger, I, 276 ff.). It became more common in later writers (Bonnet, 641; Taylor, 127; Pei, 263), and Grandgent (51) has seen in it a new analytical passive inflection, appearing as early as the time of Tertullian (A.D. 160–240). It has been shown, however, that Grandgent is in error on this point.[89] The fact that the longer forms were known so early and were used side by side with the shorter, without differentiation in meaning, as well as the fact that all the regular passive forms flourish down until the eighth century, has led to the conclusion that the truly analytical passive did not appear until the middle of the eighth century.[90]

The cases where the perfect tenses of *sum* are used as auxiliaries in Codex Bezae are:

fui for **sum**: *non fuerunt ausi interrogare eum*, L 20.40; *sortitus fuit sortem*, A 1.17. Note the small number of instances for this tense (cf. note 90).

fueram for **eram**: *nondum missus fuerat in carcerem*, J 3.24; *ihs nondum fuerat honoratus*, J 7.39; *Lazarus qui mortuus fuerat*, J 12.1; *responsum . . . fuerat super eum*, L 2.26.

fuero for **ero**: this substitution is more frequent than any: *quem osculatus fuero ipse est*, Mt 26.48; *qui . . . confessus fuerit me . . . hunc filius hominis confundetur*, L 9.26; and Mt 10.23; 13.48; 22.24; 23.15; 24.32; 28.14; J 3.27; 5.7; 6.65; 11.25; 12.32; 13.19; 14.29; L 5.35; 12.8; 16.4; 17.4; 20.28; 22.47; Mk 13.11,28; 14.9,29,44; A 3.22; 15.1.

fuerim for **sim**: no instances found.

fuissem for **essem**: *si quis confessus fuisset Xpm eum esse*, J 9.22; *non fuisset frater meus mortuus*, J 11.21,32; *si non . . . locutus eis fuissem*, J 15.22; *cum facta fuisset uox*, L 9.36; *cum pergressi fuissent totam insulam*, A 13.6.

Periphrasis for the future tense:[91]

One of the most common ways of expressing futurity in Late Latin was to use *incipio* with an infinitive. This seems to be an attempt on the part of writers to

[88] Possibly a case of dittography for *tradit*.
[89] H. Muller, "The Passive Voice in Vulgar Latin," *Romanic Review*, 15(1924), 68–93.
[90] *Ibid.*, pp. 70–71: "although . . . the later writers [no more than Livy, however] seem to have shown a greater liking for these more rounded forms, this shifting of tenses was a general characteristic of Latin from its early period and had evidently nothing to do with the disappearance of the synthetic passive. Indeed, the most important tense, the tense that was surely most used, viz., the perfect, was, in all periods down to the eighth century, the least affected by it." P. 68: ". . . this analytical or Romance passive, far from being a characteristic of spoken or vulgar Latin, did not appear, and hence presumably was not evolved, until the end of the Merovingian period [third quarter of the eighth century]."
[91] Thielmann, "*Habere mit dem Infinitiv, etc.*," *AR*, 2(1885), 48–89, 157–202. Leumann-Hofmann, 556 ff.; Mørland, 144–45.

express the Greek μέλλειν (Löfstedt, 210). Thielmann calls the construction an Africanism (*loc. cit.* 85 ff.), which Löfstedt denies. It occurs frequently in Codex Bezae, substituting for the simple future as well as for the active periphrastic conjugation: *filius hominis incipiet pati ab eis,* Mt 17.13; *incipiet filius hominis tradi in manus hominum,* Mt 17.22; *dicebant . . . exitum eius quem incipit conplere,* L 9.31; *fugere haec omnia quae incipient fieri,* L 14.29; *ipse erat qui incipiebat saluare Israhel,* L 24.21; and many others.

Another periphrasis that prevailed widely was *habeo* with an infinitive (Grandgent, 57; Salonius, 282 ff., Thielmann, *loc. cit.*). *Habeo dicere* originally meant *habeo quod dicere,* and was thus used by Cicero; later it came to mean *debeo dicere;* and finally it represented the simple future, out of which usage developed the Romance future. Codex Bezae, however, shows but very few cases where this construction is used, two where the original meaning of the phrase is intended, and four where it is used with future significance (Rönsch, 447). It appears as future in the following: *misit eos . . . in omnem locum . . . ubi habebat uenire,* L 10.1; *quia inde habebat transire,* L 19.4; *omnes uos scandalizari habetis* (D, σκανδαλίσασθαι), Mk 14.27; *eum accipere habetis,* A 1.5. In these instances the Greek has some form of μέλλειν, except where otherwise indicated.

Moods

Infinitive

In Codex Bezae, as in other Late Latin writings, the infinitive often replaces *ut* and the subjunctive in expressions of purpose (Grandgent, 51; Bonnet, 647; Leumann-Hofmann, 580). The number of instances where *ut* is used is 207 against 132 cases of the infinitive, which shows that the latter usage was making serious inroads on the classical construction. The infinitive of purpose is common in Greek, and doubtless exerted a strong influence on translation literature. Some examples follow: *uenimus adorare,* Mt 2.2; *ueni mittere pacem,* Mt 10.34; *ascendit in montem . . . orare,* Mt 14.23; *sedebat . . . uidere finem rei,* Mt 26.58; *eo parere locum uobis,* J 14.2; *unxit me euangelizare,* L 4.18; *descendi eripere eos,* A 7.34; *conuenerunt . . . uidere de sermone hoc,* A 15.6; and many others.

The use of the infinitive after adjectives is confined in Codex Bezae to *idoneus* and *dignus.* The latter, at least, was not followed by the infinitive in prose until the time of the Elder Seneca (Leumann-Hofmann, 578). There are very few instances of this construction: *cuius non sum idoneus calciamenta portare* (D missing), Mt 3.11; *non sum dignus uocari* (ἄξιος κληθῆναι) *filius tuus,* L 15.19; *ut digni habeamini* (καταξιωθῆτε) *fugere,* L 21.36; *cuius non sum dignus soluere* (ἱκανὸς λῦσαι) *corregiam,* Mk 1.7; *non sum dignus . . . soluere* (ἄξιος . . . λῦσαι), A 13.25.

Facilis and *difficilis,* commonly followed by the supine (Leumann-Hofmann, 601), take the infinitive in the following cases: *quid . . . est facilius dicere,* Mt 9.5; *facilius est . . . transire . . . quam . . . introire,* Mt 19.24; Mk 10.25; *difficile est . . . introire,* Mk 10.24. Both are common with the infinitive, however, in classical authors (*Thes. Ling. Lat.,* V, 1083, 18 ff.; VI, 58, 40 ff.).

In a few places there are traces of the influence of the Greek articular infinitive: *propter quod esset iuxta Hierusalem et putare quia . . .* (διὰ τὸ εἶναι . . . καὶ δοκεῖν), L 19.11; *factus est in eo fabulari eos et conquerere* (ἐν τῷ ὁμειλεῖν . . . καὶ συνζητεῖν), L 24.15.

A finite verb is incorrectly used for the infinitive in the following: *qui uolunt . . . salutationes in foro facitis*, Mk 12.38; *scis testimonium nostrum uerum est*, 3 J 12; *oratio esset bidebatur (uidebatur)*, A 16,13; *existimans effugisset custodias*, A 16.27.

The infinitive is employed occasionally where a finite verb should be: *dicentes Dne si in tempore hoc restituere regnum Istrahel*, A 1.6; *ds . . . praeordinauit te ut cognosceris . . . et uidere . . . et audire*, A 22.14; and *contigit . . . ut . . . introire eos . . . et loqui*, A 14.1, where the infinitives correspond to the Greek of the corresponding στίχοι.

For the replacement of regular infinitive constructions by clauses with *quod, quoniam*, etc., see p. 60.

Participle

The functions of the participle were greatly extended in Vulgar Latin, and especially so in Biblical texts, where the Greek exerted a strong influence. We find in Codex Bezae extensive use of the participle as equivalent to a clause correlative with the main clause.[92] This is so common that a few references will suffice: *magi . . . uenerunt . . . dicentes*, Mt 2.1,2; *angelus apparuit . . . dicens*, Mt 2.13; *iratus est . . . et mittens*, Mt 2.16; *euntes . . . praedicate*, Mt 10.7; and Mt 4.22,23; 9.9,13,25; 11.2; etc.

Another common usage is the substitution of a participle for an adverbial clause of time, circumstance, cause, etc. This, too, needs little illustration: *orantes . . . non uana loquimini*, Mt 6.7; *uidentes . . . timuerunt*, Mt 9.8; *transiens in ciuitatem esuriit*, Mt 21.18; *et ueniens ille arguet mundum*, J 16.8; *hoc iam tertium manifestatus est Ihs . . . surgens a mortuis*, J 21.14; *uidentes . . . cognouerunt de uerbo*, L 2.17; etc.

In a few instances a participle is equivalent to an adverb: *uenerunt festinantes*, L 2.16; *festinans* (σπεῦσον) *descende*, L 19.5*; *coepit . . . gaudentes laudare*, L 19.37.

The replacement of the correlative participle by a *cum* clause is common, especially in the Acts; cf. the following references: *in diebus his cum surrexisset Petrus . . . dixit*, A 1.15; *cum stetisset . . . Petrus . . . et elebabit* (perf.) . . . *et dixit*, A 2.14; *cum statuisset (statuissent) eos in medio interrogabant*, A 4.7; *cum surrexissent . . . iubenes (iuuenes) inuoluerunt eum et cum extulisset sepelierunt*, A 5.6; *cum exclamasset (exclamassent) uoce magna compresserunt aures eorum*, A 7.57. The Greek invariably has the participle in such cases.

Another common phenomenon is the replacement of the infinitive by the participle after verbs of beginning and ending. This is an imitation of the Greek usage (Plater-White, 39):[93] *cum consummasset Ihs praecipiens*, Mt 11.1; *cum . . . cessasset loquens*, L 5.4; *cum consummasset loquens*, L 7.1; *non cessauit osculans mihi pedes*, L 7.45; *coeperunt quaerentes* (συνζητεῖν) *ab illo signum*, Mk 8.11*; *homo hic non cessabit* (perf.) *uerba loquens*, A 6.13; *commouentes et turbantes . . . non cessabant*, A 17.13; *cessauerunt percutientes*, A 21.32.

The present participle with forms of *esse* is used analytically to form a finite tense (Leumann-Hofmann, 605; Löfstedt, 245 ff.). In classical Latin *esse* with the present participle nominative is possible only in cases where the participle has become an adjective, e.g., *sapiens*, etc. In Late Latin this usage was extended to participles

[92] Bonnet finds a similar usage in Gregory (p. 650): "Placé à la fin d'une proposition le participe present . . . prend la valeur d'une proposition novelle jointe à la principale par *et*."

[93] Though ἄρχομαι is followed by the infinitive in N.T., as Professor Hatch notes.

which had not become adjectives; in Biblical Latin it was possibly due to Greek influence (Leumann-Hofmann, 606). A few typical cases in Codex Bezae are given: *et erat incipiens . . . interpraetari*, L 24.27; *erat . . . docens eos*, Mk 1.22; *et erat praedicans . . . et daemonia eiciens*, Mk 1.39; *in quo erat . . . iacens*, Mk 2.4; *erat praecedens Ihs*, Mk 10.32; *erat sedens cum ministros*, Mk 14.54; *noluerunt oboedientes esse patres nostri*, A 7.39.

The present participle is found sometimes as the equivalent of the indicative. This usage was due to the widespread employment of the nominative absolute, and also to the fact that in cases where forms of *esse* were used with the participle they tended to drop out, leaving the participle standing alone (Leumann-Hofmann, 606; Löfstedt, 158, 249). Bonnet (650–51) asserts that clauses formed with the participle alone are not exactly independent, "mais jointe par *que* ou *et* à d'autres principales." This is not true, however, of all cases in Codex Bezae: *et ascendens in nauem ad illos et cessauit uentus*, Mk 6.51; *et ipse ascendens in nauem . . . et uenit*, Mk 8.10; *angelus Dni adstitit Petro et lux refulgens in illo loco*, A 12.7; *saecuti sunt . . . Paulum et Barnaban qui loquentes cum illis persuadentes eis*, A 13.43; *sacerdotes . . . coronas . . . adferentes cum turba bolentes* (*uolentes*) *immolare*, A 14.13. In all these instances D has the finite verb, so that this phenomenon seems peculiar to the Latin text.

In the following references a finite verb appears in d where the Greek has a participle: *hic respiciens . . . et uidit* (ἰδών) . . . *rogabat*, A 3.3; and Mt 26.42; L 21.12; A 4.21; 6.4; 12.21; 14.21; 19.25; 20.13.

A participle instead of the noun *inscriptio* is required in Mk 15.26; *erat . . . causa criminis eius inscriptio* (ἐπιγεγραμμένη).

The participle is replaced by an infinitive in *loquebantur cum craecos euangelizare* (εὐαγγελιζόμενοι) *Dnm Ihm Xpm*, A 11.20; very likely in an attempt to represent the idea of purpose, which was (erroneously, no doubt) thought to reside in the Greek participle, as Professor Hatch suggests.

Gerund, gerundive, and supine

These forms are not numerous in Codex Bezae. They were generally replaced by other constructions in Late writers (Grandgent, 48–49).

The genitive of the gerund is used to express the Greek dependent or qualifying infinitive (Plater-White, 112): *qui habet aures audiendi* (ὦτα ἀκούειν) *audiat*, Mt 13.9; L 8.8; *dedit illis potestatem curandi . . . et eiciendi* (ἐξουσίαν θεραπεύειν . . . ἐκβάλλειν), Mk 3.15; *nec manducandi spatium habebant* (φαγεῖν εὔκαιρος), Mk 6.31.

The ablative of the gerund replaces the present participle as a rendering of the Greek present participle (Plater-White, 112; Löfstedt, 159): *obtulit eis paecunias rogando et dicendo* (παρακαλῶν καὶ λέγων), A 8.19; *misi ad te rogando uenire te* (παρακαλῶν), A 10.33; *quae reditum multum praestabat dominis suis per hoc diuinando* (μαντευομένη), A 16.16; *ut . . . docerem per domos et publice testificando* (διαμαρτυρούμενος), A 20.21.

The accusative of the gerund is found with *ad* to show purpose. The Greek has πρός or εἰς and the infinitive, except where otherwise indicated: *qui uidet mulierem ad concupiscendum eam*, Mt 5.28; *ligate manipulos ad comburendum*, Mt 13.30; *tradent eum . . . ad castigandum . . . inludendum . . . crucifigendum*, Mt 20.19; *ad sepeliendum me fecit*, Mt 26.12; *cum stabitis ad orandum* (προσευχόμενοι) Mk 11.25. There is one instance where *ad* has been omitted: *aures audiendum*, Mk 7.16.

The gerundive construction appears in but one instance: *facient signa . . . ad seducendos . . . electos*, Mk 13.22.

The supines are very rare. The following instances look as though they may be cases of the supine in *-um*, but they are doubtful (cf. Plater-White, 115): *surdis praestat auditum*, Mk 7.37; *quisquis . . . potum dederit uobis calicem aquae*, Mk 9.41. The supine in *-u* does not occur at all; the phrase *uado piscatu* in J 21.3 is probably intended for an accusative, the horizontal stroke over the *u* having been lost.

Imperative (cf. also remarks under Future, p. 54)

The imperative is found in its regular forms throughout. There are some cases however, where the indicative and imperative have been confused. The imperative for the indicative is found in: *quae uidi . . . haec loquor . . . quae uidistis . . . haec facite*, J 8.38;[94] *amodo cognoscite eum et uidistis eum*, J 14.7; *cum produxerint fructum . . . scitote iam quia . . . aestas est*, L 21.30. The Greek has the indicative in all these cases. The indicative, or the subjunctive, for the imperative may occur: *cum feceritis quae dico dicitis* (λέγεται=λέγετε), L 17.10; *paenitentiam agite et baptizetur* (βαπτισθήτω), A 2.38.

The imperative takes the place of a participle in one instance, the error being phonological, perhaps: *tolle* for *tollens* in L 19.22.

Subjunctive

As in practically all other points, so in his use of the indicative and subjunctive moods the scribe of Codex Bezae is somewhat careless. It is hard to determine the influence of the Greek here. Many cases of confusion are due to translation from the Greek, but on the other hand there are also many places where the two differ. The following references give some of the typical errors which are found.

Indicative for **subjunctive**

- in clauses of purpose: *ut ubi ego sum et uos eritis*, J 14.3; and Mt 13.15; L 8.17; 14.8,9,29.
- in a clause of result: *ut filium suum . . . dedit*, J 3.16.
- in indirect questions: *sciebat Ihs qui sunt*, J 6.64; *interrogauerunt eum . . . quomodo uidit*, J 9.15; and J 11.57; L 4.34; 12.11; 13.25.
- in contrary-to-fact conditions: *bonum erat ei si non esset natus*, Mt 26.24; *hic si esset propheta sciebat*, L 7.39; and J 8.39,42; 14.28; 15.19,22,24; L 17.6. This occurs occasionally in classical Latin.
- in less vivid future conditions: *si . . . dixerit . . . et incipiat . . . ueniet Dms*, Mt 24.48–50; *si non . . . moriatur solum manet*, J 12.24; also Mt 15.14; J 15.6.

Subjunctive for **indicative**

This is less common than the opposite tendency, but in the following cases the indicative should be used: *numquid accenditur lucerna . . . et non super candalabrum ponatur*, Mk 4.21; *donec alius exurrexerit rex qui non meminisset ipsius Ioseph*, A 7.18; *in quo tempore natus esset Moyses*, A 7.20; *qui . . . loquatur tibi*, A 10.32.

[94] Perhaps due to a misunderstanding of the Greek, in which both moods have the same form, as Professor Hatch notes.

There is no apparent reason for the confusion in any of these instances except the first, where D has ἵνα . . . τεθῇ.

Moods in substantive clauses

The infinitive and accusative construction was largely replaced in Late Latin by the use of a substantive clause introduced by *quod*, *quia*, or *quoniam* (Grandgent 41, 50; Bonnet, 659 ff.; Löfstedt, 117 ff.; Salonius, 321 ff.). In Codex Bezae *quod*[95] is comparatively rare in this usage, being found but 30 times, while *quia* is used 133 times and *quoniam* 92 in the same capacity. They translate the Greek ὅτι. Some examples are given: *quia: uidens quia delusus est*, Mt 2.16; *nolite putare quia ueni dissoluere*, Mt 5.17; *putant quia . . . exaudientur*, Mt 6.7; *creditis quia possum hoc facere*, Mt 9.28; *nolite putare quia ueni mittere pacem*, Mt 10.34; *legistis . . . quia sacerdotes . . . uiolant*, Mt 12.5; *intellegitis quia . . . dixi*, Mt 16.11; *cognouerunt quia de ipsis dicit*, Mt 21.45; *cognoui quia durus es homo*, Mt 25.24; *bene dixisti quia uirum non habes*, J 4.17; etc. It will be noted that the indicative mood alone is used, which is unusual in view of the fact that others have found both moods (cf. Salonius, 306; Bonnet, 662). The same is true of the examples with *quoniam* which follow: *ut sciatis quoniam filius . . . habet*, Mt 9.6; *dicentes quoniam adpropinquauit*, Mt 10.7; *scis quoniam pharisaei . . . scandalizati sunt*, Mt 15.12; *scitote quoniam prope est*, Mt 24.33; and Mt 27.3; J 3.33; 9.20; L 8.53; etc.

Moods with conjunctions

cum and **dum**

Temporal *dum* and *cum* were often confused in Late Latin (Salonius, 316; Leumann-Hofmann, 743–44). This fact may account for the following cases where the subjunctive, instead of the usual indicative, follows *dum* in the meaning of "while": *dum accusaretur . . . nihil respondebat*, Mt 27.12; *dum sacerdotio fungeretur . . . accidit*, L 1.8; *in eo dum populus esset . . . uidit*, L 5.1; *dum esset in una ciuitatium*, L 5.12; *dum aporiarentur de eo duo uiri adsisterunt*, L 24.4; *dum inpleret cursum . . . dicebat*, A 13.25. The indicative is found once: *dum intra se . . . haesitabat Petrus*, A 10.17.

The confusion in temporal clauses may explain the substitution of *dum* for *cum* causal in *quomodo potestes* (*potestis*) *bona loqui dum maligni estis*, Mt 12.34.

Dum meaning "until," with the idea of anticipation or expectancy, is regularly followed by the subjunctive, with the exception of J 21.22: *si eum uolo sic manere usque dum uenio* (ἕως ἔρχομαι).

Cum is substituted for *dum*, "while," in: *cum . . . dormirent homines uenit . . . inimicus*, Mt 13.25; *ambulate ergo cum habetis lumen*, J 12.35; *numquid possunt fili sponsi cum habeant sponsum secum ieiunare*, L 5.34; *cum esset Petrus in atrium uenit ad eum una*, Mk 14.66; *cum fuissent Salamina adnuntiabat uerbum Di*, A 13.5; and Mt 25.10; J 17.11; L 8.42; 9.18,29; 10.38; 11.27; 17.11,14; Mk 2.14 10.17.

In one instance *cum* takes the place of *dum*, "until": *non gustabunt mortem usque cum uideant filium*, L 9.27.

Cum when referring to the future usually has the indicative (Leumann-Hofmann,

[95] *Quod* is rare as a conjunction in other usages also, being found only 11 times in a causal sense in addition to the usage here mentioned. Cf. p. 62, *infra*.

750), but is found once in Codex Bezae with the subjunctive, due to the Greek in D: *uenient . . . dies cum tollatur ab eis sponsus* (ὅταν ἀρθῇ), Mt 9.15.

Temporal *cum* is not replaced by *dum* in Codex Bezae, although this substitution occurs in other similar texts (cf. Taylor, 133).

donec

The moods after *donec*, "until," are regular. The indicative refers to an actual occurrence: *stella . . . praecedebat eos donec uenit et stetit*, Mt 2.9; *nescierunt donec uenit diluuium*, Mt 24.39; *adnuntians expeditionem . . . donec oblata est*, A 21.26; the subjunctive denotes anticipation (*Thes. Ling. Lat.*, V, 1996, 54 ff.): *ibi manete donec exeatis*, Mt 10.11; *linum . . . non extintinguet donec eiciat ad uictoriam iudicium*, Mt 12.20; and Mt 5.18; 10.23; 13.33; 16.28; 17.9; 18.30,34; 22.44; 23.39; 24.34; L 13.35; Mk 6.10; 9.1; 12.36; 13.30; A 2.35.

priusquam, antequam, postquam

These conjunctions are rare in Codex Bezae and are followed by their usual moods, *priusquam* and *antequam* taking the subjunctive in anticipation, *postquam* always the indicative.

ut

The usual subjunctive follows *ut* in purpose and result clauses, with the exception of the instances noted on p. 59. The subjunctive is also regular in substantive clauses.

Temporal *ut* is found 31 times in Codex Bezae, and is regularly followed by the indicative (Leumann-Hofmann, 758), with the exception of the following instances: *ut adpropiasset Hierosolyma*, Mt 21.1; *factum est . . . ut adpropiaret porte* (*portae*, dat.) *ciuitatis*, L 7.12. In both places D has the indicative. In the case of *ut accepissent* (λαβόντες) *mandatum . . . proficiscebatur*, A 17.15, the subjunctive is correct, however, since *ut* here means "as soon as" (Leumann-Hofmann, 758).

Ut is in one instance omitted in a substantive clause: *comminatus est eis nemini dicerent de illo*, Mk 8.30.

7. Miscellaneous Peculiarities in Construction

Adjectives

Cardinal numerals are in general use throughout Codex Bezae where the ordinals should be employed. This usage is a Hebraism which comes into the Latin through the Greek (Plater-White, 21). The following instances occur: *secundus et tertius usque ad septem*, Mt 22.26; *inluscente in una sabbatorum*, Mt 28.1; *ueniunt mane una sabbati*, Mk 16.2; J 20.19; L 24.1; A 20.7.

Pronouns

Very commonly throughout the MS. the antecedent of a relative pronoun is omitted: *fili estis qui occiderunt prophetas*, Mt 23.31; *ut faciam uoluptatem qui me misit*, J 4.34; *erit consummatio quae dicta sunt*, L 1.45; *sunt nobiliores qui Thessalonicae sunt*, A 17.11; and J 5.10; L 3.7; 6.4; 24.33; Mk 3.34; 10.23; A 4.21; 6.1; 16.10,13; 22.11.

Omission of the relative is far less frequent: *dicit . . . Martha soror defuncti erat*, J 11.39; *arbor ficui maledixisti aruit*, Mk 11.21;[96] *secernite mihi Barnaban et Saulum ad opus uocaui eos*, A 13.2.

Conjunctions

The employment of a conjunction to introduce a direct quotation is common in Biblical Latin, and in other translation literature. This construction is of frequent occurrence in the Greek (the so-called recitative ὅτι), and its use in Latin is due to imitation. *Quia*, *quoniam*, *quod*, and *ut* are the conjunctions so used in Codex Bezae (cf. Salonius, 329; Leumann-Hofmann, 721, *quod;* 726, *quia;* 753, *quoniam*). *Quia* and *quoniam* are used in the large majority of instances (89 and 84 times respectively), while *quod* and *ut* are found but seldom (7 and 3 times respectively). A few examples will suffice to illustrate this common usage: *dixit . . . quia Di filius sum*, Mt 27.43; *dixit . . . quia post tres dies resurgam*, Mt 27.63; *dixerunt ei quia omnes quaerunt te*, Mk 1.37; *dicentes quoniam fantasma est*, Mt 14.26; *dicens quoniam sic mihi fecit Dms*, L 1.25; etc.

Verbs

1. A very characteristic mark of Biblical Latin is the use of the expression *et factum est*, "and it came to pass," in a transitional sense to introduce a new paragraph. The construction is common in Hebrew, and passed into Greek in the Septuagint Version of the O.T. (καὶ ἐγένετο). From the Greek it naturally passed into the Latin versions (Süss, 103–07).[97]

Factum est in this sense is generally followed by a temporal clause with *cum*, *dum*, or *ut*, or by the ablative absolute; and the main clause follows, construed in the ways indicated below:

With the indicative: this is by far the most common construction with *factum est: et factum est cum consummasset Ihs praecipiens . . . transiit inde* (καὶ ἐγένετο . . . μετέβη), Mt 11.1; *et factum est ut conpleti sunt dies ministerii eius tunc abiit*, L 1.23; and Mt 9.10; 13.53; 17.1; 19.1; 26.1; L 1.8,41; 2.1,15,46; 7.1; 8.40; 9.18,29,33,57; 10.38; 11.27; 17.14; 18.35; 19.5,29; 20.1; 24.4,30,51; Mk 1.9; 2.15; A 2.1,2. Sometimes the indicative clause is joined to *factum est* by *et: factum est . . . dum populus super eum esset . . . et uidit* (ἐγένετο . . . καὶ ἴδεν), L 5.1,2; *factum est . . . ut adpropiaret porte* (dat.) *ciuitatis et ferebatur . . . filius*, L 7.12; and L 5.12; 8.1; 9.28,51; 11.1; 14.1; 17.11; 24.15; A 5.7.

With the accusative and infinitive: *factum est . . . Ihu baptizato . . . aperiri caelum et descendere spm sanctum* (ἐγένετο . . . ἀνοιχθῆναι . . . καὶ καταβῆναι), L 3.21,22; *et factum est iterum eum sabbatis ambulare per sata* (αὐτὸν . . . διαπορεύεσθε [*sic*]), Mk 2.23; *factum est . . . per omnem ciuitatem transire uerbum Dni* (ἐγένετο . . . διελθεῖν), A 13.44; and L 5.17; 6.1,12; 9.37; 19.15; A 22.17.

In one instance *factum est* is followed by a substantive clause with *ut: factum est . . . ut moreretur pauper et ductus est in sinus Abrahae* (ἐγένετο δὲ ἀποθανεῖν), L 16.22.

There are two cases where *erit* is used in a sense somewhat similar to *factum est*,

[96] Professor Hatch suggests that this may be a case of haplography, *ficui* = *fici cui*. The text would then read: *arbor fici cui maledixisti aruit*. For the phrase *arbor fici* cf. the Vulgate *fici arborem*, Mt 21.19.

[97] This is also the view of J. H. Moulton, who has an excellent discussion of ἐγένετο in his *Grammar of New Testament Greek*, vol. I, *Prolegomena*, pp. 16 f.

but with reference to the future, naturally; the Greek is ἔσται: *erit in nouissimis diebus . . . effundam spm meum*, A 2.17; *erit omnis quicumque inuocauerat nomen Dni saluus erit*, A 2.21.

2. *Facio* is sometimes used in a causal sense with the infinitive, usually of an intransitive verb. This became quite common in Late Latin, especially among the Ecclesiastical writers, who used the construction as a translation of the Greek ποιέω with an infinitive (Kaulen, 278; *Thes. Ling. Lat.*, VI, 117, 82 ff.).[98] Examples in Codex Bezae are: *faciam uos fieri piscatores hominum*, Mt 4.19; Mk 1.17; *solem suum oriri fecit*, Mt 5.45; *facite homines recumbere*, J 6.10; *caecos faciebat uidere*, L 7.21; *possidere eos fecit terram allophoelorum*, A 13.19.

3. *Opus est* in Late Latin had given way almost entirely to the personal construction *opus habeo*, on the analogy of the usage *necesse habeo* found in Cicero, Caesar, and other classical authors (Leumann-Hofmann, 436; Salonius, 263). A few cases of this are found in Codex Bezae: *abs te opus habeo baptizari* (D lacking), Mt 3.14; *Dms eorum opus habet* (χρείαν ἔχει), Mt 21.3; *eme quorum opus habemus*, J 13.29; *non opus habet ut . . .* (χρείαν ἔχεις), J 16.30; *non habent opus qui salui sunt medico* (χρείαν ἔχουσιν), L 5.31; *scit quoniam opus habetis horum* (χρῄζεται), L 12.30.

The older usage, *necesse habeo*, has been noted in a few places: *non necesse habent fortes medico*, Mt 9.12; *non necesse habent ire*, Mt 14.16; *non necesse habet . . . labare* (*lauare*), J 13.10.

4. It is interesting to note here what Harris has called a peculiar form of the verb *habeo*.[99] He points out five instances of its occurrence, which we shall take up in order. The first is in Mt 5.46: *si . . . dilexeritis diligentes uos quam mercedem habebetis*, which we are asked to regard as a peculiar present form. However, the Greek has ἕξεται (i.e. ἕξετε), and *habebetis* is doubtless future, *i* and *e* being commonly confused (pp. 17, 18). But even regarding the form as a present there is little reason to call it a peculiar form, since dittography is common in this MS.[100]

Harris' second instance (in Mt 6.1, not 6.2) is *habebitis*, where the Greek is ἔχετε. He wants us to regard this as a present; but there is no difficulty in taking it as a future, since the two tenses are confused frequently (p. 54). The same holds true of the third case in J 6.53. *Habebitis* in J 16.22 (the fourth instance) is clearly not a peculiar form of the present, but a future, D having ἕξετε.

His last instance, *habebebat enim orationem*, A 18.18, is clearly dittography. In view of the facts presented, it is difficult to see how Harris could ever have made the statement that "these five instances will show, and especially the last, that we are not dealing with a palaeographical blunder, but with an actual verb form."[101]

5. It should be noted that verbs are sometimes confused as to person, but the instances are rare:

3rd for 1st: *in quod intuitus considerabat* (κατενόουν) *et uidi*, A 11.6; and *dixit*, 11.8; *coepisset*, 11.15; *uenerunt* (D lacking),[102] 21.16; *surrexit* (D lacking), 22.11. Except where D is lacking, the Greek has first person forms.

3rd for 2nd: *scis omnia et non opus habet* (ἔχεις) *ut . . .* , J 16.30; and *descendet*,

[98] The best treatment of this usage is by Thielmann, "*Facere mit dem Infinitiv*," *AR*, 3(1886), 177–206; especially, pp. 186 ff.

[99] *Codex Bezae*, p. 260.

[100] Cf. *extintinguet*, Mt 12.20; *locututus*, J 6.63; *loquituitur*, J 7.46; etc.

[101] *Loc. cit.*

[102] This may be correct, but the Greek MSS. are not in agreement at this point.

L 10.15; *putat,* L 18.8 (may be haplography for the plural *putatis;* D has no corresponding verb here); *locutus est,* A 4.25. The Greek is second person in all these instances.

2nd for 3rd: *non contendet . . . confringes . . . extintinguet* (all with the same subject), Mt 12.20; *mna tua decemnas adquisiuis,* L 19.16. In the first of the above examples D also has the second person.

1st singular and 3rd plural: this confusion is the result of phonetic difficulty with final *m* and *nt.*[103] In the following, *erant* should be first person singular: *tres uiri superuenerunt ad domum in qua erant,* A 11.11. The instances where the first person singular is used for the third person plural are: *mundus odit eos quoniam non sum* (εἰσὶν) *de hoc mundo,* J 17.14; *sicut uultis ut faciam* (ποιῶσιν) *uobis homines,* L 6.31; *et exquiram* (ἐκζητήσωσιν) *residui hominum D$\overline{m}$,* A 15.17; *isti homines perturbam* (ταράσσουσιν) *nostram ciuitatem,* A 16.20.

[103] Page 21, *supra.* Harris (chap. xii) quotes Sittl, *Die lokalen Verschiedenheiten der lateinischen Sprache,* p. 70, "Auslautendes NT wird nur in Italien durch nasales M ersetz." Cf. Lindsay, *The Latin Language,* p. 124. This evidence adds to the probability that we are not to consider Gaul as the place where Codex Bezae was written.

Chapter III

CONCLUSION

The language of the Latin Text of Codex Bezae does not vary materially in character from that of other literary remains from the same approximate period (saec. iv–vii).[1] This has been shown by the numerous references in the text to other works where the same phenomena appear. There are, however, a few general differences between d and the other works referred to. Our MS. shows unmistakable signs of having been written by a careless and ignorant scribe, and many errors in such things as number and case are found which can not easily be duplicated elsewhere. There are also peculiar syntactical phenomena which arise from the influence of the Hebrew and the Greek upon Biblical Latin.

The phonology of the MS. presents few irregularities. The change *i*>*ei* (p. 18) is rare in Late Latin; *d*>*p* (p. 20) may be palaeographical, since it is attested in no other place; and for *m*>*p* (p. 21) there seems to be no ready explanation. Another strange phonological feature is the insertion of a *t* between *s* and *r* in the word *Istrahel,* which appears regularly in this form throughout the text, *Israhel* being found but ten times (p. 22).

Some of the outstanding Hebraisms which are noted in the MS. are the confusion of the neuter plural with the feminine singular (p. 27),[2] the use of abstract nouns in the plural with concrete force (p. 32), the employment of *in* with the ablative to show means or instrument (p. 48), the use of *in* with the accusative in a factitive sense (p. 48), the practice of using cardinal numerals for ordinals (p. 61), and finally the use of the phrase *et factum est* to introduce new paragraphs (p. 62).

The influence of the Greek on the language of d is very considerable, as has been indicated throughout, and only the most outstanding Grecisms need be summarized here. Greek gender has influenced the scribe in several instances (p. 27). The genitive absolute in Latin occurs only in Ecclesiastical texts, a clear case of Greek influence (p. 33). While some Latin poets of the classical period use the genitive after certain verbs in imitation of the Greek, the instances are rare; but the phenomenon is common in Codex Bezae (pp. 34, 35). The genitive after comparatives is another clear Grecism (p. 35). The extensive employment of the demonstrative pronouns for the definite article (p. 41) can be traced to the Greek. The word *μέλλειν* presented a problem to Latin translators, and the solution was a periphrastic future tense with *incipere* or *habere* and the infinitive (p. 55). The Greek articular infinitive has left its mark on the Latin text of Codex Bezae (p. 56). The Greek recitative *ὅτι* (p. 62) is responsible for the use of conjunctions such as *quia* and *quoniam* to introduce direct speeches.

Clark (*Acts,* 205 ff.) has listed some stylistic peculiarities in the Bezan text of the Book of Acts which tend to show that its translator was perhaps a different person.

[1] Precisely how much Codex Bezae deviates from classical usage in comparison with each separate Late Latin work of the same general period, it might be important to know; but such a prodigious series of statistical comparisons as a study of that kind would involve, lies far outside the scope of the present modest attempt to compare the usage of Codex Bezae with classical Latin only.

[2] Yet something of the same sort appears also in the Greek.

He has noted a somewhat peculiar manner of using the *nomina sacra*, and also some differences in vocabulary. A few more points tending toward the same conclusion have appeared from our study. The use of *ipse* as an article is found only in Acts (p. 41), and the peculiar and sometimes awkward replacement of the correlative participle by a *cum* clause (p. 57) is also characteristic of that book as distinct from the Gospels.

In regard to the bearing which the language of d has upon the provenience of the MS. we can come to no clear decision. All we can do is point out a few characteristics of the language which may strengthen the probability of certain hypotheses, while weakening that of others, and this method we shall follow in drawing up our conclusions.

As stated in the introductory chapter, it was long supposed that Codex Bezae was written in Gaul. The external evidence seemed to point in that direction, and scholars produced internal evidence as well to back up this position. But Lowe, after a thorough study of the MS. from the palaeographical point of view, has shown that the hypothesis was scarcely tenable; and Ropes has strengthened this opinion from the historical point of view. The final blow was struck by Brightman, when he showed that the liturgical notes in the margin of the MS. had no connection whatsoever with the Gallic church ritual. Thus the external evidence for the Gallic origin of our MS. was demolished. From our study of the language of d we can show that internal evidence is also deficient. The confusion between the vowels *i* and *e*, and *o* and *u*, is especially frequent in writings from Gaul (pp. 17, 18), but neither of these features is outstanding in Codex Bezae. The phonological difficulty with final *m* and *nt* (p. 64) is not Gallic but rather Italian. Harris's conclusions on the weakening of intervocalic consonants (p. 23) have been shown to lack adequate support, and furthermore, this phenomenon is not exclusively characteristic of Gallic manuscripts. Scrivener's contention that certain constructions in Codex Bezae "look more like French than Latin" has been shown to be ill taken, for the same constructions are found elsewhere throughout the Empire (p. 47, note 72).

While this study does not deal with the vocabulary of the Latin text, it should be mentioned here that some have argued for the Gallic origin of Codex Bezae on the ground that certain words appear which are characteristic exclusively of that form of Vulgar Latin used in Southern Gaul. But Harris (*Codex Bezae*, 16 26) has already shown how utterly groundless any such assumptions are.

There is one feature, however, in which Codex Bezae seems to display what might be a characteristic of Gallic Latin, i.e., the fact that verbs of the third conjugation tend to go into the second (p. 29). In this single trait the *Peregrinatio* (which is known to be a product of Gaul) and Codex Bezae agree against the general tendency observed elsewhere. Nevertheless, the cumulative evidence indicates that there is little ground for assuming that any of the linguistic phenomena of the MS. are peculiar to Gaul, or to any other particular locality. Harris and Scrivener are both guilty of attempting to localize certain forms and constructions which actually were prevalent in practically all parts of the Empire. There was no appreciable dialectalization before the close of the eighth century.[3]

[3] H. F. Muller, *A Chronology of Vulgar Latin, Beihefte zur Zeitschrift für Romanische Philologie*, 78(1929). Cf. also Muller and Taylor, *Chrestomathy of Vulgar Latin*, Heath, 1932, p. 21: "It is a well-known fact . . . that the language of the documents of this period (immediately

Having noted these facts about the language of d and its relation to Gaul, we are ready to say that, with all external evidence pointing away from Gaul, and with the internal evidence strengthening this position, Codex Bezae is almost certainly not Gallic in origin.

Southern Italy can also be practically eliminated. There are certain historical difficulties (p. 14); Lowe has objected on palaeographical grounds (p. 14); and we should expect a scribe from that locality to have a better command of Greek and Latin than the writer of our MS. displays.

This leaves us two alternatives, either to agree with Ropes that the MS. belongs to Sicily, or with Clark that it belongs somewhere in the East, most probably Egypt. The former view fits perfectly into the historical situation, and satisfies all the other requirements for the production of a MS. such as Codex Bezae: Sicily was bilingual, the church was Greek and employed the Byzantine rite, etc. The main difficulty here, pointed out by Clark, is that whoever wrote the MS. knew little Greek and Latin, a situation which is distinctly improbable in Sicily, where we should expect the scribe to know at least one of the languages well. We have seen evidence of this in our study. That the scribe knew little Latin has appeared from the great number as well as the character of the errors that may be observed on almost every page (p. 38). Also the great number of Grecisms, and the evident difficulty which the scribe had in turning the Greek into idiomatic Latin, tend to show the same thing. That the scribe did not know Greek any too well has been shown by Clark (*Acts*, p. lviii). These facts have caused Clark to maintain that the scribe's native tongue was neither Latin nor Greek, but some third language, and to turn to a trilingual area for the provenience of the MS. Because Egypt fulfils historical requirements, and other facts add to the probability (pp. 12, 13), he favors that locality.

There is little to choose between these two positions. Both have much to commend them. We may say, however, having definitely eliminated the Far West from consideration, that the view which regards Egypt as the home of Codex Bezae has a slight advantage over that which looks to Sicily, when we add the weight of linguistic evidence to that already adduced from other sources.

In conclusion, one more possibility suggests itself. We have seen that Codex Bezae certainly arose in an area where both Greek and Latin were none too perfectly known. It is also likely that it would have been used only in such an area, for any scholarly community would have found it distasteful. Perhaps we need to look for something like a Roman military colony in a region imperfectly Hellenized. Clark has already mentioned Palestine as a possible locality for the origin of the MS.,[4] and there is nothing in his view which would prevent the acceptance of this alternative. We do know that Hadrian drove the Jews out of Jerusalem, and the colony which he established there continued to exist throughout the centuries. Jerusalem also became a center of Christianity, albeit not an outstanding one. Between 408 and 450 a series of churches was established by Eudoxia, the wife of

---

preceding the age of Charlemagne), corrupt from the point of view of Latin though they may be, does not differ in its essentials, whether the documents originate from one region, Northern France, or another, Italy. . . . The regional peculiarities must have consisted mostly of colloquial expressions, local terms, which the written language had little occasion to record."

[4] *Supra*, p. 12.

Theodosius II, and in 451 the city became a patriarchate.[5] Codex Bezae could very well have fitted the needs of such a community.

It is strange, too, that while there were doubtless many copies of the scriptures which were better and more carefully written than Codex Bezae, these have perished, while our MS. seems to have been preserved with some care through the vicissitudes of the years. This would seem to indicate that for some reason the book was especially reverenced. Such reverence might be less unreasonable if, as a matter of fact, this was the very copy of the New Testament used by the Christian church in Jerusalem in the fifth and sixth centuries, and thus one which must have acquired a sort of sacredness which led men to preserve it despite its egregious faults.[6]

This view accords with what has already been said about the history of the MS. In 638 A.D. Jersualem was taken by the Mohammedans,[7] and the MS. could very well have begun its westward journey at that time, carried by some fugitive, the journey which finally ended in France where Beza found the Codex.[8]

[5] *RE*, IX, 954; cf. also Mommsen, *Provinces of the Roman Empire*, tr. by W. P. Dickinson, I, 244; and Milman, *History of Latin Christianity*, 1883, I, 108.

[6] The suggestion that Codex Bezae might have been composed for some such trilingual community as Jersualem must have been for a long time after the establishment of the military colony under Hadrian, and the observation that some quality other than correctness of literary tradition must be posited in order to explain its survival, when many far better manuscripts perished, was first made to me by Professor Oldfather.

[7] *RE*, IX, 954; Milman, *op. cit.*, II, 209–10.

[8] Cf. *supra*, pp. 9 and 15.

BIBLIOGRAPHY[1]

I. On the Date and Provenience of Codex Bezae

A. *Books*

CHASE, FREDERIC HENRY, *The Old Syriac Element in the Text of Codex Bezae*, Macmillan, 1893.

CLARK, ALBERT C., *The Acts of the Apostles*, Oxford, 1933.

HARRIS, J. RENDEL, *A Study of Codex Bezae*, Cambridge, 1891; in *Texts and Studies*, edited by J. A. Robinson, vol. II, no. 1.

——————, *Four Lectures on the Western Text of the New Testament*, Cambridge, 1894.

KENYON, FREDERIC G., *Handbook to the Textual Criticism of the New Testament*, Macmillan, 1912.

LOWE, E. A., *Codices Lugdunenses Antiquissimi*, Lyons, 1924.

——————, *Codices Latini Antiquiores*, vol. 2, no. 140, pp. 7, 47, Oxford, 1935.

ROPES, JAMES HARDY, *The Text of Acts*, Macmillan, 1926; in *The Beginnings of Christianity*, Jackson and Lake, Part I, vol. 3.

SCRIVENER, FREDERICK H., *Bezae Codex Cantabrigiensis*, Cambridge, 1864.

B. *Articles*

BRIGHTMAN, F. E., "The Marginal Notes of Lections," *Journal of Theological Studies*, 1(1899–1900), 446–54.

BURKITT, F. C., "The Date of Codex Bezae," *Journal of Theological Studies*, 3(1901–02), 501–13.

CHANTRAINE, P., "A Review of Clark's *Acts*," *Revue de Philologie*, 61(1933), 214–15.

CHAPMAN, J., "The Order of the Gospels in the Parent of Codex Bezae," *Zeitschrift für die neutestamentliche Wissenschaft*, 6(1905), 339–46.

KENYON, F. G., "Review of Codex Bezae," *Journal of Theological Studies*, 1(1899–1900), 293–99.

LIETZMANN, H., "Die Chester-Beatty-Papyri des Neuen Testaments," *Die Antike*, 11(1935), 139 ff.

LAKE, KIRSOPP, "On the Italian Origin of Codex Bezae," *Journal of Theological Studies*, 1(1899–1900), 441–45.

LOWE, E. A., "The Codex Bezae," *Journal of Theological Studies*, 14(1912–13), 385–88.

———, "The Codex Bezae and Lyons," *ibid.*, 25(1924), 270–74.

MERCATI, G., "On the Non-Greek Origin of the Codex Bezae," *Journal of Theological Studies*, 15(1913–14), 448–51.

QUENTIN, H., "Le Codex Bezae à Lyon au IXe siècle?" *Revue Bénédictine*, 23(1906), 1–23.

SANDERS, H. A., "A Papyrus Fragment of *Acts* in the Michigan Collection," *Harvard Theological Review*, 20(1927), 1 ff.

SOUTER, A., "The Original Home of Codex Claromontanus (D^{paul})," *Journal of Theological Studies*, 6(1904–05), 240–43.

II. Books Cited in the Linguistic Section

(Listed in alphabetic order of abbreviations used in footnotes)

AR = *Archiv für lateinische Lexikographie und Grammatik*, vols. 1–15 (the individual articles are cited in the text).

Baehrens = W. A. BAEHRENS, *Sprachlicher Kommentar zur Vulgärlateinischen Appendix Probi*, Halle, 1922.

Bechtel = Ed. BECHTEL, *Sanctae Silviae Peregrinatio*, Diss., Chicago, 1902.

Bonnet = MAX BONNET, *Le Latin de Grégoire de Tours*, Paris, 1890.

Dessau = H. DESSAU, *Inscriptiones Latinae Selectae*, Berlin, 1892–1916.

Diehl = E. DIEHL, *Inscriptiones Latinae Christianae Veteres*, Berlin, 1925–31.

[1] Works referred to only occasionally are cited in full in the text, and do not appear in this bibliography.

Draeger = A. Draeger, *Historische Syntax der lateinischen Sprache*, Leipzig, 1878.

Georges, *Lex.* = K. E. Georges, *Lexikon der lateinischen Wortformen*, Leipzig, 1890.

Grandgent = C. H. Grandgent, *An Introduction to Vulgar Latin*, Boston, 1922.

Kaulen = Franz Kaulen, *Sprachliches Handbuch zur biblischen Vulgate*, Freiburg im Breisgau, 1904.

Kühner = Raphael Kühner, *Ausführliches Grammatik der lateinischen Sprache*, Hannover, 1878.

Leumann-Hofmann = *Stolz-Schmalz lateinische Grammatik*, neu bearbeitet von Manu Leumann und Joh. Bapt. Hofmann, München, 1928 (*Müller Handbuch*, II, 2).

Lindsay, Pl. = W. M. Lindsay, *The Syntax of Plautus*, Oxford, 1907.

Löfstedt = Einar Löfstedt, *Philologischer Kommentar zur Peregrinatio Aetheria*, Uppsala, 1911.

——— *Synt.* = *Syntactica* (*Studien und Beiträge zur historischen Syntax des Lateins*). I. *Über einige Grundfragen der lat. Nominalsyntax*, Lund, 1928.

——— *Verm. Stud.* = *Vermischte Studien zur lateinischen Sprachkunde und Syntax*, Lund, 1936.

Mørland = Henning Mørland, *Die Lateinische Oribasiusübersetzungen* (*Symbolae Osloenses Fasc. Supplet. V*), Oslo, 1932.

Neue-Wagener = Friedrich Neue, *Formenlehre der lateinischen Sprache*, 3rd edition, by C. Wagener, Leipzig, 1902, vol. I.

Pei = Mario A. Pei, *The Language of the Eighth-Century Texts in Northern France*, Diss., College of the City of New York, 1932.

Pirson = J. Pirson, *La langue des inscriptions latines de la Gaule*, Bruxelles, 1901.

Plater-White = W. E. Plater and H. J. White, *A Grammar of the Vulgate*, Oxford, 1926.

Rönsch = Hermann Rönsch, *Itala und Vulgata*, Marburg, 1875.

Salonius = A. H. Salonius, *Vitae Patrum*, Lund, 1920; in *Acta Societatis Humaniorum Litterarum Lundensis, II.*

Schuchardt = Hugo Schuchardt, *Der Vokalismus des Vulgärlateins*, Leipzig, 1866.

Seelmann = Emil Seelmann, *Die Aussprache des Latein*, Heilbronn, 1885.

Sommer = Ferdinand Sommer, *Handbuch der lateinischen Laut- und Formenlehre*, 2nd ed., Heidelberg, 1914.

Süss = Wilhelm Süss, *Studien zur lateinischen Bibel*, Tartu, 1932; in *Acta et Commentationes Universitatis Tartuensis, B, Humaniora*, XXIX (1933).

Svennung = J. Svennung, *Untersuchungen zu Palladius und zur lateinischen Fach- und Volkssprache*, Uppsala, 1935.

Taylor = Pauline Taylor, *The Latinity of the Liber Historiae Francorum*, Diss., Columbia University, 1924.

Väänänen = Veikko Väänänen, *Le Latin Vulgaire des Inscriptions Pompéiennes*, Helsinki, 1937.

III. Lexicographical Works Cited

Georges, *Ausf.* = Karl Georges, *Ausführliches lateinisch-deutsches Handwörterbuch*, 8th ed. by Heinrich Georges, Hannover und Leipzig, 1912.

Thes. Ling. Lat. = *Thesaurus Linguae Latinae, editus auctoritate et consilio academiarum quinque Germanicarum, Berolinensis, Gottingensis, Lipsiensis, Monacensis, Vindobonensis*, Leipzig, 1900 to date (*A—ignotus*).

IV. Not Cited[2]

Bassett, E. L., "The Genitive Absolute in Latin," *Classical Philology*, 40(1945), 108–14.

von Dobschutz, E., "Das Decretum Gelasianum," *Texte und Untersuchungen zur Geschichte der Altchristlichen Literatur*, 38(1912), 99 ff.

Vrusch, Bruno, "Orthographica, Lexica, et Grammatica," in *Gregarii Turonensis Opera, Monumenta Germaniae Historica, Scriptores Rerum Merovingicarum*, Vol. I, Hannoverae, 1885, pp. 912–63.

[2]These titles came to my attention too late for citation in the text.

INDEX VERBORUM

EXPLANATION OF LISTING[1]

THIS INDEX has been prepared as an aid to scholars who might desire to investigate more thoroughly the linguistic phenomena of the Latin text. Every occurrence of every word is listed, in all the various inflectional forms, making it a simple matter to trace peculiarities of morphology and syntax in any particular case, tense, or mood.

The various forms of the words are listed in the order usually found in the paradigms. In nouns, the singular is listed first, then the plural. No indication of case is given, except when it is not evident from the position of the form in the listing. E.g. *puero* between *puerum* and *pueri* could be nothing else than ablative singular; but *pueris* after *puerorum*, assuming that the accusative plural does not occur, could be either dative or ablative, and will be marked accordingly.

Forms of adjectives and pronouns are listed across, first the nominative singular masculine, feminine, and neuter, then the genitive, etc. Here again position will be the clue to form in most cases, e.g. *boni* between *bonum* and *bonae* is masculine genitive singular, while the same form between *bonae* and *bono* would be neuter genitive singular.

Verbs are listed first in the indicative mood, in the usual order of tenses, then in the subjunctive mood, followed by the imperative, infinitive, participle, gerundive, and gerund. The passive voice is listed immediately after the active for each tense.

Because of the large number of variant spellings there are numerous cross references. It is hoped that these will facilitate the finding of any unusual forms. Words which have more than one spelling are usually listed under the form which is most common in the MS. regardless of whether it is the "correct" form or not.

Sincere efforts have been made to prevent errors, but in spite of extreme care there are doubtless mistakes. For these I take full responsibility.

ABBREVIATIONS AND SYMBOLS

ab.	ablativus	ind.	indicativus	praep.	prepositio
ac.	accusativus	indec.	indeclinabile	praes.	presens
adi.	adiectivus	indef.	indefinitum	pron.	pronomen
adv.	adverbium	inf.	infinitivum	quoq.	quoque
caus.	causale	interr.	interrogativum	rec.	recitative
col.	colophon	loc.	locativus	rel.	relativum
con.	coniunctio	m.	masculinum	s.	singularis
coni.	coniunctivus	mix.	mixta	sup.	supinum
d.	dativus	n.	nominativus	subst.	substantivum
exclam.	exclamatorius	neu.	neutrum	s.v.	sub verbo
f.	femininum	nih.	nihil	temp.	temporalis
fut.	futurum	nom.	nomen	v.	vide
g.	genitivus	part.	participium	verb.	verbum
imv.	imperativus	perf.	perfectum	voc.	vocativus
inc.	incertum	pl.	pluralis		

( ) Indicates the original of a form on which a correction has been made by one of the annotators of the MS.

[ ] Indicates a form as corrected by an annotator.

⟦ ⟧ Indicates a reference which occurs in the portion of the MS. added in the ninth century, which is not a part of the original text.

[1] Following, in general, but with a few variations due to the unusual character of the text, the system recommended by W. A. Oldfather, "Suggestions for Guidance in the Preparation of a Critical Index Verborum for Latin and Greek Authors," *T&PAPA*, 68 (1937), 1–10.

INDEX VERBORUM

a, *v.* **ab.**

Aaron L 1.5; A 7.40.

ab, a, abs **ab** (*c.ab.*) Mt 2.1,7; 3. [[6]],13; 5.13; 6.2; 8.30; 9.15,22; 10.17,22,28; 12.12,43; 13.12,35; 15.1,28; 17.13,18*bis*,25,26; 19.4,8, 12; 20.20; 23.7; 24.21,27,31; 25.28,29,32,34; 26.29; 27.45,57*bis;* J 4.10,52; 5.34,41,44; 6.64; 7.18,29,51; 8.26,44; 10.5; 11.51,53; 12.36,37; 15.4,27; 16.4; [[19.38]]; 20.1; L 1.2,38; 2.15,21; 3.19; 4.13,15,35*bis*,42; 5.2,15,35; 6.13,17,19, 29,30; 7.21,30; 8.18,29,33,37,43,44,49; 9.33, 39,45; 10.7,21,42; 11.16,24; 12.4,15,48,54,58; 13.12,17,29*bis;* 16.22; 18.3,34; 19.24,26*bis*,42; 20.4,6; 21.17,20; 22.16,41,45; 23.8,51; 24.31 *bis*,51; Mk 1.5,26,34,42; 2.20; 3.8*bis*,22; 4.25; 5.8,35; 7.1; 8.11; 9.21,25,26; 10.6; 12.38; 13.13,19; 14.35,43,52; 15.43; 16.3, [[11]]; III J 12*bis;* A 1.4,9; 2.5,24; 3.2,5; 4.36; 5.16,38 *bis*,39; 6.10; 10.22; 11.27; 12.1,5,10; 13.4,13, 39; 14.8,15,19; 15.3,4,38; 16.2; 17.27; 18.1, 2,7,21; 19.9*bis*,12; 21.27; 22.12; **ab** (*c.ac.*) L 4.1; 9.8; Mk 1.9; A 5.15; 16.18; **ab** (*c.indec.*) Mt 1.17; 20.29; L 10.30; 24.13,47; A 10.23; 12.25; 15.2; **ab** (*c.adv.*) L 14.18; **ab** (*c.ac. et ab.*) A 17.9; **a** (*c.ab.*) Mt 1.17,22; 2.15,16*ter*, 17; 3.8; 4.1*bis;* 5.18; 11.7,12,19,25,27,29; 12.6, 38,42; 14.2,8,24,26; 15.8; 16.6,21; 17.9,25*bis;* 18.7,19; 19.1,20; 20.8,21*bis*,23*ter;* 21.42,43; 22.31,44; 23.35; 24.31,32; 25.33*bis*, 34,41*bis;* 26.39,47,64; 27.12,38*bis*,64; 28.4,14; J 3.25; 4.9; 5.19,24,30; 6.45,46,65; 7.17,28; 8.9,28, 40,42; 9.16,32,33; 10.18*bis*,32; 11.18; 12.1, 21; 13.3; 14.10,21; 15.15,26*bis;* 16.13,22,28, 30; [[18.3,28,34]]; 20.9; 21.2,6,8*bis*,14; L 1.11, 26,45,52,70; 2.1,26,36; 3.7; 4.2,38,41; 5.3, 8,36; 6.34; 7.24,35; 8.2,12,14,27,29,38,46; 9.7 *bis*,22*bis;* 10.22; 11.4,50,51,*bis;* 12.1,20,57; 13.15,16,27; 16.16; 17.20,25,29; 18.21; 19.3; 20.46; 21.16,24,26; 22.18,42,45; 23.5,33*bis*, 49,55; 24.2,41; Mk 1.13; 2.21; 3.7; 5.15,26, 29,34; 6.14,16,22; 7.4,6,17; 8.15,31*bis;* 9.9,10; 10.12; 11.12,20; 12.11,25,34; 13.27,28; 14.36, 40,43*bis;* 15.38,45; [[16.19]]; A 1.11,12,22*bis*, 25; 2.22,25,33; 3.15,19,26; 4.9,10,11; 5,39,41; 6.9; 7.3,13,16,45; 8.6,7,10; 10.17,22,29,30,33 *bis*,37,38,41*bis*,42; 11.11,19; 12.14,19,20,23; 13.13,23,31,33,34,45; 14.8; 15.1,2,7,11,18,20, 29,33,38,40; 16.6,14; 17.3,13,15,19,31; 18.6; 19.12; 20.3,6,9,17,18,24,26; 21.3,7,25,35; 22.11; **a** (*c.ac.*) Mt 27.24; L 12.36; 20.42; Mk 13.27; A 11.23; 13.8,14; 16.38; 18.16; 21.21; **a** (*c.ac. et g.*) L 24.27; **a** (*c.g.*) Mk 6.21; A 16.11; **a** (*c.adv.*) Mt 27.51; **a** (*c.indec.*) Mt 1.17; 21.11; J 7.42; Mk 1.9; 2.3; A 3.24; 10.38; **abs** (*c.ab.*) Mt 3.14; 5.29; 18.8,9; J 12.49; 17.7,8; A 10.22. *v.quoq.* **abante, abintus, abinvicem, aforis, alonge, amodo.**

abalieno **abalienabatur** L 10.40; **abalienetis** L 12.29.

abante L 19.4.

abba Mk 14.36.

Abel Mt 23.35; L 11.51.

abeo **abit** Mt 13.46; 14.25; 19.22; 26.14; **abibat** J 4.50; **abiebat** Mt 24.1; **abii** Mt 25.25; J 9.11; **abiit** Mt 4.24; 9.7; 12.1; 13.25; 16.4; 18.30; 19.15; 26.(42),44; 27.60; J 4.3,28,47; 5.15; 6.1,3; 8.1; 9.7; 10.40; 11.28,54; 12.19,36; L 1.23,39; 4.30,42; 5.25; 8.33; 15.15; 19.12; 22.4; Mk 1.35; 2.12; 5.20; 6.1,46; 7.24; 8.13; 10.22; 14.10,39; 15.46; A 12.17; **abierunt** Mt 2.9; 8.32; 20.4; 22.5,22; 28.16; J 6.66; 7.53; 11.46; [[18.6]]; 20.10; L 1.15; 8.33; 9.56; 10.30; 24.24; Mk 6.32; 12.12; 14.16; A 5.18; **abierant** J 4.8; 6.22; **abiero** J 14.3; **abiret** L 4.42; 9.51; **abieritis** Mt 10.5; L 21.8; **abisset** Mk 6.28; 7.30; A 5.26; **abi** Mt 2.20; **abire** [[J 18.8]]; L 6.1; 8.31,37; 13.33; 24.28; A 1.25; [4.15]; 16.7; 17.14; **habire** (A 4.15); **abiens** (*m.*) [Mt 26.42]; L 14.31; **abeunte** (*m.*) A 1.10; **abeuntes** (*m.n.*) Mt 8.33; 21.6; 27.66; L 13.32; 24.13; Mk 11.4; **abientes** (*m.*) L 8.14; 22.13; **abeuntes** (*f.n.*) Mk 16.1; **abeuntes** (*m.ac.*) Mk 6.33; **abeuntibus** (*m.*) Mt 11.7.

aberto, *v.* **auerto.**

abet, *etc.,* *s.v.* **habeo.**

Abia L 1.5.

abicio **abiciam** J 6.37; **abiecit** A 18.16.

Abillianes **abillianetis** L 3.1.

abintus Mt 23.28; L 11.39; Mk 7.21,23.

abinuicem **abinuice** A 12.20; **abinuicem** Mt 25.32; J 5.44; A 15.39.

Abiud L 3.23.[1]

Abiuth Mt 1.13*bis*.

abluo **ablui** J 9.11,15; **abluit** J 9.7; **ablue** J 9.7,11; A 22.16.

abnego **abnegabis** Mt 26.34; **abnegauis**

---

[1] The names in the genealogy in Codex Bezae do not correspond with our versions in vss. 23-30; therefore all are included under vs. 23 by Scrivener.

(*fut.*) L 22.61; **abnegauitur** (*fut.*) L 12.9; **abneget** Mt 16.24; L 9.23.

abominatio L 16.15; **abominationem** Mt 24.15; Mk 13.14.

Abraam, Abraham **Abraam** Mt 3.9; J 8.33; L 13.28; **Abraae** (*d.*) Mt 3.9; **Abraam** (*voc.*) L 16.27; **Abraham** Mt 1.17; J 8.37,39 *ter*,40,52,53,56,57,58; L 1.55,73; 3.8,34; 16.25, 29; A 3.13,25; 7.2,4,16,17,32; 13.26; **Abrahae** L 13.16; 16.22; **Abrahae** L 3.8; **Abraham** L 16.23; 19.9; 20.37; Mk 12.26; **Abraham** (*voc.*) L 16.24,30.

abrenuntio **abrenuntiat** L 14.33; **abrenuntiare** L 9.61.

abripio **abripiebat** L 8.29.

abs, *v.* **ab.**

abscensio **abscensionem** A 21.21.

abscido **abscide** Mt 18.8; Mk 9.43,45.

abscindo, abscidit ⟦J 18.10,26⟧; **absciderat** Mt 27.60.

abscod-, *v.* **abscond-.**

abscondo **abscondebat** L 1.24; **abscondi** Mt 25.25; **abscodisti** L 10.21; **abscondisti** Mt 11.25; **abscondit** Mt 13.33,44; 25.18; J 8.59; 12.36; L 13.21; A 7.24; **abscondistis** L 11.52; **absconsum est** L 19.42; **abscondi** Mt 5.14; **absconditum** (*n.*) Mk 4.22; **absconsum** (*n.*) Mt 10.26; L 8.17; 12.2; 18.34; **absconso** (*m.d.*) Mt 13.44; **absconsa** (*ac.*) Mt 13.35; **absconse** (*adv.*) J 7.10.

abstineo **abstineant** A 15.20; **abstinere** A 15.29.

abstraho **abstrahant** A 20.30.

absum **absit** L 20.16; A 11.8.

abundantia **abundantia** (*ab.*) Mt 12.34; L 6.45; 12.15; 21.4.

abundo **abundat** Mk 12.44; **abundant** L 15.17; **abundabant** A 16.5; **abundabit** Mt 13.12; **habundabit** Mt 25.29.

abutor **abusi sunt** L 7.30.

abyssus **abyssum** L 8.31.

ac, *v.* **atque.**

accaetum, *v.* **acetum.**

accedo **accedit** L 12.33; **accedunt** Mt 9.14; 15.1; Mk 11.27; **accessit** Mt 4.3; 17.7; 20.20; 26.7; 27.58; Mk 1.31; 12.28; A 12.13; 18.2; **accesserunt** Mt 4.11; 5.1; 9.28; 13.36; 14.15; 15.30; 17.24; 18.1; 19.3; 21.14,[23]; 22.23; 24.1,3; 26.17,60; J 12.21; L 13.31; Mk 6.35; 10.35; **adcessit** Mt 17.14; **adcesserunt** (Mt 21.23); **accederet** A 7.31; **accede** Mt 20.28; **accedere** Mk 2.4; A 10.28; **accedens** (*m.*) Mt 18.21; 19.16; 20.28; 21.28,30; 25.20, 22,24; 26.39,[49]; 28.2,18; L 7.14; 10.34; 22.47; 23.52; Mk 14.45; **accedens** (*f*) Mt 9.20; L 8.44; **accedente** (*m.*) L 9.42; **accedentes** (*m.n.*) Mt 13.10,27; 14.12; 15.12,23; 16.1; 17.19; 26.[49],50; L 8.24; 9.12; 23.36; **accentes** (*m.n.*) L 20.27; **accedentes** (*f.n.*) Mt 28.9.

accendo **accendit** L 15.8; **accenditur** Mk 4.21; **accensum est** L 12.49; **accendens** (*m.*) L 8.16; 11.33.

acceptor A 10.34.

accerso **accersisti** A 10.29; **accersibit** (*perf.*) A 7.14; **accersi** A 10.5,32; 11.13; **accersire** A 10.22.

accido **accidit** (*perf.*) L 1.9; Mk 9.21; **accidisset** Mk 6.21.

accipio J 5.34,41; **accipis** L 20.21; **accipit** Mt 10.38; 13.20; J 3.32; 4.36; 6.57; 7.23; 12.48; 13.20*quater;* 21.13; L 9.39,48; 11.10; A 7.38; **accipitis** J 5.43; **accipiunt** Mt 17.24, 25; 26.52; L 8.13; (A 19.2); **accipiebant** A 8.17; **accipiam** J 10.17; **accipiet** Mt 10.41; 19.29; J 16.14,15; L 18.30; Mk 10.30*bis;* **accipietis** Mt 21.22; J 5.43; 16.24; Mk 11.24; A 1.8; [2.38]; **accipient** L 10.10; 20.47; Mk 12.40; **accepi** J 10.18; A 20.24; **accepit** Mt 2.14, ⟦21⟧; 14.19; 15.36; 25.16,17; J 3.33; 6.11; 13.12; ⟦19.27⟧; L 2.28; 7.16; Mk 8.6; 12.20,21; 15.23; A 10.22; **accepimus** Mt 16.7; L 5.5; **accepistis** Mt 10.8; 16.9,10; A 2.23; 7.53; 19.2; **acceperunt** Mt 12.14; 20.9,10; 25.1,3,4; 27.9,30; J 6.24; 12.13; 17.8; ⟦19.23, 40⟧; Mk 4.36; 12.22; A 10.47; **acceptus est** L 4.24; A 10.35; **acceperat** Mt 25.18,20,22, 24; **acceperit** L 9.48; 18.17; **acceperitis** J 6.53, 56; **acceperint** L 9.5; 10.8; **accipiat** L 20.28; Mk 12.19; A 8.19; **accipiant** J 6.7; L 16.4,9; A 8.15; **acciperent** Mt 20.10; **accepissem** Mt 25.27; **accepisset** ⟦J 18.3; 19.30⟧; **accepissent** A 17.15; **accepturi erant** J 7.39; **accipe** Mt 2.20; L 16.6,7; A 7.59; **accipite** Mt 26.26; J ⟦18.31; 19.6⟧; 20.22; L 22.17; Mk 14.22; A 2.38; **accipere** Mt 5.40; 11.14; 15.26; 16.5; 21.34; J 3.27; 6.21; 14.17; L 11.54; 19.12; Mk 7.27; A 1.5; 3.5,21; 10.43; 15.14; **accipiens** Mt 13.31; 17.27; 26.26,27; 27.24,48; J 13.4, 5,30; L 4.15; 9.16; 20.29; 22.17,19; 24.30,43; Mk 9.36; 14.22,23; 15.46; A 16.3; **accipiens** (*f.*) Mt 13.33; J 12.3; L 7.37; 13.21; **accipientem** (*m.*) L 19.15; **accipientes** (*m.n.*) Mt 20.11; 21.35,39; 27.6; J 5.44; A 2.46; 17.9; **accipientes** (*f.n.*) Mt 25.3; **accipientium** (*m.*) L 24.31; **acceptum** (*m.ac.*) L 4.19; **accepta** (*ab.*) Mt 28.15; A 2.33; **accepto** Mt 27.7;

28.12; L 13.19; A 16.24; **acceptis** (*m.ab.*) Mk 6.41.

acclamo **adclamabant** A 12.22.

accubitus **adcubitum** L 14.8; **adcubitos** L 11.43; 14.7; **addubitos** L 20.46.

accurro **adcurrit** Mk 10.17; 15.36; **accucurrit** A 16.29; **adcucurrit** Mk 5.6; **adcurrens** (*f.*) A 12.14.

accusatio A 4.32; **accusationem** [[J 18.29]].

accuso **accusant** Mk 15.4; **accusabant** Mk 15.3; **accuset** J 5.45; **accusent** A 19.38; **accusarent** Mt 12.10; Mk 3.2; **accusaretur** Mt 27.12; **accusaturus sum** J 5.45; **accusare** J 8.4; L 6.7; 11.54; 23.2; **accusari** A 19.40; **accusantes** (*m.n.*) L 23.10.

Aceldemach A 1.19.

acetum **acetum** (*ac.*) [[J 19.30]]; L 23.36; **acaeto** [[J 19.29]]; **aceto** Mt 27.48; [[J 19.29]]; Mk 15.36.

Achaia **Achaie** (*g.*) A 18.12; **Achaiam** A 18.2,27; 19.21.

Achas L 3.23.

Achim Mt. 1.14*bis*.

acquiro **adquiro** L 18.12; **adquisiuis** L 19.16; **adquisibit** A 20.28; **adquisiuit** L 19.18; **adquirite** L 21.19.

actio **actioni** L 23.51.

actus **actus** (*n.pl.*) [[col. Mk]]; col. III J; **actos** A 19.18.

acus **acus** (*g.*) Mt 19.24; L 18.25; Mk 10.25.

Acyla, *v.* **Aquila.**

ad, *con.*, *v.* **at.**

ad, *praep.* (*c.ab.*) Mt 17.19; L 2.52; Mk 10.20; A 15.22; 20.19; **ad** (*c.ac.*) Mt 2.12; 3. [[5,7]],10,13*bis*,14,17; 4.3,6; 5.1,13,23,28; 9.14, 28,38; 10.6,13; 11.28; 12.20; 13.2,30,36,48; 14.15,21,25,28,29; 15.1,24,30; 17.[14],14,27; 18.1; 19.3,8,14; 20.19,20; 21.1,14,19,23,32, 34; 22.3,4,5,9,16*ter*,23,34; 23.37; 24.3,33; 25.9, 10,36,39; 26.7,12,14,18*bis*,40,45,49,50,55,57; 27.4,7,19,27,58,62; J 3.20,21,25,26*bis*,(26),34; 4.15,30,35,40,47,48,49; 5.33,35,40,45; 6.5*bis*, 16,17,21,28,34,35,37*bis*,44,45,65,68; 7.3,33, 45,50*bis*; 8.2,12,31,33,57; 9.13; 10.3,35,41; 11.3,4,15,19,21,29,32,45,46; 12.19,21,22,32; 13.1,3,6,28; 14.3,6,12,18,23*bis*,28*bis*; 16.5,7 *bis*,10,17,28; 17.5,11,13; [[18.13,16,18,24,29, 37,38; 19.2,9,33,39]]; 20.1,2,3,10,11,12*bis*,17 *ter*,27; 21.4,21,22,23; L 1.13,16,17,18,19,27, 28,34,43,55,61; 2.15,17,18,20,34,48,49,52, 3.2, 9,12; 4.6,11,21,23,26*bis*,31,40,43; 5.1,2,4,3,14, 27,30,31,33,34,36; 6.3,9,47; 7.6,20*bis*,38,39, 40,44,50; 8.4*ter*,5,12,13,19,22,35,47; 9.3,12, 13,14,23,33,41,43,47,57,59; 10.2,18,23,26,29, 32,33,39; 11.1,5,39,53; 12.1,3,11,13,15,16,22, 41,47,58*bis*; 13.6,34; 14.3,5,6,7*bis*,12,23,26, 28,32; 15.3,18,20,22; 16.1,20,26,30,31*bis*; 17.1,4,16,22; 18.3,7,9,16*bis*; 19.7,8,13,29,37, 39,42,44; 20.2,3,5,10,19,23,34,41,45; 21.12, 15,38; 22.15,23,45,52*ter*,56,69; 23.1,4,7,14,15, 22,28,42,48,52; 24.1,5,10,14,17,18,22,25,29, 32,44,50; Mk 1.5,32,33,38,40,45; 2.2,3,13*bis*, 14; 3.4,7,8,13*bis*,31; 4.1*bis*,38; 5.13,15,19, (21),21,22; 6.25,30,45,50,51; 7.1,25,31; 8.9, 16; 9.5,14*bis*,17,19; 10.1,5,7,14,26,35,37*bis*, 40*bis*,50; 11.1,7,25,27,33; 12.2,3,4,12,18,36; 13.22; 14.10,48,53,54,62,66; 15.27*bis*,43,46; 16.2,5; III J 14; A 1.7,21; 2.7,12,29,34,37*bis*, 38; 3.1*bis*,2,4,10,12,19,22*bis*,25; 4.1,4,8,19,23 *bis*,24,30,35; 5.3,8,9*bis*,10*bis*,21,23,29,35; 6.2; 7.3,6,31,33,55,56,58; 8.14,20; 10.13,15,17,21, 22,25,28*bis*,33*bis*,48; 11.3*bis*,9,11*bis*,14,21, 24,30; 12.5,8,10,12,15*bis*,20,21; 13.2,11,15*bis*, 31,36,39,46*bis*; 14.1,11,13,14,15,26; 15.2,4,7, 19,25,33,36,38; 16.16,19,29,36,37,39,40; 17.2, 5*bis*,6,14,15*bis*,19,21; 18.2,6*bis*,12,14,21; 19.2 *bis*,15,25,31; 20.6,18*bis*; 21.6,11,13,16,18,32, 39,40; 22.11,13; **ad** (*c.indec.*) J 6.67; L 1.73, 80; A 1.8; 3.25; 7.40; **ad** (*c.nih.*) L 10.40; **at** (*c.ac.*) (Mt 17.14); J 21.9; A 21.37. *v.quoq.* **adinuicem, usque ad.**

Adam L 3.38.

adaperio **adaperti sunt** L 24.45; **adaperite** Mk 7.34; **adaperiens** (*m.*) A 17.3.

adaquo **adaquat** L 13.15.

adc-, adq-, *v.* **acc-, acq-.**

addo **adde** L 17.5.

addubitos, *v.* **accubitus.**

adduco [[J 19.4]]; **adducunt** J 8.3; 9.13; [[18.28]]; **adducent** L 12.11; **adduxit** [[J 19.13]]; L 4.9; 10.34; **adduxistis** J 7.45; L 23.14; A 19.37; **adduxeunt** L 22.66; **adduxerunt** Mt 21.7; [[J 18.13]]; L 2.22; 4.29; 22.54; 23.1; Mk 11.7; 14.53; A 6.12; 17.19; 18.12; 20.12; 21.16; **adduxissent** A 5.27; **adduc** L 5.4; 9.41; 14.21; **adducite** Mt 21.2; L 15.23; 19.27, 30; Mk 11.2; **adducere** J 10.16; A 5.28; **adduci** L 18.40; A 5.21; 21.34; **adducentes** (*m.n.*) L 19.35.

adfacio **adfecerunt** Mk 12.4.

adfero **adferet** (*praes.*) Mk 4.8; **adferent** (*praes.*) Mk 7.32; **affertis** [[J 18.29]]; **adferunt** Mk 8.22; 10.13; **adferebant** L 4.40; Mk 1.32; A 4.34; **adferet** J 12.24; 15.2*bis*,5; **adferent** L 8.14; **adtuli** Mk 9.17; **adtulit** Mt 14.11; J 4.33; Mk 6.28; A 4.37; **attulit** L

12.16; adtulerunt Mk 9.20; A 19.19; attulerunt Mk 12.15; adlatum est Mt 14.11; adferat J 15.2; adferatis J 15.8,16; adferret L 23.26; adtulissent A 5.2; adfers J 20.27*bis;* L 13.7; adferte Mt 14.18; 17.17; J 21.10; L 15.22; Mk 9.19; 12.15; adferi Mk 6.27; adferens (*m.*) A 17.20; adferentes (*m.n.*) L 5.18; Mk 2.3; A 14.13; adferentes (*f.n.*) L 24.1.

adficio adficient Mk 13.12.

adfigo adfixerunt Mk 15.24; adfixi erant Mk 15.32; adfigeretur Mk 15.15; adfige Mk 15.13,14; adfixum (*m.*) A 2.23.

adfligo adfligor L 16.24; adfligeris L 16.25.

adgeniculor adgeniculans (*m.*) Mt 17.14; Mk 10.17; adgeniculantes (*m.n.*) Mt 27.29.

adgnosco A 19.15; adnoscit J 14.17; adgnoscitur Mt 12.33.

adgredior adgreditur A 18.10; adgressi sunt A 19.13; adgressi (*n.*) A 6.12.

adhereo (adhaereo) adherebat A 8.13; adherebit Mk 10.7; adhesit L 10.11; 15.15; adherere A 5.13; 10.28; adherentes (*m.n.*) A 14.4.

adhibeo adhibita (*ab.*) A 13.46.

adhuc Mt 5.41; 11.12; 15.16; 17.5; 18.16; 19.20; 20.28*bis;* 26.47,65; 27.63; J 7.33; 12.35; 13.33; 14.19; 16.12; [[20.1]]; L 1.15; 8.49; 9.42; 13.8; 14.22,26,32; 15.20; 16.2; 18.22; 20.36; 22.47,60,71; 23.53; 24.6,41; Mk 5.35; 12.6; 14.43,63; A 2.26; 10.44; 12.23; 18.18; 21.35.

adicio adiciebat A 2.47; adiciebantur A 5.14; adicietur L 19.26; Mk 4.25; adicientur L 12.31; adiecit L 3.20; A 12.3; adiectae sunt A 2.41; adicere L 12.25; adiciens (*m.*) L 19.11.

adimpleo adinplebatur L 2.40; adinpleuitur L 3.5; adimpleuit J 16.6; A 13.22; adinpleuit A 5.3; adimpleantur Mk 14.49; adimpleretur [[Mt 2.23]]; adinpleretur J 12.38.

adinpleo, *v.* adimpleo.

adinuicem J 4.33; 6.52; 16.17; [[19.24]]; L 4.36; 6.11; 8.25; 20.14; Mk 4.41; 12.7; 16.3; A 4.15; 21.14.

adiubo, *v.* adiuuo.

adiuro Mt 26.63; Mk 5.7; A 19.13.

adiuuo adiubauit L 1.54; adiubet L 10.40; adiubarent L 5.7; adiuba Mt 15.25; adiuua Mk 9.24; adiuuate A 21.28.

adleuo adlebans (*m.*) J 17.1.

adlido adlidit L 9.39; adlisit L 6.48,49; 9.42.

adligatum, *v.* alligo.

adloquor adloquitur A 22.2; adlocutus est A 21.40; adloquentibus (*m.d.*) L 7.32.

admarus (amarus) admare (*adv.*) L 22.62.

admirabilis admirabiles (*m.s.*) Mk 12.11.

admiror admiramini A 3.12; 13.41; admirabatur Mk 11.18; 15.44; admirabantur Mk 6.2; 7.37; 10.26; A (2.7); 4.13; admirarentur Mk 2.12.

admitto admisit L 8.51; Mk 5.19,37.

adnumero adnumeratus erat A 1 17.

adnuntiator A 17.18.

adnuntio A 17.3, 23; adnuntiat [J 4.25]; A 17.30; adnuntiatur A 13.38; adnuntiabant A 8.4; 13.5; adnuntiauo J 16.25; adnuntiabit Mt 12.18; J 16.15; adnuntiauit (*fut.*) J 16.13, 14; adnuntiabit (*perf.*) L 8.47; adnuntiauit J (4.25); 20.18; L 14.21; A 5.25; 11.13; 12.14; adnuntiabimus A 15.36; adnuntiauerunt L 8.36; A 3.24; adnuntiatum est A 17.13; adnuntiem A 20.27; adnuntiarem A 20.20; adnuntiarent A 4.2; adnuntia Mk 5.19; adnuntiare L 4.19; adnutiare L 4.18; adnuntians (*m.*) A 21.26; adnuntiantes (*m.n.*) L 13.1; adnuntiantes (*m.ac.*) A 15.27.

adnuo adnuit (*perf.*) A 18.20; adnuens (*m.*) L 1.22.

adorator adoratores (*n.*) J 4.23.

adorno adornatum (*m.*) L 11.25.

adoro adoramus J 4.22; adoratis J 4.22; adorabat Mt 9.18; 15.25; 18.26; adorabantur A 11.23; adorabis Mt 4.10; L 4.8; adorauitis J 4.21; adorauit J 9.38; Mk 5.6; A 10.25; adorauerunt Mt 2.11; 14.33; 28.9,17; J 4.20, 23; adoraueris Mt 4.9; L 4.7; adorem Mt 2.8; adorent J 12.20; adorare Mt 2.2; J 4.20,24; A 7.43; adorans (*f.*) Mt 20.20; adorantes (*m.n.*) J 4.24; adorantes (*m.ac.*) J 4.23.

adpono adponuntur L 10.8; adponam Mk 14.25; adposuit Mt 13.24; A 19.21; adposuerunt Mk 8.6; adpositus est A 13.36; adposita est A 11.24; adponam L 11.6; adponerent Mk 6.41; 8.6; adponere L 9.16; adponi Mk 8.7.

adpraehendo adprehendet L 16.13; adpraehendit Mt 14.31; J 6.17; 8.20; L 5.9; A 16.33; adprehendit [[J 19.1]]; adpraehenderunt A 1.16; 16.19; adprehenderunt A 18.26; adpraehenderit Mk 9.18; adpraehendant J 12.35; adpraehenderent J 7.32; 11.57; L 20.20; adprehendissent A 21.30; adpraehendere J 7.30,44; 10.39; L 20.26; A 12.3; adpraehendens (*m.*) L 14.4; adprehendens (*m.*) L 9.47; adpraehendentes (*m.n.*) L 23.26; A 18.17; adpraehensum (*m.ac.*) Mk 12.3,8; A 3.7; 17.19; adprehensum A 12.4; adpraehensam Mk 1.31; adpraehendi (*inc.*) Mk 8.23.

adpraetio adpraetiauerunt Mt 27.9; adpraetiati (*m.g.*) Mt 27.9.

adprehendo, *v.* adpraehendo.

adpropinquo adpropinquat L 21.28; adpropinquauit Mt 4.17; 10.7; L 10.11; 11.20; 21.20; 22.1; A 7.17; appropinquait [[Mt 3.2]]; adpropinquaret Mk 11.1; adpropinquasset Mt 21.34; A 21.33.

adpropio adpropiat Mt 24.31; adpropiant L 15.1; adpropiauit Mt 26.45; L 10.9; 21.8; Mk 1.15; adpropiauerunt L 24.28; adpropiaret L 7.12; 18.35; A 10.25; adpropiasset L 18.41; 19.29,41; adpropiassent Mt 21.1; adpropians (*m.*) L 24.25; adpropiantibus (*m.ab.*) L 19.37; A 10.9.

adpud, *v.* apud.

adque, *v.* atque.

adquisitio A 19.25; adquisitionem A 19.24.

adripio adrripuerunt A 6.12.

adsenso adsensum est A 5.36.

adsequor adsecuto (*m.d.*) L 1.3; adsecuti (*n.*) A 4.13.

adsertio adsertionem (A 4.3).

adseruatio adseruationem [A 4.3]; adseruatione A 5.18.

adseruo adseruabant A 12.6.

adsideo adsidens (*f.*) L 10.39.

adsimulo adsimilauimus (*fut.*) Mk 4.30; adsimulati (*n.*) A 14.11.

adsisto L 1.19; adsistebant A 1.10; adsistet Mt 26.53; adsistit A 4.10; 12.7; adsisterunt L 20.1; 24.4; A 4.1,26; 10.17; adsistere L 2.22; adsistans (*m.*) A 22.20; assistens (*m.*) [[J 18.22]].

adsto adstabat Mk 15.39; astabant L 19.24; adstitit L 2.9; adstantium (*m.g.*) L 12.1.

adsum adest Mk 4.29; adesse A 20.16.

adsumentum adsumentum (*ac.*) Mk 2.21.

adsumo adsumit L 11.26; 15.2; adsumam J 14.3; adsumetur Mt 24.40,41*bis*; L 17.34,35,36; adsumpsit Mk 9.2; 10.32; 14.33; A 21.26; adsumpsistis A 7.43; adsumptus est A 1.11,22; assumptus est [[Mk 16.19]]; adsumptum est A 10.16; adsumerent A 15.38; adsume Mt 18.16; A 21.24; adsumere A 15.37; adsumens (*m.*) L 4.5; 9.10,28; 18.31; adsumpto (*m.ab.*) Mk 5.40; A 15.39; adsupto (*m.ab.*) A 12.25; 20.14; adsuptis (*m.ab.*) A 17.5.

adsumptio adsumptionis L 9.51.

adsuo adsuit Mk 2.21.

adtendo, adtendebat A 3.5; adtendite Mt 6.1; 10.17; 16.6,12; L 12.1; 17.3; 20.46; 21.34; A 5.35; attendite Mt. 16.11; A 20.28.

adtingo adtingitis L 11.46; adtigero Mk 5.28.

adtraho adtraxerit J 6.44.

aduena L 24.18; aduene (*n.pl.*) A 17.21.

aduenio aduenit (*perf.*) Mt 3.13; L 8.19; 19.16; aduenerunt A 11.27; 18.5; aduenerant L 22.52; aduenirent L 2.6; aduenissent A 14.27; 15.1; 17.10; aduenire A 10.33; aduenions (*m.*) L 14.21; aduenientem (*m.*) A 18.21; aduenientes (*m.n.*) L 7.4,20; 8.35.

aduentus Mt 24.27,37,39; aduentus (*g.*) Mt. 24.3; L 21.7; 23.42; aduentu A 7.52.

aduersarius Mt 5.25; aduersario (*d.*) Mt 5.25; aduersario (*ab.*) L 12.58; abuersario L 18.3; adversarii L 13.17.

aduerso aduersantes (*m.n.*) L 21.15.

aduersum, *v.* aduersus.

aduersus (*praep.c.ac.*) Mt 10.35*bis*; 12.32; 20.11; 26.59; [[J 18.29]]; L 3.13; Mk 3.6; 9.40; 14.55,56; A 4.26*bis*; 6.1,13; 14.2*bis*; 16.22; 17.20; 19.16; 21.28; aduersum Mt 5.11, 23; 10.35; 12.30,32; [[J 19.11]]; Mk 11.25; 14.57; A 6.13; 16.39*bis*.

adulescens (*m.*) Mk 14.51; adulescentes (*m.g.*) A 7.58; adulescentior (*m.*) L 15.12,13.

adulter, adultera (*f.n.*) Mt 12.39; adultera (*f.ab.*) Mk 8.38; adulteri L 18.11.

adulterium, adulterii Mt 5.32; 19.9; adulterio (*ab.*) J 8.4; adulteria (*n.*) Mt 15.19; Mk 7.22.

adultero, adulteres Mk 10.19.

aduoco, aduocauit L 23.20; aduocauerit A 2.39; aduocasset Mk 10.42; aduocans (*m.*) Mt 10.1; 18.2,32; L 7.19; 15.26; 16.5; Mk 7.14.

aduoluo, aduoluens (*m.*) Mt 27.60; aduol Mk 15.46.

adynatus A 14.8.

Aebraeos, *s.v.* Hebraeus.

aedebat, *s.v.* 1. edo.

aedificator aedificatoribus (*ab.*) A 4.11.

aedifico aedificat Mt 27.40; Mk 15.29; aedificatis Mt 23.29; L 11.47,49; A 7.49;

aedificabant L 17.28; **aedificabo** [Mt 16.18]; A 15.16; **aedificauo** (Mt 16.18); **aedificauit** (*fut.*) Mt 21.33; **aedificabit** (*perf.*) L 7.5; **aedificauit** A 7.47; **aedificata est** L 4.29; **aedificare** Mt 26.61; L 14.28,29,30; **aedificanti** (*m.d.*) L 6.48,49; **aedificantes** (*m.n.*) Mt 21.42; L 20.17; Mk 12.10.

aeditua **aedituam** A 19.35.

aeger **aegrum** (*m.*) L 7.10; **aegros** Mk 6.13.

Aegyptius A 21.38; **Aegyptium** (*m.*) A 7.28; **Aegyptio** (*m.*) A 7.24; **Aegyptiorum** (*m.*) A 7.22.

Aegyptus **Aegypti** A 7.10,11,40; 13.17; **Aegyptum** A 2.10; 7.9,10,15,34,39; **Aegypto** Mt 2.13,14,15,19; A 7.12,17,34,36.

Aelamita **Aelamitae** (*n.*) A 2.9.

aelemosynae, *s.v.* **elemosyna.**

aemulatio **aemulatione** A 13.45.

aemulator **hemulatores** (*n.*) A 21.20.

aemulor **hemulati** (*m.n.*) A 7.9.

Aenon **Aeno** (*ab.*) J 3.23.

Aenos L 3.38.

Aenox L 3.37.

aeo, *s.v.* **is.**

Aephesum, *s.v.* **Ephesus.**

aepulatio (epulatio) **aepulationem** L 14.13; A 5.17; **aepulatione** L 7.25.

aepulor **aepulemur** L 15.23; **aepulans** (*m.*) L 16.19; **aepulare** L 12.19; **aepulari** L 15.24,32.

aequalis **aequalem** (*m.*) J 5.18; **aequalem** (*neu.*) A 11.17; **aequales** (*m.ac.*) Mt. 20.12.

aeramentum **aeramentorum** Mk 7.4.

aes **aes** (*ac.*) Mt 10.9; Mk 6.8; 12.41; **aera** (*ac.*) Mk 12.42.

aesitauerit, *s.v.* **haesito.**

aestas Mt 24.32; L 21.30; Mk 13.28.

aestuo **aestuauerunt** Mt 13.6.

aestus L 12.55; **aetus** (*ac.pl.*) Mt 20.12.

aetas **aetatem** J 9.21,23; L 12.25; **aetate** L 2.52.

aeternus **aeterna** (*f.n.*) J 12.50; 17.3; **aeternae** (*g.*) J 6.68; **aeterni** Mk 3.29; **aeternum** (*m.*) Mt 18.8; 25.41; **aeternam** Mt 19.16,29; 25.46*bis;* J 3.16,36; 4.14,36; 5.24,39, 40; 6.27,40,47,54; 10.28; 12.25; 17.2; L 10.25; 18.18,30; Mk 9.45; 10.17,30; A 13.46,48; **aeternum** Mt 21.19; J 4.14; 6.51,58; 8.35*bis*, 51; 11.26; 12.34; 14.16; L 1.55; Mk 11.14; **aeterna** (*neu. ac.*) L 16.9.

aeuum **aeuum** (*ac.*) J 13.8; **aeuo** Mk 10.30.

aff-, *v.* **adf-.**

aforis Mt 23.27,28; L 11.39,40.

Agabus A 11.28; 21.10.

ager Mt 13.38; 27.8*bis*; A 4.37; **agri** Mt 13.36; L 12.28; **agrum** Mt 13.44; 22.5; 26.36; 27.7,10; J 4.5; L 14.18; **agro** Mt 13.24,27,31, 44; 24.18,40; L 11.6; 17.7,31,36; 23.26; Mk 13.16; **agros** Mt 19.29; L 8.34; 15.15; Mk 5.14; 10.29,30.

agg-, *v.* **adg-.**

agnosco **agnoscitis** J 8.43.

agnus **agnos** L 10.3.

ago J 11.41; L 18.11; **agit** J 3.20; L 22.26; 24.21; **agitis** A 15.29; **agunt** A 17.7; **aguntur** A 19.38; **agent** L 7.25; A 20.21; **egit** L 23.41; Mk 14.23; **egimus** L 23.41; **egistis** A 3 17; **egerunt** Mt 12.41; J 5.29; **actum est** L 23.15; **egerant** Mk 6.30; **egerit** L 17.3; **egeritis** L 13.3; **agant** A 17.30; **agerent** Mk 6.12; **egissent** L 10.13; **agite** [[Mt 3.2]]; A 2.38; 3.19; **agere** L 3.13; 22.23; A 5.35; 19.36; **agens** (*m.*) Mt 15.36; 26.27; Mk 8.6,7; **agente** (*m.*) L 2.2; **agenti** (*m.*) L 15.7,10; **acti** (*neu.*) Mk 5.33.

agonia **agonia** (*ab.*) L 22.44.

agricola **agricula** J 15.1; **agricolis** L 20.9; **agricolas** L 20.10,16.

Ainan L 3.37.

aio **ait** Mt 4.7; 16.23; 17.11,23; 19.16; 20.7,23; 21.27; 22.13,43; 25.21,23,41; 26.34, 62; 27.11; J 6.20; 14.1; Mk 1.38,41; 2.5,10,14, 17,19,25; 3.3; 4.11,13,35; 5.19,30,36,39,41; 6.16,25,31,37; 7.6,18,29,34; 8.1,12,17,21,24, 26; 9.12,24,36,39; 10.5,14,20,23,24,27,38,42, 52; 11.2,21,22,33; 12.15,16,17,24,32,43; 13.1, 5; 14.6,18,20,24,27,29,30,32,34,37,41,45,48, 61,63,67; 15.9,12; A 2.38; 7.1,31; 10.28,30,31; 11.28; 15.36; 16.37; 17.22; 19.25,35; 20.18; 21.37.

ala **alas** Mt 23.37; L 2.28; 13.34.

alabaster **alabastrum** Mt 26.7; L 7.37; **alabastro** Mk 14.3.

alapa **alapam** Mt 5.39; [[J 18.22]]; **alapas** [[J 19.3]]; **alapis** Mk 14.65.

albus Mt 28.3; **album** (*m.*) Mt 5.36; **albae** (*n.*) J 4.35; **alba** (*n.*) Mt 17.2; L 9.29; **albis** (*neu.ab.*) J 20.12.

Alexander A 4.6; 19.33; **Alexandri** Mk 15.21; **Alexandrum** A 19.33.

Alexandrinus A 18.24; **Alexandrinorum** (*m.*) A 6.9.

[2] See p. 73, note 1.

7.9; 12.37,44; 18.17,29; 21.32; Mk 3.28; 8.12; 9.1,41; 10.15,29; 11.23; 12.43; 13.2,30; 14.9, 18,25,30; [[16.20]].

amica amicas L 15.9.

amicio amictus Mk 14.51.

amictus amictu L 24.4; amitibus (*ab.*) (A 2.24).

amicus Mt 11.19; J 3.29; 11.11,14; [[19.12]]; L 7.34; 11.6,8; amicum L 11.5; ame (Mt 26.50); amice Mt 20.13; 22.12; [26.50]; L 14.10; amie L 11.5; amici J 15.14; L 23.12; III J 15; A 19.31; amicis L 12.4; amicos J 15.15; L 7.6; 14.12; 15.6; 16.9; III J 15; amicis J 15.13; L 15.29; 21.16; A 10.24; 16.39.

Aminadab L 3.33.

amitibus, *v.* amictus.

ammoneo ammonitus [[Mt 2.22]].

amo J 21.15,16,17; amas J.11.3; 21.16,17 *bis;* amat J 12.25; amant Mt 6.5; 23.6; amabat J 11.5,36; 15.19; amantium (*m.*) L 20.46.

amodo Mt 23.39; 26.29,64; J 13.19; 14.7; L 1.48; 12.52; 22.18,69.

Amos L 3.23.[3]

amoueo amotus fuero L 16.4.

Amphipolis Amphipolim A 17.1.

amphora amphorae (*g.*) Mk 14.13.

amplifico amplificant Mt 23.5.

amplus amplius Mt 5.37; 11.9; ampliorem (*m.*) J 15.2; amplius L 12.48; 20.47; amplius (*adv.*) Mt 5.47; 22.46; 27.23; J 6.35, 66; 21.6; L 3.13;5.14; 7.26; 12.4; 20.40; Mk 5.4; 7.37; 9.8; 11.14; 14.31; 15.5; A 4.17; 15.28; 20.18.

ampulla ampullam Mk 14.3.

amputo amputabit (*perf.*) Mk 14.47.

an Mt 27.4; J 7.17; [[18.34]]; L 7.19,20; Mk 11.30; 13.35*bis.*

ana (*praep.c.ac.*) L 9.3.

Ananias A 5.1,5; 22.12; Ananian A 5.3.

ancilla [[J 18.17]]; L 1.38; Mk 14.69; ancillae (*g.*) L 1.48; ancillas A 2.18; ancillis Mk 14.66.

Andreas Mt 10.2; J 6.8; 12.22; Mk 13.3; A 1.13; Andreae (*g.*) L 4.38; Mk 1.29; Andreae (*d.*) J 12.22; Andream Mt 4.18; L 6.14; Mk 1.16; 3.18.

anethum anethum (*ac.*) Mt 23.23.

anetius anetios A 16.37.

angario angariauerunt Mt 27.32; Mk 15.21; angariauerit Mt 5.41.

angelus Mt 1.20,24; 2.13,19; 28.2,5; J 12.29; L 1.11,13,19,26,28,30,35,38; 2.9,10; 22.43; Mk 16.6; A 5.19; 7.30; 10.7; 12.7,8,10, 15,23; angeli A 6.15; 7.35; angelum Mt 11.10; L 1.18,34; 7.27; Mk 1.2; A 11.13; 12.9,11; angelo L 2.13,21; A 7.38; 10.22; angeli Mt 4.11; 13.39,49; 18.10; 22.30; 24.36; 25.31; L 2.15; Mk 1.13; 12.25; 13.32; angelorum Mt 26.53; L 9.26; 12.8,9; 15.10; 24.23; A 7.53; angelis Mt 4.6; 25.41; L 4.10; 20.36; angelos Mt 13.41; 24.31; J 20.12; Mk 13.27; angelis Mt 16.27; L 16.22; Mk 8.38.

angulus anguli (*g.*) Mt 21.42; L 20.17; Mk 12.10; A 4.11; angulis (*ab.*) Mt 6.5.

angustiae angustiis (*ab.*) Mt 24.9.

angustus angustam L 13.24.

anima Mt 12.18; 26.38; J 12.27; L 1.46; 12.23; Mk 14.34; A 3.23; 4.32; 20.10; animae Mt 16.26*bis;* Mk 8.36; animae L 12.22; A 2.43; anime (*d.*) L 12.19; animam Mt 2.20; 10.28*bis*,39*bis;* 16.25*bis;* 20.28; J 10.11,15,17, 24; 12.25*bis;* 13.37,38; 15.13; L 2.35; 6.9; 9.24*bis;* 12.4,20; 14.26; 17.33; Mk 3.4; 8.35; 10.45; A 2.27; 20.24; anima Mt 22.37; L 10.27; Mk 8.37; 12.30,33; anima (*voc.*) L 12.19; animae A 2.41; animis Mt 11.29; animas L 21.19; A 14.2,22; 15.24; animabus A 7.14; 14.27; anim A 15.26.

animaequus animequi (*n.*) J 16.33; animaequior (*m.*) Mk 10.49; animequior (*m.*) L 23.43.

animatio animatione A 17.11.

animus A 12.20.

Anna L 2.36; 3.2.

Annas [[J 18.24]]; A 4.6; Annam [[J 18.13]].

annus anni J 11.49,51; [[18.13]]; annum L 4.19; 13.8; A 11.26; anno L 3.1 A 18.11; anni L 2.42; 13.7,16; annorum L 2.37; 3.23; 8.42; Mk 5.42; A 4.22; 7.23; annos J 5.5; 8.57; L 2.36; 13.11; 15.29; A 7.36; 19.10; annis Mt 9.20; L 4.25; 8.43; Mk 5.25; A 7.6,30, 42; 13.18,20,21.

ante (*c.ac.*) Mt 5.12,24; 6.2; 8.29; 10.18; 11.10*bis*,26; 17.14; 24.38; 25.32; 27.11,29; J 3.28; 5.7; 7.50; 10.4,8; 12.1; 13.1; 17.24; 20.4; L 1.76; 7.27; 9.52; 10.1; 21.12; 23.54; Mk 1.2; 5.33; 6.41; 11.4; 13.9; 14.68; 15.42; A 3.13; 5.21,36; 7.4; 12.6,14; 13.24; 14.13; 18.17; ante (*c.indec*) J 8.58; 11.55; ante (*c.adv.*) J 6.62; 7.51; 9.13; anti (*c.ac.*) A 21.38; *v.quoq.* abante.

---

[3] See p. 73, note 1

antecedo antecedebat L 22.47; antecedebant L 18.39; antecedes L 1.76; antecedet L 1.17; antecedent Mt 21.31; antecedens (*m.*) L 19.4.

antequam Mt 1.18; 26.34; J 12.28; 13.19; 14.29; 17.5; L 2.21; 11.38.

anti (*praep.c.ac.*) A 16.9.

anticus, *v.* antiquus.

Antiocensis Antiocensem (*m.*) A 6.5.

Antiochia Antiochiam A 11.19,20,22,26 *bis*,27; 13.14; 14.21,26; 15.22,23,30; 18.22; Antiochia A 13.1; 14.19; 15.35.

antiquus anticus L 9.8; antiquum (*m.*) A 21.16; antiquis (*m.ab.*) Mt 5.21,33; A 15.7; antiquis (*f.ab.*) A 15.21.

anulus anulum L 15.22.

aperio aperit J 10.3; aperiebat L 24.32; aperiam Mt 13.35; aperietur L 11.9,10; aperuit J 9.14,17,21,26,30,32; 11.37; [[19.34]]; A 5.19; 12.14; 14.27; 16.14; aperta est A 12.10; apertum est L 1.64; aperti sunt Mt 3.16; 9.30; J 9.10; L 24.31; apertae sunt Mk 7.35; aperta sunt Mt 27.52; A 16.26; aperiant L 12.36; aperiantur Mt 20.33; aperuisset A 12.16; aperuissent A 5.22; aperi Mt 25.11; L 13.25; aperire J 10.21; A 18.14; aperiri L 3.21; aperiens (*m.*) Mt 5.2; 17.27; A 10.34; aperiens (*neu.*) L 2.23; aperientes (*m.n.*) Mt 2.11; A 5.23.

apertus apertum (*neu.ac.*) A 10.11; apertos Mk 1.10; A 7.56; apertas A 16.27.

apex Mt 5.18; apicem L 16.17.

apo aptus L 9.62.

Apollonia Apolloniam A 17.1.

Apollonius A 18.24.

aporia L 21.25.

aporior aporiarentur L 24.4.

apostolatus apostolatus (*g.*) A 1.25.

apostolus J 13.16; apostoli (*n.*) L 9.10; 17.5; 22.14; Mk 6.30; A 4.33; 5.41; 8.14; 11.1; 15.6, 23; apostolorum Mt 10.2; [[col. Mk]]; col. III J; A 2.42; 4.35,37; 5.2,12; 6.6; 8.18; 16.4; apostolis A 1.2; 15.22; apostolos L 6.13; 11.49; 24.10; A 1.26; 2.37,43; 5.18,34,40; 8.1; 15.2; apostolis A 2.14; 4.36; 14.4; 15.4.

apotheca L 12.24; apothecas L 12.18.

appareo apparuit Mt 1.20; 2.13; Mk 9.4; [[16.9,14]]; A 16.9; apparens (*m.*) A 1.3; apparentis (*m.g.*) Mt 2.7.

appello appellatus est Mt 27.8.

applico applicauimus A 20.15.

applonto applontat Mk 9.18.

appropinquo appropio, *v.* adp-.

apto aptauerunt Mt 25.7.

apud (*c.ac.*) adpud J 4.40; apud Mt 13.56; 26.55; 28.15; J 14.17,25; L 1.30,37; 18.27; Mk 9.19; A 5.34; 18.3; 19.14; 21.4,16; aput Mt 6.1; 18.20; 19.26; 22.25; J 8.38*bis*; 12.28; 17.5; 21.23; L 18.4; 20.29; Mk 9.10; 10.27 *bis*; 12.20; 14.49; A 2.27,29,31,47; 10.6; 13.1; 14.25; 21.7; 22.1,15; aput (*c.ab.*) Mt 19.26.

aqua J 5.7; [[19.34]]; aquae [Mt 10.42]; J 4.14; 5.3; 7.38; L 22.10; Mk 9.41; 14.13; aque (Mt 10.42); aquae L 8.25; aquam Mt 14.28; 27.24; J 4.7,10,11,14,15,46; 13.5; L 7.44; 16.24; Mk 9.22; A 10.47; aqua Mt 3.11, 16; 17.15; J 4.13,14; L 3.16; Mk 1.7,10; A 1.5; 11.16; aquae J 3.23; aquas Mt 14.29; aquis Mt 8.32.

1. aquila aquilae (*n.*) Mt 24.28; L 17.37.

2. Aquila Acylam A 18.2; Acyla A 18.7; Aquila A 18.18; Aquilas A 18.26.

aquilo aquilone L 13.29.

ara aram A 17.23.

Arabus Arabi (*n.*) A 2.11.

Aram L 3.33.

aratrum aratrum (*ac.*) L 9.62.

arbitror arbitrabatur A 7.25; arbitrari J 5.45.

arbor Mt 3.10; 12.33; 13.32; L 3.9; 6.43*bis*, 44; 13.19; Mk 11.21; arborem Mt 12.33*bis*; arborum Mt 3.10; L 3.9; arbores L 21.29; Mk 8.24; arboribus Mt 21.8; Mk 11.8.

arca arcam Mt 24.38; L 17.27.

Archelaus [[Mt 2.22]].

archisynagogus L 13.14; Mk 5.22; A 18.8; archisynagogi Mk 5.38; archisynagogo Mk 5.36; archisynagogum A 18.17; archisynagogo L 8.49; Mk 5.35; archisynagogi A 13.15; archisynagogae (*n.*) A 14.2.

ardeo ardet J 15.6; ardens (*f.*) J 5.35; ardentes (*f.n.*) L 12.35.

area aream Mt 3.12; L 3.17.

areo arunt [Mt 13.6]; harunt (Mt 13.6); aruit [Mt 21.19,20]; J 15.6; Mk 11.21; haruit (Mt 21.19,20).

Areopagita A 17.34.

aresco arescit Mk 9.18.

argentarius A 19.24.

argenteus argenteos Mt 27.3,9; argentea A 19.24.

argentum A 3.6; argenti A 7.16; argento A 17.29; argentum Mt 10.9; 25.18,27; 27.5.

argumentum argumentis (*ab.*) A 1.3.

arguo arguet J 16.8; arguantur J 3.20; argueretur L 3.19; argue Mt 18.15.

aridus aridum (*n.*) L 8.6; aridam Mt 12.10; [23.15]; L 6.6,8; Mk 3.1,3; 11.20; haridam (Mt 23.15); arido (*neu.*) L 23.31; aridorum (*m.*) J 5.3; arida L 11.24.

Arimathia Arimathia (*ab.*) Mt 27.57; [[J 19.38]]; L 23.51; Mk 15.43.

Aristarchus A 20.4; Aristarchum A 19.29.

Arius Arii A 17.22; Arium A 17.19.

arma armis (*ab.*) [[J 18.3]].

armatura armaturam L 11.22.

armo armatus L 11.21.

aro arantem (*m.*) L 17.7.

aroma aromata (*ac.*) L 23.56; Mk 16.1; aromatibus [[J 19.40]].

Arphaxad L 3.36.

ars artis A 17.29.

artifex artefices (*n.*) A 19.38; artificibus (*d.*) A 19.24; artifices (*voc.*) A 19.25.

artificium artificium (*ac.*) A 18.3.

arundinem, *s.v.* harundo.

as asse Mt 10.29.

Asaph L 3.23.

ascedo, *v.* ascendo.

ascendo J 7.8; 20.17; ascendimus Mk 10.33; A 21.15; ascendunt L 24.38; ascendebant J 12.20; A 3.1; ascendi J 20.17; ascendit Mt 3.16; 5.1; 14.23; 15.39; J 5.1; 7.10,14; 21.11; L 2.4; 9.28; 19.4; Mk 3.13; 8.13; 15.8; A 2.34; 7.23; 10.9; ascendimus Mt 20.18; L 18.31; A 20.13; ascenderunt Mt 13.7; J 7.10; 21.3; L 2.42; 5.19; 8.22; 18.10; Mk 4.7; A 1.13; 10.4; 13.31; ascenderant Mk 15.41; ascenderit Mt 17.27; ascenderet A 21.12; ascedisset A 18.22; ascendisset A 20.11; ascende L 14.10; ascendite J 7.8; ascendere Mt 14.22; Mk 6.45; A 15.2,4; ascendens (*m.*) Mt 9.1; 13.2; 15.29; 20.17; 21.5; J 10.1; L 5.3; 8.37; 19.28; Mk 1.10; 4.1; 6.51; 8.10; ascendentem (*m.*) J 6.62; Mk 4.8; ascendente (*m.*) Mk 5.18; ascendentes (*m.n.*) J 6.17; Mk 6.32; 10.32; A 21.2; ascendentibus (*m.ab.*) Mt 14.32.

asellus asellum J 12.14.

Aser L 2.36.

Asia A 19.27; Asiae (*g.*) A 19.26; Asiam A 2.9; 19.1,10,22; 20.4,18; Asia A 16.6; 20.16; 21.27.

Asiarchas Asiarcharum A 19.31.

asina asinae (*g.*) J 12.15; asinam M 21.2, 5,7.

asinarius asinaria (*f.n.*) Mt 18.6.

asinus asinum L 13.15.

aspectus Mt 28.3.

asper aspra (*neu.n.*) L 3.5.

aspicio aspicis Mk 12.14; aspiciebat Mk 12.41; aspexi A 22.13; aspiciant J 17.24; aspice Mk 13.1; A 3.4; 4.29; aspie A 22.13; aspiciens (*m.*) L 9.16,62; 21.1; Mk 6.41; 7.34; 8.24; 10.21; aspiciens (*f.*) Mk 14.67; aspicientes (*m.n.*) A 1.10,11.

aspie, *s.v.* aspicio.

Asron L 3.33.

assumo, *v.* adsumo.

assus assi L 24.42; assum A 20.13,14.

asto, *v.* adsto.

astrum astrum (*ac.*) A 7.43.

at (*praep.*), *v.* ad.

at (*con.*) ad J 4.32; 8.11*bis;* 9.15,17,27,28, 38; 20.25; 21.6*bis;* L 3.13,14; 4.43; 5.11,33; 6.9; 7.4,40*bis*,43; 8.10,21,24,30,32,46,48,52; 9.13,19,21,59,60; 10.26,27,29,30,37; 11.2,7,15, 28,46; 12.14; 13.8,23; 14.4,6,16; 15.27,28,31; 16.6,7*bis*,30; 17.6,37; 18.19,20,21,27 29,38,39 *bis*,41; 19.17,22; 20.5,16,17; 21.8; 22.9,10,25, 33,34,35,36,38,57,58,67,70,71; 23.5,21,22,23; 24.5,17,19,25,32,38; Mk 1.45; 3.5; 5 40; 6.49; 7.6,28,36; 8.19,20,33; 9.12,21,32,34,39; 10.3, 20,22,36,39,48; 11.6; 12.16; 14.11,19,31,46, 52,68,69,71; 15.13,14; A 3.5; 4.21,24; 5.8,33; 7.2,23,25; 8.4; 10.14,22; 12.6,15*bis;* 13.51; 16.31; 19.3; 20.18; 21.20,32,37; at [[Mk 16.8]].

Athenae Athenis (*ab.*) A 17.15,16; 18.1.

Athenensis Athenenses (*m.n.*) A 17.21; Athenenses (*m.uoc.*) A 17.22.

atque et ac adque A 7.29,58; 13.26; ac L 12.20; Mk 6.17; A 8.12; 10.23; 13.18; 20.31.

atramentum atramentum (*ac.*) III J 13.

atrium atrium (*ac.*) Mt 26.3; [[J 18.15]]; Mk 14.54,66,68; 15.1,16; atrio J 10.16; L 22.55.

Attalia Attaliam A 14.25.

attendo *v.* adtendo.

audeo audebat J 21.12; Mk 12.34; audiebat A 7.32; ausus est Mt 22.46; fuerunt ausi L 20.40.

audio J 5.30; L 9.9; 16.2; audis Mt 21.16; 27.13; audit Mt 13.(18), 19,20,22,23; J 3.29; 5.24; 6.45; 8.47; 9.29,31*bis;* [[18.37]]; L 6.47; 10.16*quater;* Mk 2.17; audimus A 2.8; 17.32; auditis Mt [11.4]; 13.17; J 8.47; 10.20; 14.24;

31*bis;* 21.4,6,8,9,11,13,15,16,18,21,24,25,26, 28,29*bis*,30*bis*,32*bis*,34,35,37,38; 22.5,6,8,11, 12,14,18,19,27,29,31,34,39,41; 23.4,5,6,8*bis*, 12,13*bis*,16,18,23,24,25,27,28; 24.2,3,6,8,13, 17,19,20,22,29,31,32,35,36,43,48,49; 25.2,4,5, 8,9,12,16,18,19,22,24,26,29,31,33,38,46; 26.5, 6,8,10,11,17,18,20,23,24,25,26,29,32,33,41,47, 50,56,57,58,59,61,63; 27.4,6,7,11*bis*,15,16,17, 19,20*bis*,21*bis*,23,24,26,32,35,39,44,45,46,47, 49,50,54,55,57,61,62,65,66; 28.1,2,3,4,5,9,11, 15,16,17; J 3.18,19,21,23,29,30,31,36; 4.4,6 *bis*,14,39,42,43,46,51; 5.2,5,7,9,17,29,34,35, 36; 6.2,4,6*bis*,10,11,12,13,15,[16],17,39,53,67, 68,71; 7.2,6,7,10,14,18,27,29,31,32,37,39,40, 44,46; 8.1,2,3,5*bis*,6,7,9,10,13,14,15,35*bis*,40, 41,50,55,59; 9.9,14,16,21,29,40,41; 10.2,5,6, 10,12,16,21,22,24,38,41; 11.1,2,4,5,10,13*bis*, 18,19,20,31,32,37,38,46,49,51,55,57; 12.2,6, 10,14,16,20,23,24,33,37,41,42; 13.1,7,23,28, 30,36; 14.10,11,17,19,21,26; 15.7,11,15,22,24, 26; 16.4,5,7,10,11,20,21,22; 17.3,13,14,20,25; 18.2,⟦5,7,10,14,15*bis*,16,18*bis*,22,23,25,28,36, 39,40; 19.9,12,13,14,15,17,18,19*bis*,23,25,29, 33,38*bis*,39,41; 20.1⟧,4*bis*,11,16,20,24,31; 21.1,4,8,18,19,20,21,25; L 1.6,8,11,22,26,29, 39,56,57,62,64,76,80; 2.1,4,6,8,17,19,26,35,40, 41,47,50,51; 3.1*bis*,7,9,11,12,14,15,16,17,19, 21,23; 4.1,3,16,21,24,28,30,33,38*bis*,40*bis*,41, 42; 5.1,2,3,4,5*bis*,8,10*bis*,13,14*bis*,15,16,17,20, 22,24,27,31,33,34,35,36; 6.1,2,3,4,8,9,11,12, 30,39,40,41*bis*,46,48,49; 7.2,6*bis*,9,12,13,14, 16,21,24,28,30,36,39,41,44,45,46,48,50; 8.4,9, 10,11,12,13,14,15,16,19,20,22,23,24,25,26,28, 30,31,32,33*bis*,34,35,37*bis*,38,39,40,44,45,47, 50,51,52,54,56*bis;* 9.1,6,7,8*bis*,9*bis*,11,12*bis*, 13,14,16,19,20*ter*,23,24,25,27,28,30,31,32*bis*, 34*bis*,36,37,41,42*bis*,43*bis*,45,47,48,49,50,51, 54,55,58,59,60,61*bis*,62; 10.1,2*bis*,5,7,10,12, 16,17,18,20,21,23,25,28,30,31,32,33,37,38*bis*, 40*bis*,41; 11.11,14,16,17,18,19,20,22,24,27,29, 34,37*bis*,38,39*bis*,45,47,48,53; 12.1,4*bis*,5,8,9, 10,11,13,15,16,20,22,25,27,28,31,39,45*bis*,47, 48*ter*,50,52,54; 13.1,5,6,10,12,14,15,16,23,28, 35; 14.7,12,15,25,28,34; 15.1,3,6,7,11,14,17 *bis*,20,21,22,25*bis*,28*bis*,30,32; 16.1,3,6,7,14, 15,17,19,20,22*bis*,25*ter*,27,29,31; 17.1,7,14,15, 16,17,20; 18.1,3,6,7,9,15*bis*,16,20,22,23,24,25, 28,31,34,35,36,37,40,41; 19.8,9,11,12,13,14, 19,24,26,28,36,37,39,40,42,45,46,47; 20.1,3,9 *bis*,10*bis*,11,13,14,18,19,23,25,26,27,35,37,39, 40,41,45; 21.1,2,4,7,9,11,12,16,20,28,33,35, 36,37; 22.1,2*bis*,3,7,13,23,24,26,27,31,32*bis*, 38,39,40,41,43,44,47,48,49,51,52,54*bis*,55,56, 60,61,63,69,70; 23.2*bis*,3*bis*,4,6,7,8,9*bis*,10,11, 12,13,14,17,18*bis*,20,24,25*bis*,26,27,28,32,34, 35,36,38,39,40,41,43,45,49,54,55,56; 24.1*bis*, 2,3,5,6,13,14,16,18,21,24,31,36,37,41,48,49, 50*bis;* Mk 1.7,16,29,30,32; 2.5,6,10,18,20,21, 24,27; 3.6,7,27,29; 4.11,15,34*bis*,36; 5.5,6,11, 14,16,19,31,33,34,36,40,42; 6.15*bis*,16,19,29, 55; 7.6,7,11,20,21,25,26; 8.1,9,20,28*bis*,29*ter*, 35,38; 9.23,27; 10.6,13,14,18,21,24,26,27,29, 30,31,32,39,40,49,50,51,52; 11.8*bis*,17,26,29; 12.5,7,15,17,24,26,29,31,42; 13.7,10,13,14,17, 28,31,32,37; 14.1,4,6,7,17,21,31,38,44,48,51, 61,63,64,69; 15.4,5,6,7,9,12,15*bis*,16,25,26,37, 39,40,44,46,47; ⟦16.9,12,16,17,20⟧; A 1.5,[15 *bis*]; 2.7,14,26,30,38,47,[47]; 3.1,4,6,11*bis*,12, 14,18,23; 4.1,5,13,15,18,19,22,23,24,32,36; 5.1, 3,5,6,8,17,21,25,34,39,42; 6.1,4,9,10; 7.1,6, 11,14,25,27,42,47,54; 8.3,6,9,11,16,20; 10.4,7, 9,10,19,25*bis*,33,34,46; 11.4,8,10,13,15,17,18, 20,25,27*ter*,29*bis;* 12.3,6,7,8*bis*,14,15,17,18,20, 21,24; 13.1,2,8,14,23,28,37,44*bis*,50; 14.1,2,4, 5,7,9,11,13,14,19,21,23,24,27; 15.2*bis*,4*bis*,6, 8,11,13,16,33,34*bis*,38,39,40,41*bis;* 16.1,4,6,7, 8,12,13,15,18*bis*,25,26,28,35,37,38*bis;* 17.1,11, 13,14,15,18,22,32,34; 18.4,6,9,14,15,24,26,27; 19.4,7,8,10,15,17,19,23,27,28,30,32,33,34,39; 20.1,3,4*bis*,7,9,10,14,17; 21.3,4,5,7,13,15,17, 18*bis*,21,27,29,34,35,39*bis;* 22.2,11,17; **(a)utem** Mt 25.6; **aum** (J 6.16); **aute** Mt 23.3; A 20.12; **autes** L 8.25; **tem** L 8.32.

autrus (A 2.38).

auxilior **auxiliari** A 16.9.

auaritia Mk 7.22.

auello **auellere** [Mt 12.1].

aueo **habe** Mt 26.49; 27.29; L 1.28; 23.37; Mk 15.18; **haue** ⟦J 19.3⟧; **habete** Mt 28.9.

auerto **auertaris** Mt 5.42; **abertatur** (A 3.26); **auertatur** [A 3.26]; **auertantem** (*m.*) L 23.14.

auis **aues** (*n.*) Mt 13.32; Mk 4.32.

Azor Mt 1.13,14; L 3.23.

azymus **azymorum** Mt 26.17; L 2.42; 22.1; Mk 14.12; A 12.3; 20.6.

Babylon **Babylonis** Mt 1.12,17*bis;* A 7.43.

bade, badis, *s.v.* **uado.**

baiulo (**baiolo**) **baiulat** L 14.27; **baiulabat** J 12.6; **baiolabatur** (A 3.2); **baiulabatur** [A 3.2]; **baiolauit** L 11.27; **baiulauerunt** J 10.31; **baiolare** J 16.12; L 10.4; A 15.10; **baiulari** A 21.35; **baiulans** (*m.*) ⟦J 19.17⟧; L 22.10.

baptisma Mt 21.25; Mk 11.30; **baptisma** (*ac.*) L 3.3; 7.29; Mk 10.39; A 13.24; 18.25; 19.3,4; **baptismate** A 1.22.

baptismum (*ac.*) ⟦Mt 3.7⟧; L 12.50; Mk 1.4; 10.38; A 10.37.

baptismus L 20.4; baptismos Mk 7.4.

baptista [[Mt 3.1]]; 14.2; L 7.20,33; Mk 6.14; baptistae (*g.*) Mt 11.12; 14.8; Mk 6.24, 25; baptiste (*g.*) L 7.27; baptistam Mt 3.13; 16.14; L 7.18; 9.19; Mk 8.28; baptista Mt 11.11; 17.13.

baptizo Mt 3.11; L 3.16; Mk 1.7; baptizat J 3.26; 4.1; baptizor Mk 10.38,39; baptizamini Mk 10.39; A 1.5; 11.16; baptizabat J 3.22; 4.2; baptizabantur [[Mt 3.6]]; J 3.23; Mk 1.5; A 8.12; 18.8; baptizabit Mt 3.11; L 3.16; baptizauit (*fut.*) Mk 1.8; baptizauit (*perf.*) A 1.5; 11.16; 19.4; baptizatus est (Mt 3.16); L 11.38; Mk 1.9; A 8.13; 16.33; baptizati estis A 19.3; baptizati sunt A 2.41; 19.5; baptizata est A 16.15; baptizati erant A 8.16; baptizatus fuerit [[Mk 16.16]]; baptizetur A 2.38; baptizentur Mk 7.4; A 10.47; baptizaretur Mt 3.13; baptizatus esset L 3.21; baptizare A 22.16; baptizari Mt 3.14; L 3.7,12; 12.50; Mk 10.38; A 10.48; baptizans (*m.*) J 3.23; 10.40; Mk 1.4; baptizantes (*m.n.*) Mt 28.19; Mk 7.8; baptizatus [Mt 3.16]; baptizato (*m.ab.*) L 3.21; baptizati L 7.29,30.

bapulo, *v.* uapulo.

Barabbas Mt 27.16; [[J 18.40]]; Mk 15.7; A 15.22; Barabbam Mt 27.26; L 23.18; Mk 15.11; Barabban Mt 27.17,20,21; [[J 18.40]]; Mk 15.15.

Barachias Barachiae (*g.*) L 11.51; Barachie (*g.*) Mt 23.35.

Bariesus Bariesuam A 13.6.

Bariona, *s.v.* Petrus.

Baritimeas Mk 10.46.

barius, *v.* uarius.

Barnabant, *s.v.* Barnabas.

Barnabas A 1.23; 4.36; 12.25; 13.1,46; 14.7, 14; 15.35,37,39; Barnabae A 11.30; Barnabae A 15.2; Barnabam A 13.50; 15.12; Barnaban A 13.2,7,43; 14.12, 20; 15.36; Barnabant A 11.22; Barnaba A 15.2,22,25.

Bartholomeus Mt 10.3; A 1.13; Barthilomeum Mk 3.18; Bartholomeum L 6.14.

bascellum bascellum (*ac.*) L 22.10.

basiliscus (J 4.46).

basis bases (*n.*) [A 3.7]; uases (*n.*) (A 3.7).

beatus Mt 11.6; 16.17; 24.46; L 6.4; 7.23; 12.43; 14.14,15; ueatus L 11.27; beata L 1.45; beatam L 1.48; beati Mt 5.3,4,5,6,7,8,9,10, 11; [13.16]; J 13.17; 20.29; L 6.20,21,22; 10.23; 11.28; 12.37,38; ueati (Mt 13.16); beatae L 23.29.

Bedsaida L 9.10; 10.13; J 12.21; Bessaidan Mk 6.45; Betsaida Mt 11.21.

Beelzebul et Belzebul Beelzebul L 11.15, 18,19; Mk 3.22; Belzebul Mt 10.25; 12.24,27.

bello, *v.* uello.

bellum bellorum Mt 24.6; Mk 13.7; bella Mt 24.6; Mk 13.7.

Belzetha [J 5.2].

bene Mt 15.7; J 4.17; 8.48; 13.13; [[18.23]]; L 6.26; 20.39; Mk 7.6,9,37; 12.28,32; [[16.18]]; A 10.33; 15.29; melius J 4.52; A 10.28.

benedico benedicebat Mk 10.16; benedicetur (A 3.25); benedicentur [A 3.25]; benedixit Mt 14.19; J 6.11; L 2.28,34; 9.16; 22.19; 24.30,50; Mk 6.41; 14.22; benediceret L 24.51; benedicite Mt 5.44; L 6.28; benedicens (*m.*) Mt 26.26; J 21.13; L 1.64; 22.17; benedicentem (*m.*) A 3.26; benedictus Mt 21.9; 23.39; J 12.13; L 1.42,68; 13.35; 19.38 *bis;* Mk 11.9; benedicta L 1.28*bis*,42; benedictum Mk 11.10; benedicti (*m.g.*) Mk 14.61; benedicti (*voc.*) Mt 25.34.

benefacio benefacitis L 6.33; benefacite Mt 5.44; L 6.27,35; benefacere Mt 12.12; Mk 3.4; 14.7; benfacere L 6.9; benefaciens (*m.*) A 10.38; 14.17; benefacientibus (*m.d.*) L 6.33.

beneficium beneficio (*ab.*) [A 4.9]; benefacio (A 4.9).

beneplaceo beneplacui Mt 3.17; beneplacitum (*n.*) L 10.21; 12.32.

benesentio benesensi L 9.35.

beneuolo beneuolentes (*m.n.*) L 6.36.

Beniamin A 13.21.

benio *v.* uenio.

beniuolus Mt 5.25; L 6.36; ueniuoli (*n.*) L 22.25.

berbum, beruum, *v.* uerbum.

bermibus, *s.v.* uermis.

Beroea Beroean A 17.10,13.

Beryensis (*m.*) A 20.4.

Bessaida, Bethsaida, Betsaida, *v.* Bedsaida.

bestia uestias A 11.6; besteis Mk 1.13.

Bethania J 11.18; Bethaniam Mt 21.17; J 11.17; 12.1; L 24.50; Mk 11.1, 11; 14.3; Uethaniam Mk 8.22; Bethania Mt 26.6; J 11.1; L 19.29; Mk 11.12.

Bethleem Mt 2.1,5,6,8,16; J 7.42; L [2.4], 15; Uethleem (L 2.4).

Betphage Mt 21.1; L 19.29.

bi, *v.* ibi.

bibo bibit J 4.13, [14]; L 5.30; uiuit J 4.14; bibimus L 13.26; bibam Mt 26.42; [[J 18.11]]; uiuam Mt 26.29*bis;* bibes L 17.8; bibet L 1.15; uibet J 6.54,56; bibetis Mt 20.23; L 12.29; Mk 10.39; bibebant L 17.27, 28; uiuit J 4.12; bibimus A 10.41; uiberunt Mk 14.23; bibero Mk 10.39; uiueritis J 6.53; biberint [[Mk 16.18]]; bibam L 17.8; 22.18; Mk 14.25; bibat Mt 24.49; J 7.37; bibatis L 22.30; bibiturus sum [Mt 20.22]; uiuiturus sum (Mt 20.22); Mk 10.38; bibite Mt 26.27; bibere Mt 20.22; 27.34; J 4.7,9,10; L 12.45; Mk 10.38; 14.25; 15.23; uiuere Mt 27.34; bibens (*m.*) Mt 11.18,19; L 7.33; uibens (*m.*) L 7.34; bibentes (*m.n.*) Mt 24.38; uibentes (*m.n.*) L 10.7.

bideo, *v.* uideo.

biduus biduum (*neu.ac.*) Mt 26.2; Mk 14.1; uiduum (*neu.ac.*) J 4.43; uiduo (*neu.*) J 4.40.

bimatus bimatu Mt 2.16.

bini binos L 10.1; uinos Mk 6.7.

bis (*verb.*), *s.v.* uolo.

bis L 18.12.

Bithynia Bithyniam A 16.7.

biuicare, *s.v.* uiuifico.

blasfemia, blasfemo, *v.* blasphemia, blasphemo.

blasphemia Mt 23.31*bis;* Mk 7.22; blasphemiam J 10.33; blasfemiae Mt 15.19; blasphemiae Mk 3.28; blasphemias L 5.21; Mk 14.64.

blasphemo blasphemas J 10.36; blasphemat Mt 9.3; Mk 2.7; blasphemabat L 23.39; blasfemabant Mk 15.29; blasphemabant Mt 27.39; blasphemauit Mt 26.65; blasphemauerit Mk 3.29; blasphemauerint Mk 3.28; blasfemantes (*m.n.*) L 22.65; blasphemantes (*m.n.*) A 13.45; blasphemantes (*m.ac.*) A 19.37; blasphemantibus (*m.*) A 18.6.

blasphemus blasphema (*ac.*) A 6.11.

Blastus Blasto (*d.*) A 12.20.

Boanerges L 6.14; Boanges (*ac.*) Mk 3.17.

bolentes, *s.v.* uolo.

bonus Mt 12.35; 19.17; 20.15; J 10.11,14; L 6.45; 12.42; 18.19; 23.50; Mk 10.18; uonus J 7.12; 10.11; A 11.24; bona L 6.43; bonum Mt 13.38; 17.4; 18.8,9; 26.24; L 9.33; 14.34; Mk 7.27; 9.5,42,43,45,47,50; 14.21; boni (*neu.*) Mt 19.16; bonum Mt 3.10; 12.33; L 3.9; 18.19; Mk 10.18; bonam Mt 12.33; 13.8, 23; L 8.8,15; 10.42; Mk 4.8,20; uonam L 6.37; bonum Mt 13.24,27,37; 26.10; L 6.45; 11.13; Mk 14.6; bono (*m.*) Mt 12.35; L 6.45; bono (*neu.*) Mt 19.17; J 10.33; L 8.15; A 6.3; bone Mt 25.21,23; L 18.18; Mk 10.17; uone L 19.17; bonorum (*m.*) L 1.53; bonos Mt 5.45; 22.10; L 6.43; bonas Mt 13.45; bona Mt 5.16; 12.34*bis*,35; 24.47; J 5.29; 10.32; L 11.13; 12.19; 16.25; bonis (*m.*) L 21.5; meliora (*neu.ac.*) Mt 13.48; optime (*voc.*) L 1.3.

Boos L 3.32.

bos, *s.v.* tu.

bos bobis (*n.s.*) L 14.5; bouem L 13.15; boum L 14.19.

bracchium J 12.38; brachio (*ab.*) L 1.51; A 13.17.

breuio breuiabuntur Mt 24.22; breuiauit Mk 13.20; breuiasset Mk 13.20; breuiati essent Mt 24.22.

breuis breui (*neu.ab.*) A 10.33.

buccella buccellam J 13.26*bis*,30; bucellae L 22.44.

bulba (uulua) bulbam L 2.23.

byssus byssum L 16.19.

cabe, *v.* caueo.

cadauer Mt 24.28.

cado cadit Mt 17.15; cadebant L 16.21; cadet Mt 10.29; L 11.17; cadent Mt 15.27; 24.29; L 21.24; caecidit (J 11.32); Mk 4.5,7; A 13.11; cecidit Mt 26.39; [J 11.32]; L 5.12; 8.6,7,8,14; 13.4; 17.16; Mk 4.4,8; 14.35; A 1.26; 5.10; 10.10,44; 11.15; 15.16; 19.6; 20.9, 10; ceciderunt Mt 13.4,5,7,8; 17.6; 21.35; [[J 18.6]]; A 12.7; caeciderit L 20.18; ceciderit Mt 12.11; L 20.18; cecidisset A 5.5; cadite L 23.30; cadere L 16.17; cadens (*m.*) Mt 4.9; 18.26,29; L 8.41; cadens (*neu.*) J 12.24; cadentem (*m.*) L 10.18; cadentes (*m.n.*) Mt 2.11; cadentes (*f.n.*) Mk 13.25.

caecidit, etc., *s.v.* cado.

caecus Mt 12.22; 15.14; J 9.2,13,19,20,24, 25; L 6.39; 18.35; Mk 10.46,51 A 13.11; caeci J 9.32; 11.37; Mk 8.23; caeco J 9.17; Mk 10.49; caecum Mt 15.14; J 9.1; L 6.39; Mk 8.22; cecae (*voc.s.m.*) Mt 23.26; caeci Mt 9.27,28; 11.5; 15.14; 20.30; 21.14; J 9.39, 40,41; L 7.22; caecorum J 5.3; 10.21; caecis L 4.18; caecos Mt 15.14,30,31; L 7.21; 14.13, 21; caeci Mt 23.16,17,19,24.

caedo caedis [[J 18.23]]; caedebant Mk 11.8; 14.65; A 18.17; caeciderunt Mk 12.3,5; caedere Mt 24.49; caedi A 16.22; caedens (*m.*) A 22.19; caesum (*m.*) Mt 27.26; L 18.33;

captiuus captiuui (*n.*) L 21.24; captiuis (*d.*) L 4.18.

capto captarent Mt 22.15.

captura capturam L 5.4; captura L 5.9.

capud, *v.* **caput.**

caput capud A 16.12; caput Mt 14.11; capitis Mt 10.30; L 7.38; capiti [[J 19.2]]; capud Mt 27.39; J 20.7,12; Mk 6.28; A 4.11; caput Mt 5.36; 14.8; 21.42; 26.7; 27.29,30,37; J 13.9,10; L 7.46; 9.58; 20.17; Mk 6.24,25,27; 12.10; 14.3; 15.19; A 18.6; 21.24; capite [[J 19.30]]; L 12.7; 21.18; Mk 12.4; A 18.18; capita (*ac.*) Mt 24.31; L 21.28; Mk 15.29.

carbo carbones (*ac.*) J 21.9.

carcar, *s.v.* **carcer.**

carcer carceris A 5.19; 16.23,24,26,27*bis*, 36; carcerem Mt 11.2; 14.10; 18.30; 25.43,44; J 3.24; L 12.58; 22.33; 23.19,25; Mk 6.17,28; A 5.21,22,23,25; 8.3; 12.4,6; 16.23,37,39; carcare L 3.20; carcere Mt 14.3; 25.36,39; A 12.5,17; 16.40; 22.19; carcares (*ac.*) L 21.12.

caritas Mt 24.12; J 17.26; caritatem J 5.42; L 11.42; caritate J 15.9,10*bis;* A 5.31.

caro Mt 16.17; 19.6; 24.22; 26.41; J 6.51, 55,63; L 3.6; Mk 10.8; 13.20; 14.38; A 2.26, 31; carnis J 17.2; carnem J 6.52,53,54,56; 8.15; A 2.17; carne Mt 19.5; Mk 10.8; A 2.30; carnes (*ac.*) L 24.39.

carus caram A 20.24; caro (*neu.*) Mt 26.9; karissimus Mk 9.7; carissimum (*m.*) Mk 12.6.

Caryoto, *v.* **Iudas.**

castellum castellus L 19.30; castellum (*ac.*) Mt 21.2; J 11.30; L 8.1; 9.10,52,56; 10.38; 17.12; 24.13,28; Mk 11.2; castello J 7.42; 11.1; L 5.17; castella (*ac.*) Mt 9.35; 14.15; L 9.12; 13.22; Mk 6.6.

castigo castigandum (*m.*) Mt 20.19.

castra castra (*ac.*) A 21.34; castris A 21.37.

castro castrauerunt Mt 19.12.

catellus catelli (*n.*) Mk 7.28; catellis (*d.*) Mk 7.27.

catena catenae (*n.*) A 12.7; catenis (*ab.*) L 8.29; Mk 5.3,4; A 12.6; 21.33.

cathedra cathedra (*ab.*) Mt 23.2; cathedras Mt 21.12; 23.6; L 19.45; 20.46; Mk 11.15; 12.39.

catillus catilli L 11.39.

caueo cabe Mk 9.25.

causa Mt 19.10; Mk 15.26; A 10.21; causae (*g.*) L 23.4; A 19.40; causam Mt 19.3; 27.37; [[J 18.38; 19.4,6]]; L 8.47; 23.22; A 4.21; 13.28; causa Mt 5.22; 15.9; [19.9]; A 19.32.

cce, *s.v.* **ecce.**

cecae, *s.v.* **caecus.**

cedo cedit Mt 15.17; L 8.5.

Cedrus Cedri J 18.1.

celer cileriter A 17.15; celerius L 14.21; cilerius A 12.7.

cena J 13.2; cenae (*g.*) Mt 20.28; L 14.17; caenae [Mt 20.28]; caene (Mt 20.28); cenam J 12.2; L 5.29; 14.12,16; Mk 6.21; cena Mt 27.62; J 13.4; 21.20; L 14.24; cenis (*ab.*) Mt 23.6; L 11.43; 20.46.

cenaculum cenaculum (*ac.*) A 10.9.

Cenchra Cenchris (*ab.*) A 18.18.

ceno cenem L 17.8; cenare Mt 20.28.

census census (*g.*) Mt 22.19; censum Mt 17.25; 22.17.

centiens centies, centiens (Mk 10.30); centies [Mk 10.30].

centum Mt 13.8,23; 18.12,28; J [[19.39]]; 21.11; L 15.4; 16.6,7; Mk 4.8,20; 6.40.

centuplus centuplum (*m.*) L 8.8; centuplum (*neu.ac.*) Mt 19.29.

centurio Mt 27.54; L 7.6; 23.47; Mk 15.39; A 10.22; centurionis L 7.2; centurionem Mk 15.44; centurione Mk 15.45; centurionibus (*ab.*) A 21.32.

centus A 1.15.

cerno cerneret L 22.31.

certor certabatur L 22.59; certamini L 13.24.

certus certum (*neu.n.*) A 21.34; certo (*neu.ab.*) A 2.36.

ceruical ceruical (*ac.*) Mk 4.38.

ceruix ceruices (*ac.*) A 15.10; ceruices (*voc.*) A 7.51.

cesso cessabant A 5.42; 17.13; cessabit (*perf.*) A 6.13; cessauit L 7.45; 11.1; Mk 4.39; 6.51; A 20.1; cessauerunt L 8.24; A 21.32; cessas A 13.10; cessasset L 5.4.

ceterus cetero (*neu.ab.*) Mt 26.45; ceteri Mt 27.49; L 11.2; 18.11; Mk 3.21; 10.41; ceterae L 24.10; caeteris (*m.d.*) [[Mk 16.13]]; ceteros A 16.30; ceteris (*m.ab.*) A 5.13; 17.9; ceteris (*neu.ab.*) L 12.26.

cetus ceti (*g.*) Mt 12.40; L 11.30.

Chaldeus Chaldeorum A 7.4.

Chanaa Chanaam A 7.11; 13.19.

Chananaeus Mt 10.4; Chananaea (*f.n.*) Mt 15.22.

6.56; A 11.2; 14.6; 15.21; 16.4; 20.23; **ciuitatibus** Mt 11.1; 14.13.

ciuo, *s.v.* **cibus.**

cladium, *s.v.* **gladius.**

clam Mt 1.19.

clamo **clamat** Mt 15.23; **clamatis** J 13.13; **clamant** L 18.7; **clamabat** Mt 15.22; J 7.28, 37; 12.44; L 8.8; 18.39; Mk 10.48; A 16.17; **clamabant** Mt 20.31; 21.9; 27.23; J 12.13; [[19.6, 12,15]]; Mk 11.9; 15.14; A 19.32; 21.34; **clamabit** Mt 12.19; **clamabunt** L 19.40; **clamauit** Mt 14.30; J 11.28,43; 12.17; L 8.54; 22.34; A 7.60; 16.28; **clamauerunt** Mt 20.30; J 9.18,24; [[18.40]]; L 17.13; 23.21; Mk 6.49; 15.13; A 19.28; **clamassent** A 10.18; **clamare** Mk 10.47; **clamans** (*m.*) Mt 27.50; L 23.46, 47; Mk 1.26; 5.7; 9.26; **clamans** (*f.*) A 21.36; **clamantis** (*m.*) [[Mt 3.3]]; L 3.4; Mk 1.3; **clamantes** (*m.*) Mt 9.27; A 8.7; 14.14; 16.22, 39; 17.6; 18.13; 21.28; **clamantia** L 4.41; **clamantium** (*m.*) A 19.34; **clamantes** (*m.*) Mt 21.15.

clamor Mt 25.6.

clamys, *s.v.* **chlamys.**

clarifico **clarificabant** A 4.21; **clarificauit** A 3.13; **clarificauerunt** A 11.18; 21.20.

claritas **claritatis** A 7.2; **claritatem** A 12.23; **claritate** A 22.11.

clarus **clare** (*adv.*) Mk 8.25.

Claudius A 18.2; **Claudio** (*ab.*) A 11.28.

claudorum, *s.v.* **clodus.**

clauis **clauem** L 11.52; **clauorum** J 20.25 *bis;* **claues** Mt 16.19.

Cleopas L 24.18; **Cleope** (*g.*) [[J 19.25]].

clibanus **clibanum** L 12.28.

clodus A 3.2; **clodum** Mt 18.8; Mk 9.45; **clodi** Mt 21.14; L 7.22; A 8.7; **claudorum** J 5.3; **clodos** Mt 15.30,31; L 14.13,21.

cludo **cluditis** Mt 23.13; **cludes** (Mt 6.6); **cluserunt** Mt 13.15; **cluserit** L 13.25; **clusa est** Mt 25.10; **clusum est** L 4.25; 11.7; **clusae sunt** A 21.30; **cludens** (*m.*) [Mt 6.6]; **clusum** (*m.*) A 5.23; **clusis** (*neu.ab.*) J 20.19,26.

coaceruo **coaceruati** (*n.*) A 12.12.

coccineus **coccineam** Mt 27.28.

codrantes *s.v.* **quadrans.**

coepi **coepit** Mt 4.17; 11.7,20; 16.21,22; 26.37; J 13.5; L 4.21; 5.14; 7.15,24; 9.12; 11.29,38; 12.1; 14.30; 15.14; 19.37,45; Mk 1.45; 4.1; 5.18,20; 6.2,34; 8.25,31,32; 10.32, 47; 11.15; 12.1; 14.33,69,71,72; 15.8; A 18.26; **coipit** Mk 10.28; **coeperunt** Mt 12.1; 26.22; L 5.21; 6.1; 7.49; 11.53; 14.18; 15.24; 22.23; 23.2; Mk 2.23; 6.55; 8.11; 10.41; 14 19,65; 15.18; A[2.4]; 19.14; **coiperunt** (A 2.4); **coeperat** A 16.27; **coeperit** L 12.45; **coepisset** A 7.19; 10.37; 11.15.

cofinas, *s.v.* **cophinus.**

cogitatio **cogitationem** L 9.47; **cogitatione** L 1.51; **cogitationes** (*n.*) Mt 15.19; L 24.38; Mk 7.21; **cogitationes** (*ac.*) Mt 9.4; 12.25; L 5.22; 6.8; 11.17.

cogito **cogitat** L 14.31; **cogitatis** Mt 9.4; 16.8; J 11.50; L 5.22; Mk 2.8; 8.17; **cogitabat** L 1.29; 12.17; **cogitabant** Mt 16.7; L 6.11; 20.5,14; 24.1; Mk 8.16; 11.31; A 5.33; **cogitauerunt** J 12.10; **cogitauerant** J 9.22; **cogitarent** Mk 2.8; **cogitare** L 5.21; 11.38; Mk 13.11; **gogitare** Mt 10.19; **cogitante** (*m.*) Mt 1.20; A 10.19; **cogitantes** (*m.*) J 13 22; Mk 2.6; A 17.19; **cogitantium** (*m.*) L 3.15.

cognatio **cognationem** A 7.14; **cognatione** L 1.61; A 7.3.

cognatus [[J 18.26]]; **cognata** (*n.*) L 1.36; **cognati** (*n.*) L 1.58; **cognatis** (*m.ab.*) L 2.44; 21.16; A 10.24.

cognomino **cognominatur** A 1.23; 10.5,18, 32; 11.13; 12.12,25; 15.37; **cognominauit** L 6.14*bis;* **cognominatus est** L 6.15; A 4.36.

cognosco J 10.14,15; **cognoscit** Mt 11.27 *bis;* J 10.15; L 10.22; **cognoscitis** Mt 24.32; **cognoscitur** L 6.44; **cognoscebant** A 3.10; 4.13; **cognoscam** L 1.18; **cognoscetis** J 8.32; 14.20; Mk 4.13; 13.28; **cognoscunt** J 10.14; **cognoui** Mt 25.24; J 5.42; 17.25; **cognouisti** L 19.44; **cognouit** Mt 1.25; J 4.1,53; 6.61; 16.19; 17.25; Mk 5.30; **cognouimus** J 6.69; 8.52; 16.30; **cognouistis** J 8.55; 14.7,9; **cognouerunt** Mt 17.12; 21.45; J 7.26; 8.27; 12.16; 16.3; 17.7,25; L 1.22; 2.17; 24.31 Mk 6.33, 54; 12.12; A 17.13; **cognotus est** L 24.35; **cognoscas** L 1.4; **cognoscat** J 17.23; **cognoscatur** J 7.51; **cognatis** [[J 19.4]]; **cognoscant** J 17.3; A 21.24; **cognoscerent** L 24.16; **cognouisset** Mk 15.45; A 12.14; **cognouissent** Mt 14.35; Mk 6.38; A 4.24; **cognosceris** A 22.14; **cognoscite** J 14.7; **cognoscere** Mk 4.11; **cognoscens** (*m.*) L 3.16; 5.22; 20.23; 23.7; **cognoscentes** (*f.n.*) L 9.11; **cognito** (*neu.ab.*) Mk 2.8; 8.17; A 19.34.

cogo **cogunt** Mt 11.12; **cogitur** Mt 11.12; **coegit** Mt 14.22; Mk 6.45; **coxerunt** L 24.29; **coge** L 14.23.

cohors [[J 18.12]]; **cohortis** A 21.31; **cohortem** Mt 27.27; **cohortem** Mk 15.16; [[J 18.3]].

concito concitauerunt A 17.8.

concludo conclusit A 16.24; concluserunt L 5.6.

concolligo concolligent Mt 24.31.

conculco conculcetur Mt 5.13; conculcatum est L 8.5.

concupio concupiui L 22.15.

concupiscentia concupiscentia (*ab.*) L 22.15; concupiscentias J 8.44.

concupisco concupiscatis L 17.22; concupiscendum Mt 5.28.

concurro concurrerunt Mk 6.33; concurreret Mk 9.25.

concursio A 21.30.

concursus concurso (*ab.*) A 19.40.

concutio concusseritis L 3.14.

condemno J 8.11; condemnabit [Mt 12.42]; L 11.31; condemnabunt Mt 12.41; 20.18; condemnauit (Mt 12.42); J 8.10; condemnabitur ⟦Mk 16.16⟧; condemnauerunt Mk 14.64; condemnassetis Mt 12.7; condemnaueris Mt 12.37; condemnet L 12.58; condemnemini L 6.38; condemnare L 6.38.

condio condietur Mk 9.50.

condiscipulus condiscipulis (*d.*) J 11.16.

condoleo condoluit Mk 6.34.

conduco conduxit Mt 20.7; conducere Mt 20.1.

confero conferitis L 24.17; conferebant A 4.15; 17.18; contulit A 18.27.

confestim J 6.21; 11.44; 13.30,32; L 1.63; 5.6,13,25; 8.47*bis*,55; 12.36,54; 13.13; 14.5; 18.8,43; 19.11; Mk 2.2; 4.17; 5.29,42; 10.52; 15.1; A 3.7; 5.10; 12.23; 13.11; 16.33; comfestim Mk 9.15; A 14.2.

conficio confectus erit L 6.40.

confido confidet L 11.22; confidit Mt 27.43; confide Mt 9.2,22; confidete Mk 6.50; confidens (*m.*) L 18.9; confidentes (*m.ac.*) Mk 10.24; confidenter Mk 7.35.

confinis (*f.*) A 18.7.

confirmo confirmauit A 11.2; confirmatus est L 16.26; confirma L 22.32; confirmans (*m.*) A 15.41; 17.3; 18.23; confirmante (*m.*) ⟦Mk 16.20⟧; confirmantes (*m.n.*) A 14.22.

confiteor Mt 11.25; confitebantur J 12.42; confitebor Mt 10.32; confitebitur Mt 10.32; L 12.8; confessus est L 22.6; confessus fuerit L 12.8; Mk 8.38; confiter L 10.21; confessus fuisset J 9.22; confitentes (*m.n.*) ⟦Mt 3.6⟧; Mk 1.5; A 19.18.

conflictatio A 7.11; conflictatione A 11.19; conflictationes (*ac.*) A 14.22; conflictationibus A 7.10.

conflictio L 21.25.

confondaris, *s.v.* confundo.

conforto confortians (*m.*) L 22.43.

confringo confringes (Mt 12.20); confringet [Mt 12.20]; confringetur L 20.18; confractos L 4.18.

confundo confundor L 16.3; confundetur L 9.26; Mk 8.38; confundebatur L 9.7; confundebantur L 13.17; confunderunt A 21.27; confusa est A [2.6]; 21.31; confusus fuerit L 9.26; confondaris (Mt 20.28); confundaris [Mt 20.28]; confusa (*f.n.*) A 19.32.

confusio confusionem A 19.29; confusione L 14.9.

congaudeo congaudebant L 1.58; congaudete L 15.9; cumgaudete L 15.6.

congredior congredi Mt 5.40.

congrego Mt 25.26; congregat Mt 23.37; J 4.36; L 11.23; congregant J 15.6; congregabo L 12.18; congregabit [Mt 3.12]; L 3.17; congregauit (*fut.*) Mk 13.27; congregabunt Mt 13.41; congregabuntur Mt 24.28; 25.32; L 17.37; congregauit (Mt 3.12); congregauerunt Mt 27.27; J 6.13; 11.47; congregata est Mk 4.1; congregati sunt Mt 22.34; 26.3,57; L 22.66; A 4.5,26; congregatae sunt Mt 13.2; erant congregati L 5.17; congregem L 12.17; congreget J 11.52; congregate J 6.12; congregare Mt 23.37; L 13.34; congregans (*m.*) Mt 2.4; 25.24; L 15.13; congreganti (*f.d.*) Mt 13.47; congregata (*f.n.*) Mk 1.33; congregato (*m.ab.*) L 8.4; congregati Mt 28.12; congregatos L 24.33; congregatis (*m.*) Mt 27.17; congregatis (*f.*) L 11.29.

coniam, *v.* quoniam.

coniungo coniungetur Mt 19.5; coniunxit Mt 19.6; Mk 10.9.

conl-, *v.* coll-, for words not listed here.

conlactaneus A 13.1.

conloquor conloquebantur L 4.36; 9.30; conlocutus est L 22.4; conloquentes (*m.n.*) A 18.12.

conmendo commendo L 23.46; conmendauerunt L 12.48; A 14.23.

conminor, *v.* comminor.

conmittens, *s.v.* committo.

conor conatur L 16.16.

conpareo conparuit L 24.31.

conpes compedes (*ac.*) Mk 5.4; conpedibus L 8.29; Mk 5.4.

(*f.ab.*) L 4.13; consummati (*m.n.*) J 17.23; consummatis (*m.ab.*) L 2.43; 4.2.

contaminatio contaminationibus (*ab.*) A 15.20.

contamino contaminarentur [[J 18.28]].

contegerat contegerit, *s.v.* contingo.

contego contexta (*f.n.*) [[J 19.23]].

contemno contemnet L 16.13; contemnatur Mk 9.12; contemnatis Mt 18.10.

contemptor contemptores (*voc.*) A 13.41.

contendo contendet Mt 12.19.

contenebrico contenebricauit Mk 13.24.

contentio L 22.24.

contentionor contentionabatur A 12.21.

contestor contestabatur A 2.40.

contineo continent L 8.15; contenebant L 22.63; continuerunt Mk 9.10; continentem (*f.*) A 15.23; continenti (*neu.ab.*) L 8.1; contenentes (*m.n.*) L 22.54.

contingo contigit A 4.5; 11.26; 14.1; 16.16; contegerat A 3.10; contigerant L 24.14; contegerit A 7.40; contingeret A 20.16; contingat J 5.14; L 1.38; contingere L 8.19.

continuo Mt 13.5,20,21; 14.22,27,31; 20.34; 21.3; 24.29; 25.15; 26.49; 27.48; [[J 19.34]]; L 2.13; 4.39*bis;* 14.31; 17.7; 21.9; 22.60; Mk 1.20,30; 6.54; 9.24; 11.3; A 12.10; 21.30.

contra (*c.ac.*) Mt 21.2; 27.61; L 8.26; 9.50; 11.23; 21.10*bis;* Mk 11.2; 12.41; 13.3,8*bis;* A 17.7; 18.13; 20.15; contra (*c.adv.*) L 19.30; *v.quoq.* incontra.

contradico contradicit [[J 19.12]]; contradicebant A 13.45; contradicere L 21.15; A 4.14; contradicentem (*neu.*) L 2.34; contradicentes (*m.n.*) A 13.45.

contradictio contradictione A 19.36.

contrarius Mt 14.24; Mk 6.48.

contribulo contribulat L 9.39; contribulant L 8.45.

contristo contristatus est Mt 14.9; J 21.17; Mk 6.26; contristata est Mk 14.34; contristati sunt Mt 17.23; 18.31; contristare Mk 6.26; contristari Mt 26.37; Mk 14.19; contristatus Mk 10.22; contristati (*n.*) Mt 26.22; L 24.33.

contubernium contubernia (*ac.*) Mk 6.39.

contumelia contumeliam A 5.41; contumeliis (*ab.*) Mk 12.4.

conturbo conturbabit (*perf.*) L 9.42; Mk 9.20; conturbatus est J 11.33; 13.21; L 1.12; conturbata est L 12.27; L 1.29; conturbati estis L 24.38; conturbati sunt Mk 6.50; conturbetur J 14.1,27; conturbantes (*m.n.*) A 21.13.

conualesco conualescebat L 2.40; A 19.20 *bis;* conualescebant L 23.23.

conuenio conuenit Mk 3.20; 10.1; conueniunt [[J 18.20]]; conueniebat A 5.16; conueniebant L 5.14,15; Mk 1.45; conueniet L 5.36; conuenit Mk 5.21; A 2.6; 5.9; 20.14; conuenerunt Mt 27.62; Mk 2.2; 6.30; 7.1; 14.53; A [1.21]; 15.6; 16.35; conuerat [[J 18.2]]; conuenerant A 2.37; conuenerint Mt 18.19; A 19.32; conuenirent Mt 1.18; conuenissent A 1.6; conuenire L 5.17; 9.37; A 21.22; conuenisse A 10.27; conueniens (*m.*) Mt 20.2; conueniens (*f.*) Mk 14.59; conuenientia(*n.*) Mk 14.56; conuenti (*n.*) A 21.18.

conuenticulum Mt 26.59; conuenticulo (*d.*) Mt 5.22; conuenticulis (*ab.*) Mt 10.17.

conuentus conuentus (*n.pl.*) A 19.38.

conuerat, *s.v.* conuenio.

conuerso conuersantes (*m.n.*) A 15.29.

conuerto conuertimur A 13.46; conuertimini A 3.19; conuertuntur A 15.19; conuertet L 1.16; conuertetur A 2.20; conuertit A 7.42; conuersus est L 4.14; 8.55; conuersa est J 20.14; conuersi sumus A 10.41; conuersi sunt A 7.39; conuertar A 15.16; conuertatur Mt 24.18; L 17.31; conuertamini Mt 18.3; A 14.15; conuertantur Mt 13.13,15; J 12.40; Mk 4.12; A 16.39; conuerte Mt 5.39; 26.52; conuertere L 1.17; 22.32; conuertentes (*m.n.*) A 17.5; conuersus Mt 9.22; 16.23; J 11.38; 21.20; L 7.9,44; 9.55; 10.23; 14.25; 22.61; 23.28,42; Mk 5.30; 8.33; A 12.11; 16.18; conuersa (*n.*) J 20.16; conuersi (*n.*) L 7.10; conuersantibus (*m.ab.*) Mt 17.22.

conuicior conuiciabantur Mk 15.32.

conuinco conuincebat A 18.28.

conuiuium conuiuiis (*ab.*) Mk 12.39.

conuiuo conuiuens (*m.*) A 1.4.

conuoco conuocat L 15.6,9; conuocauit A 11.2; 19.25; 20.1; conuocauerunt Mk 15.16; A 5.21; conuocans (*m.*) Mt 15.10,32; 20.25; L 9.1; 23.13; Mk 10.16; 12.43; conuocantes (*m.n.*) A 6.2; conuocata (*ab.*) Mk 8.34; conuocatis (*m.ab.*) Mk 3.23; 6.7; 8.1; A 10.24.

cooperio cooperuimus Mt 25.38; coperit L 8.16; erat coopertum L 9.45; coperiens (*m.*) L 23.11; cooperiente (*m.ab.*) [[Mk 16.20]]; coperientes (*m.n.*) L 22.64; coopertum (*n.*) L 12.2; 24.32; coopertum (*neu.ac.*) Mt 10.26.

coperio, *v.* cooperio.

cophinus cophini (*n.*) L 9.17; cofinos Mt 14.20; 16.9; Mk 6.43; 8.19; cophinos J 6.13.

crucifixistis A 2.36; 4.10; **crucifixerunt** [[J 19.18]]; L 23.33; 24.20; Mk 15.27; **crucifixus est** [[J 19.20,32,41]]; **crucifigatur** Mt 26.2; 27.22,23; **crucifigerent** Mt 27.26,31; Mk 15.20; **crucifigeretur** [[J 19.16]]; **crucefixissent** Mt 27.35; **crucifixissent** [[J 19.23]]; **crucifige** [[J 19.6*bis*,15]]; L 23.21*bis;* **crucifigite** [[J 19.6]]; **crucifigere** [[J 19.10]]; **crucifigi** L 23.23; 24.7; A 13.29; **crucifixum** (*m.*) Mt 28.5; [[Mk 16.6]]; **crucifigendum** (*m.*) Mt 20.19.

crus **crura** (*n.*) [[J 19.31]]; A 3.7; **crura** (*ac.*) [[J 19.32,33]].

crux **cruci** Mk 15.13,14,15,24; **crucem** Mt 10.38; 16.24; 27.32; [[J 19.17,19,25]]; L 14.27; 23.26; Mk 8.34; 15.21; **cruce** Mt 27.40, 42; [[J 19.31]]; Mk 15.30,32.

cubiculum **cubiculo** (*ab.*) Mt 6.6; 24.26; A 12.20.

cubile **cubili** (*ab.*) L 11.7; **cubilia** (*ac.*) L 9.58.

cubitus **gubitum** L 12.25; **cubitos** Mk 12.39; **cubitis** J 21.8.

culex **culicem** Mt 23.24.

culpa **culpa** (*ab.*) Mt 12.5.

cultor **cultorem** L 13.6; **cultoribus** (*d.*) Mt 21.33.

-cum (*v.quoq.* **mecum, secum, tecum, nobiscum, uobiscum**) Mt 1.23; 12.30*bis*,45; 15.30; 17.17; 20.13; 25.3; 26.11,23,29,38,40; 28.20; J 3.26; 4.26; 7.33; 8.29; 9.37; 13.8,18, 33; 14.9,16; 15.27; 16.4,32; 17.24; 21.3; L 1.28; 5.34; 8.51; 9.49; 11.7,23*bis;* 12.13; 15.31; 22.15,28,33,53; 23.43; 24.24,29,44; Mk 6.3; 8.14; 9.1,8,38; 14.7,18,20,33; III J 15; A 1.21, 22; 11.12; 15.38; 16.3; 18.10; 21.16,18; 22.11.

cum (*praep.c.ab.*) Mt 2.3,11; 4.21; 5.25,41; 9.10,11,15; 12.3,4,41,42; 13.20,29; 14.7; 16.27; 17.3; 18.23; 19.10; 20.2,20; 21.2; 22.16; 24.30, 31,49,51; 25.4,10,19,27,31; 26.18,36,47,51,55, 58; 27.19,34,38,41,44,54,66; 28.8,12; J 3.22; 4.27*bis;* 6.3,22,66; 9.40; 11.16,31,33,54; 12.2, 17; 17.11,12; 18.1, [[2,3,5,15,18,26; 19.18,32, 40]]; 20.7,24,26; L 1.56,58,66,72; 2.5,13,36,40, 51; 5.19,30; 6.3,17; 7.6,11,12,36; 8.1,13,38, 45; 9.18,30,32*bis*,39; 10.17,37; 11.31,37; 12.46, 58; 13.1; 14.9,25,31; 15.2,29,30; 17.15,20; 19.23; 20.1; 22.14,37,52,55,56,59; 23.11,32; 24.1,5,10,15,29,33,52; Mk 1.13,20,36; 2.15,16 *bis*,19,25,26; 3.5,6,7,14; 4.16,36; 5.18,24,40; 8.10,34,38; 9.4,14,24,47; 10.30,46; 11.11; 13.26*bis;* 14.14,43*bis*,48,62,67; 15.1,7,23,27, 31,32,41; [[16.10]]; A 1.4,14,26; 2.14,28,29; 3.8,11; 4.13,14,27,29,31; 5.1,17,21,26; 6.9,10; 7.9,38; 10.20,23*bis*,38,41,45; 11.3,12,21; 13.7, 17,31,43; 14.4*bis*,5,13,23,27,28; 15.4,22*bis*,25, 33,35; 16.32,34,39,40; 17.11,18,34; 18.8,14,18, 20,26*bis;* 19.8,38; 20.19; 21.5,17,18,24,26,29; **cum** (*c.ac.*) L 1.39; 22.11; Mk 9.4; 14.54; A 3.4; 5.26; 7.19*bis*,45; 11.20; 12.21; 14.20; 16.4; 18.17; 19.38; **cum** (*c.mix.*) Mk 1.29; **cum** (*c.indec.*) Mt 26.20; Mk 14.17; **cum** (*c.nih.*) L 6.4; **con** L 24.31.

cum (*con.c.ind.*) Mt 2.8; 5.11; 6.2,6; 10.19, 23; 12.3,43; 13.32,48; 15.2; 19.28; 23.15; 24.15,32,33; 25.10,31; 26.29; J 4.1,21,23,25, 45; 5.7,25; 7.10,27,31; 8.28,44; 9.4*bis*,5; 10.4; 11.41; 12.16,35,36; 13.12,31; 14.29,30; 15.26; 16.4,13,21*bis*,25; 21.18; L 2.21,22,39,42; 5.35; 6.13,22; 8.13; 9.26,34; 10.35; 11.2,24,34*bis;* 12.11,54,58; 13.28; 14.8,10*bis*,12,13,29; 15.9; 16.4,9; 17.10; 21.9,20,30,31; 22.14,66; 23.26, 33; Mk 2.25; 4.29,31; 8.38; 9.36; 11.25; 12.25; 13.4,7,11,14,28,29,36; 14.7,25; A 1.3; 7.17; 10.32; 18.27; 19.21; 21.16; (*c.coni.*) Mt 1.19; 9.15; 11.1; 13.25,26,53; 14.19,23,34,35; 15.35; 17.14; 19.1; 20.10; 21.34; 26.1; 27.31,35; J 4.9, 40,47; 5.13; 6.12,16,19,24; 7.9,14; 8.7,9; 9.6; 10.33; 11.6,20,28,43,51; 13.2*bis*,21; 17.11,12; 18.1,[[3,22,38; 19.6,8,13,23,26,30,33; 20.1]],11, 19,20,22; 21.11,15,19; L 1.63; 2.6,27,29,43; 3.19,21; 5.4,34; 6.6; 7.1,6,12; 8.6,7,8,33,40, 42; 9.18,27,29,33,36; 10.38; 11.1*bis*,13,27; 13.16; 14.1; 15.14; 16.14,23; 17.11,14; 18.35, 41; 19.5,28,29,41; 20.36; 22.40,53; 23.7,12,46, 50; 24.6,23,30,44,51; Mk 1.32,37; 2.4,5,14,20; 3.11,21; 4.10,15,16,35; 5.21; 6.21,24,28,35,38, 46,47,53; 7.2,4,17,30; 8.1; 9.9,25,28,33; 10.17, 42,47; 11.1,11*bis*,12,13,15,19,20; 12.34,42; 14.3,35,66,67,69; 15.41,42,45; A 1.3,9,13,15; 2.1,14,30; 3.8,13,26; 4.7,15,24,30,31,37; 5.2,5, 6*bis*,10*bis*,17,19,21*bis*,22,25,26,27,34,40; 6.6; 7.2,12,14,21,24,31*bis*,36,55,57,60*bis;* 8.5,12, 14,15,18; 10.18,23,25,37; 11.18,20,21,23,26, 30; 12.3,6,9,10*bis*,12,13,14,16,17,18,19,20,21, 23; 13.3,5,6,7,12,13,14*bis*,16,24,27,36,45,48; 14.14,19,20,23,27; 15.1,4,7,30,31,32,33; 16.7, 8,13,18,19,20*bis*,21,30,38,39*bis*,40*bis;* 17.1,6, 10,22,24,26,29,34; 18.2,7,12,21,22,23,26; 19.2 *bis*,5,6,8,9,28,31,35,41; 20.2,3,5,10,11,15,17, 18; 21.6,11,14,19,20,27,30,31,32,33,34,35,37, 40; 22.2,13,20.

cumgaudeo, *v.* **congaudeo.**

cumi Mk 5.41.

cumque **cumquae** (A 2.6); **cumque** Mk 6.22,25; [A 2.6].

cunctatio **cunctatione** A 10.29.

cupiditas **cupiditatis** A 17.29; **cupiditate** L 12.15.

cupidus **cupidi** (*n.*) L 16.14.

cupio **cupiebat** L 15.16; **cupierunt** Mt 13.17; **cupiens** (*m.*) L 16.21.

cura J 10.13; L 10.40; A 20.24; **curam** L 10.34,35; 12.42.

curatio **curationem** A 4.30.

curiosus **curiosa** (*n.ac.*) A 19.19.

curo **curas** Mk 12.14; **curat** J 12.6; **curatur** A 17.25; **curabat** L 9.11; A 5.13; **curabantur** L 6.18; A 5.16; 8.7; **curabit** (Mt 12.15,22); L 7.21; **curauit** Mt 4.24; 12. [15],16, [22]; 14.14; 15.30; 19.2; 21.14; L 13.14; Mk 1.34 *bis;* 6.5; **curati estis** L 17.14; **erant curatae** L 8.2; **curaret** L 6.7; Mk 3.2; **cura** L 4.23; **curate** Mt 10.8; L 10.9; **curamini** L 13.14; **curare** Mt 10.1; 12.10; 17.16; L 8.43; 9.1; 14.3; **curari** L 5.15; 13.14; **curans** (*m.*) Mt 4.23; 9.35; **curantes** (*m.n.*) L 9.6; **curatum** (*m.*) A 4.14; **curandi** Mk 3.15.

curro **currit** J 20.2; **currebant** J 20.4; **cucurrerunt** Mt 28.8; **currens** (*m.*) Mt 27.48; L 15.20; **currentes** (*m.n.*) A 19.28.

cursus **cursum** A 13.25; 16.11; 20.24.

custodia **custodiam** A 12.10; **custodia** Mt 5.25; L 12.38; **custodias** L 2.8; A 16.27.

custodio **custodit** L 11.21; **custoditis** A 7.53; **custodiunt** L 11.28; **custodiebam** J 17.12; **custodiebat** Mk 6.20; **custodiebant** Mk 15.25; **custodiabatur** L 8.29; A 12.5; **custodiet** J 12.25; **custodient** J 15.20; **custodiui** Mt 19.20; J 17.12; L 18.21; **custodiuit** A 16.30; **custodierunt** J 15.20; **custodierit** J 8.51; 12.47; **custodiant** L 4.10; **custodirent** A 21.25; **custodite** Mt 23.3; **custodire** A 12.4; **custodiens** (*m.*) A 21.24; **custodientes** (*m.n.*) L 2.8.

custos **custodes** (*n.*) Mt 28.4; **custodes** (*ac.*) Mt 27.65; **custodibus** Mt 27.66; 28.11.

cyminum **cyminum** (*ac.*) Mt 23.23.

Cyprius A 4.36; **Cyprium** (*m.*) A 21.16; **Cyprii** A 11.20.

Cyprus **Cyprum** A 11.19; 13.4; 15.39; 21.3.

Cyrene **Cyrenen** A 2.10.

Cyrenensis (*m.*) A 13.1; **Cyrenensem** (*m.*) L 23.26; **Cyrinenses** (*m.n.*) A 11.20; **Cyrenensium** (*m.*) A 6.9.

Cyreneus **Cyrenium** (*m.*) Mt 27.32; Mk 15.21.

Cyrenius **Cyrenio** (*ab.*) L 2.2.

daemon **daemones** (*n.*) Mt 8.31.

daemoniacus Mt 12.22; **daemoniacum** (*m.*) Mt 9.32; **daemoniaci** Mt 8.28; **daemoniacos** Mt 4.24; **daemoniacis** (*m.*) Mt 8.33.

daemoniosus L 11.14.

daemonium Mt 17.18; J 10.21; L 4.35; 9.42; Mk 7.29; **daemonio** L 8.29; **daemonium** Mt 11.18; J 7.20; 8.48,49,52; 10.20,21; L 4.33; 7.33; 8.35; 9.1; Mk 7.26,30; **daemonio** Mt 9.33; L 8.29; Mk 5.15,16; **demonio** Mk 5.18; **daemonia** L 4.41; 8.2,30,33,38; 10.17,20; Mk 5.12; **daemoniorum** Mt 12.24; L 11.15; Mk 3.22; A 17.18; **damonia** L 13.32; **daemonia** Mt 10.8; 12.24,27,28; L 8.27; 9.49; 11.15,18, 19,20; Mk 1.34*bis*,39; 3.15,22; 6.13; 9.38; [16.17]; **demonia** Mk 1.32; [[16.9]].

daemonizor **daemonizatur** Mt 15.22.

Damascus **Damascum** A 22.11.

damno **damnabunt** Mk 10.33; **damnatus est** Mt 27.3.

Daniel **Danielum** Mt 24.15.

Dauid Mt 1.17*bis*,20; 9.27; 12.3,23; 15.22; 20.30,31; 21.9,15; 22.42,43,45; J 7.42*bis;* L 1.27,32; 2.4,5,11; 3.31; 6.3; 18.38,39; 20.41, 42,44; Mk 2.25; 10.47; 11.10; 12.35,36,37; A 1.16; 2.25,29,34; 4.25; 13.22,34,36; 15.16; **Dauit** L 1.69; Mk 10.48; A 7.45; 13.22.

dauit, *v.* **dauid.**

dauo, *etc.*, *s.v.* **do.**

de (*c.ab.*) Mt 1.18,20,21,24; 2.8,15; 3.[[4]],9, 13.16*bis*,17; 4.6,25; 5.19,37; 8.28,33,34; 9.16; 10.42; 11.7,10; 12.14,33,34,35*bis*,37*bis;* 13.41, 49,52; 14.13,14,29; 15.7,11,18*bis*,19,22,27*bis;* 16.1,11,*bis*,12*bis*,14,28; 17.5,9,13; 18.6,14,19, 28,35; 19.17; 20.24,28*bis;* 21.8,21,25*bis*,31,45; 22.16,31,42; 23.33,34; 24.1,17,29,36; 25.8; 26.24,45,62; 27.9,13,21,29,40,42,53,55; 28.2,8, 11; J 3.20,25,27,31*quater;* 4.6,7,14,22,30,39, 47,54; 5.31,32*bis*,36,37,40,46; 6.11,13,23,26, 31,32*bis*,33,38,41*bis*,42,50,51*bis*,58,61; 7.7,12, 13, 17, 25, 31, 32, 38, 39, 40, 41, 42, 48*bis*, 52*ter;* 8.13,14,18*bis*,23*quater*,26,41,42,44*bis*,59; 9.6, 16,17,18,21,22,40; 10.13,16,25,26,28,29,33,39, 41; 11.1*bis*,13*bis*,19,55; 12.3,4,9*bis*,16,17*bis*, 20,27,28,32,34,41,42*bis;* 13.1,4,5,18,22,24; 15.19*ter*,22,26; 16.2,8*ter*,9,10,11,14,15,19*bis*, 25,26; 17.6,9,14,15*bis*,16*bis;* [[18.19*bis*,23,34, 36; 19.2,24]]; 20.2; 21.2,10,12,24; L 1.1,4,5*bis*, 15,27,71,74; 2.4*bis*,5,17*bis*,18,27,33,36,37,38, 48; 3.8,15,19*bis*,22; 4.10,14,22,37,38; 5.15; 6.2,42*ter*,44*ter*,45*ter;* 7.6,17,24,27; 8.2,3,27,35; 9.5,9,11,35,37,38,45,54; 10.7,11,18; 11.1,6,13, 16,27,31,45,53; 12.7,13,15,26; 13.1,10; 14.24; 15.16,26,29; 16.2,4,9,17,21*bis*,30; 17.2,7,29; 18.31; 19.3,8,22,29,37,39*bis;* 20.4,5,10,39; 21.4 *bis*,5,11,18; 22.3,32,37,43,71; 23.6,7,8*bis*,26, 37,39; 24.4,14,19,24,27,44,49; Mk 1.10,11,25, 29,30; 2.6; 3.21; 5.2*bis*,16,17,23,27,30; 6.43, 52,54; 7.1,6,15,20,21,25,26,28,29,31,33; 8.11,

19,30; 9.7,9,17,39; 10.41; 11.8,19,30,31; 12.2, 26,28,44; 13.1,15,25,32; 14.21; 15.17,21,30,32, 35; [[16.8,9]]; A 1.1,3,4,16; 2.29,(30); 3.22,23; 5.2,24*bis;* 6.9; 7.3,4,24,37,40,52; 8.12; 10.11, 19; 11.2,5,9,22; 12.7,11,17*bis*,20; 13.29*bis*,44, 50,51; 14.17; 15.6,19; 16.39,40; 17.2,32,33; 18.12,15,25; 19.8,16,23,33,40; 20.9; 21.16,21, 24,25; de (*c.n.*) L 7.3; de (*c.ac.*) Mk 6.33; A 2.30; 12.23; 15.5; 20.17; de (*c.indec.*) Mt 22.28; 26.14,47; J 6.71; 11.19; L 22.47; Mk 14.10; A 22.18; de (*c.ab. et ac.*) Mk 10.10; A 15.2; *v.quoq.* deintus, delonge, deretro, desub, desubito, desuper, desursum.

dea deae (*g.*) A 19.27; deam A 19.37.

dealbo dealbatis (*neu.d.*) Mt 23.27.

deambulo deambulante (*m.*) Mk 11.27.

debenio, *v.* deuenio.

debeo debes Mt 18.28; L 16.5,7; debet Mt 23.18; [[J 19.7]]; Mk 13.14; debemus A 17.29; deuetis J 13.14; debebat Mt 18.28; L 7.41; debuimus L 17.10; debebatur Mt 18.30; debitum (*neu.ac.*) Mt 18.32,34; debita (*neu.ac.*) L 11.4.

debilis deuilem (*m.*) Mk 9.43; debiles (*m.ac.*) L 14.13,21.

debitor Mt 18.24; [23.16]; deuitor (Mt 23.16); debitores L 7.41; 13.4; debitorum L 16.5; debitoribus (*d.*) L 11.4.

Decapoleus Decapoleos Mk 7.31.

Decapolis Decapolim Mt 4.25; Decapoli Mk 5.20.

decedo decessit Mk 1.42; decesserit Mk 12.19.

decem Mt 18.24; 20.24; 25.1; L 13.4,11,16; 14.31; 15.8; 17.12,17; 19.13*bis*,16,17,24; Mk 10.41; (A 2.14).

decerto decertarent [[J 18.36]].

decet decens (*neu.*) Mt 3.15.

decimo L 18.12; decimatis Mt 23.23; L 11.42.

decimus decima (*ab.*) A 19.9.

declino declinauit L 24.29; declinare L 9.12.

decollo decollaui Mt 14.2; L 9.9; Mk 6.16; decollauit Mt 14.10; Mk 6.28.

decorus decorum (*n.*) Mt 23.27.

decumbo decumbebat Mk 1.30.

decurio L 23.50; Mk 15.43.

deduco deducebant A 5.26; deducent L 19.44; deducentibus (*m.ab.*) A 21.5; deductus A 22.11.

deductor deductores (*ac.*) A 13.11.

defero delatus est Mt 4.1.

deficio defecistis L 22.35; deficiat L 22.32; defecerit L 16.9; deficere Mt 26.37; L 18.1; deficientem (*m.*) L 12.33; deficientium (*m.*) L 21.26.

defino definisset A 17.26.

defuctus, *s.v.* defungor.

defungor defuctus est A 7.15; defunctus est A 2.29; defuncti (*m.g.*) J 11.39; defuncto (*m.ab.*) Mt 2.19.

deinde J [[19.27]]; 20.27; L 16.7; Mk 4.17,28 *bis;* 13.9.

deintus L 11.7.

deiungo deiungat Mk 10.9.

deleo deleantur A 3.19.

delictum delicti Mk 3.29; delicta (*ac.*) Mk. 11.25,26.

delonge Mt 26.58; 27.55; L 17.12; Mk 8.3.

deluculo, *s.v.* diluculum.

deludo deludebant L 23.36; delusus est Mt 2.16; delusissent Mt 27.31; deludentes (*m.n.*) Mt 27.41.

dem-, *v.* daem-, for all words not listed here.

demando demandabit L 4.10.

demergo demergi Mt 14.30; 18.6; demersus A 20.9.

Demetrius A 19.24,38; Demetrio (*d.*) III J 12.

demitto, *v.* dimitto.

demonstro demonstrauit (*fut.*) Mk 14.15; demonstraui J 15.15; demonstrauit [[Mt 3.7]]; J 20.20; L 2.15.

demoror demorantur A 2.10; demorabatur A 12.19; demorabantur A 14.28; 15.35; demorati sumus A 20.6; demorati sunt A 18.2; demorari A 10.48; demorantes (*m.n.*) A 16.12.

denarius denario Mt 20.13; denarium 22.19*bis;* Mk 12.15; denario Mt 20.2; denariorum Mt 18.24; J 6.7; A 19.19; denarios Mt 18.28; 20.9,10; L 7.41*bis;* 10.35; denariis J 12.5; Mk 6.37.

dendibus, *s.v.* dens.

denego deneget Mk 8.34.

dens dentem Mt 5.38; dente Mt 5.38; dentium Mt 13.42,50; 22.13; 24.51; 25.30; L 13.28; 19.27; dentibus (*ab.*) Mk 9.18; dendibus A 7.54.

denuntiatio denuntiatione A 5.28.

deorsum Mt 4.6; 20.28; 27.51; Mk 15.38; A 2.19; diosum L 4.9; zosum A 20.9.

14; 17.24,30; 19.11; 21.19; 22.14; **dei** Mt 3.16; 4.3,4,6; 5.9,34; 8.29; 12.4,28*bis;* 14.34; 15.3,6; 16.16,23; 19.24; 21.12,43; 22.16,21,29; 23.22, 39; 26.61,63; 27.40,43,54; J 3.18,34,36; 4.10; 5.25,42; 6.28,29,33,45,69, 8.47; 9.3; 10.35,36; 11.4*bis*,27,40,52; 12.41,43; [[19.7]]; 20.31; L 1.6,8,19,35,78; 2.40; 3.38; 4.3,4,9,34,41,43; 5.1; 6.4,20; 7.30; 8.1,10,11,15,21; 9.2,11,20, 43,60,62; 10.9,11,12; 11.20*bis*,42; 12.6,8,9,31; 13.18,20,28,29; 14.15; 15.10; 16.15,16; 17.20*bis*, 21; 18.16,17,24,25,29; 19.11; 20.21,25; 21.4, 31; 22.16,18,69,70; 23.35,51; 24.19; Mk 1.1,3, 14,15,24; 2.26; 3.11,35; 4.11,26,30; 5.7; 7.8, 9,13; 8.33; 9.1,47; 10.14,15,23,25,24;[4] 11.22; 12.17,24,34; 14.25; 15.39,43; [[16.19]]; A 1.3; 2.11,23,33; 4.19,24,31; 6.2; 7.43,46,55*bis*,56; 8.10,12,14; 10.31; 11.1,2,23; 12.22,24; 13.5, 7,43; 14.4,22,26; 16.6,17; 17.13,29; 18.11; 19.8,20; 20.24,27; **deo** Mt 22.21; J 5.18; 9.24; 16.2; L 2.14; 16.13; 17.18; 18.43; 20.25,36; Mk 12.17; A 2.47; 3.8; 5.4,29,39; 7.20; 12.23; 14.23; 16.25; 17.23; **deum** Mt 4.7,10; 5.8; 9.8; 15.31; 19.26; 22.37; 26.63; 27.43; J 5.18; 6.46; 8.27,41; 9.31; 10.33; 11.22; 13.3; 14.1; 17.3; 21.19; L 1.16,30,37,64; 2.13,20,28,52; 4.8,12; 5.25; 7.16,29; 10.27; 13.13; 17.15; 18.2,4,27, 43; 19.37; 20.37*ter;* 23.47; 24.53; Mk 2.12; 5.7; 10.27; 12.30; III J 11; A 3.9; 4.19,21,24; 6.11; 10.22,46; 11.18; 12.5; 13.16,26; 14.15 *bis;* 15.10,17,19; 16.14; 18.7,13; **deo** Mt 22.31; J 3.21; 5.44; 6.46; 7.17; 8.40,42,47; 9.16,33; 13.3; 16.30; L 1.26,47; 2.38; A 5.39; 10.4,33, 41,42; 13.12,36; 18.8,21; 20.21; **dii** J 10.35; A 14.11; 19.26; **deos** J 10.35; **deo** (*inc.*) A 7.40.

dexter (*adi.*) Mt 5.29; **dextram** J [[18.10]]; 21.6; L 22.50; **dextera** (*f.*) A 3.7; **dextera** (*subst.*) **destera** (Mt 6.3); **dextera** [Mt 6.3]; **dexteram** L 20.42; 22.69; Mk 10.37,40; 12.36; 14.62; 16.5; A 2.34; 7.55,56; **dextram** Mk 15.27; **dextera** Mt 27.29; A 2.33; **dextra** A 2.25; **dextris** (*ab.*) Mt 20.21,23; 22.44; 25.33, 34; 26.64; 27.38; L 1.11; 23.33; [[Mk 16.19]].

diabolus Mt 4.5,8,11; 13.39; J 6.70; 13.2; L 4.3,6,13; 8.12; **diabolo** (*d.*) Mt 25.41; **diabolo** (*ab.*) Mt 4.1; A 10.38; **diauolo** J 8.44; **diabole** A 13.10.

Diana A 19.28,34; **Dianae** (*g.*) A 19.24,27, 35.

diauolo, *s.v.* **diabolus.**

dicitum, *s.v.* **digitus.**

dico Mt 3.9; 5.18,22,26,28,32,34,39,44; 6.2,5; 10.15,23,27,42; 11.9,11,22,24; 12.6,31, 36; 13.17,30; 16.18,28; 17.12,20; 18.3,10,13, 18,19,22; 19.9,23,24,28; 21.21,27,31,43; 23.36, 39; 24.2,34,47; 25.12,40,45; 26.13,21,29,34, 64; J 4.35; 5.19,24,25,31,[31],34; 6.26,32,47, 53,56; 7.7; 8.34,51,58; 10.1,7,25; 12,24,27; 13.16,18,19,20,21,33,38; 14.12; 15.15; 16.7,20, 23,26; 21.18; L 3.8; 4.24,25; 5.24; 6.27,46; 7.8,9,14,26,28,47; 9.27; 10.12,24; 11.8,9,51; 12.4,5,8,22,27,37,44,51,59; 13.3,5,24,27,35; 14.24; 15.7,10; 16.8,9; 17.10,34; 18.8,14,17, 29; 19.26,40; 20.8; 21.3,32; 22.16,18,34,37,59; Mk 2.11,27; 3.28; 5.41; 8.12; 9.1,13,41; 10.15, 29; 11.23,24,29,33; 12.43; 13.2,30,37; 14.9,18, 25,30; A 5.38; 14.10; **dicis** J 8.5,13,33,52; 9.17; 12.34; 14.9; 16.29; [[18.34,37]]; L 8.45; 12.41; 18.19,20; 22.60; 23.3; Mk 5.31; 10.18; 14.68; 15.2; **dicit** Mt 4.6,10,19; 9.6,9,28,37; 12.13,44; 13.29,52; 14.31; 15.34; 16.15; 17.20, 25*bis;* 18.22,32; 19.8,17,18,20,21; 20.6,8,21, 28; 21.13,16,19,31,42,45; 22.8,12,20,21,37; 25.34; 26.18,25,31,35,36,38,40,45,52,64; 27.13, 22,23,65; 28.10; J 4.7,9,11,15,16,17,19,21,25, 26,28,29,34,49,50; 5.6,7,8,32; 6.5,8,12,42; 7.6, 42,50; 8.22,25,27; 11.7,11,13,23,24,25,27,39 *bis*,40,44; 12.4,22; 13.6,8,9,10,22,24,25,29,31, 36*bis*,37; 14.5,6,8,9,22; 16.17,18; [[18.4,5,17 *bis*,26,38*bis;* 19.5,6,9,10,14,26,27,35,37]]; 20.2, 13,15*bis*,16*bis*,17,29; 21.3,5,7,10,12,15*ter*,16 *ter*,17*ter*,19,21,22; L 5.20,22,24,27; 6.8,10; 9.33; 11.5,7,24,45; 17.7; 18.4,6; 20.37,42*bis;* 22.11; Mk 1.44; 6.38; 8.29; 12.37; 14.14; A 2.17,25; 7.7,49; 12.8; 13.34,35; 15.17; 21.11; **dicimus** J 8.48; L 9.54; **digimus** A 21.23; **dicitis** Mt 15.5; 16.2,15; 23.30; J 4.20,35; 8.54; 9.19,41; 10.36; 13.13; L 6.46; 7.33,34; 9.20; 11.18; 12.54,55; 17.10; 22.11,70; Mk 7.11; 8.29; 14.71; **dicunt** Mt 9.28; 11.16,18, 19; 13.27,28,51; 14.17; 15.12,33; 16.13; 17.10; 19.3,7,10; 20.7,22,33; 21.16,31,41; 22.21,42; 23.3; 27.22; J 7.26; 8.4; 11.8,34; 12.22; 16.29; 20.13; 21.3; L 9.18; 20.27,41; 24.23; Mk 1.30; 2.18; 3.32; 4.38; 5.31; 6.35,38; 8.27; 9.11; 10.35; 11.28; 12.16,18,35; 14.12; **dicitur** Mt 4.18; 10.2; 13.55; 26.3,14,36; 27.17,22,33; J 4.5,25; 5.2; 9.11; 11.16,54; 14.5; [[19.13,17]]; 20.16,24; 21.2; L 7.11; 9.10; 22.1; Mk 4.11; A 3.2; 6.9; **dicebat** Mt 9.21,24; 14.4; J 5.18; 6.6,65,71; 8.23,31; 9.9; 10.6; 12.44; L 2.38; 3.7; 6.5,20; 8.29; 9.23; 10.2; 12.54; 13.6,14,18; 14.7,12; 16.1,5; 18.1; 20.9; Mk 1.7; 3.23; 4.2, 9,21,24,26,30; 5.8; 6.4,18; 7.9,14,20; 9.1,31; 12.38; 15.14; A 11.16; 13.25; 15.2; **dicebatis** L 17.6; **dicebant** Mt 12.23,24; 26.5; 27.41,47; J 4.42; 5.10; 6.14,42; 7.11,12*bis*,25,31,40,41 *bis;* 8.19,22,25; 9.8,9,16*bis*,17; 10.20,21,24,41; 11.36,47,56; 12.29*bis;* [[19.3,21]]; 20.25; L 4.22; 5.36; 6.2,39; 9.31; 22.64,65; 23.5,35; 24.10; Mk 2.16,24; 3.21,22,30; 4.41; 6.14,15

[4] Order of verses in MS.

7.26,27,31,60; 8.9; 10.26; 11.4; 12.7; 15.38; 16.9,28; 19.4,21,26; 20.23; 21.40; **dices** L 12.16; **dicens** (*f.*) Mt 3.17; 15.22,25; 17.5; 21.10; 27.19; J 11.28,32; 12.28; ⟦19.24⟧; 20.14; L 9.35; 15.9; 18.3; Mk 5.28; 7.28; 9.7; A 16.15,17, **dicentis** (*m.*) [Mt 13.14]; **dicentem** (*m.*) Mt 1.22; 2.15,17; ⟦3.3⟧; 4.14; 12.17; 13.35; 21.4; 26.61; 27.9; L 23.2; Mk 14.58; A 6.14; 7.59; 22.18; **dicentem** (*f.*) A 11.7; **dicente** (*m.*) Mt 22.31; L 9.34; 11.14,53; **dicentes** Mt 2.2; 8.29,31; 9.14,27; 10.7,12; 12.10, 38; 13.(14),36; 14.15,26,33; 15.1,23; 16.7; 17.10; 18.1; 19.25; 20.12,30,31; 21.20,23,25; 22.16,23,24; 24.3,5; 25.37,44; 26.8,17; 27.23, 29,40,54,63; 28.13; J 4.31; 6.52; 7.15; 9.19; 10.33; 12.13,21; ⟦18.40; 19.6,12⟧; L 1.66; 3.10,14; 4.36; 5.21,26,30; 7.4,16; 8.24,25,49; 10.17; 13.25,31; 15.2; 19.14,38; 20.5,14,21,28; 21.7,8; 22.66; 23.2,18,37; 24.29; Mk 1.27; 2.6; 3.11; 5.12,35; 6.2; 7.5,37; 8.28; 9.11; 10.26; 11.9,31; 12.18; 13.6; 15.13,29; A 1.6; 2.7,12, 13,47; 4.16; 5.23; 7.35,40; 8.10; 11.3,18; 13.15; 14.11,18; 15.5; 16.39*bis;* 17.6,7,19; 18.13; 19.13,14,28; 21.14,20; **dicentes** Mt 9.33; 21.9; 25.9, [11]; J 11.3; L 24.23; **dicetes** (*f.*) (Mt 25.11); **dicentia** L 4.41; **dicentium** (*m.*) L 2.13; 21.5; **dicentibus** (*m.*) Mt 12.48; L 7.32; **dicentes** (*m.*) Mt 21.15; L 24.34; A 6.13; 16.35; **dicentes** (*m.voc.*) Mt 23.16; **dicto** (*m.ab.*) Mt 26.30; Mk 14.26; **dicendo** (*ab.*) A 8.19; **dix** L 9.3; A 22.13.

Didymus J 11.16; 14.5; 20.24; 21.2; L 6.15.

dies J 5.1; 6.4; 7.2,14; 9.4; 11.9; 16.21; ⟦19.31⟧; L 9.12,51; 21.34; 22.1,7,66; 23.54; 24.29; Mk 6.21; A 2.20; 21.27; **dies** (*f.*) L 6.13; **diei** Mt 20.12; J 7.37; L 2.42,44; A 2.15; **diem** Mt 20.2; 24.38; 25.13; 26.29; 27.15,64; 28.15; J 4.45; 7.8*bis*,10; 8.56; 11.56; 12.7,12; 13.1,29; L 1.20,80; 9.37; 17.27; 19.42; 21.37; 23.17; 24.21; Mk 13.2; 14.25,58; 15.6; A 1.2, 22; 2.29; 4.5; 10.30; 17.17,31; 18.21; **dieum** A 10.40; **die** Mt 10.15; 11.22,24; 12.36; 13.1; 20.6,19; 24.36,42; 26.5; J 4.45; 6.54; 7.11,37; 11.9,53; 12.20; 14.20; 16.23; 20.19; L 1.59; 2.37,41; 6.4,23; 13.14,15,16; 14.5; 17.4,29,30, 31; 18.7; 23.12,42; Mk 4.27; 5.5; 6.2; 13.32; 14.2; A 2.41; 5.42; 7.8,26; 10.24; 12.18,21; 13.14; 16.13; 20.16,26,31; 21.5,18,26; **die** (*f.*) Mt 22.23; 24.50; J 6.22,39,40,44; 11.24; 12.12, 48; 16.26; 20.19; L 4.42; 7.11; 12.46; 18.33; 24.7,13,46; Mk 2.20; 4.35; 8.31; 11.12; 14.12; A 7.28; 8.1; 10.9,23,30; 14.20; 16.11*bis*,35*bis;* 20.7,15,18; **dies** Mt 9.15; 15.32; 24.22*bis*,37; L 1.23; 2.6,21,22; 5.35; 13.14; 17.22; 19.43; 21.6; 23.29; Mk 2.20; A 2.1; 12.3; **dies** (*f.*) L 21.22; **dierum** Mt 24.29; L 5.17; 8.22; 17.22; 20.1; A 21.26; **dies** Mt 4.2; 12.40*bis;* 16.21; 17.1,23; 26.61; 27.63; J 11.6,17; 12.1; 20.26; L 1.24,75; 2.46; 9.22,28; 15.13; Mk 2.1; 9.2, 31; 10.34; 13.20*bis;* A 1.3,5; 3.24; 5.36; 7.45; 10.41,48; 15.36; 16.12,18; 17.19; 18.18; 20.6 *bis;* 21.4,15,38; **diebus** Mt 2.1; ⟦3.1⟧; 9.15; 11.12; 23.30; 24.19,38; 27.40; 28.20; L 1.5,8, 18,25,39; 2.1,36,43; 4.2*bis*,25; 5.35; 6.12; 9.36; 11.30; 17.26*bis*,28; 21.23; 23.7; 24.18; Mk 1.9,13; 8.1; 13.17,19,24; 15.29; A 1.15; 2.1,17; 3.1; 5.37; 6.1; 7.41; 11.27; 13.31,41; 15.7,30.

diescessus **diescessum** A 20.29.

diffamo **diffamauerunt** A 21.21; **diffamatus est** L 16.1; **diffamare** Mk 1.45.

differo **differitis** L 12.7,24; **differebatur** A 10.11.

difficilis **difficile** (*neu.n.*) L 1.37; **difficile** (*adv.*) Mt 19.23; L 18.24; Mk 10.23,24.

digimus, *s.v.* **dico.**

digitus **digiti** L 16.24; **dicitum** J 20.25,27; **digito** Mt 23.4; J 8.6,8; L 11.20; **digitorum** L 11.46; **digitos** Mk 7.33.

dignus Mt 10.10,11,37,38; L 3.16; 7.4,6; 10.7; 15.19,21; Mk 1.7; A 13.25; **digna** Mt 10.13; **dignum** L 23.15; **dignum** (*m.*) Mt 3.8; L 3.8; **digni** Mt 22.8; L 20.35; 21.36; A 5.41; **dignos** A 13.46; **digna** L 12.48; **dignior** (*m.*) Mt 20.28; **digne** L 23.41.

dilato **dilatant** Mt 23.5.

dilectio **dilectionem** J 15.13; **dilictionem** J 13.35.

dilectus **dilectissimis** (*m.ab.*) A 15.25.

diligentia **diligentia** (*ab.*) A 5.23.

diligo J 14.31; **diligis** Mt 22.37; J 21.15; **diligit** Mt 10.37; 15.8; J 3.35; 5.20; 10.17; 14.21*bis*,23*bis*,24; 16.27; L 7.5,42; **diligitis** J 14.15; L 6.32; 11.43; **diligunt** L 6.32; **diligebat** J 13.23; ⟦19.26⟧; 20.2; 21.7,20; **diligebatis** J 8.42; **diligam** J 14.21; **diliges** Mt 5.43; 19.19; 22.39; **dililges** L 10.27; **diligis** Mk 12.30,31; **diliget** L 16.13; **diligetur** J 14.21; **dilexi** J 13.34; 15.9,12; 17.23; **dilexisti** J 17.23,24,26; **dilexit** J 13.1; 15.9; Mk 10.21; **dilexistis** J 16.27; **dilexerunt** J 3.19; **dilixeritis** Mt 5.46; **diligatis** J 13.34*bis;* 14.28; 15.12; **diligite** Mt 5.44; J 15.17; L 6.27,35; **diligere** Mk 12.33 *bis;* **diligens** (*m.*) J 13.1; **diligentes** (*m.ac.*) Mt 5.46; L 6.32*bis;* **diligenter** Mt 2.8; L 1.3; 15.8; Mk 14.44; A 16.23; 18.25; **diligentius** A 18.26 **dilectus** Mt 3.17; 12.18; 17.5; L 9.35; Mk 1.11; **dilectum** (*m.*) L 20.13.

dilubium, *v.* **diluuium.**

6.40; **discumberent** Mk 6.39; **discubueris** Mt 20.28; **discubueritis** Mt 20.28; **discumbere** Mt 14.19; 15.35; Mk 8.6; **discumbentis** (*m.*) Mt 26.7; **discumbente** (*m.*) Mt 9.10; **discumbentium** (*m.*) Mt 22.10; **discumbentes** (*m.*) Mt 22.11; **discumbentibus** (*m.*) J 12.2; Mk 14.18.

discupio **discupiuntur** (A 6.1).

discus **disco** (*ab.*) Mt 14.11; Mk 6.25,28.

discutio **discutietur** A 19.39.

dismitto, *v.* **dimitto.**

dispargo **dispargit** Mt 12.30; J 10.12; L 11.23; **dispargentur** Mk 14.27; **disparsi** Mt 25.26; **disparsit** L 1.51; 15.13; **disparsi sunt** J 11.52; **dispersi sunt** A 5.37; 8.1; **dispersi erant** A 8.4; **dispargamini** J 16.32; **dispargentur** Mt 26.31; **dispersi** (*n.*) A 11.19.

dispartior **dispartiebantur** A 2.45.

dispereo **disperibit** A 3.23.

dispergo, *v.* **dispargo.**

dispersio **dispersionem** J 7.35.

dispertio **dispertitur** Mk 3.26.

dispicio **dispiciuntur** [A 6.1].

dispono L 22.29; **disposuit** L 22.29; A 7.44; **disposuerat** A 20.13.

dispositio **dispositionis** A 3.25; 7.8; **dispositiones** (*ac.*) A 7.53.

disputo **disputabat** A 17.17; 18.4,19; 20.7; **disputabit** (*perf.*) A 17.2; **disputauit** A 3.25; **disputans** (*m.*) A 19.8,9; **disputante** (*m.*) A 18.28; 20.9; **disputantibus** (*f.ab.*) A 18.6.

disquiro **disquirebant** Mk 9.34.

disrumpo **disrumpit** L 9.39; **disrumpet** Mk 2.22; **disrumpebat** L 8.29; Mk 5.4; **disrupit** Mt 26.65.

dissensio J 7.43; 10.19; **dissensionem** L 23.19; **dissensiones** (*ac.*) L 21.9.

dissero **disserebat** Mk 4.34; **disertus** A 18.24.

dissipo **dissipans** (*m.*) L 16.1.

dissit, *s.v.* **discedo.**

dissolbantur, *s.v.* **dissoluo.**

dissoluo **dissoluit** Mt 27.40; **dissolbantur** Mt 15.32; **dissoluit** A 19.41; **dissoluere** Mt 5.17*bis;* 26.61.

distraho **distrahebant** A 2.45; **distraxerunt** A 7.9; 19.33.

distribuo **distribuebantur** A 4.35.

dit, *s.v.* **dico.**

diuasto **diuastabat** A 8.3.

diuersorius, *v.* **deuersorius.**

diues (*m.*) Mt 19.23; 27.57; L 16.1,19,22; 18.23; Mk 10.25; 15.43; **diuitis** (*m.*) L 12.16; 16.21; **diuitem** (*m.*) Mt 19.24; L 18.25; **diuitibus** (*m.d.*) L 6.24; **diuites** (*m.*) L 1.53; 14.12; 21.1.

diuido **diuidet** Mt 24.51; L 11.22; 12.46; **diuidetur** L 12.53; **diuidentur** L 12.52; **diuisit** L 15.12; Mk 6.41; **diuiserunt** Mt 27.35; Mk 15.24; **diuisus est** Mt 12.26; L 11.18; **diuisa erat** A 14.4; **diuidatur** Mk 3.24,25; **diuisa** (*f.n.*) Mt 12.25; **diuisum** Mt 12.25; L 11.17; **diuisi** (*n.*) L 12.52.

diuidus **diuidi** (*n.*) A 2.3.

diuino **diuinando** (*ab.*) A 16.16.

diuinus **diuinum** (*neu.n.*) A 17.27 29.

diuisio **diuisionem** L 12.51.

diuitiae **diuitiarum** Mt 13.22; L 8.14.

diurnus **diurnum** (*neu.ac.*) A 17.28; **diurno** (*neu.*) A 6.1.

diuulgo **diuulgabant** Mt 9.31; **diuulgatum est** Mt 28.15; **diuulgare** L 5.14.

dixeribus, *s.v.* **dico.**

do J 8.18; 10.15,28; 13.34; 14.27*bis;* L 4.6; 10.19; 19.8; A 3.6; **dat** (Mt 5.42); J 3.34; 5.36; 6.27,32,37; 8.18; 10.11; 14.27; 21.24; Mk 4.8; A 7.25; **datis** J 15.27; **datur** A 8.18; **dabat** Mt 15.36; L 9.16; 15.16; 24.30; Mk 15.36; A 2.4; **dabant** Mt 13.8; [[J 19.3]]; Mk 15.23; **dabo** Mt 4.9; 16.19; [20.4] J 4.14, [14]; 6.51; L 4.6; 21.15; Mk 6.23; A 2.19; 13.33,34; **dauo** (Mt 20.4); (J 4.14); Mk 6.22; **dabis** A 2.27; 13.35; **dabit** Mt 16.26; 24.29; J 11.22; 16.23; L 1.32; 11.8,11*bis*,12,13; 16.12; **dauit** J 14.16; 15.26; L 17.18; 20.16; Mk 8.37; 12.9; 13.24; **dauimus** Mk 6.37; **dabunt** Mt 24.24; L 6.38; **dabitur** Mt 12.39; 13.12; 16.4; 21.43; 25.29; L 6.37; 8.18; 11.9,29; Mk 8.12; **dedi** J 13.15; 17.8,14,22; **dedis** J 17.24; **dedisti** J 17.2*bis*,4,6*bis*,7,8,9,11,12,22,24; [[18.9]]; L 7.44,45; 15.29; 19.23; **dedit** Mt 9.8; 10.1; 14.19; 21.23; 25.15; 26.27,48; J 3.16,35; 4.5, 12; 5.22,26,27,36; 6.11,31,32,39; 7.19,22; 10.29; 12.49; 13.3; [[18.11,22; 19.9]]; 21.13; L 6.4; 7.15; 9.1; 10.35; 18.43; 19.13; 20.2; 22.19; Mk 2.26; 3.15; 4.7; 6.28*bis*,41; 8.6; 14.22,23; A 3.16; 5.32; 7.5,8,10; 10.40; 11.17, 18; 12.23; 13.20,21,47; 14.2; 15.8; **dedistis** Mt 25.35,42; **dederunt** Mt 27.10 34; 28.12; L 12.48; A 1.26; **dederat** [[J 18.14]]; L 19.15; 22.47; Mk 14.44; **dederant** J 11.57; **datus est** A 20.9; **data est** Mt 28.18; Mk 6.2 **datum est** Mt 13.11*bis;* 14.11; 19.11; J 12.5; L 8.10; Mk 4.11; A 4.12; **dederit** Mk 9.41; A 17.25; **datum fuerit** J 3.27; 6.65; Mk 13.11; **det**

Mt 5.31; J 15.16; L 3.11; **daret** J 13.29; L 1.74; A 11.17; **darent** L 2.24; 20.10; Mk 12.2; A 19.31; **dedisset** J 4.10; **esset datum** [[J 19.11]]; **da** Mt [5.42]; 14.8; 17.27; 19.21; J 4.7, 10,15; 6.34; 9.24; L 6.30; 11.3; 12.58; 14.9; 15.12; 18.22; Mk 6.25; 10.21,37; A 4.29; **date** Mt 10.8; 14.16; 25.8,28; L 6.37; 9.13; 11.41; 12.33; 15.22; Mk 6.37; A 8.19; **dare** Mt 14.7; 19.7; 20.14,23,28; 22.17; 24.45; 26.15; J 6.52; L 1.77; 11.7,13; 12.32,42; 20.22; 22.5; 23.2; Mk 10.4,40,45; 12.14; 14.11; A 5.31; 7.5,38; **dari** Mt 14.9; 26.9; L 8.55; Mk 5.43; 14.5; **dans** (*m.*) Mt 26.26; J 6.33; Mk 6.7; A 3.8; 14.3,17; **datum** (*neu.ac.*) L 11.13; **data** Mk 13.34; **dato** A 16.23; **data** (*ac.*) L 11.13; **dabite** L 11.8.

docenta, *s.v.* **ducenti.**

doceo doces Mt 22.16; J 9.34; L 20.21*bis;* Mk 12.14; **docet** A 21.28; **docebat** Mt 13.54; J 7.14; L 4.15; 5.3,27; Mk 1.21; 2.13; 4.2; 9.31; 10.1; 11.17; A 18.25; **docebant** A 5.21; 15.1; **docebit** J 14.26; L 12.12; **docui** [[J 18.20]]; **docuisti** L 13.26; **docuit** Mt 5.2; J 8.28; L 11.1; **docuerant** Mk 6.30; **docti erant** Mt 28.15; **docuerit** Mt 5.19; **docerem** A 20.20; **docerent** A 4.2,18; **doce** L 11.1; **docete** Mt 28.19; **docere** Mt 11.1; J 7.35; Mk 4.1; 6.2,34; 8.31; A 1.1; 5.28; **docens** (*m.*) Mt 4.23; 9.35; 26.55; J 6.59; 7.28; 8.20; L 4.31; 13.10,22; 19.47; 21.37; 23.5; Mk 1.22; 6.6; 12.35,38; 14.49; A 11.2; 18.11; 21.21; **docentem** (*m.*) Mt 21.23; **docente** (*m.*) L 5.17; 20.1; **docentes** (*m.n.*) Mt 15.9; 28.20; Mk 7.7; A 5.25,42; 15.35; **docentes** (*m.ac.*) A 14.19; **doctus** Mt 13.52; A 18.25; **docta** (*ab.*) Mt 14.8.

dociuilis dociuiles (*m.n.*) J 6.45.

doctor Mt 23.8,10; L 10.25; A 5.34; **doctores** L 7.30; 11.53; A 13.1; **doctoribus** L 11.46,52; **doctores** Mt 23.10; L 5.17; 14.3; **doctoribus** L 11.45.

doctrina J 7.16; Mk 1.27; **doctrinae** (*g.*) A 17.4,19; **doctrinam** Mk 1.22; **doctrina** Mt 16.12; 22.33; J 7.17; [[18.19]]; L 4.32; Mk 4.2; 6.2; 11.18; A 2.42; 5.28; 13.12; **doctrinas** Mt 15.9; Mk 7.7; **doctrinis** A 14.7.

doleo dolentes (*m.n.*) L 2.48.

dolor dolore A 4.2; **dolorum** Mt 24.8; Mk 13.8.

dolosus dolose (*adv.*) A 5.4.

dolus Mk 7.22; **dolus** (*g.*) A 13.10; **dolo** (*ab.*) Mt 26.4; L 20.20; Mk 14.1.

domesticus domestici (*n.*) Mt 10.36; **domesticos** Mt 10.25.

domicilium domicilium (*ac.*) Mk 5.3; **domicilia** (*ac.*) A 5.18.

dominor dominantur Mt 20.25; L 22.25; Mk 10.42; **dominatus** A 19.16.

dominus Mt 10.25; 12.8; 18.25,27,32,34; 20.8; 21.3,40; 22.44; 24.42,45,46,48,50; 25.19, 21,23,26; 28.6; J 13.13,14; 15.15; 20.28; 21.7 *bis*,12,16; L 1.25,28,32,48,58,68; 2.15; 6.5; 11.39; 12.37,42*bis*,43,45,46; 13.15; 14.23; 16.3,8; 18.6; 19.31,34; 20.13,15,42; 22.31; 24.34; Mk 2.28; 3.23; 5.13; 12.9,29*bis*,36; 13.20,35; [[16.19]]; A 1.21; 2.17,34,39,47; 3.22; 7.7,31,49; 10.36; 12.11,17; 13.47; 14.2; 15.17; 16.10,14,40; 17.24; 18.9; **domini** Mt 1.20,24; 2.13,19; [[3.3]]; 21.9; 25.18,21,23; 28.2; J 12.13, 38; L 1.6,9,11,15,38,43,66,76; 2.9,23,24,26,39; 3.2,4,6; 4.18,19; 10.39; 11.28; 12.47; 13.35; 16.5; 19.38; 22.61; Mk 1.3; 11.9; 12.14; A 2.20,21,38; 3.19; 4.33; 5.9,19; 6.7,8; 7.30; 8.16; 10.48; 11.16,21; 12.7,23; 13.10,11,12,44, 46,48,49; 14.10; 15.11,26,35,36,40; 16.32; 18.4,8,25; 19.5,10,13,17,23; 20.28; 21.13,14; **domino** Mt 5.33; 18.31; 22.44; L 1.17; 2.22, 23; 14.21; 16.5; 17.5; 20.42; 22.49; Mk 11.3; 12.36; 14.14; A 2.34; 5.14; 13.2; 15.18; 16.15; 20.19; **dominum** Mt 4.7,10; 9.38; 10.24; 22.37, 43,45; J 11.2; 20.2,13,17*bis*,18,20,25; L 1.16, 46; 4.8,12; 10.2,27; 12.36; 19.8; 20.37,44; 23.40,42; Mk 12.30,37; A 2.25,36; 4.26; 5.42; 7.55; 11.17*bis*,20,21,23,24; 13.32; 16.4; 18.5; 20.21; 21.20; **domino** Mt 1.22; 2.15,17; 21.42; J 13.16; 15.20; L 1.45; Mk 12.11; [[16.20]]; A 2.22; 13.44; 14.3; 16.31,34; 18.8; 20.24; **domine** Mt 9.28; 11.25; 13.27; 14.28,30; 15.22,25,27; 16.22; 17.4,15; 18.21; 20.31,33; 21.30; 25.11*bis*,20,22,24,37,44; 26.22; 27.63; J 4.11,15,19,49; 5.7; 6.34,68; 8.11; 9.36,38; 11.3,12,21,27,32,34,39; 12.21,38; 13.6,8,9,25, 36,37; 14.5,8,22; 20.15,16; 21.15,16,17,20,21; L 2.29; 5.8,12; 6.46*bis;* 7.6; 8.24*bis;* 9.54,61; 10.17,21,40; 11.1; 12.41; 13.8,23,25*bis*,26; 17.37; 18.41; 19.8,16,18,20; 22.33,38; Mk 7.28; 9.22; 10.51; A 1.6,24; 4.24,29; 7.59,60; 10.4,14; 11.8; 22.19; **domini** A 16.19; **dominorum** Mt 15.27; **dominis** L 16.13; A 16.16; **domini** A 16.30.

domo domare Mk 5.4.

domus Mt 10.13; 12.25; 21.13*bis;* 23.38; J 4.53; 12.3; L 11.17; 13.35; 14.23; 19.46*bis;* Mk 3.25*bis;* 11.17*bis;* 13.35; A 2.36; 10.6; 11.14; 16.15,31; 18.7; **domus** (*g.*) Mt 10.6; 15.24; L 6.49; 22.11; Mk 14.14; **domui** Mt 10.12; L 6.48; 10.5; 15.25; A 7.46; **domum** Mt 2.11; 9.6,7,23,28; 10.12; 12.4,29*bis*,44*bis;* 13.36; 17.25; 19.29; 24.43; J 7.53; 8.35; L

1.23,33,40,56; 4.38; 5.24,25; 6.4,48,49; 7.10, 36,44; 8.39,41,51; 9.4,61; 10.5,7,38; 11.17,24; 14.1; 15.6,8; 16.27; 22.10,12,54; Mk 1.29; 2.9, 11,26; 3.20,27*bis;* 5.19,38; 7.17,24,30; 8.26 *bis;* 9.28; 10.10,30; 13.15,34; 14.3; A 2.2; 7.10, 47,49; 10.17,22,32; 11.11,12; 12.12; 16.15,32, 34; 17.5; 18.7; **domo** Mt 5.15; 9.10; 13.57; 24.17; 26.6; J 11.20,31; 14.2; L 1.27,69; 2.5; 5.29; 7.6,37; 8.27; 10.7*bis;* 12.52; 17.31; 19.5, 9; Mk 2.1,15; 6.4; 8.3; 13.15; A 7.20; 10.30; 11.13; 18.8; 19.16; **domu** A 16.34; **domi** (*loc.*) Mk 9.33; A 5.42; **domus** (*voc.*) A 7.42; **domum** (*g.*) A 4.34; **domos** L 18.29; 20.47; Mk 12.40; A 2.46; 8.3; 20.20; **domus** L 16.4; **domibus** Mt 11.8.

donec (*c.ind.*) Mt 2.9; 24.39; A 7.18; 21.26; **donec** (*c.coni.*) Mt 5.18*bis*,26; 10.11,23; 12.20; 13.33; 14.22; 16.28; 17.9; 18.30,34; [22.44]; 23.39; 24.34; L 13.35; Mk 6.10; 9.1; 12.36; 13.30; 14.32; A 2.35; **ponec** (Mt 22.44).

dono **donauit** Mk 15.45; L 7.42,43; **donari** A 3.14.

donum Mt 23.19; A 10.45; **donum** (*ac.*) Mt 23.19; J 4.10; Mk 7.11; A 11.17; **dono** Mt 23.18.

dormio **dormis** Mk 14.37; **dormit** Mt 9.24; J 11.12; L 8.52; Mk 5.39; **dormitis** L 22.46; **dormiebant** Mt 25.5; **dormibit** (*perf.*) A 7.60; **dormiuit** J 11.11; A 13.36; **dormirent** Mt 13.25; **dormite** Mt 26.45; Mk 14.41; **dormiens** (*m.*) Mk 4.38; A 12.6; **dormientium** (*m.*) Mt 27.52; **dormientes** (*m.*) Mt 26.40,43; L 22.45; Mk 13.36; 14.37,40; **dormientibus** (*m.*) Mt 28.13.

dormitio **dormitione** J 11.13.

dormito **dormitauerunt** Mt 25.5.

douerius A 20.4.

drachma **drachmam** L 15.9; **drachmas** L 15.8.

dubito **dubitant** A 10.20; **dubitasti** Mt 14.31; **dubitauerunt** Mt 28.17.

ducatus **ducatus** (*g.*) L 3.1; **docatum** L 2.2; 22.26.

ducenti **ducentorum** (*m.*) J 6.7; **docenta** A 19.19; **ducentis** (*m.*) Mk 6.37; **ducentis** (*neu.*) J 21.8.

duco **ducit** Mk 9.2; A12.10; **ducebant** A 17.15; **ducebatur** L 4.1; [8.29]; **ducebantur** L (8.29); 23.32; **ducent** J 21.18; **ducentur** L 21.12,24; **duxi** L 14.20; **duxerunt** Mt 26.57; 27.2,31; L 23.26; Mk 15.1,16,20; **ductus est** L 16.22; **duxerit** Mt 19.9; Mk 10.11,12; **ducat** Mt 15.14; **duxisset** Mk 6.17; A 5.19; **ducere** L 6.39; **ducite** Mk 14.44; **ducens** (*m.*) L 13.15; **ductus** Mt 21.29; 27.3.

dum (*c.ind.*) Mt 12.34; 13.4; J 5.7; L 12.58; 19.13; Mk 4.4,27; A 10.17; **dum** (*c.coni.*) Mt 27.12; L 1.8; 5.1,12; 12.50; 24.4; Mk 6.45; A 11.15; 13.25.

duo Mt 8.28; 9.27,28; 10.29; 18.8,19,20; 19.5,6; 20.21,30; 24.40,41; 26.61; 27.38; J 11.6; 21.2; L 7.41; 9.13,30; 12.52; 17.34,35,36; 18.10; 23.32; 24.4,13; Mk 10.8*bis;* A 1.10; **duae** Mt 24.41; L 23.55; **duo** Mt 5.41; **duorum** (*m.*) Mt 18.16; **duum** (*m.*) J 8.17; **duobus** (*m.*) L 16.13; [[Mk 16.12]]; **duos** Mt 4.18, 21; 14.17,19; 18.9,16; 21.2; 26.37; J 6.9; [[19.18]]; 20.12; L 2.24; 7.19; 9.16,32; 10.35; 15.11; 19.29; Mk 6.38,41; 9.47; 11.1; 14.13; A 1.23; 7.29; 12.6; 19.10,22; **duo** (*m.*) Mk 9.45; 15.27; **duas** Mt 10.10; 18.8; 27.51; L 3.11; 5.2; 9.3; Mk 6.9; 9.43; 15.38; **duo** Mt 25.15,17*bis*,22*ter;* L 21.2; Mk 5.13; 12.42; **duobus** Mt 20.24; 21.31; 27.21; L 12.6,52; Mk 6.41; A 1.24; 10.7; **duabus** A 12 6; 19.34; 21.33; **duobus** Mt 22.40; **duo** (*fem.*) L 22.38.

duodecim Mt 9.20; 10.1,2,5; 11.1; 14.20; 19.28*bis;* 20.17; 26.14,20,47,53; J 6.13,67,70, 71; 11.9; 20.24; L 2.42; 6.13; 8.1,42,43; 9.1,12, 17; 18.31; 22.3,30*bis*,47; Mk 3.14; 5.25,42; 6.7,43; 8.19; 9.35; 10.32; 11.11; 14.10,17,20,43; A 1.26; 6.2; 7.8; 19.7.

duplus **duplum** (*m.*) Mt 23.15.

duritia **duritiam** Mk 10.5; [[16.14]].

durus Mt 25.24; J 6.60; **durum** (*neu.ac.*) Mt 19.8; **durae** (*voc.*) A 7.51.

dux Mt 2.6; A 1.16; **ducem** A 5.31; **duces** Mt 15.14; **duces** (*ac.*) L 21.12; **duces** (*voc.*) Mt 23.16,24.

e, *praep.*, *s.v.* **ex.**

Eber L 3.35.

Ebraeice, Ebraice, *s.v.* **Hebraice.**

ebrietas **ebrietate** L 21.34.

ebriosus **ebriosis** (*m.ab.*) Mt 24.49.

Ebrius **Hebrii** (*pl.*) A 2.15.

ecce Mt 1.20,23; 2.1,9,13,19; 3.16,17; 4.11; 8.29,32,34; 9.2,3,10,18,20,32; 10.16; 11.8,10, 19; 12.2,10,18,41,42,46,47,49; 13.3; 15.22; 17.3,5*bis;* 19.16,27; 20.18,30; 21.5; 22.4; 23.34,38; 24.23,25,26*bis;* 25.6,20,22,25; 26.45, 46,47,51,65; 27.51; 28.2,7,9,11,20; J 3.26; 4.35; 5.14; 7.26; 11.3,36; 12.15,19; 16.29,32; [[18.21; 19.4,5,14,26,27]]; L 1.20,31,36,38,44, 48; 2.9,10,34,48; 5.12,18; 6.2,42; 7.25,27,34, 37; 9.30,38; 10.3,19; 11.31,41; 13.7,11,16,30, 32,35; 15.29; 17.21*bis*,23*bis;* 18.28,31; 19.2,8, 20; 22.10,21,31,38,47; 23.50; 24.4; Mk 1.2;

18.21; 19.21; 22.1,13,17; me (*ab.*) Mt 3.11; 10.32,37,38; 11.6,29; 15.5,8; 17.27; 25.41; 26.31,39; J 4.9; 5.30,31,32*bis*,36,37,39; 6.56 *bis;* 7.17,28; 8.14,18*bis*,28,42; 10.18,25,38; 12.49; 13.38; 14.10*ter*,11,20,29,30; 15.2,4,5*bis*, 6,7,27; 16.33; 17.21,23; ⟦18.34⟧; L 3.16; 5.8; 7.23; 8.46; 12.8; 13.27; 22.37,42; 24.44; Mk 1.7; 6.22; 7.6,11; 9.39; 14.6,36; A 13.33; 22.17; **mecum** Mt 12.30*bis;* 20.13; 26.23,38,40; J 8.29; 13.8,18; 15.27; 16.32; 17.24; L 11.7,23 *bis;* 12.13; 15.31; 22.28; 23.43; Mk 9.1; 14.18, 20; A 11.12; 22.11; **nos** Mt 9.14; 17.19; 19.27; 28.14; J 4.22; 6.42,69; 8.41,48; 9.21,24,28,29, 40; 11.16; 12.34; 17.11,22; ⟦19.7⟧; 21.3; L 9.13; 11.4; 18.28; 23.40,41; 24.21; Mk 9.28; 10.28; 14.58; III J 12; A 2.8,32; 3.12,15; 4.9, 20; 5.32; 6.4; 10.33,39,47; 13.32; 14.15; 15.10; 20.6,13; 21.7,12,25; **nostri** Mt 9.27; 20.30,31; **nostrorum** A 17.27; **nobis** Mt 3.15; 8.29; 13.36; 14.22; 15.15,33; 19.27; 20.12; 21.25; 24.3; 25.8,9,11; 26.63; J 4.12,25; 6.34,52; 10.24; 14.8*bis*,9,12; 16.17; ⟦18.31⟧; L 1.2,69,74; 2.15, 48; 4.34; 7.5; 9.13,33; 10.11,17; 11.3,4,45; 13.25; 17.5,13; 20.2,22,28; 22.8; 23.18; 24.32 *bis;* Mk 1.24; 9.22; 10.35,37; 11.31; 12.14*bis*, 19; 13.4; 14.15; 16.3; A 2.37,39; 6.2,14; 7.38, 40; 10.41,42; 11.13,17; 13.26,47; 15.8,25,28; 16.9,10,16,21; 19.25,27; 21.23; **nos** Mt 8.31 *bis;* 13.56; 15.23; 17.4; 20.7; 22.25; 27.4,25; J 9.4,34; L 1.71,78; 4.34; 7.20; 11.1*bis*,2,4*bis;* 12.41; 16.26; 19.14; 20.6,29; 21.34; 23.30*bis;* 24.22; Mk 1.24; 5.12; 9.5,22; 12.20; A 1.17, 21; 2.29; 3.4,12; 5.28; 7.4,27,35,40*bis;* 10.33; 11.15; 14.11,22; 15.9; 16.10,17,37*ter*,39; 20.5, 14; 21.5,11,13,15,16,17; **nobis** [Mt 28.13]; L 1.1; 7.16; A 1.22; 2.22; 11.27; 13.26; 15.7, 24; 16.16; 20.7; **nobiscum** Mt 1.23; L 9.49; 24.24,29; Mk 6.3; 9.38; A 1.21,22; 21.16,18; **nouis** (Mt 28.13); J 17.21; **nobis** (*inc.*) A 16.15; **m-** L 22.37.

egredior **egreditur** Mt 15.11; **egrediebatur** Mk 1.5; **egrediebantur** L 3.7; Mk 11.19; **egressi sunt** Mk 5.14; **egressus esset** Mk 10.17; **egredientibus** (*m.ab.*) Mt 20.29; Mk 6.54; **egressus** Mt 14.14; 18.28; 20.3; Mk 1.45; 6.1; A 12.17; **egressi** (*n.*) Mt 12.14.

egrotus (*aeg-*) **egrotos** ⟦Mk 16.18⟧.

eicio Mt 12.27,28; L 11.19,20; 13.32; **eicis** Mt 8.31; **eicit** Mt 12.26,35; J 10.3; L 11.15; Mk 3.22,26; **eiciunt** Mt 12.27; A 16.37; **eiciebat** Mk 1.34*bis;* **eiciebant** Mk 6.13; **eicient** J 16.2; L 6.22; 11.19; ⟦Mk 16.17⟧; **eiecit** Mt 12.24; 21.12; 26.51; Mk 1.12; **eiecerunt** Mt 21.39; J 9.34,35; L 4.29; Mk 12.8; A 13.50; **eiecerat** ⟦Mk 16.9⟧; **eiecerit** J 10.4; **eiecta est** Mt 9.25; **eiciam** L 6.42; **eiciat** Mt 9.38; 12.20; **eiciant** Mt 10.1; **eiciatur** J 9.22; **eiciantur** J 12.42; **eiceret** Mk 7.26; **eicerent** Mk 9.18; **eice** L 6.42; **eicite** L 19.27; **eiecite** Mt 10.8; **eicere** L 6.42; 11.15,18; 19.45; Mk 3.23; 9.18,28; 11.15; **eici** L 13.28; **eiciens** (*m.*) L 10.35; Mk 1.39; 5.40; 14.47; **eicientem** (*m.*) L 9.49; Mk 9.38; **eiectum** (*m.*) A 7.58; **eiecto** (*neu.*) Mt 9.33; L 11.14; **eiciendi** Mk 3.15.

Eleazer Mt 1.15; L 3.23.

elebauit, *s.v.* **eleuo.**

elego **elegit** (*perf.*) L 10.42; **electus** L 23.35.

elemosyna Mt 6.4; **elemosynam** Mt 6.2,3; L 12.33; A 3.2,3,10; **aelemosynae** A 10.4,31.

eleuo **elebauit** L 1.69; Mk 1.31; **eleuabit** Mk 9.27; **elebabit** A 2.14; **eleuate** J 4.35; **eleuans** (*m.*) L 6.20; **eleuans** L 11.27; **eleuatis** (*m.ab.*) J 6.5.

Eliacim L 3.23*bis*.

elido **elisus** Mk 9.20.

Eliecib Mt 1.13.

eligo **eligebant** L 14.7; **elegi** Mt 12.18; J 6.70; 13.18; 15.16,19; **elegisti** A 1.24; **elegit** Mk 13.20; A 1.2; 13.17; 15.7; **elegistis** J 15.16; **elegerunt** A 6.5; **eligans** (*m.*) A 7.20; **eligens** (*m.*) L 6.13; **electi** (*n.*) Mt 20.16; 22.14; **electorum** (*m.*) L 18.7; **electos** Mt 24.22,24,31; Mk 13.20*bis*,22,27; A 15.22,25.

elingebant, *v.* **lingo.**

Elisabed L 1.7,13,24; **Elisabet** L 1.5,36,40, 41*ter*,57.

Eliseus, Eliseo (*ab.*) L 4.27.

Eliud L 3.23.

Ellada, *v.* **Hellas.**

eloquium **eloquia** (*ac.*) A 7.38.

eloquor **eloquebatur** A 18.25; **eloqui** A 2.4.

emendo **emenda** L 17.3; **emendans** (*m.*) L 23.16,22.

emineo **eminentibus** (*m.ab.*) Mt 20.28.

emitto **emittit** Mt 13.52.

Emmor A 7.16.

emo **emit** Mt 13.44,46; **emebant** L 17.28; **emet** L 22.36; **ememus** J 6.5; **emi** L 14.18,19; **emerunt** Mt 27.7; Mk 16.1; **emamus** L 9.13; **emant** Mt 14.15; Mk 6.36; **emerent** J 4.8; **eme** J 13.29; **emite** Mt 25.9; **emere** Mt 25.10; **ementes** (*m.ac.*) Mt 21.12; L 19.45; Mk 11.15.

emorior **emortua** (*ab.*) Mk 3.5.

emundatio **emundatione** Mk 1.44.

emundo **emundatis** (*neu.ab.*) A 15.9.

enarro **enarrauit** A 10.8; **enarrabit** A 16.10; **eterrabit** A 12.17.

enauigo **enauigauimus** A 20.6; 21.3; **enauigarunt** A 14.26; **enauigassemus** A 20.15.

encenia J 10.22.

enim Mt 1.18,20,21; 2.2,5,6,13,20; 3. [[2,3]], 9,15; 4.6,10,17*bis;* 5.12,13,18,19,21,29,46; 6.7; 9.5,13,16,21,24; 10.10,13,17,20,26,35; 11.13,18,30; 12.6,8,33,37,40,50; 13.12,15,17; 14.3,4,24; 15.2,4,19,27; 16.2,3,25,27; 17.15, 20; 18.7,10,11,20; 19.12,14,22; 20.1,16; 21.26, 32; 22.14,16,28,30; 23.3,4,5,8,9,17,19,39; 24.5, 6,7,21,24,27,37,38,45; 25.29,35,42; 26.9,10, 11,12,28,31,43,52; 27.18,19,23,43; 28.5,6; J 3.17,19,20,24,34*bis;* 4.8,18,37,42,44,45,47; 5.13,19,20,21,22,26,36,46*bis*,47; 6.27,33,40, 55,64,71; 7.1,4,5,39; 8.24,42*bis;* 9.22; 11.30, 31; 12.43,47; 13.10,11,13,29,35; 14.30; 15.5, 14; 16.7,13,27; [[18.13; 19.6,31,36]]; 20.9,17; 21.7,8; L 1.15,18,30,44,48,76; 2.10; 3.8; 4.10, 43; 5.9,10; 6.23,38,44,45,48; 7.5,6,33; 8.17, 18,29*quater*,30,36,37,40,42,46,52; 9.14,24,25, 26,39,44,50; 10.7,24; 11.2,10,30; 12.2,7,12,23, 30*bis*,34,58; 14.14,24; 16.2,13,28; 17.21,24, 25; 18.16,17,23; 19.10,21,26,48; 20.6,19,33,36 *bis*,38; 21.4,8,9,10,15,23,26; 22.16,18,37,47, 71; 23.8,15,22,41; Mk 1.22,38; 2.15; 3.10,21, 35; 4.22,25; 5.8; 6.14,17,18,20,31,48,52*bis*,55; 7.3,10,19,27; 8.35,36; 9.6*bis*,31,34,39,40,41, 49; 10.14,22; 11.13,18,32; 12.12,14,23,25,44; 13.6,7,8,11,19,22,33,35; 14.2,7,40,56; 15.10, 14; 16.3, [[8*bis*]]; III J 14; A 1.11,20; 2.15*bis*, 25,34*bis*,39; 4.3,20,27,34; 5.26,36; 6.2,14; 7.31,33,34,40; 8.1,7*bis*,16; 10.16,37,46; 12.9, 20; 13.8,27,33,36,39,47; 14.20,22; 15.21,28; 16.3,28; 17.15,20,23,28*bis;* 18.18,28; 19.24, 32,35,37; 20.10,13,16*bis*,27; 21.3,13,22,25,36.

enuntio **enuntiauit** A 11.2.

enutrio **enutrierunt** L 23.29.

eo Mt 21.30; J 11.11; 14.2,19; **ibat** L 7.6, 11; 19.28; 22.39; 24.15; Mk 5.24; A 3.11; **ibant** J 6.21; 12.11; L 2.3,41; 7.11; 14.25; 24.28; Mk 6.31; A 5.41; 17.10; **ibo** L 15.18; **ibit** L 11.5; **ibimus** J 6.68; **ibunt** Mt 25.46; **iit** Mt 21.29,30; **iero** J 16.7*bis;* **hieris** L 9.57; **eam** Mt 26.36; J 16.7; L 9.59; **eat** Mt 5.29; **eamus** Mt 26.46; J 11.7,15,16; 14.31; Mk 1.38; 6.31; 14.12,42; **eatis** J 15.16; **eant** Mt 28.10; **iret** A 11.22; **irent** L 17.14; **ierit** L 16.30,31; **ieritis** L 17.23; **ite** Mt 8.32; 10.6; 20.4,7; 21.2; 22.9; 25.9,41; [26.18]; 27.65; 28.10,19; L 10.3; 17.14; 19.30; Mk 6.38; 11.2; 14.13; [[16.7]]; A 5.20; **itte** (Mt 26.18); **ire** Mt [[2.22]]; 14.16; 16.21; J 6.67; 7.35*bis;* L 22.33; Mk 9.47; A 19.21; **iens** (*m.*) L 9.53; **euntem** (*m.*) A 1.11; **eunte** (*m.*) L 19.36; **euntes** (*m.n.*) Mt 2.8; 9.13; 10.7; 11.4; 13.28; 22.15; L 7.19,22; 9.12,13,52; 19.32; 22.8; Mk 6.36, 37; [[16.13,15]]; **euntes** (*f.n.*) Mt 14.15; 28.7; **euntibus** (*m.d.*) [[Mk 16.12]]; **euntibus** (*m.ab.*) L 7.24; 9.57; A 16.16; **euntibus** (*f.ab.*) Mt 28.11.

eo (*adv.*) Mk 7.37.

eo quod [[J 19.38]].

Ephesius **Ephesium** (*m.*) A 21.29; **Ephesi** A 18.27; **Ephesii** A 20.4; **Ephesiorum** (*m.*) A 19.28,34; **Ephesi** (*voc.*) A 19.35.

Ephesus **Ephesi** A 19.26; **Aephesum** A 18.26; **Ephesum** A 18.19,24; 19.1,17; 20.16, 17; **Epheso** A 18.21.

Epicurius **Epicuriorum** A 17.18.

episcopatus **episcopatum** A 1.20.

episcopus **episcopos** A 20.28.

epistula **epistulam** A 15.23,30; **epistulae** *col.* III J.

equalis **equales** (*m.n.*) L 20.36.

eradico **eradicetis** Mt 13.29; **eradicabitur** Mt 15.13.

Erastus **Erastum** A 19.22.

eremus **eremum** (*neu.ac.*) A 21.38; **eremo** (*neu.*) J 6.31.

ergo Mt 1.17; 3.8,10; 5.23,48; 6.2,8; 9.38; 10.16,26,31,32; 12.12,26,28; 13.18,27,40,56; (14.27); 15.33; 17.10,26; 18.4,29,31,33; 19.6, 7; 20.9; 21.40; 22.9,28,43,45; 23.3,20; 24.15, 26,42; 25.3,13,27,28; 26.54,63; 27.22,64; J 3.25,29; 4.1,5,9,28,40,45,46,48,52,53; 5.10,15; 6.3,5,10*bis*,11,14,21,24,28,30*bis*,32,34,35,41, 42,52,60,61,66; 7.3,6,11,15,23,25,28,30,33,35, 45; 8.12,19,21,22,24,25,28,31,36,38,39,41,42, 52,57,58; 9.7,8,10*bis*,11,12,15,16,17,19,24,25, 26,30*bis*,41; 10.7,19,20,31; 11.3,6,12,14,16,17, 20,21,33,36,38,41,45,47,54,55,56; 12.1,3,4,7,9, 17,21,29,34,35*bis*,44,50; 13.6,12,14,22,24,25, 30,31; 16.17,22; [[18.3,6,7,8,10,11,12,16,17,19, 25,27,28,29,31*bis*,33,37,39; 19.1,5,6,8,10,13, 16,20,21,23,24,26,29,30,31,32,38,40,42]]; 20.2, 3,6,8,10,11,17,19,21,25,26; 21.5,7*bis*,9,15,21, 23; L 3.8,9; 4.7; 5.7; 7.31,42; 8.18; 10.2,36,40; 11.13,35,48; 12.7,20,40; 13.14,18; 14.33; 16.11,27; 17.22; 18.26; 19.16,23; 20.5,15,17, 33; 21.14; 23.16,22; Mk 10.9; 12.9,14,20,23, 27; 13.23,33,35; 15.12; A 1.6,18,21; 2.32,33, 36,37,41; 3.19; 4.17; 5.39; 6.3; 10.23,29,32,33 *bis;* 11.2; 13.38,40; 14.3; 15.2,10,27; 16.5,10, 36; 17.12,17,20,23,29; 19.3,38; 21.22,23.

erigo **erigam** A 15.16; **erexit** J 8.7; **erecta**

est L 13.13; **erigite** L 21.28; 23.11; **erigere** L 13.11; **erigens** (*m.*) J 8.10.

eripio **eripuit** A 7.10; 12.11; **eripere** A 7.34.

Erodes, *v.* **Herodes.**

erogatio **erogationem** L 14.28.

erogo **erogauerat** Mk 5.26; **erogasset** L 15.14; **eroga** A 21.24.

erro **erratis** Mt 22.29; Mk 12.24,27; **errauit** Mt 18.12; **errauerunt** Mt 18.13; **erretis** L 21.8; **errauerit** Mt 18.12.

error Mt 27.64; **errores** (*n.*) Mk 4.19.

eructo **eructabor** [Mt 13.35]; **eructuauor** (Mt 13.35).

erudio **eruditus est** A 7.22.

eruo **erue** Mt 5.29; 18.9.

Esaias (**Eseias**) Mt 15.7; J 12.41; L 4.17; Mk 7.6; **Eseias** J 12.39; **Esaiae** (*g.*) Mt 13.14; J 12.38; L 3.4; **Esaiam** Mt 1.22; ⟦3.3⟧; 4.14; 12.17; Mk 1.2.

esca ⟦Mt 3.4⟧; J 4.34; 6.55; **escam** J 4.32; 6.27*bis;* **esca** Mt 10.10; L 12.23; **escas** Mt 14.15; J 4.8; L 3.11; 9.13; Mk 7.19.

espondens, *s.v.* **respondeo.**

espuo **espuent** L 18.32.

essed, *s.v.* **sum.**

esuffocarent, *v.* **suffoco.**

esurio **esuriunt** L 6.21; **esuriet** J 6.35; **esurietis** L 6.25; **esurii** Mt 25.42; **esuriui** Mt 25.35; **esuriit** Mt 4.2; 12.3; 21.18; L 4.2; 6.3; Mk 2.25; 11.12; **esurierunt** Mt 12.1; **esuriens** (*m.*) A 10.10; **esurientem** (*m.*) Mt 25.37,44; **esurientes** (*m.n.*) Mt 5.6; **esurientes** (*m.ac.*) L 1.53.

et Mt 1.17*bis*,19,21,23*bis*,24,25*bis;* 2.2,3,4*bis*,6,8*bis*,9*bis*,11*quinquiens*.12,13*ter*,14*bis*,15,16*ter*,18*ter*,20*bis*, ⟦21*bis*,22,23; 3.2,4*bis*,5*bis*,6,7,⟧9,10,11,12*bis*,14,16*quater*,17; 4.2*bis*,3*bis*,5,6*bis*,8*bis*,9,10,11*bis*,13*bis*,15,17,18,19*bis*,21*ter*,22,23*quater*,24*septies*,25*quinquiens*; 5.1,2,6,11*bis*,12,13,15,16,18,19,23,24*bis*,25*bis*,29*bis*,39,40*bis*,41,42,43,44*bis*,45*ter*,46,47*bis;* 6.2,4,5*ter*,6*bis;* 8.27*bis*,28,29*bis*,32*ter*,33,34*bis;* 9.1*bis*,2,3,4,5,6*bis*,7,8,9*ter*,10*ter*,11,13,14,15*bis*,16,17*ter*,18,19*bis*,20,22*bis*,23*ter*,24,25,26,27*bis*,28*ter*,29,30*bis*,33*bis*,35*quinquiens*,36; 10.1*ter*,2*ter*,3*ter*,4*ter*,5*bis*,11,14,15,16,17,18*bis*,21*ter*,22,25,26,27,28*ter*,29,30,32,33,35*bis*,36,38*bis*,40,42; 11.1*bis*,4,5*ter*,6,9,12,13,14,17*bis*,18,19*quinquiens*,21*ter*,22,23,25*ter*,27*bis*,28,29*bis*,30; 12.1*bis*,3,4,5,7,9,10*bis*,11*bis*,13*bis*,14,15*bis*,18,20,21,22*quater*,23,25,29*bis*,30,31,32,33*bis*,35,37,38,39*bis*,40*ter*,41*bis*,42*bis*,43,44*bis*,45*quater*,46,47,49*bis*,50*bis*; 13.1,2*bis*,3,4*ter*,5,6,7*bis*,8,10,12*bis*,13*bis*,14*quinquiens*,15*sexiens*,16,17*quater*,19*bis*,20,22*ter*,23*bis*,25*bis*,26,29,30*bis*,32*bis*,34,36,40,41*bis*,42*bis*,44*ter*,46*ter*,47,48,49,50*bis*,52,53,54*ter*,55*quater*,56,57*bis*,58; 14.2*bis*,5,6,9*bis*,10,11*ter*,12*ter*,13,14*ter*,15,17,19*ter*,20*ter*,21,22*bis*,23,24,26,29,30,31,32,34,35*bis*,36*bis;* 15.1,3, [4],4,6,10,11,16,17,21*bis*,22,23,26,27,28,29*bis*,30*quater*,31*ter*,32*ter*,33,34*bis*,35,36*ter*,37*ter*,38,39*bis*; 16.1*bis*,3,4*bis*,5,6*bis*,9,10,11,12,17,18*ter*,19*bis*,21*quinquiens*,22*bis*,24*bis*,27; 17.1*quater*,2,3*bis*,4*bis*,5,6,7*quater*,9,10,12,13,14*bis*,15,16*bis*,17,18*ter*,20*bis*,21,23*ter*,24*bis*,25*bis*,27*ter;* 18.2,3*bis*,5,6,8,9*bis*,12*bis*,13,15,17*bis*,[18],21,25*quater*,26,27,28,29,30,31,33*bis*,34,35; 19.1*bis*,2*bis*,3*bis*,4,5*quater*,7,9,12*bis*,13,14,15,16,19*bis*,21*ter*,25,27,28,29*bis*,30; 20.3,4*ter*,5,6*bis*,7,8,10,12*bis*,14*bis*,16,17*bis*,18*ter*,19*quater*,20,21,23,24,25,27,28*septiens*,29,30*bis*,32*bis*,34*ter;* 21.1,2*bis*,3*bis*,5,7*quater*,8,9,10,12*quinquiens*,13,14*ter*,15*ter*,16*bis*,17*bis*,19*quater*,20,21*ter*,22,23*ter*,24*bis*,27*bis*,28,30,31,32*bis*,33*quinquiens*,35,36,38,39*bis*,41,42,43,45*bis*,46; 22.1,3*bis*,4*bis*,6,7*bis*,9,10*ter*,12,13*ter*,16*ter*,20,21,22*bis*,24*bis*,25*bis*,26*bis*,27,32*bis*,33,35*bis*,37*bis*,38,40,46; 23.1,2,3*bis*,4*bis*,5,6,7*bis*,9,12,13,15*ter*,17,18,20,21*bis*,22*bis*,23*septiens*,25*ter*,26,27*bis*,28*bis*,29*bis*,30,32,34*quinquiens*,35,37*bis;* 24.1*bis*,3*bis*,4,5,6,7*ter*,9*bis*,10*ter*,11*bis*,12,14*bis*,18,19,22,23,24*quater*,27,29*ter*,30*quater*,31*quater*,32,33,35,36,38*bis*,39*bis*,40,41*bis*,43,44,45,49*bis*,50,51*ter;* 25.1*bis*,2,5,7,9*bis*,10*bis*,14,15*bis*,16,17*bis*,18,19,20,21,22,23,24,25*bis*,26*bis*,27,28,29*bis*,30*bis*,31,32*bis*,33,35*ter*,36*ter*,37*bis*,38*bis*,39,40,41*bis*,42*bis*,43*quater*,44*bis*,46; 26.1,2,3,4*bis*,7,9,13,18,19*bis*,21,22,26*bis*,27*bis*,30,31,35,36,37*ter*,38,39*bis*,40*ter*,41,43,44*bis*,45*ter*,49*bis*,50,51*ter*,53,55*bis*,57,58,59,60*ter*,61*bis*,62,64; 27.2*bis*,3,5*bis*,9,10,11,12*bis*,14,20,25*bis*,28*bis*,29*ter*,30*bis*,31*bis*,[31],33,34*bis*,36,37,38,40*ter*,41*bis*,42,44,48*ter*,49,51*ter*,52*bis*,53*bis*,54*bis*,55,56*ter*,57,58,59,60*bis*,61,62,64*bis;* 28.1,2*bis*,3,4,7*bis*,8*bis*,9*bis*,10,12,14*bis*,15,17,18*bis*,19*bis*,20; J 3.19,20,22*ter*,23*ter*,26*ter*,27,29,31,32*bis*,35; 4.1,2,3,10*ter*,11,12*ter*,13,16,17,18,20,23*bis*,24*bis*,27*bis*,28*bis*,30*bis*,34,35*bis*,36*ter*,37,38,40,41,42,45,47*bis*,48,50,51,52,53*bis;* 5.1,3,5,6,8*bis*,9*ter*,10,11,12,14,15,16,17,18,19*bis*,20*bis*,21*bis*,24*bis*,25*bis*,26,27,29,30,32,33,35,37,38,39,40,43,44,46; 6.3,5,9,11*ter*,13,15*bis*,17*bis*,19*bis*,21,22,24,25,26*ter*,29,30,33,35,36*bis*,37,40*bis*,42*bis*,43,44,45*bis*,49,50,51,53,54*bis*,56*ter*,57*ter*,58,60,64,65,66,67,69*bis*,70*bis;* 7.3*bis*,4,10,11,12,14,16,18,19,20,21*bis*,22,26*bis*,28*quater*,29,30,31,32*bis*,33,34*bis*,35,36*bis*,37*bis*,42,45*bis*,47,51,52*ter*,53; 8.2,3,4,7,8,9*bis*,11,14*ter*,

[5] Order of verses in MS.

34,35*bis*,37,38,39*ter*,41,42,43,44*ter*,46*bis*,47*bis*,48,49,51,52,53; Mk 1.4,5*ter*,6*ter*,7,9*bis*,10*bis*,11,12,13*quater*,15*bis*,16*bis*,17*bis*,18,19*ter*,20*bis*,21*bis*,22,23*bis*,24,25*bis*,26*bis*,27*quater*,28,29*bis*,30,31*ter*,32,33,34*quinquiens*,35,36*bis*,37,38*ter*,39*bis*,40*bis*,41*ter*,42*bis*,43,44*bis*,45*bis*; 2.1*bis*,2*bis*,3,4*bis*,6,9*bis*,11*bis*,12*quater*,13*ter*,14*ter*,15*ter*,16*sexiens*,17,18*quinquiens*,19,20,21,22*ter*,23*bis*,25*ter*,26*bis*,28; 3.1*bis*,2,3*bis*,4,5*ter*,7*bis*,8*quinquiens*,9,11*bis*,12,13*ter*,14*bis*,15*bis*,16,17*ter*,18*octiens*,19*bis*,20*bis*,21*bis*,22*bis*,23,24,25,26,27,28,31*ter*,32*quater*,33,34*bis*,35*bis*; 4.1*ter*,2*bis*,4*ter*,5*ter*,6*bis*,7*quater*,8*sexiens*,9*bis*,10,11,12*quater*,13*bis*,15*bis*,16,17*bis*,18,19*ter*,20*quinquiens*,21*ter*,24,25*bis*,26,27*quinquiens*,29,30,32*bis*,33,35,36*ter*,37*bis*,38*bis*,39*quinquiens*,40,41*quater*; 5.1,2,3,4*bis*,5*ter*,6,7*bis*,9*bis*,10,12,13*quater*,14*ter*,15*quater*,16,17,18,19*ter*,20*ter*,21,22*bis*,23*bis*,24*ter*,25,26,27,29*bis*,30*bis*,31,32,33*ter*,34,37*ter*,38*ter*,39*bis*,40*ter*,41,42*ter*,43*bis*; 6.1*bis*,2*quater*,3*sexiens*,4*ter*,5,6*ter*,7,8,9,10,11,12,13*bis*,14*ter*,17*bis*,19*bis*,20*quater*,21*ter*,22*ter*,23,24,26*bis*,28*quater*,29*bis*,30*ter*,31*quater*,32,33*quater*,34*ter*,35*bis*,36*bis*,37*ter*,38*ter*,39,40*bis*,41*quinquiens*,42*bis*,43*bis*,44,45,46,47*bis*,48*quater*,49,50*bis*,51*quater*,53,54,56*ter*; 7.1*bis*,2,3,4*quinquiens*,5*bis*,6,8*bis*,9,10*bis*,13,14*bis*,17,18*bis*,19,23,24*ter*,25,26,27*bis*,28,29,30*bis*,31,32*ter*,33*bis*,34*bis*,35*ter*,36,37*ter*; 8.1,2,3,4,5,6*quinquiens*,7*ter*,8*ter*,10*ter*,11*bis*,12,13,14,15*bis*,16,19,21,22*ter*,23*ter*,24,25*ter*,26*ter*,27*ter*,30,31*quinquiens*,32,34*ter*,36,38*ter*; 9.1,2*quinquiens*,3,4*bis*,5*ter*,7*bis*,8,9,10,11,12*bis*,13*bis*,14*bis*,15*bis*,16,17,18*sexiens*,19,20*ter*,21,22*bis*,24,25*ter*,26*ter*,27,28,29*bis*,30,31*ter*,32,33,35,36,37,38,39,42,43,44,45,46,48,50; 10.1*ter*,2,4,5,6,7*ter*,8,10,11,12*bis*,13,14*bis*,16*bis*,17*bis*,19,21*quater*,22,23,24,26,28*bis*,30*quinquiens*,31,32*ter*,33*quater*,34*ter*,35*ter*,37*bis*,38,39,41*bis*,42*bis*,44,45*bis*,46*ter*,47*bis*,48,49,51,52*bis*; 11.1*bis*,2*ter*,3*bis*,4*bis*,5,6,7*ter*,8,9*bis*,10,11*bis*,12,13*bis*,14,15*quinquiens*,16,17,18*bis*,19,20,21,22,23*bis*,24*bis*,25*bis*,27*quater*,28,29*bis*,31,33; 12.1*sexiens*,2,3*bis*,4*ter*,5*ter*,6*bis*,7,8*bis*,9*bis*,11,12*ter*,13*bis*,14*bis*,16*bis*,17*bis*,18*bis*,19*ter*,20*ter*,21*ter*,22*ter*,26*bis*,28*bis*,30*tcr*,32*bis*,33*quinquiens*,34*bis*,35,36,37*ter*,38*ter*,39*bis*,40,41,42,43; 13.1*bis*,2*bis*,3*quater*,4,5,6,7,8*bis*,9*ter*,10,11,12*quater*,13,15,16,17,18,20,21,22*bis*,24,25*bis*,26*bis*,27*bis*,28,29,31,32,34*bis*; 14.1*ter*,3*bis*,4,5*bis*,7,9,10,11*bis*,12*bis*,13*bis*,14,15*bis*,16*quinquiens*,18*bis*,19*bis*,22*quater*,23*ter*,24,26,27,30,31,32*bis*,33*quinquiens*,34,35*bis*,36,37*ter*,38,39,40*bis*,41*quater*,43*quinquiens*,44,45*bis*,46,47*bis*,48,49,50,51,53*quater*,54*bis*,55*bis*,56,57,58,59,60,61,62,63,65*quater*,66,67*bis*,68*bis*,69,70,71,72*ter*; 15.1*quinquiens*,2*bis*,3,7,8*bis*,16,17*bis*,18,19*bis*,20*ter*,21*bis*,22,23*bis*,24,25,27*bis*,29*ter*,30,31,32*bis*,33,34,35,36*quater*,38,39,40*quater*,41,42,43*bis*,44,45,46*ter*,47; 16.1,2,3,4*bis*,5*bis*,6,⟦7,8*bis*,10,11*bis*,13,14*bis*,15,16,18*bis*,19*bis*,20⟧; III J 12*ter*,13,14; A 1.1,2,3*bis*,4,5,7,8*quater*,9*bis*,10*bis*,11,13*sexiens*,14*ter*,15,17,18*bis*,19,20*bis*,21,23*bis*,24,25,26*ter*; 2.1*bis*,2*bis*,3*bis*,4*bis*,6,7,8,9*quinquiens*,10*quater*,11,12*bis*,14*ter*,17*quater*,18*bis*,19*bis*,20,21,22*bis*,23,26*bis*,29*bis*,30,33*ter*,36*bis*,37*bis*,38*bis*,39*bis*,40,41,42*ter*,43,44,45*ter*,46*bis*,47; 3.1,2,[3],3,4,6,7*quater*,8*ter*,9*bis*,10*bis*,11,13*ter*,14*bis*,16*ter*,17*bis*,19,20,24*ter*,25*bis*; 4.1,2,3*bis*,4,5*bis*,6*quinquiens*,[7],8,10,12,13*bis*,16,19,20,23*bis*,24*quinquiens*,25,26*bis*,27*bis*,28,29*bis*,30*bis*,31*ter*,32*ter*,33,34,35,37; 5.2*bis*,3,4,5,6,7,9,10*ter*,11*bis*,12*bis*,14,15*ter*,16,17,18*ter*,20,21*quinquiens*,22*bis*,23,24,25,27,28,31*bis*,32*bis*,33,35,36,37*ter*,38*bis*,40*bis*,42*bis*; 6.3,4,5*noniens*,7*bis*,8*bis*,9*ter*,10,11,12*quater*,13*bis*,14,15*bis*; 7.2,3*ter*,4*quater*,5*bis*,6*bis*,7*ter*,8*quinquiens*,9*bis*,10*quinquiens*,11*ter*,13*bis*,14,15*bis*,16*ter*,17,20,21,22*bis*,24*ter*,26*bis*,27,29,30,(30),31,32*bis*,33,34*ter*,35*ter*,36*ter*,38,39,41*ter*,42*bis*,43*ter*,46,51*ter*,52*bis*,53,54,55,56*bis*,57*bis*,58,59*bis*,60*bis*; 8.1*bis*,2,3,6,9,12,13*quater*,14,17,19*ter*; 10.4*bis*,5*bis*,7,8,9*bis*,10,11*bis*,12*ter*,13*bis*,14,15,16,17*bis*,18,20*bis*,22*bis*,23,24*bis*,25,26*bis*,27*bis*,28,29,30*ter*,31*bis*,32,35,38*bis*,39*bis*,40,41*bis*,42*ter*,45*bis*,46,47; 11.1*bis*,2*quater*,3,5*bis*,6*quater*,7*bis*,8,10,11,12*bis*,13*bis*,14,15,18*bis*,19*bis*,20,21,22,23*bis*,24*ter*,26*bis*,30; 12.2,3*bis*,7*ter*,8*ter*,9*bis*,10*quater*,11*ter*,12*bis*,14*bis*,16*bis*,17*bis*,19*bis*,20*bis*,21,22,23*quater*,24,25; 13.1*quinquiens*,2*bis*,3*bis*,5*bis*,7*bis*,9*bis*,10,11*quinquiens*,12,14,15*bis*,16*bis*,17,18,19,20*bis*,21*bis*,22,25,26,27*bis*,28,29*quater*,32,33*bis*,35,36*bis*,39,41*ter*,43*ter*,45*ter*,46*bis*,48*ter*,49,50*quinquiens*,52; 14.1*bis*,2*bis*,3,4,5*ter*,6*ter*,7*ter*,8,9,10*ter*,13,14*bis*,15*quater*,17*ter*,18*bis*,19*quater*,20,21*ter*,22,23,25,26,27*bis*; 15.1*bis*,2*quinquiens*,3*bis*,4*bis*,6,7*ter*,8,9*bis*,11,12*ter*,15,16*ter*,17*bis*,20*ter*,22*ter*,23*ter*,25,27*bis*,28,29*ter*,30,31,32*bis*,35*ter*,36,38,41; 16.1,2,3,4*ter*,5,6,7,9*bis*,10,11,13,14,15*bis*,17*bis*,18*bis*,19*bis*,20,21,22,24,25,26,27*bis*,29*bis*,30*bis*,31*bis*,32,33*ter*,34*ter*,35*bis*,36,37,39*bis*,40*ter*; 17.1*bis*,2,3*ter*,4*quinquiens*,5,6*ter*,7,8*bis*,9*bis*,10,12*quater*,13*quater*,14,15,17*ter*,18*ter*,19,21,23*bis*,24*bis*,25*bis*,26,28*ter*,29,34*bis*; 18.2*ter*,3*bis*,4*ter*,5,6*bis*,7,8*bis*,9,10,11*bis*,12,13,15*bis*,16,18*bis*,19,21*bis*,22*ter*,23*bis*,25*bis*,26*quater*,28; 19.2,6*bis*,8,9,10,12*bis*,14*bis*,15,16*bis*,17*ter*,18,19*bis*,20*bis*,21*bis*,22*bis*,26*bis*,27,28,29*ter*,32,35,36,38*bis*,41; 20.1,2,3,4*quater*,6,8,9,10*bis*,11*bis*,12,15*ter*,18,19*bis*,20

exeo exit Mt 17.21; 24.27; exeunt Mt 15.18*bis*,19; L 4.36; Mk 7.20; exiebat [[Mt 3.5]]; L 6.19; exiebant J 8.9; L 4.22,41; A 8.7; exies [Mt 5.26]; L 12.59; exiet Mt 2.6; J 10.9; Mk 10.12; exient Mt 13.49; exibi (Mt 12.44); exiui [Mt 12.44]; J 8.42; 16.28; 17.8; L 11.24; existi J 16.31; exibit J 10.39; L 4.35; A 7.4; 10.23; 15.40; 17.33; 18.27; exiit Mt 8.34; 9.26; 13.1,3; 17.18; 20.1,6; 21.17; J 4.43; 11.31; 18.1, [[38; 19.4,5]]; Mk 1.26; 4.3; 7.19, 29; 9.26; 11.11; 14.68; A 11.25; 16.18; 20.1; exiuit J 3.22; 8.59; 11.44; 13.3,30,31; [[18.16, 29; 19.17,34]]; 20.3; 21.23; L 2.1; 4.14,37; 7.17; 8.5,44; 17.29; A 1.21; 14.20; exibimus A 16.13; existis Mt 11.7,8,9; L 7.24,25,26; 22.52; Mk 14.48; exierunt Mt 25.1; 26.30; J 4.30; 12.13; 21.3,9; L 8.27; Mk 3.21; 8.11; 14.26; A 16.40; exierat Mk 5.30; exierant L 8.2,38; exierit Mt 12.43; L 11.24; exeas A 16.18; exeatis Mt 10.11; Mk 6.10; exeant L 21.21; exiret A 19.12; exisset Mk 6.24; A 12.9; exissent L 8.33; Mk 11.12; A 12.10; 16.40; exi L 4.35; 5.8; 8.29; 13.31; 14.21,23; Mk 1.25; 5.8; 9.25; A 7.3; 22.18; exite Mt 25.6; L 9.4; A 16.39; exire Mt 24.26; J 8.9; L 6.12; Mk 9.29; A 16.3,39; 19.1,14; 20.7; exisse L 8.46; Mk 7.30; exiens (*m.*) Mt (5.26); 15.21; 20.5; 24.1; L 1.22; 4.42; 5.14; 14.18; 15.28; 22.39,62; Mk 7.31; exiens (*f.*) Mt. 15.22; exeunte (*m.*) A 3.11; exeuntes (*m.n.*) Mt 8.28,32; 9.31; 10.14; 22.10; 27.32,53; L 9.5,6; 10.10; Mk 3.6; 5.13; 6.11,12; A 15.24; 16.36; 18.26; 21.5,17; exientes (*m.*) L 5.2; Mk 6.34; exeuntes (*f.n.*) Mt 28.8; [[Mk 16.8]]; exeuntibus (*m.ab.*) Mt 9.32; Mk 5.2; pexiuit A 18.23; xibunt A 7.7.

exercitus exercitui A 7.42; exercitum Mt 22.7; exercitu L 21.20; 23.11.

exestuo exestuauit Mk 4.6.

exhorior, *v.* exorior.

exhortatio exhorationis A 4.36; exhortationis A 13.15.

exhortor exhortabatur [A 2.40]; exortabatur (A 2.40); exhortati sunt A 15.32; exhortantes (*m.n.*) A 14.22; exhortatus A 20.1; exortatus A 20.2.

exibeo exibere A 17.31.

exibit, *etc.*, *s.v.* exeo.

exigo exigebam L 19.23; exigatis L 3.13.

exilio exiliuit A 14.10; exilierunt A 14.14; exsiluisset A 3.8; exiliens (*m.*) Mk 10.50; A 10.25.

eximo exime Mk 9.47.

exinde Mt 4.17; 16.21; [[J 19.12]]; A 13.21.

existo existimare A 17.29; existimans (*m.*) A 16.27; existimantes (*m.n.*) A 14.19.

exitus exitum L 9.31; exitus (*ac.*) Mt 22.9.

exorcista exorcistarum A 19.13.

exorcizo exorcizare A 19.14.

exorior exhortus est Mk 4.6; exhortum est Mk 4.5; exhorti sunt A 16.40; exhorta sunt (Mt 13.5); exorta sunt [Mt 13.5].

exortor, *v.* exhortor.

expauesco expauescebant L 2.47; expauerunt L 8.56; Mk 9.15; 16.5.

expectatio expectatione L 21.26; expectationi (*ab.*) A 12.11.

expecto expectas A 22.16; expectamus Mt 11.3; L 7.19,20; expectabat L 23.51; expectabant A 20.5; expectare A 1.4; expectans (*m.*) L 2.25; Mk 15.43; A 3.5; 10.24; expectans (*f.*) L 1.21; expectante (*m.*) A 17.16; expectantes (*m.n.*) L 3.15; 8.40; expectantium (*m.*) J 5.3; expectantibus (*m.d.*) L 12.36.

expedio expedit Mt 5.29; 18.6; 19.10; J 11.50; 16.7; [[18.14]]; expedior A 10.34; expediebat L 17.2; expedita (*ab.*) A 21.7.

expeditio expeditionem A 21.26.

expello expulit A 7.45; expelleret Mk 5.10; expellere Mt 17.19.

expeto expetiuit L 22.31.

expiro exspirauit L 23.46; expirauit Mk 15.37; A 12.23; expirasse Mk 15.39.

explico explicit *col.* Mt; *col.* J; *col.* L; [[*col.* Mk]]; *col.* III J.

expono exponebat A 11.4; exposuit A 15.14; exposuerunt A 18.26; exposuerit A 13.41; expositus esset A 7.21; exponi A 7.19; exponentes (*m.n.*) A 15.5; exponentes (*m.ac.*) A 15.12; expostura (*f.n.*) A 21.3.

expostulo expostulabunt L 12.48.

exprobro exprobant L 23.11; exprobabunt L 6.22; exprobrauit [[Mk 16.14]]; exproprari L 9.22.

expuo expuens (*m.*) Mk 7.33; 8.23.

exquiro exquiram A 15.17; exquisiuit Mt 2.7,16; exquiretur L 11.51; exquirat L 11.50.

exsilio, *v.* exilio.

exspecto, *v.* expecto.

exspiro, *v.* expiro.

exsurgo exsurget Mt 12.42; 24.7; L 11.31; exurget L 21.10; exsurgent Mt 24.11,24; Mk 13.22; exurgent A 20.30; exurrexit Mk 5.42; exurrexerit A 7.18; exurgat Mk 4.27; exsur-

23.44; Mk 15.33; facta sunt Mt 17.2; 18.31; 28.11; J 10.22; [[19.36]]; L 23.48; 24.18,21; Mk 9.3; fecerat Mk 5.32,33; 15.7; factum erat A 4.22; 5.7; fecerit J 5.19; L 13.9; Mk 2.25; 3.35; A 15.12; fecerimus A 3.12; feceritis J 15.14; L 17.10; factus fuerit Mt 23.15; 24.32; factum fuerit J 13.19; 14.29; faciam J 4.34; 6.38; L 6.31; 18.41; 20.13; faciem Mt 27.22; faciat Mt 16.26; L 3.11; Mk 9.39; faciamus Mt 17.4; J 6.28; L 3.12; A 4.16; faciatis Mt 23.15; J 13.15; A 15.20; faciant J 6.15; faceret L 8.42; 10.38; 17.11; A 7.19; faceritis J 8.39; facerent L 2.27; 19.48; fecerim J 13.12; feceris Mk 10.19; A 16.28; feceritis A 15.29; fecisset Mt 13.26; Mk 5.20; A 7.36; 21.33; fecissent A 14.21; 15.33; 18.23; factus esset A 12.18; facta esset A 2.6; factum esset J 6.16; Mk 4.35; 5.16; 6.47; 11.19; 15.42; factae essent Mt 11.21,23; L 10.13; facta fuisset L 9.36; esset facturus J 6.6; fac J 13.27; L 4.23; 7.8; 10.28,37; 15.19, 21; 23.35; Mk 15.30; A 7.40; 21.23; facite Mt 3. [[3]],8; 12.33*bis;* 23.3; J 6.10; 8.38; L 3.4,8; 6.31; 12.33; 16.9; Mk 1.3; facere Mt 5.36; 6.1; 9.28; 12.2; 20.15; 23.3,23; J 5.19,27,30; 7.17; 8.44; 9.16,33; 11.37; 15.5; L 1.72; 12.4, 51; 17.10; Mk 3.4; 6.5; 7.12; 8.35; 9.3; 15.31; A 1.1; 4.28; 5.4,34; 7.44; 16.21,30; 18.21; 19.14; 20.13; 22.10; fecisse J 12.18; faciens (*m.*) L 10.25; 13.22; 18.18; Mk 8.13; A 8.9; 11.2; 13.44; 15.17; 19.24; faciens (*f.*) Mt 3.10; L 3.9; 6.43*bis;* facienti (*f.*) Mt 21.43; facientem (*m.*) Mt 24.46; J 5.19; L 12.43; faciente (*m.*) Mt 6.3; facientes (*m.ac.*) Mt 13.41; A 14.19; facientibus (*m.*) A 10.9; factus L 10.32; 22.44; A 1.18; 7.32; 10.4; 16.29; factum (*m.*) L 18.24; factam L 3.22; 23.19; Mk 11.20; 15.17; A 13.32; factum Mt 16.2; (21.4); Mk 14.58 *bis;* facto Mt 14.6; 26.6; A 12.18; facta Mt 13.21; L 4.42; 6.48; Mk 1.32; 4.17; 14.17; A 15.2; 16.35; facto Mt 14.15,23; 20.8; 26.20; 27.57; J 21.4; A 18.6; 21.40; factae L 24.22; faetae L 24.5; facta (*ac.*) J 3.19; 12.37; L 4.23.

facula faculae (*n.*) A 20.8.

facultas facultates (*ac.*) A 2.45.

faenerator faeneratori L 7.41.

faenero faeneratis L 6.34; faenerant L 6.34; faenerate L 6.35.

faenum Mt 13.26; J 6.10; faenum (*ac.*) Mt 14.19; L 12.28; Mk 6.39.

faenus faenus (*ac.*) Mt 18.27.

faetae *s.v.* facio.

falsus falsum (*n.*) 18.14; falsi (*m.*) A 13.10; falsum (*neu.*) Mt 19.18; 26.59; L 18.20; Mk 10.19; 14.56,57; falsi Mt 26.60, 61; falsa Mt 15.19; falsos A 6.13.

falx falcem Mk 4.29.

fama Mt 9.26; L 4.14,37.

familia familiam Mt (20.11); 24.45.

famis L 4.25; 15.14; Mk 13.8; A 7.11; famem A 11.28; fame L 15.17; fames (*n.*) Mt 24.7; L 21.11.

famulus famulorum A 10.7.

fantasma, Farao, farisaeus, *etc.*, *v.* phantasma, Pharao, pharisaeus, for words not listed here.

fanu, *s.v.* manus.

Fanuel L 2.36.

Fares L 3.33.

farina farinae (*g.*) L 13.21; farinam Mt 13.33.

fatigo fatigentur Mk 8.3; fatigatus J 4.6; fatigati (*n.*) Mt 9.36.

fatuus fatue (*voc.*) Mt 5.22.

fax facibus [[J 18.3]].

febricito febricitans (*f.*) Mk 1.30.

febris J 4.52 Mk 1.31 febri (*d.*) L 4.39; febri (*ab.*) L 4.38.

feidelis, *v.* fidelis.

fel felle Mt 27.34.

femina feminam Mt 19.4; Mk 10.6.

fenestra fenestram A 20.9.

ferbens *s.v.* ferueo.

fere J 6.10.

fermento fermentetur Mt 13.33; fermentatum est L 13.21.

fermentum fermento (*d.*) Mt 13.33; L 13.21; fermento (*ab.*) Mt 16.6,11,12; L 12.1; Mk 8.15*bis.*

fero ferebant Mk 14.4; ferebatur L 7.12; tulit Mt 24.39; J 11.41; [[19.38]]; Mk 10.14; tulistis Mk 8.20; tulerunt Mt 14.12,20; 15.37; J 8.59; 11.41; 20.2,13; Mk 6.29; tuleritis L 9.3; ferretur A 2.2; tulisset A 21.11; ferte L 19.24; ferre Mk 6.55; ferens (*m.*) [[J 19.39]]; ferentes (*m.n.*) A 5.16; 15.29; ferenda (*neu. ac.*) Mt 23.4.

ferreus ferream A 12.10.

ferueo ferbens (*m.*) A 18.25.

festinatio festinationem L 1.39.

festino festinabat A 20.16; festina A 22.18; festinans (*m.*) L 19.5,6; festinantes (*m.n.*) L 2.16; festinanter L 7.4.

festuca festucam L 6.41,42*bis.*

firmo firmauit L 9.51; firmatae sunt A 3.7.

flagello flagellabunt Mt 10.17; flagellauit [[J 19.1]].

flagellum flagellis (*ab.*) L 18.33; Mk 15.15.

flagrum flagris (*ab.*) Mt 27.26.

flamma flamma (*ab.*) A 7.30.

fleo fleuit L 19.41; 22.62; fleuimus Mt 11.17; flere Mk 14.72; flentem (*f.*) Mk 5.38; flentibus (*m.d.*) [[Mk 16.10]].

fletus Mt 13.42,50; 22.13; 24.51; 25.30.

flo flantem (*m.*) L 12.55; flante (*m.*) J 6.18.

fluctus fluctus (*ac.*) Mk 4.37; fluctibus Mt 14.24.

flumen L 6.48,49; flumen (*ac.*) A 7.21; 16.13; flumina (*n.*) J 7.38.

fluor fluent J 7.38.

fluxus fluxum Mt 9.20.

fobeam, *s.v.* fouea.

fodio fodiit Mt 21.33; fodit Mt 25.18; L 6.48; fodiam L 13.8; fodit Mk 12.1; fodere L 16.3.

folium folia (*n.*) Mt 24.32; Mk 13.28; folia (*ac.*) Mt 21.19; Mk 11.13*bis*.

fons J 4.6,14; Mk 5.29; fontem J 4.6.

foramen foramen (*ac.*) Mt 19.24; L 18.25; Mk 10.25.

forans (*adv.*), *v.* foras.

foras (*praep.c.ab.*) Mt 10.14; 21.17; foras (*adv.*) Mt 5.13; 12.47; 23.25,26,30; 25.30; J 9.34; 11.43; 15.6; [[18.29; 19.4*bis*,13]]; L 8.20; 13.28; 14.35; 22.62; 24.50; Mk 3.32; 14.68; A 5.34; 16.30; forans L 1.10.

forensis forenses (*m.ac.*) A 17.5.

foris (*adv.*) Mt 12.46; 13.48; J 12.31; [[18.16]]; 20.11; L 5.14; 13.25; Mk 1.45; 3.31; 4.11; 5.40; 11.4; A 12.13; *v.quoq.* aforis.

fornicatio fornicatione J 8.41; A 21.25; fornicationes (*n.*) Mt 15.19; Mk 7.22.

fors forte (*adv.*) Mt 13.29; 20.28; 27.64; L 1.9; 3.15; 4.11; 9.13; 10.31; 12.58; 14.8,12, 29; A 5.39; 16.39; 17.17,27; fortius L 23.5.

forsitan forsitam L 11.20; 20.13; A 11.18; 12.15; 18.14.

fortis (*m.*) L 11.21; fortis (*m.g.*) Mt 12.29; Mk 3.27; fortem (*m.*) Mt 12.29; Mk 3.27; fortes (*m.n.*) Mt 9.12; fortior (*m.*) Mt 3.11; L 3.16; 11.22; Mk 1.7; fortiter L 23.10; A 18.28.

forum forum (*ac.*) A 16.19; foro Mt 11.16; 20.3; L 7.32; 11.43; 20.46; Mk 7.4; 12.38; A 16.35; 17.17; foros Mt 23.7.

fouea foueam Mt 15.14; fobeam L 6.39.

fracmentorum, *s.v.* fragmentum.

fractio fractionis A 2.42; fractione L 24.35.

fragmentum fracmentorum Mk 8.20; fragmentorum Mt 14.20; 15.37; J 6.12,13; L 9.17; Mk 6.43; 8.8,19.

frango fregi Mk 8.19; fregit Mt 15.36; 26.26; L 22.19; Mk 6.41; 8.6; 14.22; fregerunt [[J 19.32,33]]; frangerentur [[J 19.31]]; fregisset A 20.11; frangere A 20.7; frangens (*m.*) Mt 14.19; fracto (*m.ab.*) Mk 14.3.

frater Mt 5.23; 10.2*bis*,21; 12.50; 18.15,21; J 6.8; 11.2,21,23,32; L 15.27,32; 17.3; 20.28 *bis;* Mk 3.35; 6.3; 12.19*bis;* 13.12; fratris Mt 14.3; L 3.1,19; 6.41,42; Mk 6.17,18; fratri Mt 5.22*bis*,24; 18.35; 22.24*bis*,25; L 6.42; 12.13; 20.28; Mk 12.19; fratrem Mt 4.18,21; 10.21; 17.1; 18.15; L 6.14*bis;* Mk 1.16,19; 3.17; 5.37; 13.12; A 12.2; fratre J 11.19; frater A 21.20; 22.13; fratres Mt 12.46,47,48, 49; 13.55; 22.25; 23.8; J 7.3,5,10; L 8.19,20, 21; 20.29; Mk 3.31,32,33,34; 12.20; A 11.1,2, 12; 15.23; 17.10,14; 21.17; fratrorum Mt 25.40; fratrum A 10.23; fratribus Mt 28.10; A 11.29; 12.17; 15.3,23; 18.18; fratres Mt 4.18,21; 5.47; 19.29; J 20.17; 21.23; L 14.12, 26; 16.28; 18.29; 22.32; Mk 10.29,30; A 7.23, 25; 11.2; 14.2; 15.1,32,36; 16.40; 17.6; 21.7; fratribus Mt 20.24; L 21.16; A 1.14; 3.22; 7.13,37; 15.22,33,40; 16.2; fratres A 1.16; 2.29,37; 3.17; 5.38; 6.3; 7.2,26; 13.15,26,38; 15.7,13; 20.18; 22.1.

fraus fraudem Mk 10.19.

fremo fremebant Mk 14.5; fremuerunt A 4.25.

frequenter [[J 18.2]]; L 5.33; Mk 9.22.

fretum fretum (*ac.*) J 6.17.

frico fricantes (*m.n.*) L 6.1.

frigidus frigidae (*g.*) Mt 10.42.

frigus [[J 18.18]].

froferet, *s.v.* profero.

1. frons frondes (*ac.*) Mk 11.8.

2. frons frontes (*ac.*) L 23.48.

fructifer fructifera (*ac.*) A 14.17.

fructifico fructificat Mt 13.23; Mk 4.28; fructificant L 8.15; Mk 4.20.

fructus Mt 21.19; J 15.16; L 1.42; fructum Mt 3.8,10; 12.33*bis;* 13.8,26; J 4.36; 12.24;

generis A 13.26; **genus** A 7.19; **genere** Mt 13.47; Mk 6.4; 7.26; A 4.6,36; 7.24.

Geraseni **Gerasenorum** Mt 8.28; L 8.26, 37; Mk 5.1.

germino **germinant** Mt 24.32; **germinet** Mk 4.27; **germinasset** Mt 13.26; L 8.7,8.

gero **gesserunt** A 19.19.

Gesamini Mk 14.32; **Gethsamini** [Mt 26.36]; **Getsamini** (Mt 26.36).

gigno **genui** L 3.22; A 13.33; **genuit** Mt 1.12*bis*,13*ter*,14*ter*,15*ter*,16; A 7.8,29; **genuerunt** L 23.29.

gladius L 2.35; **cladium** L 22.36; **gladium** Mt 10.34; 26.51,52*bis;* [[J 18.10,11]]; Mk 14.47; **gladio** Mt 26.52; L 22.49; A 12.2; 16.27; **gladii** L 21.24; **gladiis** (*ab.*) Mt 26.47, 55; L 22.52; Mk 14.43,48.

gloria J 8.54; L 2.9,14; 14.10; 19.38; **gloriae** (*g.*) Mt 19.28; 25.31; **gloriam** Mt 4.8; 16.27; J 5.41,44*bis;* 7.18*bis;* 8.50; 9.24; 11.4,40; 12.41,43*bis;* 17.22,24; L 2.32; 4.6,15; 9.32; 17.18; 18.43; 24.26; Mk 8.38; A 7.55; **gloria** Mt 24.30; 25.31; J 12.28; 17.5; L 9.27,31; 12.27; 21.27; Mk 10.37; 13.26.

glorifico **glorificabo** J 12.28; **glorificauit** (*fut.*) J 13.32*bis;* 16.14; **glorificaui** J 12.28; **glorificasti** J 17.10; **glorificauerunt** Mt 9.8; 15.31; **glorificent** Mt 5.16; **glorificetur** J 11.4; 12.23; 14.13; **glorificentur** Mt 6.2; **glorificatus est** J 12.16; 13.31*bis;* 15.8; **glorifica** J 12.28; 17.1.

gloriosus **gloriosis** (*neu.ab.*) L 7.25.

gnosco, *v.* **nosco.**

gogitare, *s.v.* **cogito.**

Golgotha Mt 27.33; [[J 19.17]]; Mk 15.22.

golligit, *s.v.* **1. colligo.**

Gomorra **Gomorrae** (*g.*) Mt 10.15.

grabastis, *s.v.* **grauo.**

grabattus **grabattum** J 5.8,9,10,11,12; L 5.19,24,25; Mk 2.4,9,11; **grabatto** Mk 2.12; **grabattis** (*ab.*) Mk 6.55; A 5.15.

gradus **gradus** (*g.*) A 7.5; **gradum** A 12.10; **grados** A 12.10; **graduus** A 21.35; **gradibus** A 21.40.

Graecus **Crecus** A 16.3; **Graeca** Mk 7.26; **Graeco** (*m.ab.*) A 16.1; **Craeci** A 19.10; **Graeci** J 12.20; A 18.17; **Graecorum** (*m.*) A 17.4; **Grecorum** J 7.35; A 14.1; 17.12; **Crecis** (*m.d.*) A 20.24; **Graecis** A 20.21; **Grecis** A 19.17; **Craecos** A 11.20; **Graecos** A 18.4; **Grecos** J 7.35; A 21.28; **Grecis** (*m.*) A 6.1; **Graecis** (*f.*) L 23.38; **Grece** (*adu.*) [[J 19.20]]; A 21.37.

grandis **grandis** (*f.*) L 4.25; **grande** (*neu. ac.*) Mk 14.15.

granum J 12.24; **grano** Mt 13.31; L 13.19; Mk 4.31; **granum** Mt 17.20; L 17.6; Mk 4.28.

gratia L 2.40; 6.32,33,34; A 4.33; **gratiae** (*g.*) L 4.22; A 14.3; 20.24; **gratiam** L 1.30; 17.9; A 2.38,47; 7.10,46; 11.2,23; 15.11; **cratia** A 14.26; **gratia** L 2.52; A 6.8; 13.43; 15.40; **gratias** Mt 15.36; 26.27; J 11.41; L 18.11; Mk 8.6,7; 14.23; **gratis** (*adv.*) Mt 10.8 *bis;* J 15.25.

grauis **graui** (*m.ab.*) A 20.9; **graues** (*m.n.*) A 20.29; **grauia** (*neu.ac.*) Mt 23.4; **grauiora** (*neu.ac.*) Mt 23.23; **grauiter** Mt 13.15.

grauo **grabastis** (A 3.14); **grauastis** [A 3.14]; **grauentur** L 21.34; **grauati** (*n.*) Mt 26.43; L 9.32; Mk 14.40.

Grecus, *v.* **Graecus.**

grex Mt 8.30,32; J 10.16; L 8.32,33; Mk 5.11,13; **gregis** Mt 26.31; **gregi** A 20.28,29; **gregem** Mt 8.31; L 12.32.

gubitum, *v.* **cubitum.**

gurges **gurgitem** Mt 12.11.

gusto **gustabit** J 8.52; L 14.24; **gustabunt** Mt 16.28; L 9.27; Mk 9.1; **gustasset** A 20.11; **gustare** A 10.10; **gustans** (*m.*) Mt 27.34.

habe **haue**, *v.* **aueo.**

habeo **abeo** L 12.50; **habeo** Mt 3.14; J 4.17,32; 5.7,36; 8.26,49; 10.16,18*bis;* 16.12; [[19.10*bis*]]; L 7.40; 11.6; 12.17; 14.18; 16.28; A 3.6; 20.24; 21.13; **habes** Mt 25.25; J 4.11 *bis*,17,18; 6.68; 7.20; 8.48,52,57; 13.8; L 12.19; 18.22; Mk 10.21; **abet** L 19.26; **habet** Mt 5.23; 9.6; 11.15,18; 12.11; 13.9,12*ter*,21, 27,43,44; 21.3; 25.29; J 3.29; 4.44; 5.6,24,26; 6.9,47,54; 9.21,23; 10.20; 11.9; 12.48; 13.10; 14.21,30; 15.13; 16.15,21,30; [[19.11]]; L 3.11 *bis;* 5.24; 7.33; 8.8,18*bis;* 9.58; 11.8; 14.28,35; 15.4; 17.9; 19.24,26,31,34; 20.24; 22.36*bis;* 24.39; Mk 2.10; 3.22,26,29; 4.9,23,25*ter;* 7.16; A 14.9; 15.21; **hauet** L 22.37; **habemus** Mt 3.9; 14.17; 26.26,65; J 8.41; 13.29; [[19.7,15]]; L 3.8; 22.71; **abetis** Mk 4.40; **habetis** Mt 15.34; 16.8; 26.11*bis;* 27.65; J 5.38,42; 6.56; 12.35,36; 21.5; L 6.24; 12.30; 24.41; Mk 6.38; 8.5,17; 11.25; 14.7*bis*,27; A 1.5; **habent** Mt 9.12; 14.16; 15.32; 21.26; J 15.22; L 5.31*bis;* 8.13; 9.58; 14.14; 15.7; 16.29; 18.24; 22.25; Mk 2.17; 4.17; 8.2; 10.23,42; A 7.1; 15.21; 19.38; 21.25; **habebam** J 12.28; 17.5; L 19.20; **hababa** (Mt 13.5); **habebat** Mt [[3.4]]; 13.[5], 46; 18.25; 21.28; J 13.29; L 8.27; 10.1; 13.6; 15.11; 16.1; 19.4; 23.17; Mk 4.6; 5 3,26; 7.25;

Herodianus **Herodianis** (*m.ab.*) Mt 22.16; Mk 3.6; 12.13.

Herodias **Herodiades** (*g.*) Mk 6.22; **Herodiadis** Mt 14.6; **Herodiadem** Mt 14.3; **Herodiaden** Mk 6.17; **Herodiade** L 3.19.

hesito **hisito**, *v.* **haesito.**

hic Mt ⟦3.3⟧; 8.27; 9.3; 10.22; 11.10; 12.23, 24; 13.19,20,22,23,55; 14.2*bis;* 15.8; 16.20; 17.5; 18.4; 21.10,11,38,42; 24.13; 26.23; 27.37, 54,58; J 3.26; 4.42,47; 6.14,42,46,50,52,58,60, 71; 7.15,18,25,26,31,35,40,41,46; 9.2,3,8,9,16, 19,20,24,33; 11.37*bis*,47; 12.21,34; 13.24; 14.19; 15.5; 17.21,25; ⟦18.30⟧; 21.21,23,24; L 1.32,36,66; 2.25,34; 4.22,36; 5.21; 7.27,39, 49; 8.25,41; 9.9,24,35,48; 14.30; 15.2,24,32; 16.1,25; 17.18; 18.11,14; 19.2,9; 20.14,17; 22.56,59; 23.22,38,41,47,51; Mk 2.7; 3.35; 6.3,16; 7.6; 9.7; 12.7,10,21; 13.13; 14.69; 15.26,39; A 1.18; 3.3,10,12; 4.9,10,11; 6.5,13, 14; 7.36,37,38,40; 8.10; 10.6,32,36,38; 11.22; 13.7,31; 14.9; 17.3,18,24; 18.13,25,26; 19.25, 26,38; 20.5; 21.28; **haec** Mt 13.54; 21.42; 22.20; 24.34; 26.8,12,13; J 6.39,40; 7.49; 8.4; 11.4; 12.30; 17.3; L 1.29; 2.2,36,37; 4.21; 7.44,45,46; 8.9,11; 11.29; 18.5; 21.3,4,32; 22.53; Mk 1.27; 12.16,43,44; 13.30; 14.8,9,35; A 2.6,39; 16.17; 17.19; 21.11; **hoc** Mt 1.22; 17.21; 19.26; 20.28; 22.38; 24.14; 26.9,13,26, 28,56; 27.8,46; 28.14,15; J 3.19,29; 6.29,61; 12.5; 15.12; 16.17,18; L 1.34,43,61; 2.12; 5.14; 7.17; 15.26; 18.36; 20.17; 22.19; Mk 9.21,29; 10.27; 12.30; 14.22,24; A 1.19; 2.12, 14,16; 4.22; 5.38; 10.16; 11.10; 12.3; 19.4,10, 17; **huius** Mt 13.15; 27.24,25; J 11.9; 12.31; 14.30; 16.11; L 16.24; 19.34; Mk 7.8,13; 9.37; A 4.8; 5.28; 13.17,23; 17.28; 19.35; **huius** J 15.13; L 7.31; 11.31; A 13.26; 17.30; **huius** L 16.8; 20.34,35; A 1.17,25; **huic** Mt 13.14,54,56; 17.20; 20.14; 21.21; J 5.38; 10.3; 13.24; 14.22; L 7.8; 14.9; 17.6; 19.19; 21.23; Mk 6.2; 11.23; A 10.43; **huic** Mt 10.12; 12.45; L 10.5; 11.30; 13.32; Mk 8.12; **huic** Mt 22.39; **hunc** Mt 26.61; 27.32; J 5.6; 6.27,34,58; 7.8, 27; 9.29,31,39; 10.36; 16.21,28*bis;* 17.3,18 *bis;* ⟦18.29,40; 19.8,12,20⟧; 21.21; L 9.13,26, 48; 12.5; 13.8; 16.28; 19.14; 20.12,13; 22.42; 23.2,14,18*bis;* 24.20; Mk 7.29; 14.36,58*bis;* A 2.23,29,32,36; 3.16; 5.31,37; 7.35*bis;* 10.30, 40; 12.4; 13.29,38; 15.38; 16.3; 18.27; 21.28; **hunt** A 21.28; **hanc** Mt 11.16; 15.32; 16.18; 21.23; J 4.15; 12.27; L 4.6,23; 7.44; 11.50; 12.41; 13.6,16; 15.3; 20.2,9,19; Mk 4.13; 12.10; A 1.16; (2.40); 3.16; 4.37; 7.4; 8.19; 13.32; 15.2,31; **hoc** Mt 9.28; 13.28; 19.5,11; 21.4,43; 23.34; 26.24,61; J 3.18; 4.18,54; 5.16, 18,28; 6.6,65; 7.39,50; 8.40,47; 9.23; 10.6,17, 18; 11.7,11,26,51; 12.6,18*bis*,27,33,39; 13.28; 14.13; 15.19; 16.15; ⟦18.34,37*bis*,38⟧; 20.20, 22; 21.14,19; L 1.18; 2.15; 3.20; 4.43; 6.3,32, 33; 7.4,8; 9.21,45; 10.11,28; 11.19,49; 12.18, 22,39,56; 16.2; 21.9; 22.15,17,23,37,47,51; 23.46; Mk 1.38; 2.17; 5.32; 10.7; 13.11; A 3.6,12*bis*,19; 4.7; 7.60*bis;* 16.16,18; 17.23; 19.5; 21.23; **hoc** J 4.20,21; 6.51; 8.23*bis*,26; 12.25; 13.1; 17.6,9,11*bis*,13,14,16; ⟦18.36*bis*⟧; 20.30; L 19.42; 23.4; 7.7,29; 15.6; 19.40; **hac** Mt 10.23; 12.41,42; 26.29,31,34; J 4.13; 12.27; L 11.51; 13.7; 17.25,34; 19.9; Mk 8.38; 14.30; A [2.40]; 4.27; 18.10; 19.23,25; **hoc** J 4.27,37; 6.66; 8.11; 9.30; 10.16; 13.35; 15.8; 16.19*bis*,30; L 9.45; 10.20; 12.10; 13.16; 18.29,30; Mk 5.36; 10.22,30; A 1.6; 4.17; 5.24,28; 6.3; 17.32; **hi** Mt 20.21; ⟦J 18.21⟧; L 8.14,15,21; 17.17; 20.47; Mk 4.15,16,18,20; 10.42; A 1.6,14; 2.7,41; 16.17; 17.6,11; **hii** Mt 13.38; 20.12; 25.46; Mk 12.44; A 2.15; 15.13; **hae** Mt (13.56); 23.36; **haec** Mt 10.2; 15.20; 16.22; 24.8,34; J 6.9; 10.21; 12.16; ⟦19.36⟧; 20.31; L 1.20; 12.31; 21.7,32; 24.11, 17,21; Mk 6.2; 7.23; 13.4*bis*,8,30; ⟦16.17⟧; A 7.1; 17.20; **horum** (*m.*) Mt 18.10; 25.40,45; L 17.22; **horum** (*neu.*) J 5.20; 7.40; 14.12; L 5.33; 12.30; 18.34; 21.28; 24.14,48; Mk 12.31; A 5.32; 18.15; 20.24; **his** (*m.*) Mt 25.34,41; J 6.13; L 1.79; 19.24; ⟦Mk 16.10,14⟧; A 15.19; 17.17; 19.17; **hiis** (*m.*) A 1.16; 5.32; 11.29; 15.23,38; 17.17*bis;* **his** (*neu.*) A 8.6; **hos** Mt 10.5; 19.1; 26.1; ⟦J 18.8; 19.13⟧; A 1.5; 2.22; 3.24; 5.5,24,36; 16.36; 21.15,24,38; **has** Mt 15.24; Mk 13.2; **haec** Mt 4.9; 9.18; 11.25; 13.34,51, [56]; 19.20; 21.23,24,27; 23,23; 24.2, 33; J 3.22; 4.31; 5.1,14,16,19,34; 6.1,59; 7.1, 4,9; 8.20,26,28,30,38*bis;* 9.6,22; 10.19; 11.11, 28,43; 12.16*bis*,36,41; 13.17,21; 14.25; 15.11, 17,21; 16.1,3,4*bis*,6,25,33; 17.1,13; 18.1, ⟦22; 19.24,38⟧; 20.14; 21.1,19,24; L 1.19,65; 2.19; 4.28; 6.26; 7.9; 8.8; 9.9,28,34; 10.21; 11.14,27, 45,53; 12.30; 13.2; 14.6,15,21; 16.14; 17.8,30; 18.4,11,21,23; 19.11,28; 20.2,8; 21.6,12,31, 36; 23.31,49; 24.9,10,26,36; Mk 10.20; 11.28, 29,33; 13.19,29; ⟦16.12⟧; A 1.9; 4.1; 5.11; 7.30,50; 10.44; 11.18; 12.17; 13.42; 14.15,18; 15.16,17,23,27,28; 16.38; 17.8,11; 19.25,28, 41; 21.11,12; **his** Mt 10.28,29,42; 11.7; 18.14; 23.34; 27.48; J 5.3; 12.20; 17.20; L 12.4; 13.14; 17.18; 24.24; Mk 9.42; A 1.15, [21],24; 3.2; 10.7; 13.31; 16.2; 17.12; 19.19; **his** Mt 25.2; L 1.1; **his** Mt 5.37; 22.40; 24.31; J 21.24; L 2.18,33,49; 12.27; 16.26; A 14.15; 19.36; **his** (*inc.*) A 16.4.

hic (*adv.*) Mt 8.29; 12.6,41,42; 14.8,17; 16.28; 17.4*bis* (20); 20.6;24.2,23; 26.38; 28.6;

honoro **honorat** Mk 7.6; **honorauit** Mt 15.5; **fuerat honoratus** J 7.39; **honoret** J 12.26; **honora** Mt 15.4; 19.19; L 18.20; Mk 7.10; 10.19; **honorans** (*m.*) L 17.15; 18.43; **honoratus** L 7.2.

hopus, *v.* **opus.**

hora Mt 14.15; 26.45; J 4.6,21,23; 5.25,28; 7.30; 8.20; 12.23; 13.1; 16.2,4,25,32; 17.1; [[19.14]]; L 22.14,53; 23.44; Mk 11.11; 15.25; A 2.15; **ora** Mk 6.35*bis;* 14.35,41; 15.33; **horae** (*g.*) L 22.59; **horam** Mt 20.3,5,9; 25.13; 27.45,46; J 4.52; 12.27; Mk 15.33; A 3.1; **oram** J 5.35; **hora** Mt 9.22; 15.28; 17.18; 18.1; 20.12; 22.46; 24.36,44,50; 26.40,55; 27.45; J 4.52,53; 12.27; [[19.27]]; L 1.10; 2.38; 7.21; 10.21; 12.12,39,40,46; 13.31; 14.17; 20.19; 23.44; 24.33; Mk 13.11,32; 14.37; 15.34; A 10.9; 16.18,33; 19.9; 22.13; **horarum** A 5.7; **horas** J 11.9; **horis** A 19.34.

horabit, *v.* **oro.**

hordiaceus **hordiacios** J 6.9; **hordiaciis** (*m.*) J 6.13.

horreum **horreum** (*ac.*) Mt 3.12; 13.30.

hortor **hortantes** (*m.n*) A 18.26.

hortulanus J 20.15.

hortus J 18.1; **hortum** L 13.19; **horto** [[J 18.26]].

hospes **hospitem** Mt 25.44.

hospitium **hospitio** (*ab.*) A 10.23; **hospitiis** (*ab.*) A 17.21.

hospitor **hospitatur** A 10.32; **ospitatur** A 10.18; **ospitaremur** A 21.16; **ospitans** (*m.*) A 10.6.

hosteis, *s.v.* **osteum.**

hostia **hostiam** J 16.2; A 7.41; **hostias** A 7.42.

huc, *v.* **hoc** (*adv.*).

humanus **humanae** (*g.*) A 17.29; **humanis** (*f.ab.*) A 17.25.

humilio **humiliat** L 14.11; 18.14; **humiliabitur** [Mt 23.12]; L 18.14; **humiliauitur** (Mt 23.12); L 14.11; **humiliauerit** Mt 18.4; 23.12; **humiliab** L 3.5.

humilis (*m.*) Mt 11.29; **humiles** (*m.ac.*) L 1.52.

humilitas **humilitatem** L 1.48; **humilitati** (*ab.*) A 20.19.

hunt, *s.v.* **hic.**

hydria **hydriam** J 4.28.

hydropicus L 14.2.

hymnus **ymnum** A 16.25; **hymno** Mt 26.30; Mk 14.26.

hypocrisis L 12.1; **hypocrisi** (*ab.*) Mt 23.28.

hypocrita (*voc.*) L 6.42; 13.15; **hypocritae** (*n.*) Mt 6.2,5; **hypocritis** (*ab.*) Mt 24.51; **upocritis** Mk 7.6; **hypocritae** Mt 15.7; 22.18; 23.13,15,23,25,27; L 12.56; **ypocritae** Mt 23.39; L 11.39.

hysopum **hysopo** (*ab.*) [[J 19.29]].

ibi **bi** (J 12.2); **ibi** Mt 2.15; 5.23,24; 10.11; 12.10,45; 13.42,50; 15.29; 19.2; 21.17; 22.11, 13; 24.28,51; 25.30; 27.36; 28.7,10; J 3.22,23; 4.6; 5.5; 6.3,15,22,24; 10.40,42; 11.8,15,31,54; 12. [2],9; [[19.42]]; L 8.32; 9.4; 10.6; 12.18,34; 13.28; 15.13,15; 17.37; 19.27; 22.12; 23.33; Mk 1.35,38; 3.1; 6.5,33; [[16.7]]; A 7.4; 16.1; 17.14; 18.19; 19.21; 21.3; **ibit** Mk 15.39.

ibide L 17.6.

ibidem Mt 2.13; 13.58; 14.23; 26.36; 27.61.

ibit, *s.v.* **ibi.**

Iconium **Iconio** A 16.2; **Iconium** A 14.21; **Hiconio** A 13.51; **Ichonio** A 14.1; **Iconio** A 14.19.

idem **eundem** Mt 26.44; **idem** Mt 5.47; **eodem** L 6.4; Mk 10.10; **eadem** A 16.18; **eodem** L 13.1; **isdem** (*m.ab.*) Mt 2.13; 9.32.

identidem **idemtidem** [Mt 20.5; 21.30,36; 27.44]; **identidem** (Mt 20.5; 21.30,36; 27.44).

ideo Mt 12.27,31; 13.13,52; 14.2; 18.23; 24.44; J 7.22; Mk 12.24; A 13.35.

idoneus Mt 3.11.

Idumea **Idumea** (*ab.*) Mk 3.8.

igitur Mt 19.25,27; J 5.19; 6.43; 11.53; 12.19.

ignis **ignis** (*g.*) Mt 5.22; 13.42,50; L 16.24; Mk 9.43,44,46,48; A 2.3; 7.30; **ignem** Mt 3.10; 18.8; J 15.6; L 3.9; 9.54; 12.49; 22.55; Mk 9.22,45; 14.54; **igne** Mt 17.15; 25.41; **igni** Mt 3.11,12; 13.40; L 3.16,17; **igne** (*inc.*) L 17.29.

ignorantia **ignorantiae** (*g.*) A 17.30; **ignorantiam** A 3.17.

ignoro **ignoras** J 13.7; **ignorat** L 12.46; A 19.35; **ignoramus** J 9.21; A 16.39; **ignoratis** J 4.32; 7.28; **ignorabant** L 9.45; Mk 9.32; **ingnorabant** Mk 14.40; **ignorauit** L 12.48; **ignorauerunt** J 10.6; **ignorantes** (*m.n.*) A 17.23.

ignotus **ignotae** (*g.*) A 21.39; **ignoto** (*m.d.*) A 17.23.

illac, *v.* **illic.**

ille Mt 18.26,28; 22.7; 24.46,48; 26.24; 27.8,63; J 4.25,29,32; 5.11,19,35,37,38,46; 6.29,57; 7.11,29; 8.11,42,44; 9.9,11,12,15,17,

3.22; 7.44,50; 10.20; 11.49; 17.26; L 2.1; 4.2 *bis;* 5.35; 6.12; 7.42; 8.23; 9.36,57; 15.2; 19.37; 21.23; 23.7; 24.15; Mk 1.9; 2.15,19; 5.2; 6.54; 8.1,3; 9.9,14; 13.17,19,24; 14.18, 22,70; A 2.1; 7.41; 10.9; 13.43; 14.27; 15.4; 21.24; **illis** (*f.*) Mt 28.11; L 24.1; A 21.25; **illo** (*adv.*) Mt [[2.22]]; 17.20.

1. illic **illac** L 19.5; **illuc** [[J 18.2,3]]; Mk 6.33.

2. illic (*adv.*) Mt 17.27; 24.23; 26.36; 27.47; J 4.40; L 17.23; Mk 2.6; 6.10; 11.5; 13.21; 14.15; A 14.7; 17.13; **illi** L 17.21.

ill- *v.* **inl-.**

illym, *s.v.* **ille.**

imago Mt 22.20; Mk 12.16; **imaginem** L 20.24.

imber **imbrens** (*ac.*) A 14.17.

imbrex, *v.* **inbrex.**

imm-, *v.* **inm-** for words not listed here.

immolo **immolabatur** Mk 14.12; **immolarent** A 14.18; **immola** A 10.13; 11.7; **immolare** A 14.13; **immolari** L 22.7.

imperator **imperatores** (*n.*) A 5.39.

in (*c.ab.*) Mt 1.18,20,23; 2.1,2,9,13,16,19*bis*, [[22*bis*,23; 3.1*bis*,3,6]],11,12,17; 4.4*bis*,6,13,16 *bis*,21,23*bis;* 5.12,13,15,16,19,25,28,45,48; 6.1, 2*bis*,4*bis*,5*bis*,6*bis*,7; 8.32; 9.2,4,10,15,31,35; 10.9,10,11,15,16,17,20,23*bis*,27*quater*,32*bis*, 33,41,42; 11.1,6,8,11,16,20,21*quater*,22,23*bis*, 24,25; 12.1,5*ter*,11,18,19,21,27,32*bis*,36,40*bis*, 41*bis*,50; 13.1,3,7,10,13,19,21,22,24,27,30,31, 32,34,35,40,43,44,48,49,52,57*ter;* 14.1,2,3,6, 33; 15.32,33; 16.17,19*ter*,28; 17.5,21,22; 18.1 *bis*,2,4,5,6,10*bis*,12,13,14,16,[18],18,19,20*bis;* 19.5,21,28; 20.3,15,17,21,26*bis*,27,28; 21.8*bis*, 9*bis*,12,14,15,22,23,24,27,32,42*bis;* 22.1,15,16, 23,28,30*bis*,36,37*ter*,40,43,45; 23.6*bis*,9,16*bis*, 18*bis*,20*ter*,21*ter*,22*bis*,30*bis*,39; 24.5,14,15,16, 18,19*bis*,26*bis*,30,38,40,41*bis*,45,48,50; 25.3,4, 16,18,21,23,25,31,36,39; 26.5*bis*,6*bis*,13,29,31 *bis*,33,55*bis;* 27.5,29,56,59,60*bis;* 28.1,18,19; J 3.18,23; 4.14,20*bis*,21,23,24,27,37,44,52,53 *bis;* 5.1,2,3,5,13,14,26*bis*,28*bis*,35,38,39,42,43 *bis;* 6.10,31,39,40,44,45,49,53,56*quater*,59; 7.1 *bis*,11,12,18,22,23*bis*,28,37,43; 8.3,4*bis*,5,9,12, 17,20*bis*,21,24*bis*,26,31,37,44*bis;* 9.3,5,30,34; 10.22,23,25,34,38*bis;* 11.6,9,10*bis*,17,20,24*bis*, 31,56; 12.13,20,25,28,35*bis*,37,46,48; 13.1,31, 32,35; 14.2,10*ter*,11*bis*,13*bis*,14,17,20*quater*, 26,30; 15.2,4*bis*,5*bis*,6,7*bis*,8,9,10*bis*,11,16,24; 16.13, 23*bis*, 24, 25*bis*, 26*bis*, 30, 33*bis;* 17.10, 11*sexiens*, 12, 13*bis*, 17, 19, 21*ter*, 23*bis*, 26*bis*; [[18.20*bis*,26,38,39; 19.4,6,13,31,41*ter*]]; 20.4, 12,19,26,30*bis*,31*;* 21.3,20; L 1.1,5,6*bis*,8*ter*, 15,17*ter*,18,19,20,21*bis*,22,25*bis*,26,29,31,36, 39,41,44*bis*,47,51,59,61,65,66,69,75*bis*,77,78, 79,80; 2.1,7*bis*,8,11,12,14*bis*,16,19,20,21,23, 24,27,29,31,33,36,38,41,44*bis*,46*bis*,47,49,51; 3.1,2,4*bis*,7,8,15,16*bis*,17,20*bis;* 4.1,2,4*bis*,5, 7,14,15,16,18,20,21,22,23,24,25*bis*,28,31*bis*,32 *bis*,33,35,36,44; 5.1,3,5,7,9,12*ter*,14,17,18,19 *bis*,21,22,25,29,35; 6.1,6,8,10,12*bis*,17,23*bis*, 38,41*bis*,42; 7.16,18,21,23,25*ter*,27,28,32,37 *bis*,50; 8.1,5,10,13,15*bis*,22,27,43,47; 9.12,26, 27,31,34,35,36,43*bis*,48*bis*,49,57; 10.5,7,9,11, 12,13*bis*,17,20*bis*,21*ter*,26,27*ter;* 11.1,2*quater*, 4,7,15,19,20,21,22,27,30*ter*,35,38,43*ter*,53; 12.3*ter*,6,8*quater*,9*bis*,10*bis*,12,15,27,32,33,42, 45,46*bis*,51,52*ter*,53,58; 13.6*bis*,7,10,11,14*bis*, 17,26*bis*,28,29,31,35; 14.2,10,14,15,31,34,35; 15.7,10,18,21,25; 16.10*quater*,11,12,15*ter*,23*bis*, 24,25,26; 17.4,26*bis*,28,30,31*ter*,34,35,36; 18.2, 3,12,22,27,29,30,35; 19.5,9,17,20,27,30,38*ter*, 44,45,47; 20.1*bis*,2,8,20,21,26*bis*,33,37,42,46 *quater;* 21.6*bis*,8,14,19,21*ter*,23,24,25*bis*,26,27, 34,36*bis*,37*bis*,38; 22.7,16,24,26,27*bis*,28,30, 40,44,49,53,55,59; 23.4,7,9,12*bis*,14*bis*,15,29, 31*bis*,40,42,43,53*ter;* 24.4,5,6,11,13,15,18*bis*, 19*bis*,21,25,27,32,35*bis*,36,43,44,47,49,53; Mk 1.3,4,7,8,9,13,15,19,20,23*bis*,39,45; 2.1,4,6,8 *bis*,10,15,20; 3.9,34; 4.2*bis*,11,17,18,24,30,35, 36,38; 5.2,3,5*bis*,13,14,20,23,25,30; 6.2,3,4*ter*, 14,25,28,29,47*bis*,55,56; 8.1,3,17,26,27,38; 9.20,29*bis*,30,33,36,37,38,39,41,50*bis;* 10.8,21, 22,24,30*bis*,37,43,52; 11.4,9,10,13,15,23,25, 26,27,28,29,33; 12.1,2,4,11,23,25,26,32,35,36, 38*bis*,39*bis;* 13.3,6,9*bis*,10,11,14,16,17,24,28, 29,32; 14.2,6,25,49; 15.7,29,41,46*bis;* [[16.12, 17]]; A 1.3,6,7,10,14,15*bis*,20*bis*,21; 2.1,8,17, 19*bis*,20*bis*,22*bis*,25,38,41,42*bis*,46*bis*,47; 3.1, 6,10*bis*,16,25,26; 4.2,7*bis*,9,10*ter*,12*bis*,17,18, 19,24,27,30,31,32,34; 5.4*bis*,12,15*bis*,18,20,23, 25,27,28,30,31,34,37,40,42; 6.1*ter*,3,5,6,8,10 *bis*,15*bis;* 7.2,4*bis*,5,6*bis*,7,12,13,14,16,17,20 *bis*, 22, 24, 29, 30*ter*, 33, 34, 35*bis*, 36*ter*, 38*ter*, 41 *bis*,42*bis*,44,46,48; 8.1*bis*,6,8,9,16; 10.4,30*ter*, 31*bis*,33*bis*,34,35,39*bis*,48; 11.5,11,13,14,22, 27,28,29; 12.1,5,7,11,18; 13.1*bis*,5,12,15,17 *bis*,18,19,26,28,31,33,39*bis*,40,41,42,43; 14.3, 7*bis*,9,10,15,16,21,26; 15.7*bis*,12,21,26,29,30; 16.3,6,10,12,18*bis*,24,31,33,34,35; 17.16,17*bis*, 22,23,24*bis*,28,31*bis*,34; 18.5,8*bis*,10,11,18,24, 25,26,27; 19.5,9*bis*,14,16,21,23; 20.6,7,8,10, 15,16*ter*,18,21,22,23,28; 21.3,5,19,20,21,27,29, 34,40; 22.17,19; **in** (*c.ac.*) Mt 2.1,11,12,20, [[21, 22]]; 3.10,11,12; 4.1,5,8,12,24; 5.1,22,29,34, 35*bis*,36,39; 8.28,31,32,33; 9.1,6,7,17*bis*,23, 26,28; 10.5*bis*,18,21*bis*,22; 11.7; 12.4,11,25 *bis*,26,28,29,44; 13.5,8,30,33,36,50; 14.13,15,

[6] Order of verses in MS.

tibus (*neu.ab.*) Mt 24.31; incipientium (*inc.*) L 24.47.

incircumcisus incircumcisi (*voc.*) A 7.51.

incito incitabatur A 17.16; incitauerunt A 14.2.

inclino inclinauerunt L 24.5; inclinatus J 8.6,8; inclinato (*neu.ab.*) ⟦J 19.30⟧.

includo inclusit L 3.20; includens (*m.*) A 22.19.

incoho inchoo, *v.* incoo.

incola A 7.29; incolae (*n.*) A 21.12.

incolumis incolumes (*m.ac.*) Mt 15.31.

inconsutilis inconsutilis (*f.*) ⟦J 19.23⟧.

incontra L 8.22.

incoo incoauit (A 1.1); inchoauit [A 1.1].

incrasso incrassatum est [Mt 13.15]; ingrassatum est (Mt 13.15).

incredulitas incredulitatem Mt 17.20; Mk 6.6; 9.24; ⟦16.14⟧; incredulitates (*ac.*) Mt 13.58.

incredulus incredula (*f.voc.*) Mt 17.17; L 9.41; Mk 9.19.

increpo increpebat Mt 20.31; L 23.40; increpebant Mt 27.44; L 18.15,39; increpauit Mt 17.18; L 4.35,39; 9.21,55; increpa L 19.39; increpare Mt 16.22; increpans (*m.*) L 4.41.

incresco increscat Mk 4.27.

incumbo incumbebant L 23.23; incubuit L 15.20; incumbens (*m.*) J 13.25; incumbens (*f.*) L 13.11.

inde Mt 4.21; 5.26; 9.9,27; 11.1; 12.9,15; 13.53; 14.13; 15.21,29; 19.15; J 4.43; L 9.4; 12.59; 16.26; 19.4; Mk 6.1,10,11,53; 7.24; 9.30; 10.1,46; 11.15; A 13.4; 14.26; 17.1; 20.13,15; 21.17; indiė A 16.12.

indemnatus indemnatos A 16.37.

indie, *s.v* inde.

indignatio indignationis Mk 3.5; indignatione A 19.28.

indignor indignati sunt Mt 20.24; 21.15; 26.8; indignari Mk 10.41; indignans (*m.*) L 13.14.

indignus indigne (*adv.*) Mk 10.14; 14.4.

indolesco indoluisset A 16.18.

induco induxit A 21.29; inducas L 11.4; inducerent L 2.27; 5.19; induceretur A 21.37; inducere L 5.3,18.

induo induebatur L 8.27; 16.19; induerunt Mk 15.17,20; induamini L 12.22; 24.49; indueritis Mk 6.9; indutus est L 12.27; induite L 15.22; indutus A 12.21; indutum (*m.*) Mt 11.8; 22.11; Mk 16.5.

induro indurarent A 19.9.

inebrio inebriari L 12.45.

inextinguibilis (*m.*) Mk 9.43; inextinguibilem (*m.*) Mk 9.45; inextinguibili (*m.*) Mt 3.12; inextintibili (*m.*) L 3.17.

inextintibili, *s.v.* inextinguibilis.

infans L 1.41,44,66; 2.40; infantem J 16.21; L 1.59; 2.12,16,21,27; 9.47,48; 18.17; infante L 2.17; infans L 1.76; infantium Mt 21.16; infantibus L 7.32; infantes L 18.15,16; A 7.19; infantibus Mt 14.21; 15.38.

infantia infantia (*ab.*) Mk 9.21.

infatuo infatuatum (*neu.n.*) Mt 5.13; L 14.34.

infernus infernum (*neu.ac.*) L 10.15; inferno (*neu.*) L 16.23.

infero inferentur A 19.12; inferrent A 5.15.

inferus inferorum (*m.*) Mt 16.18; inferos Mt 11.23; A 2.27,31; inferiorum (*m.*) A 2.24; inferioribus (*m.ab.*) J 8.23; imam A 16.24.

infidelis (*m.*) J 20.27; infidelibus (*m.a.b*) L 12.46.

infirmis, *v.* infirmus.

infirmitas J 11.4; infirmitatis (*n.*) A 19.12; infirmitatem Mt 4.23; 9.35; 10.1; infirmitate J 5.5; L 6.17; 13.11,12; infirmitates (*ac.*) L 9.1; infirmitatibus Mt 4.24; L 5.15; 7.21; 8.2.

infirmo infirmatur J 11.3,6; infirmabatur J 11.2; infirmatus sum Mt 25.36; infirmantes (*m.ac.*) L 4.40; A 19.12.

infirmus J 4.46; 5.7; 11.1; infirmis (*m.n.*) Mt 25.43; J 5.13; infirma Mk 14.38; infirmis (*f.n.*) Mt 26.41; infirmi (*m.*) [A 4.9]; infirmum (*m.*) Mt 25.39,44; (A 4.9); infirmi L 10.9; infirmorum (*m.*) J 5.3; infirmos Mt 10.8; 14.14; J 6.2; L 9.2; Mk 6.5,56; A 5.15,16.

infra Mt 2.16.

infructuus [Mt 13.22]; infructuos (Mt 13.22).

infundo infundens (*m.*) L 10.34.

ingemisco ingemiscens (*m.*) Mk 8.12.

ingemo ingemuit Mk 7.34.

ingn-, *v.* ign-.

ingrassatum, *s.v.* incrasso.

ingratio ingratiasset A 12.21.

ingratus ingratos L 6.35.

ingredior ingrediuntur Mk 1.21; ingrediebantur A 3.2; ingressus sum A 20.18; in-

Mk 11.7; inponebat Mk 10.16; inponebant A 8.17; inpones L 4.40; imponent ⟦Mk 16.18⟧; inposuit J 9.15; L 13.13; 23.53; Mk 3.16,17; 8.25; imposuerunt ⟦J 19.2⟧; inposuerunt Mt 27.29,37; L 19.35; 23.26; Mk 15.17; inposuero A 8.19; inponeret Mt 19.13; Mk 7.32; inposuisset A 19.6; inposuissent A 13.3; inpone Mt 9.18; inponere A 15.10; inponens (*m.*) Mt 27.48; L 10.34; Mk 6.5; inponentes (*m.n.*) L 10.30; 23.37; A 18.12; impositum (*m.*) J 21.9; impositis (*f.ab.*) Mt 19.15; inpositis (*f.*) Mk 8.23; A 16.23.

inpositio inpositionem A 8.18.

inpossibilis inpossibile (*neu.n.*) Mt 17.20; 19.26; L 17.1; Mk 10.27; inpossibilia (*n.*) L 18.27.

inprobitas inprobitatem L 11.8.

inpropero inproperauerint Mt 5.11; inproperare Mt 11.20.

inproximo Mk 13.28,29.

inprudens inprudentes (*m.n.*) Mk 7.18.

inpudicitia Mk 7.22.

inpugno inpugnans (*m.*) A 12.20.

inquantum Mt 9.15; 25.40,45.

inquiro inquirentes (*m.n.*) A 10.17.

inquito inquitauerunt A 17.6.

inrideo inredebant Mk 5.40; irridentes (*m.n.*) Mk 15.31.

inrigo inrigauit L 7.44.

inritus inritum (*neu.ac.*) Mt 15.6; Mk 7.9.

inruo inruerunt A 18.12; inruerent Mk 3.10.

insanio insanis A 12.15; insanit J 10.20.

inscriptio Mt 22.20; L 23.38; Mk 15.26.

insensatus insensati (*voc.*) L 24.25.

insidiae A 20.3; insidiis (*ab.*) A 20.19.

insidior insidiabatur Mk 6.19.

insignis insignem (*m.*) Mt 27.16.

insilio insilien (*m.*) A 19.16.

insipiens insipientes (*m.n.*) Mt 15.16.

insipientia insipientia (*ab.*) L 6.11.

inspicio inspicis L 6.41; inspiciebant J 13.22; inspiciens (*m.*) L 20.17.

inspuo inspuit (*perf.*) J 9.6.

instigo instigauerunt A 13.50; instigassent A 14.19.

instita institis (*ab.*) J 11.44.

insto instabant A 18.5; instans (*m.*) L 4.39; instans (*f.*) L 2.38; 10.40; instantissime A 12.5.

insuflo insuflauit J 20.22.

insula insulam A 13.6.

insulsus insulsum (*neu.n.*) Mk 9.50.

insuper A 21.28.

insurgo insurgebat J 6.18; insurget Mk 13.8; insurgent Mt 10.21; Mk 13.12.

integritas integritatem A 3.16.

intellectus A 13.15; intellectum L 1.77; 3.16; intellecto L 2.47.

intellego intellegit Mt 13.19,23; intellegimus A 16.10; intellegetis Mt 13.14; 15.17; 16.9; Mk 7.18; intelleximus [Mt 13.51]; intellegistis Mt 16.11; Mk 8.17; intellexistis Mt 13.51; Mk 8.21; intellexerunt Mt 16.12; 17.13; L 2.50; 18.34; A 7.25; 14.6; intellexerant Mk 6.52; intellegat Mt 24.15; Mk 4.9; 13.14; intellegant Mt 13.13,15; J 12.40; L 24.45; Mk 4.12; intelligite Mt 15.11; Mk 7.14; intellegere A 7.25; intelligens (*m.*) Mk 4.9; intellegentes (*m.n.*) Mk 12.24; A 13.27; intellegentibus (*m.ab.*) L 10.21.

intemperantia intemperantiae (*g.*) Mt 23.25.

intendo intendebant A 8.6,10,11; intendere A 16.14; intendens (*f.*) L 22.56; intendentes (*m.n.*) L 4.20.

inter (*c.ac.*) Mt 2.6; 11.11; 13.25; 16.7,8; 18.15; 21.25; 23.35; 27.7; J 4.31; 6.43; 7.35; 9.16; 10.19; 11.54; L 1.28,42; 2.44; 11.51; 16.26; Mk 1.27; 5.27; 7.31; 9.16,34,50; 10.43; 11.31; 15.40; A 1.17; 12.6; 15.9; 18.12; 20.25.

intercedo intercesso (*neu.ab.*) L 22.59.

intercipio intercipere A 5.3.

interfectio interfecti (*d.*) A 8.1.

interficio interficis Mt 23.37; interficient L 11.49; interfecisti A 7.28; interfecit Mt 2.16; A 12.2; interfecistis A 2.23; 3.15; 5.30; interfecerunt A 10.39; interfectus est A 5.36; interficerent J 11.53; interficeretur A 13.28; interficere ⟦J 18.31⟧; A 5.33; 7.28; 16.27; interfici Mt 16.21; L 23.32.

interitus interitum A 13.34.

interlocutio interlocutiones (*ac.*) A 17.20.

interpono interponens (*m.*) A 18.4.

interpraetor interpraetatur J 9.7 interpraetabatur A 13.8; interpraetari L 24.27; interpraetatum (*neu.n.*) Mt 1.23; Mk 5.41; 15.22,34; A 4.36.

interrogatio interrogatione A 12.19.

interrogo A 10.29; interrogas Mt 19.17; ⟦J 18.21⟧; interrogat J 16.5; interrogant Mk 7.5; interrogamur A 4.9; interrogabat Mt 2.4;

16.13; J 4.52; L 8.45; 15.26; 18.36; 23.9; Mk 5.9; 8.23,27; 9.33; 12.28; 14.60; A 21.33; **interrogabant** L 8.9; Mk 7.17; 9.11,28; 10.2; 12.14,18; 13.3; A 1.6; 4.7; 10.18; **interrogabo** [Mt 21.24]; L 6.9; **interrogauo** (Mt 21.24); L 20.3; Mk 11.29; **interrogauit** Mt 22.35,41; 27.11; ⟦J 18.7,19⟧; L 8.30; 9.18; 18.18,41; 23.3,6; Mk 8.5,29; 9.16,21; 15.2,4,44; A 5.27; **interrocauerunt** Mt 16.1; **interrogaverunt** Mt 12.10; 17.10; 22.24; J 5.12; 9.2,15,19; L 3.10, 14; 20.21,27; 21.7; Mk 4.10; 10.10; **interrogauero** L 22.68; **interroget** J 16.30; **interrogaret** J 13.24; **interroga** ⟦J 18.21⟧; **interrogate** Mt 2.8; 10.11; J 9.21,23; **interrogare** Mt 22.46; J 16.19; 21.12; L 9.45; 20.40; Mk 9.32; 12.34; **interrogans** (*m.*) L 23.14; **interrogantem** (*m.*) L 2.46; **interrogantes** (*m.n.*) J 8.7; **interrogatus** L 17.20.

intingo **intingit** Mk 14.20; **intingat** L 16.24; **intingens** (*m.*) J 13.26; **intincta** (*ab.*) J 13.26.

intinguo **ntinguet** Mt 26.23.

intra (*c.ab.*) Mk 5.28; 6.51; A 10.17; **intra** (*c.ac.*) Mt 3.9; 9.3,21; 21.38; J 6.61; J 7.39,49; 12.17; 16.3; 17.21; 24.1; Mk 2.8.

intransmigro **intransmigrauit** A 7.4.

1. intro (*adv.*) J 20.26.

2. intro **intrat** Mt 15.11; J 10.2; **intrant** J 10.1; L 8.16; 11.26; **intrauit** (*fut.*) L 17.7; 18.17; Mk 7.25; 10.15; **intrauit** (*perf.*) L 22.3; Mk 2.1; **intrauerunt** L 9.52; Mk 5.13; 11.15; **intrauerant** J 6.22; **intraueritis** L 9.4; 10.5,8, 10; **intres** L 7.6; **intretis** Mt 26.41; L 22.40, 46; Mk 14.38; **intrent** L 21.21; **intra** Mt 6.6; 25.21,23; **intrans** (*m.*) L 7.36; 8.51; 11.37; 19.1; **intrantem** (*m.*) L 1.9; **intrantes** (*m.n.*) Mk 16.5.

introduco **introduxit** ⟦J 18.16⟧; A 21.28; **introduxerant** A 7.45.

introeo **introit** Mt 15.17; **introitis** Mt 23.13; **introibat** Mk 6.56; **introibi** L 7.44,45; **introibit** Mt (12.4); 19.23; J 6.22; 10.9; 18.1; L 21.35; **introibitis** Mt 18.3; **introibunt** L 18.24; Mk 10.23; A 20.29; **introisti** A 11.3; **introibit** (*perf.*) J 13.27; 20.5,6,8; L 1.40; 4.16; 6.4; 10.38; 19.7; 24.29; Mk 2.26; 3.1; 5.40; A (1.21; 3.8); 5.7; 10.27; 11.8; 14.20; 17.2; 18.7; 21.18,26; **introiit** Mt 21.12; 24.38; L 17.27; Mk 7.19; **introiuit** [Mt 12.4]; ⟦J 18.15, 33⟧; [A 1.21; 3.8]; **introibimus** A 11.12; **introistis** J 4.38; L 11.52; **introierunt** Mt 25.10; ⟦J 18.28⟧; L 9.34; A 5.21; 19.14; **introierit** J 10.9; L 13.25; 22.10; Mk 14.14; **introieritis** Mt 10.11; Mk 6.10; **introeas** Mk 9.25; **introeat** Mk 13.15; **introeamus** Mk 5.12; **introirent** L 8.32; **introieritis** Mt 10.5; **introisset** L 6.6; 14.1; Mk 6.22,25; 7.17; 9.28; 11.11; A 19.8; **introissent** A 1.13; 5.10; 13.14; **introire** Mt 12.29; 18.8; 19.24; 23.13; L 5.14; 8.41,51; 13.24*bis;* 14.23; 15.28; 18.25; 24.26; Mk 1.45; 9.43,45,47; 10.24; A 3.3; 14.1,22; 19.30; **introiens** (*m.*) L 1.28; A 12.17; **introiens** (*neu.*) Mk 7.15,18; **introeunte** (*m.*) L 17.12; **introeuntes** (*m.n.*) Mt 10.12; 12.45; 20.28; L 11.33; 19.30; Mk 11.2; **introeuntes** (*f.n.*) L 24.3; **introeuntes** (*m.ac.*) Mt 23.13; L 11.52; **introeuntibus** (*m.*) L 22.10.

intueor **intuemini** L 12.24,27; A 3.12; **intuens** (*m.*) Mk 10.27; **intuentes** (*m.n.*) A 4.13; **intuitus** A 3.4; 7.34,55; 11.6; 13.9; 14.9; **intuiti** (*n.*) A 6.15.

intus (*adv.*) Mt 23.25,26,27; 26.58; L 11.40; A 5.22,23; **intus in** (*c.ac.*) Mk 15.16; *v.quoq.* **abintus, deintus.**

inuado **inuaserat** ⟦Mk 16.8⟧.

inualesco **inbaliscebat** L 1.80.

inuenio ⟦J 18.38; 19.4,6⟧; L 13.7; 23.4,22; **inuenit** Mt 10.39; 12.43,44; 26.40; J 5.14; L 11.25; Mk 14.37; **inueniunt** Mk 16.4; **inueniebant** L 19.48; Mk 14.55; A 7.11; **inuenies** [Mt 17.27]; **inueniet** Mt 10.39; 16.25; J 10.9; L 11.10; 12.37,38,43; 18.8; **inueniemus** J 7.35; **inuenietis** Mt 11.29; 21.2; J 7.34,36; 21.6; L 2.12; 11.9; 19.30; Mk 11.2; **inuenient** L 13.24; **inueni** L 7.9; 15.6,9; 23.14; A 13.22; 17.23; **inuenisti** L 1.30; **inuenit** Mt 18.28; 20.3,6; 21.19; 26.43; J 9.35; 11.17; L 4.17; 22.45; Mk 7.30; 11.13; 14.40; A 10.27;**inuenimus** L 23.2; A 5.23*bis;* **inuenerunt** Mt 22.10; 26.60*bis;* 27.32; L 2.16,46; 7.10; 22.13; 24.2,3, 24,33; Mk 11.4; A 5.10,22; 13.6; 19.19; **inuentus est** L 9.36; 15.24,32; 17.18; **inuenta est** Mt 1.18; A 13.28; **inuenerit** Mt 24.46; L 15.9; **inueneritis** Mt 2.8; 22.9; **inueniat** Mt 18.13; L 15.4,8; Mk 13.36; **inueniamini** A 5.39; **inueniant** A 17.27; **inuenirent** L 6.7; 11.54; **inuenisset** A 12.19; 19.2; **inuenissent** L 24.23; Mk 1.37; A 11.26; 17.6; 18.2; **inuenire** J 14.30; A 7.46; **inueniens** (*m.*) Mt 13.44,46; (17.27); J 12.14; L 11.24; 13.6; 15.5; **inuenientes** (*m.n.*) J 6.25; L 2.45; 5.19; A 4.21; **inuentis** (*m.ab.*) A 21.4.

inuicem Mt 24.10; J 13.14,22,34*bis*,35; 15.12,17; L 7.32; A 7.26; 19.38; 21.6; *v.quoq.* **abinuicem, adinuicem, ininuicem.**

inuidia **inuidiam** Mt 27.18; Mk 15.10.

inuitator Mt 20.28*bis.*

inuito **inuitauit** L 14.9,10; **inuitauerat** L 14.12; **inuitaris** L 14.8,10; **inuitati sunt** L 14.24; **inuitatis** (*m.*) Mt 22.4; L 14.17; **inuitatos** Mt 22.3; L 14.7.

inumbro **inumbraret** A 5.15.

inundatio **inundatione** L 6.48.

inuoco **inuocatum est** A 15.17; **inuocauerit** A 2.21; **inuocare** A 19.14; **inuocans** (*m.*) A 22.16; **inuocantem** (*m.*) A 7.59.

inuolo **inuolet** J 10.10.

inuoluo **inuoluit** Mt 27.59; L 2.7; 23.53; Mk 15.46; **inuoluerunt** A 5.6; **inuolutum** (*m.*) L 2.12; **inuolutum** (*neu.*) J 20.7.

inutilis **inutilem** (*m.*) Mt 25.30; L 19.27; **inutiles** (*m.n.*) L 17.10.

iota Mt 5.18.

ipse Mt 1.21; 3.⟦4⟧,11; 6.4; 11.14; 12.50; 21.27; 25.17; 26.48; 27.57; J 4.2,12,44,53; 5.20,37; 6.6,15,20; 7.9,10; 9.21,37; 10.2; 12.49; 16.27; 18.1; ⟦19.21⟧; L 1.17,22; 2.28; 3.15,16; 4.15,30; 5.14,16,37; 6.3,8,35; 7.5; 8.1, 54; 9.51; 11.17; 15.14; 16.24; 17.11; 20.9,42; 22.41,47; 24.21,28,31,36,39; Mk 1.8; 2.25; 3.13; 4.1,38; 5.40; 6.17,45,47; 8.10,29; 9.28; 10.17; 12.36,37; 14.15,44; 15.43; A 2.34; 5.26; 7.15,31,48; 8.13; 10.42; 12.13,16; 14.12; 16.33; 17.25; 18.19; 19.22; 20.13; 21.24; **ipsa** L 1.36; Mk 5.33; **ipsum** A 10.16; **ipsius** (*m.*) Mt 5.35; 13.19; J 9.27; 15.10; Mk 6.2; A 7.18,43; 11.12; 14.3; 15.18; 19.26; **ipsius** (*f.*) L 2.35; Mk 6.22; **ipsi** (*m.*) Mt 4.10; J 9.9; 11.30; L 4.8; A 7.13,17; 13.23; **ipsum** Mt 16.24; 18.15; 19.19; 22.39; 27.42; J 4.42; 6.42; 7.4; 8.54; 9.21,23; 11.38; 13.5; 14.3,21, 22; 17.5,19; 21.1,18,25; L 4.23; 5.14; 9.23,25; 10.27; 15.17; 23.35; Mk 1.10,44; 8.34; 12.31, 33; 15.31; A 3.14,16,22; 7.5,8,35,37; 14.17; 19.4; **ipsam** Mk 3.25; A 16.19; 20.24; **ipsud** A 16.35; **ipsum** L 22.58; A 3.46; **ipso** Mt 1.20; 2.3; 9.10; J 5.26; 7.51; 9.21; 13.32; 16.13; ⟦18.34⟧; L 5.17; 11.38; 23.12; Mk 3.14; 6.14; A 2.24; 5.17,21,31; 12.5; 17.28; 18.18; 19.30; 20.10; **ipsa** L 1.29; 2.38; 7.21; 10.7,21; 12.12; 13.31; 20.19; 24.13,33; III J 12; A 8.9; 13.17; 19.33; 22.13; **ipso** L 23.40; A 11.23; **ipsi** Mt 5.5,4,[7]6,7,8; 12.27; 23.4; 25.44; J 3.28; 4.45; 17.8,11,19,21; ⟦18.28⟧; L 1.2; 2.50; 6.11; 9.36; 11.19,46,48,52; 14.1; 16.28; 18.34; 22.23; 24.35,37,52; A 2.22; 4.2,31; 5.24,32; 7.58; 8.6; 13.4; 15.32; 16.25,37; 18.15; 22.19; **ipsa** J 5.36; 10.25; **ipsorum** (*m.*) Mt 5.3,10; A 1.19; 5.36; 6.1; 11.29; 14.5; 18.26; **ipsis** (*m.*) ⟦J 18.21⟧; A 7.25; **ipsos** Mt 19.12; J 11.55,56; L 20.5; 22.23; 24.14,32; Mk 1.19; 8.7; 10.26; 11.31; 13.9; A 4.16; 10.21; 15.9, 12,17,27,29,33; 16.37; 18.11,12; 20.30; **ipsas** J 10.16; **ipsa** J 14.11; **ipsis** (*m.*) Mt 9.15; 17.22; 21.45; 26.26; J 11.37; 17.13; ⟦18.5⟧; L 3.8; Mk 9.2; 14.69; A 2.37; 3.1; 4.14; 10.10; 11.20,28; 18.26; 20.30; 21.26.

ira J 3.36; L 21.23; **ira** (*ab.*) Mt 3.8; J 11.33, 38; L 3.7; 6.10; Mk 3.5.

irascor **irascitur** Mt 5.22; **iratus est** Mt 2.16; 22.7; L 15.28; **iratus** Mt 18.34; L 14.21; Mk 1.41; **irasmini** J 7.23.

irequiro **irequisisset** A 12.19.

irr-, *v.* **inr-**.

is **id** Mk 7.2; **eius** Mt 1.21,23,25; 2.2,13, 14,20, ⟦21; 3.3,4⟧,12; 4.18,21,24; 5.1; 9.10, 19,20,21; 10.2*bis*,25*ter*,36,42; 12.19,21,26,29 *bis*,45,46; 13.10,25,32,36,41,44,55*bis*,56; 14.11, 12*bis*,15,36; 15.23,30,33; 17.1,2*bis*,19,27; 18.6, 25,29,31,32,34; 19.10; 21.35,38,45; 22.6,33,45; 24.1,31,46,51; 25.26,34,41; 26.7,51; 27.19,29 *bis*,30,32,35,37,53,64; 28.3*bis*,4,7,8,9,13; J 3.20,21,22,32,33,35; 4.2,12,27,34,47,51*bis*; 5.28,30, [32],35,37*bis*,38; 6.8,16,22,24,38,53, 54*bis*,60,61,66; 7.5,7,10,16,17,18,38,40; 8.20, 55; 9.2,3,4,6,18,20,22,23,31; 10.3; 11.3,4,8,13, 32,44; 12.3,4,13,16,50; 13.1,16,23; 14.24; 15.15; 16.17,29; 18.1, ⟦10,19,25,26; 19.2,23, 25*bis*,29,33,34,35⟧; 20.7,18,20,25*bis*,26,31; 21.2,20,24; L 1.13,14,17,23.24,31,32,33,49, 50,55,60*bis*,62,63*bis*,64,65,67,70,72,75,76,77, 80; 2.21,22,33,34,41,42,43,47,48,51; 3.1,4,7, 17; 4.22,32*bis*; 5.8,10,18,30; 6.10,14*bis*,17,19, 40,45; 7.3,11,28,38*ter*; 8.9,19*bis*,22,41,44; 9.11,29*bis*,31,32,51,53,54; 10.34*bis*,35; 11.1, 8,(8),18,21,22*bis*,54; 12.15,42,43,46*bis*,47; 13.17; 14.2; 15.20*bis*,21,22*bis*,25,28; 16.1,20, 21,23; 17.2,16,31; 19.31; 20.20,26*bis*,28*bis*; 22.44,50,51,64,71; 23.34,49,55; 24.8,23,26,47; Mk 1.7,16,19,22,33; 2.15*bis*,16,23; 3.26,27,31 *bis*,34; 4.10,32; 5.22,27,28,37; 6.1,2,3,14,27,29 *bis*,35,56; 7.17,19,25,33*bis*,35*bis*; 8.23,25,27; 9.3,21,27,28,42; 10.10,13,24*bis*; 11.14,18; 12.19*bis*,37; 14.3,4,16*bis*,44,64,65; 15.21,24, 26,45; ⟦16.7⟧; A 1.14,18, [20],22; 2.(3),29,30 *bis*,31,41; 3.7,16*bis*; 4.26; 5.7,10,20; 6.15; 7.5, 6,10,14,20,23,25,34; 8.1; 10.7,25,39,43; 12.3, 7,15; 13.8,24,31; 14.20; 15.16; 16.3,9,32,33; 17.16; 18.2; 19.12,31; 20.10; 21.19,21; 22.14 *bis*,15,16; **eius** Mt 1.19; 2.16; 9.25,26; 12.33 *bis*; 15.28; 24.32; 26.13; J 11.1,5; 16.21; L 1.5,41,58; 8.44,54,55,56; 10.10; 11.8; 13.19; 21.21; Mk 5.29; 7.26; 13.28; 14.9; A 3.25; 13.27; 16.15,19; **eius** Mt 9.16; J 8.44; **ei** (*m.*) Mt 1.20,24; 2.2,5,8,11*bis*; 3.15,16; 4.3, 6,7,8,10,11,24; 5.40; 8.27,28; 9.2,9,18,28,32; 11.2; 12.4,22,38,46; 13.10,12,27,28,51; 14.4, 17,28,33,35; 15.12,15,25,33; 16.16; 17.12,18; 18.6,21,22,24,27,28; 19.7,10,13,17,18,20,21,

[7] Order of verses in MS.

4.38; 10.8,39; 12.37,40; 13.12; 15.22,25; 17.20; [[19.31]]; L 1.16,51; 3.16; 4.27,29,30; 5.15,20, 22,25; 6.8,17,23,26; 8.12; 9.46,47; 11.17; 13.1; 15.12; 18.8,11; 20.23,33; 22.25*bis;* 23.23,24, 25,51; 24.11,16,31*bis*,36*bis*,43,45; Mk 1.39; 3.5; 4.15; 5.17; 6.52; 7.6; 9.36,44,46,48; 10.42 *bis;* 14.40; A 1.9, (20,21); 2.3, 17*bis;* 3.24; 4.4, 29,32; 5.9,15*bis;* 6.9,15; 7.19,57; 8.16; 12.20; 13.50; 14.3,27; 15.9; 16.19,24; 17.26; 19.9; 21.26; **eorum** L 4.26; **eorum** Mt 2.8; 24.31; J 10.32; L 1.77; 4.6; A 22.15; **eis** Mt 2.8; [[3.7]]; 4.19; 6.8; 9.15; 10.1; 11.4; 12.3,11,16,25; 13.11,13,24,28,29,31,52,57; 14.16,27; 15.10, 34; 16.1,6,15; 17.3,9,13,20,22,27; 18.19; 19.8, 11,13*bis*,14,15,26; 20.6,8,17,25; 21.6,13,16,21, 24,31,36,42; 22.1,20,21,29; 24.2,4,45; 25.14, 40,45; 26.10,18,19,27,31,38,45,48; 27.21,22, 23,26*bis*,65; 28.16,18; J 4.32; 5.11,17; 6.7; 7.45; 9.12,41; 10.6; 11.46; 13.12; 15.22; 16.31; 17.8,14,22,26; [[18.4,5,6,18,31,38; 19.4,5,6,15, 16]]; 20.23; L 1.22; 2.9*bis;* 4.39; 5.22; 6.5; 8.21,32; 9.1,21; 10.23; 13.2; 15.6,12; 16.15; 18.16; 19.13,46; 20.8,25; 22.19,41,47; 24.35, 44,46; Mk 2.24,26; 3.12,17,33; 4.12,34; 6.10, 37,38; 7.36; 8.15,30; 9.19; 10.3; 12.38; 15.8,11, 14; [[16.15,18,19]]; A 1.3,4,10; 2. [3],4; 4.3,17, 32; 5.13,25,40; 6.6; 7.26; 8.5,18; 11.2*bis*,4,15, 17*bis*,26; 12.10,17*bis;* 13.2,3,5,8,21,43; 14.13; 15.2,4,8,20; 16.4,23; 17.2; 19.6; 20.7,21.27; **eis** Mt 9.36; 13.3,34; 14.16; 28.9,10; L 24.11; A 7.43; **eis** A 16.14; **eos** Mt 2.8,9; 4.21; 5.2; 10.1,21,26; 12.2,15; 13.14,42,50,54; 14.25; 15.30*bis*,32; 16.4; 17.1,5,7,27; 18.17; 19.2,4, 14; 20.2,25,31,32; 21.3,14,17,41; 22.41; 25.32; 26.40,43,44; 27.10; 28.19,20; J 4.40; 6.17; 7.39; 8.31; 9.16,19; 12.19; 13.1; 17.11*bis*,12, 14,15*bis*,17,18,23; [[18.7,21,29]]; 20.22; L 2.17,18,34,46*bis*,49; 4.21,23,31,40*bis*,43; 5.7, 17,31,34,36; 6.3,9,10; 8.4,22; 9.2,3,10,11,13, 14,16,18,34,54,55; 10.1,2,18; 11.47,48,49,53; 12.16,37; 13.4; 14.5,7; 15.3; 16.29,30,31; 17.14; 18.7,15*bis;* 19.13,27; 20.3,17,23,34,41; 22.15,45,47,52; 23.14,20,22; 24.15,25,50*bis*, 51; Mk 1.21,22; 2.13; 3.5,21; 5.12,13,14; 6.7, 33,34,41,46,48,50,55; 8.3,5,10,29; 9.14,33; 10.1,13,14,16*bis*,27; 12.12; 13.12; 14.37,40; [[16.17]]; A 1.7; 2.6,11,38,40,47; 3.3,5,11,12; 4.7,8,13,15,18,19,21*bis*,23,33; 5.13,18,19,21, 22,26,27*bis*,29,33,38,39,40; 6.2; 7.6,26*bis*,34, 36,42,52; 8.14,15,17; 10.20,23,24,28,46,48*bis;* 11.2*bis*,15; 12.21; 13.2,8,15,17,18,19,46*bis*,50, 51; 14.1*bis*,5,19,23,25; 15.2*bis*,5,7,8,33,34; 16.20,22,23,24,25,30,33,34,39*bis*,40; 17.2,5,6, 9,15; 18.2,3,6,16,21; 19.2,6,13,14,15,16*bis*,17,25 *bis;* 20.6,12,18; 21.4,7,19,24,25,32,40; 22.19; **eas** J 10.3,4,27; 11.19; L 12.18; 23.28; 24.5; Mk 4.34; [[16.8]]; A 21.3; **ea** Mt 1.20; 11.25; 13.4,7,28; 23.4; J 5.36; 10.28; 13.17; 14.21; L 4.41; 6.47; 10.21; 12.24; 18.16; Mk 1.34; 15.24; A 1.3; 2.45; 17.23; **eis** Mt 2.7; 4.16; 6.1; 8.30,32; 9.4,15,28,30; 10.5; 12.39; 14.14; 17.13,24; 20.29; 22.35; 25.19; 26.21,36; **is** Mt 26.51; J 4.52; 11.46; 12.36; 15.24; 17.9, 11,12*bis*,19,23,26; [[18.9]]; 20.24,26; L 2.15, 51; 4.42; 5.35; 6.13,17; 7.6; 8.37; 9.45; 10.7; 11.15,49; 12.6; 17.15; 18.34; 22.24,50,55; 24.10,13,18,29,31,33,41,51; Mk 1.34; 2.20; 3.23; 8.1; 14.52; [[16.12]]; A 1.4; 3.5,8.11; 4.1, 32,34; 5.24; 8.11; 10.20,23; 11.3,12,21,22; 13.13,22,42; 14.15,52; 15.22,38; 16.40; 17.4, 34; 18.6,20*bis;* 19.9,12; **eis** Mt 18.12 J 5.39; L 5.2; 24.4; A 7.43; **eis** Mt 13.29; 25.16; J 6.12; 17.10; L 15.4; A 4.24; **eius** (*inc.*) L 21.20; **his** (*inc.*) A 4.22.

Isac Mt 22.32; L 3.34; 13.28; 20 37; Mk 12.26; A 3.13; 7.8*bis*,32.

Iscarioth, *s.v.* **Iudas.**

ispes, *s.v.* **spes.**

Israhel et Istrahel **Israhel** Mt 2.6,20, [[21]]; 10.6,23; 19.28; L 1.54,68; 22.30; 24.21; **Istrahel** Mt 9.34; 15.24,31; 27.9,42; J 12.13; L 1.16,80; 2.25,32,34; 4.25,27; 7.9; Mk 12.29; 15.32; A 1.6; 2.36; 4.8,10,27; 5.21,31; 7.23, 37,42; 10.36; 13.17,23,24.

Israhelitas (Istrahelitas) **Istrahelitae** (*voc.*) A 2.22; 3.12; 5.35; 13.16; 21.28.

iste Mt 18.4; 26.39,42; 27.47; J 7.36; Mk 1.28; 4.41; 12.11; 15.35; A 1.11; **ista** Mk 1.27; 4.10; 8.12; 14.4; **istud** A 5.38; **istut** Mk 14.5; **istius** (*m.*) [[J 18.17]]; **istum** Mk 14.71; A 6.14; **istam** Mt 15.15; Mk 8.2; A 5.4; **istut** Mk 10.5; **isto** A 4.10; 13.39; **ista** Mt 23.36; A 16.12,39; **isto** Mt 12.32; **isti** Mt 4.3; 21.16; 26.62; J 6.5; 17.25; L 4.3; 13.2; 19.40; 21.4; 24.44; Mk 12.40; 14.60; A 2.13; 10.47; 11.12; 13.14; 16.20; 17.7; 21.20; **istae** L 21.22; **iste** Mk 6.2; **ista** L 24.17; **istorum** (*m.*) A 1.22; **istis** (*m.*) A 4.16; **istos** J 17.20; 21.15; L 1.24; Mk 8.4; A 19.37; **istas** Mt 13.53; A 16.1; **ista** L 9.44; Mk 2.8; **istis** Mt 3.9; 5.19; 18.6; L 1.39; 3.8; 17.2; 24.18; A 5.35,38,39; 6.1; 11.27; **istis** (*neu.*) L 24.21.

Istrahel, Istrahelitas, *v.* **Israhel, Israhelitas.**

ita Mt 5.12; 8.28; 11.26; 12.22 45; 13.2,32, 40,54; 15.31; 18.35; 20.26; 23.28; 24.27,33,37, 39,46; 27.14; L 17.9; Mk 1.45; 2.12; 3.10; 4.1, 32,36,37; 8.25; 9.26; 10.43; 15.5; A 1.19; 5.15; 7.29; 12.15; 13.34,47; 14.1; 15.39; 16.26,37; 17.11; 19.10,12,16.

29,34,35,41; 13.2,5; 14.3,6,18,27,30,48,62,72; 15.5,37; A 1.1,11,21; 6.14; 13.32; 17.3; **Iesu** (*g.*) Mt 8.34; 11.2; 14.1; 27.58; J 6.22; 12.3; 13.23,25; ⟦18.32; 19.25,38*ter*,40⟧; 20.12; L 5.19; 8.35,41; 23.52,53; Mk 1.1; 15.43; A 1.14; 2.38; 3.6; 4.10,18,30,33; 5.40; 6.8; 8.12, 16; 10.48; 14.10; 15.11,26; 16.7,18; 18.4,8; 19.5,13,17; 20.25; 21.13; **Iesu** (*d.*) Mt 14.12; 17.4; 21.27; 26.17; ⟦J 18.22⟧; **Iesum** Mt 1.16, 21,25; 2.1; 14.29; 17.8; 18.1; 26.4,49,50,57,59; 27.17,20,22,26,27,54,55; 28.5; J 5.16; 6.19, 24; 11.3,21,56; 12.11,21,22; ⟦18.5,7,12,15,19, 28,33; 19.1,9,13,17,18,33,39,42⟧; 20.14; 21.21; L 1.31; 2.27; 8.28,37; 9.33; 10.29; 19.3,35; 22.47; 23.8,20,25,26; Mk 5.6,15; 6.30,55; 9.5, 8,15; 11.7,33; 14.53,55,60; 15.1,15; 16.6; A 1.16; 2.22,36; 3.13,20; 4.2,27; 5.30,42; 7.45, 55; 10.36,38; 11.17,20; 13.23; 16.4; 17.7; 18.5, 28; 19.13,15; 20.21; **Iesun** J 12.9; L 5.12; A 2.32; **Iesu** Mt 9.10,27; 17.19; 26.6,51; 27.57; ⟦J 18.15⟧; L 3.21; 24.19; Mk 2.15; 5.27; 9.4; 14.67; A 4.13; 16.31; 17.31; 18.25; 19.14; 20.24; **Iesu** (*voc.*) Mt 8.29; L 4.34; 17.13; 18.38; Mk 1.24; 5.7; 10.47; A 7.59.

Ioacim L 3.23.

Ioana L 24.10.

Ioanthas [A 4.6]; **Ioathas** (A 4.6).

Ioas L 3.23.

Ioathan L 3.23.

Iohana L 8.3.

Iohanes et Iohannes **Iohanes** J 10.40; L 1.60,63; 5.10; 7.33; 9.49,54; 11.1; A 3.1; **Iohannes** Mt 3. ⟦1,4⟧,14; 4.12; 10.2; 11.2,18; 13.55; 14.2,4; 21.32; J 3.23,24,27; 4.1; 10.41 *bis;* L 7.20; 9.7; Mk 1.4,6,14; 6.14,18; 9.38; 10.35; 13.3; A 1.5; 4.19; 10.37; 11.16; 13.13, 24,25; 19.4; **Iohannis** (*n.*) A 1.13; **Iohanis** (*g.*) J 21.16,17; L 5.33; 7.27,29; 20.4; *col.* III J.; **Iohannis** Mt 9.14; 11.12; 14.8; 21.25; J 3.25; 21.15; Mk 2.18*bis;* 6.24,25; 11.30; A [1.22]; 4.13; 12.2,12; 18.25; 19.3; **Iohani** L 7.22; **Iohanni** Mt 11.4; L 7.24; **Iohanen** *col.* J; L 1.13; 3.2,20; 6.14; 7.18; 8.51; 9.9,19,28; 16.16; 22.8; Mk 6.20; **Iohannen** Mt 3.13; 4.21; 11.13; 14.3,10; 16.14; 17.1; 21.26; *col.* Mt; J 3.26; 5.33,36; L 20.6; Mk 1.9,19,29; 3.17; 5.37; 6.17; 8.28; 9.2; 11.32; 14.33; A (1.22); 3.3,4,11; 8.14; 12.25; 13.5; 15.37; **Iohane** L 3.15; 7.24; **Iohanne** Mt 11.7,11; 17.13; Mk 10.41.

Ionas Mt 12.40; L 11.30*bis;* **Ionae** (*g.*) Mt 12.39,41*bis;* 16.4; L 11.29.

Ioppen A 10.5,8,23,32; 11.5,13.

Ioram L 3.23.

Iordanes **Iordanis** L 3.3; **Iordanen** Mt 3.⟦5⟧,13; 4.15,25; 19.1; J 3.26; 10.40; L 4.1; Mk 1.5,9; 3.8; 10.1; **Iordane** ⟦Mt 3.6⟧.

Ioseph **Iosef** L 2.16; **Ioseph** Mt 1.16,18, 19,20,24; 2.13,19; 27.56,57,59; J 4.5; 6.42; ⟦19.38⟧; L 1.27; 2.4; 3.23; 4.22; 23.50; Mk 15.40,43,45,46; A 1.23; 4.36; 7.9,13*bis*,14,18.

Ioses **Iosetis** Mk 6.3.

Iosia L 3.23.

iubenis, *v.* **iuuenis.**

iubeo **iussit** Mt 14.9; 18.25; 27.58; L [11.8]; 18.40; Mk 8.7; A 5.34; 21.19; 21.33,34; **iusserunt** A 16.22; **iussisset** Mt 14.19; 15.35; **iussissent** A 4.15; **iube** Mt 14.28; [27.64]; **iuue** (Mt 27.64).

iucunditas **iucunditate** A 2.28; 14.17.

iucundo **iucundabantur** A 7.41.

Iuda Mt 2.6; L 1.39; 2.4; 3.33; **Iudae** (*g.*) Mk 6.3.

Iudaea ⟦Mt 3.5⟧; **Iudaeae** Mt 2.1,5,6; L 1.5,65; 5.17; Mk 10.1; A 8.1; **Iudeae** (*g.*) Mt ⟦3.1⟧; 19.1; **Iudaeae** (*d.*) L 3.1; A 1.8; **Iudaeam** J 3.22; 4.3; 7.3; 11.7; L 7.17; A 2.9; 10.37; 11.1; **Iudaea** Mt ⟦2.22⟧; 4.25; 24.16; J 4.47,54; 7.1; L 6.17; 21.21; Mk 3.7; 13.14; A 11.29; 12.1; 15.1; 21.20.

Iudaeus J 4.9; ⟦18.35⟧; A 18.24; 19.34; 21.39; **Iudaeo** (*m.d.*) A 10.28; **Iudaeum** (*m.*) A 13.6; 18.2; **Iudaei** J 5.10,16,18; 6.41,52; 7.1, 11,15,35; 8.22,48,52,57; 9.18,22; 10.24,31,33; 11.8,31,36; ⟦18.20,31; 19.31⟧; Mk 7.3; A 2.5, 10; 13.45,50; 14.19; 16.20; 17.13; 18.12; 19.10; 21.11,27; **Iudei** ⟦J 19.7,12⟧; **Iudaeorum** Mt 2.2; 27.11,29,37; J 5.1; 6.4; 7.2,13; 8.9; 11.45, 55; 12.11; ⟦18.12,33,39; 19.3,19,20,21*bis*⟧; 20.19; L 7.3; 23.3,37,38,51; Mk 15.2,9,12,18, 26; A 10.22,39; 12.11; 13.5,43; 14.1*bis*,2,5; 17.1,10; **Iudeorum** ⟦J 19.21,38,42⟧; **Iudaeis** J 5.15; 8.31; 13.33; ⟦18.14,36; 19.14⟧; A 11.19; 12.3; 17.17; 18.5,19; 19.17; 20.21,24; **Iudeis** ⟦J 19.40⟧; **Iudaeos** Mt 28.15; J 3.25; 9.22; 10.19; 11.33,54; ⟦18.38⟧; A 16.3; 18.2,4, 14,28; 21.21; **Iudaeis** J 4.22; 12.9; A 14.4; 17.5; 19.13,33; 20.3,19; 22.12; **Iudaei** (*voc.*) A 2.14; 18.14; **Iudaea** (*f.s.*) Mk 1.5; **Iudeae** (*g.*) A 16.1; **Iudaea** A 12.19.

Iudas **Iuda** Mt 26.25; **Iudas** Mt 10.4; 13.55; 26.47; 27.3; J 13.29; 14.22; ⟦18.2,3,5⟧; A 1.25; 5.37; 15.22,32,34; **Iudam** A 15.27; **Iudan** L 6.16; 22.3; **Iuda** A 1.16; **Iuda** (*voc.*) L 22.48; **Iudan in Scarioth** L 6.16; **Iuda Simonis a Caryoto** J 13.2; **Iudae Simonis a Caryoto** (*d.*) J 13.26; **Iudas a Caryoto** J 12.4; **Iudas Iscariot** L 22.47; **Iudas Scariotes** Mt

L 20.6; lapidistis J 10.32; lapidauerunt Mt 21.35; A 14.5; lapidarent J 10.31; lapidarentur A 5.26; lapidassent A 14.19; lapidare J 8.5; 11.8.

lapis Mt 24.2; J 11.38; L 21.6; Mk 13.2; A 4.11; lapides (*g.*) L 22.41; lapidi A 17.29; lapidem Mt 4.6; 21.42; 24.2; 27.66; 28.2; J 8.7; 11.39,41; 20.1; L 4.11; 11.11; 17.2; 19.44 *bis;* 20.17,18; 21.6; 23.53; 24.1,2; Mk 12.10; 13.2; 15.46; 16.3,4; lapides (*n.*) Mt 4.3; L 4.3; 19.40; Mk 13.1; lapides (*ac.*) J 8.59; 10.31; lapidibus Mt 3.9; L 3.8; 21.5; Mk 5.5.

laqueus L 21.35.

lateo latuit L 8.47; latere Mk 7.24.

laterna laternis (*ab.*) ⟦J 18.3⟧.

Latinus Latinis (*f.ab.*) L 23.38; Latine ⟦J 19.20⟧.

latro J 10.1; ⟦18.40⟧; latronem Mt 26.55; L 22.52; Mk 14.48; latrones Mt 27.38,44; J 10.8; latronum Mt 21.13; L 19.46; Mk 11.17; latrones L 10.30,36; Mk 15.27.

latus latus (*ac.*) J ⟦19.34⟧; 20.20,25,27; A 12.7.

laudo laudauit L 16.8; laudare L 19.37; laudantem (*m.*) A 3.9; laudantes (*m.n.*) L 2.13,20; 24.53.

lauo labas J 13.6; labant Mt 15.2; lababant L 5.2; lababis J 13.8; laui J 13.14; labit J 13.12; lauit Mt 27.24; J 13.10; lauero J 13.8; lauerint (*coni.*) Mk 7.3; labare J 13.10; lauare J 13.5,14; lotis (*f.ab.*) Mk 7.2.

lauor lauoro, *v.* labor, laboro.

laus laudem Mt 21.16; A 2.47; 3.8.

Lazarus Lazar J 11.14; Lazarus J 11.1,2, 11; 12.1,2; L 16.20,25; Lazarum J 11.5; 12.9, 10.17; L 16.23,24; Lazare J 11.43.

Lebbeus Mt 10.3; Lebbeum Mk 3.18.

lectio lectionem A 13.15.

lector lectores (*n.*) A 16.38; lectores (*ac.*) A 16.35.

lectulus lectulis (*ab.*) A 5.15.

lectus lectum Mt 9.6; L 5.18; 8.16; Mk 4.21; 7.30; lecto Mt 9.2; 24.41; L 17.34; lectorum Mk 7.4.

legatus legatos L 14.32; 19.14.

legio L 8.30; Mk 5.9; legion L 8.36; legiones (*ac.*) Mt 26.53.

lego legis L 10.26; legit Mt 24.15; Mk 13.14*bis;* legunt L 6.44; leguntur A 13.27; legistis Mt 12.3,5; 19.4; 21.16,42; 22.31; L 6.3; Mk 2.25; 12.10,26; legerunt ⟦J 19.20⟧; legatur A 15.21; legissent A 15.31; legere L 4.16.

lenis lenes (*f.ac.*) L 3.5.

lentiamen lentiamine J 20.7; lentiamina (*ac.*) J 20.5,6.

lentium, *v.* linteum.

lepra Mk 1.42.

leprosus L 5.12; Mk 1.40; leprosi (*m.g.*) Mt 26.6; Mk 14.3; leprosi (*n.*) Mt 11.5; L 4.27; 7.22; 17.12; leprosos Mt 10.8.

Leui L 5.27,29.

leuis leue (*neu.n.*) Mt 11.30.

Leuita L 10.32; A 4.36.

leuo leuat Mt 12.11; leuabit J 13.18; L 14.5; leuabit (*perf.*) A 10.26; leuauit Mt 17.1; leuauerunt A 4.24; 14.11; leuatus est A 1.9; leuate Mt 24.31; leuare L 18.13; leuans (*m.*) L 16.23; 24.50; leuantes (*m.n.*) Mt 17.8.

lex ex J 7.23; lex Mt 11.13; J 7.51; L 16.16; leges (*g.*) L 11.53; legis Mt 23.23; L 2.27; 5.17; 6.4; 7.30; 10.25; 11.45,46 52; 14.3; A 5.34; 13.15; 21.20; legem Mt 5.17; J 7.19 *bis*,49; ⟦18.31; 19.7*bis*⟧; L 2.22,39 A 6.13; 7.53; 15.5; 18.13,15; 19.39; 21.24,28; 22.12; lege Mt 5.18; 12.5; 22.36; J 8.5,17; 10.34; 12.34; L 2.23,24; 10.26; 16.17; 24.44; A 13.39; leges (*ac.*) J 15.25.

libellus libellum Mk 10.4.

libens libenter Mk 12.37; liuenter Mk 6.20; A 13.8.

1. liber liberi (*n.*) Mt 17.26; liueri J 8.33, 36.

2. liber librum Mt 19.7; L 4.20; libro J 20.30; L 3.4; 20.42; Mk 12.26; A 1.20; 7.42; libri J 21.25; libros A 19.19.

liberatio liueratio L 21.28.

libero liberat [Mt 27.49]; liuerat (Mt 27.49); liuerabantur A 5.15; liuerabit J 8.32, 36; liberabitur Mt 24.13; liuerauit A 12.17; liberet [Mt 27.43]; liueret (Mt 27.43); libera Mt 14.30; [27.40]; L 11.4; liuera (Mt 27.40); liberatos L 1.74.

libertinus liuertinorum (*m.*) A 6.9.

libra libram J 12.3; libras ⟦J 19.39⟧.

licet Mt 12.2,10,12; 14.4; 15.26; 19.3; 20.15; 22.17; 27.6; J 5.10; ⟦18.31⟧; L 6.2,9; 14.3; 20.22; Mk 3.4; 6.18,23; 10.2; 12.14; A 2.29; 16.21; 21.37; licebat Mt 12.4; L 6.4; Mk 2.24,26.

lignum ligno (*ab.*) L 23.31; A 5.30; 10.39; 13.29; 16.24.

ligo ligabatur L 8.29; ligabant A 21.11; ligauit Mt 14.3; L 13.16; A 21.11; ligauerunt ⟦J 18.12; 19.40⟧; ligatus erat Mk 5.4; ligata erat J 11.44; ligaueris Mt 16.19; ligaueritis

Mt 18.18; ligate Mt 13.30; ligare Mk 5.3; ligari A 21.13,33; ligantes (*m.n.*) Mt 27.2; ligatus J 11.44; A 12.6; 20.22; ligatum (*neu.*) Mt 16.19; ligatum (*m.*) [[J 18.24]]; Mk 5.4; 11.2; ligatum (*neu.*) A 10.11; ligata (*neu.n.*) [Mt 18.18].

lilium lilia (*ac.*) L 12.27.

lingo elingebant L 16.21.

lingua L 1.63; A 2.26; linguae (*g.*) Mk 7.35; linguam L 16.24; Mk 7.33; lingua A 1.19; 2.6,8; 21.40; 22.2; linguae A 2.3; linguis (*ab.*) [[Mk 16.17]]; A 2.4,11; 10.46; 19.6.

lino linuit J 9.6,11.

linteum A 11.5; lentium (*ac.*) J 13.4; linteum A 10.11; lentio J 13.5; linteis (*ab.*) [[J 19.40]].

linum linum (*ac.*) Mt 12.20.

liquo liquantes (*m.voc.*) Mt 23.24.

lis lite L 23.12.

Lithostratus [[J 19.13]].

litigo litigabant J 6.52; litigantibus (*m.d.*) A 7.26.

littera litteris J 5.47; litteras J 7.15; L 16.6,7; litteris L 23.38; A 4.13.

litus litus (*ac.*) Mt 13.2,48; J 21.4; litore A 21.5.

liu-, *v.* lib-.

loco locauit Mt 21.33,41.

loculus loculum J 12.6; 13.29.

locuntur, *s.v.* loquor.

locuples locuplens L 19.2.

locus Mt 14.15; 27.33; J 4.20; [[19.20]]; L 2.7; 14.22; Mk 6.35; 15.22; [[16.6]]; A 4.31; 7.33,49; loci Mt 14.35; A 21.12; locum Mt 14.13; 20.28; 26.52; 27.33; 28.6; J 6.23; 10.40; 11.30,48; 14.2,3; [[18.2; 19.17]]; 20.7; L 4.17,37,42; 10.1,32; 14.9*bis*,10; 16.28; 23.33; Mk 1.35; 6.31,32; 15.22,47; A 1.25*bis;* 6.13, 14; 21.28*bis;* loco Mt 24.15; J 5.13; 6.10; 11.6; [[19.13,41]]; L 6.17; 9.12; 11.1; 22.40; A 7.7; 12.7; loca (*ac.*) Mt 12.43; 24.7; L 11.24; 21.11; Mk 4.5; 13.8; locis Mt 20.28; L 5.14; Mk 1.45; A 16.3.

locusta locuste (*n.pl.*) [[Mt 3.4]]; lucustas Mk 1.6.

longinquus longinquam L 15.13; 19.12; longinquo (*adv.*) A 2.39.

longus longa (*ac.*) L 20.47; longiore (*neu.*) A 18.20; longe (*adv.*) Mt 8.30; 15.8; J 21.8; L 7.6; 14.32; 15.20; Mk 7.6; 12.34; A 17.27; longius L 24.28; *v.quoq.* alonge, delonge.

loquella loquellam J 8.43.

loquor Mt 13.13; J 4.26; 7.17; 8.25,26,28, 38,45; 12.50*bis;* 14.10; 17.13; loqueris Mt 13.10; J 16.29; [[19.10]]; loquitur Mt 10.20; 12.34; J 3.31,34; 7.18,26; 8.44*bis;* 9.37; L 5.21; 6.45; Mk 2.7; loquituitur J 7.46; loquimini Mt 10.20; A 5.20; locuntur Mt 12.36; A 2.7; loquebatur Mt 13.34; J 4.27; 7.13; 8.12; L 1.64; 9.11; 24.32; Mk 2.2; 4.33, 34; 7.35; 8.32; 9.6; 14.31; L 6.10; 7.38,44; 10.7; 11.14; 16.13; 19.6,8; loquebantur L 1.65; A 4.31; 11.20; loquar J 12.49; 14.30; 16.25; loqueris J 4.27; loquetur Mt 26.13; J 9.21; 16.13*bis;* loquentur [[Mk 16.17]]; locutus sum J 8.40; 12.48,49; 14.10,25; 15.11; 16.1,4,6,25,33; [[18.20*bis*,21,23]]; L 24.44; locututus sum J 6.63; locutus est Mt 9.33; 13.3,31,34; 14.27; 23.1; 28.18; J 7.46; 8.20; 9.29; 12.29,36,41; 17.1; L 1.55,70; 24.6; Mk 6.50; [[16.19]]; A 3.21; 4.25; 7.6; locuti sunt L 24.25; A 3.24; 16.32; loquatur A 10.32; loquamini Mt 10.19; Mk 13.11; locutus fuerit A 3.22; loqueretur Mt 12.22; loquerentur A 4.18; locutus esset Mt 19.1; locutus fuissem J 15.22; loquere A 18.9; loquimini Mt 6.7; Mk 13.11; loqui Mt 12.34,46,47; J 8.26; L 1.19,20,22; 4.41; 7.15; 11.2; Mk 1.34; 7.37; 9.39; 12.1; A 2.4; 4.17,20,29; 5.40; 11.15; 13.46; 14.1; 16.6; 18.26; 21.37,39; loquens (*m.*) L 5.4; 7.1; A 6.13; loquentem (*m.*) A 6.11; 14.9; loquente (*m.*) Mt 9.18; 12.46; 17.5; 26.47; J 8.30; L 8.49; 22.47,60; Mk 5.35; 14.43; A 10.44; loquentes Mt 17.3; Mk 9.4; 13.11; A 11.19; 13.43; 20.30; loquentium (*m.*) L 24.36; loquentes (*m.*) Mt 15.31; L 20.20; A 2.6,11; 10.46; loquentibus (*m.*) A 4.1; locuti (*n.*) A 14.25; locuturum (*m.*) III J 14.

Lot L 17.28,29,32.

Lucas Lucam col. L; Lucan col. J.

luceo lucet Mt 24.27; lucebunt Mt 13.43; luceat Mt 5.15,16; lucens (*f.*) J 5.35.

lucerna J 5.35; L 11.34; Mk 4.21; lucernam Mt 5.15; L 8.16; 11.33; 15.8; lucernae L 12.35.

lucidus lucida (*n.*) Mt 17.5; lucidum (*n.*) L 11.34.

Lucius A 13.1.

lucror lucretur Mt 16.26; Mk 8.36; lucrastus es (Mt 18.15); lucratus es [Mt 18.15]; lucratus est Mt 25.16,17; lucrari L 9.25.

lucustas, *s.v.* locusta.

lugeo lugunt Mt 5.4; lugetis L 6.25; lugete L 23.28; lugentibus (*m.d.*) [[Mk 16.10]].

lumbus L 12.35; **lumbos** [[Mt 3.4]].

lumen Mt 4.16; 5.14,16; J 9.5; 11.10; 12.46; L 11.35; **lumen** (*ac.*) Mt 4.16; 24.29; J 11.9; 12.35,36*bis;* L 1.79; 2.32; 8.16; 11.33; 22.56; A 13.47; 16.29; **lumine** Mt 10.27; J 5.35; L 12.3.

luna Mt 24.29; Mk 13.24; A 2.20; **luna** (*ab.*) L 21.25.

lunaticus Mt 17.15; **lunaticos** Mt 4.24.

lupus J 10.12; **lupum** J 10.12; **lupi** A 20.29; **luporum** Mt 10.16; L 10.3.

luscus **luscum** (*m.*) Mt 18.9.

lutum **lutum** (*ac.*) J 9.6*bis*,11,14,15.

lux J 3.19; 8.12; 12.35; A 12.7; **lucis** J 12.36; L 16.8; A 22.11; **lucem** J 3.19,20*bis*,21; 8.12; A 5.21*bis;* 20.11; **luce** J 3.20.

luxuriosus **luxuriose** L 15.13.

Lybia **Lybiae** (*g.*) A 2.10.

Lycaonia **Lycaoniae** (*g.*) A 14.6.

Lycaonus **Lycaoni** (*adv.*) A 14.11.

Lydia A 16.14; **Lydiam** A 16.40.

Lysania **Lysaniae** (*g.*) L 3.1.

Lystra **Lystrae** (*d.*) A 16.2; **Lystram** A 14.20,21; 16.1; **Lystra** A 14.6; **Lystris** (*ab.*) A 14.7.

Macedo A 16.9; **Macedonibus** (*m.ab.*) A 19.29.

Macedonia **Macedoniae** (*g.*) A 16.12; **Macedoniam** A 19.21,22; 20.1.3; **Macedonia** A 16.9,10; 18.5.

maceria **maceriam** Mt 21.33.

machaera **machaerae** (*n.*) L 22.38.

macula **macula** (*ab.*) L 1.6.

Madiam A 7.29.

Magadan Mt 15.39; Mk 8.10.

Magdalene, *s.v.* **Maria.**

magicus **magika** (*ac.*) A 8.9; **magicis** (*f.ab.*) A 8.11.

magister Mt 9.11; 10.25; 17.24; 26.18; J 11.28; 13.13,14; L 6.40; Mk 14.14; **magistrum** Mt 10.24; L 6.40; 8.49; Mk 5.35; **magister** (*voc.*) Mt 12.38; 19.16; 22.16,24,36; 23.7 *bis;* J 8.4; 20.16; L 3.12; 5.5; 7.40; 8.45; 9.33, 38,49; 11.45; 12.13; 17.13; 18.18; 19.39; 20.21, 28,39; 21.7; 22.11; Mk 4.38; 9.17,38; 10.17, 20,35; 12.14,19,28,32; 13.1; **magistri** Mt 23.8; **magistrorum** L 2.46; **magistribus** (*ab.*) A 14.5.

magistratus **magistrati** (*n.*) A 16.22,35; **magistratos** A 16.19.

magnalia **magnalia** (*ac.*) A 2.11.

magnifico **magnificat** L 1.46; **magnificabat** A 5.13; **magnificabatur** A 19.17; **magnificauit** L 1.58; **magnificantes** (*m.ac.*) A 10.46.

magnitudo **magnitudine** L 9.43.

magnus Mt 20.26; 28.2; [[J 19.31]]; L 1.15,32,65; 4.36; 7.16; 9.48; Mk 16.3; A 2.20; 5.5,11; 16.26; **magna** Mt 15.28; 24.21; L 6.49; 15.14; 21.23; Mk 3.8; 4.37,39; A 4.33; 7.11; 8.1,10; 11.27; 17.4; 19.28,34; **magnum** Mt 22.38; L 16.26; A 8.8; 11.5; **magni** Mt 5.35; **magnae** A 19.27,35; **magnum** L 2.9; 8.37; A 5.36; 8.2,9,10; **magnam** L 14.16; Mk 9.14; A 11.28; 13.50; **magnum** Mt 4.16; 27.60; L 2.10; A 15.3; **magno** J 6.18; 7.37; Mk 4.41; 5.42; **magna** Mt 24.30,31; 27.46,50; J 11.43; L 1.42; 4.33,38; 8.28; 17.13,15; 23.46; Mk 1.26; 5.7; 15.34,37; A 4.33; 7.57,60; 8.7; 14.10; 16.28; 19.8; **magno** Mt 2.10; 20.28; 28.8; L 24.52; A 21.40; **magni** Mt 20.25; L 21.11; **magna** L 21.11; **magnorum** (*m.*) J 21.11; **magnos** Mk 4.32; **magnas** Mk 13.2; A 8.13; **magna** Mt 24.24; L 1.49; A 6.8; **magnis** (*f.*) L 23.23; **magna** (*inc.*) L 5.29; **maior** (*m.*) Mt 11.11*bis;* 12.6; 18.1,4; 23.11,17; J 4.12; 8.53; 10.29; 13.16*bis;* 14.28; 15.20; L 7.27,28; 9.46; 22.24,26; Mk 4.32; 9.34; 10.43; **maius** Mt 13.32; 22.36; 23.19; Mk 12.31,33; **maiorem** (*f.*) J 15.13; **maius** J 5.36; [[19.11]]; **maiores** (*m.n.*) Mk 10.42; **maiores** (*f.ac.*) L 12.18; **maiora** J 5.20; 14.12; **maius** (*adv.*) Mt 20.31; **magis** Mt 10.6,25,28; 18.13; 27.24; J 3.19; 5.18; 12.43,13.14; [[19.8]]; L 5.15; 11.13; 12.28; 18.14,39; 22.26; Mk 3.4; 5.26; 6.51; 7.36; 9.42; 10.26,48; 15.11,14; A 4.19; 5.14,29.

magus A 13.8; **magum** A 13.6; **magi** Mt 2.1; **magos** Mt 2.7; **magis** Mt 2.16*bis*.

Malchus [[J 18.10]].

maledico **maledicit** Mt 15.4; **maledixisti** Mk 11.21; **maledixerunt** J 9.28; **maledixerit** Mk 7.10; **maledicentes** (*m.n.*) A 19.9; **maledicentibus** (*m.d.*) Mt 5.44; **maledicentes** (*m.*) L 6.28; **maledictus** L 6.4; **maledicti** (*n.*) J 7.49; **maledicti** (*voc.*) Mt 25.41.

malefacio **malefacit** III J 11; **malefaciat** A 18.10; **malefacere** L 6.9; Mk 3.4.

malefactor [[J 18.30]].

Maleleel L 3.37.

maletracto **maletractauerunt** A 14.2; **maletractare** A 12.1.

malignus Mt 13.19; A 19.12,15; **maligni** (*m.g.*) Mt 13.38; **malignum** (*neu.*) Mt 5.11;

19.15; 22.13; J 10.39; L 6.1; Mk 5.23; 7.2,5; 8.23; 13.2; 14.58; A 12.7,11; 17.25; 19.26.

Marcus A 12.12,25; 15.37; **Marcum col.** L; [[**col.** Mk]]; **Marco** A 15.39.

mare J 6.18; Mk 4.41; **maris** Mt 4.15; 14.24; 18.6; J 6.17; **mari** Mk 4.39; **mare** Mt 4.18; 8.32; 13.1; 14.25,26; 15.29; 17.27; 21.21; 23.15; J 6.1,16,19,22,25; 21.1,7; L 5.27; 17.2,6; Mk 1.16*bis;* 2.13; 4.1*ter;* 5.21; 6.48,49; 7.31; 9.42; 11.23; A 4.24; 10.6,32; 14.15; 17.14; **marem** Mk 3.7; **mare** (*ab.*) L 21.25; Mk 5.13; 6.47; **mari** (*ab.*) Mt 4.18; 13.47; Mk 5.13; A 7.36; **maris** (*n.*) Mt 8.27.

margarita margaritam Mt 13.46; **margaritas** Mt 13.45.

Maria Mt 1.16; 13.55; 27.56,61; 28.1; J 11.2,20,32; 12.3; [[19.25]]; 20.11; L 1.27,34, 38,39,46,56; 2.19; 8.2; 10.39,42; 24.10; Mk 15.40,47; **Mariae** (*g.*) J 11.1; L 1.41; Mk 6.3; A 12.12; **Mariam** Mt 1.20; J 11.19,28,31,45; L 2.16,34; **Maria** Mt 1.18; 2.11; L 2.5; A 1.14; **Maria** (*voc.*) J 20.16; L 1.30; **Maria Magdalena** J 20.18; L 24.10; **Maria Magdalenae** [[J 20.1]]; **Maria Magdalene** Mt 27.56, 61; 28.1; [[J 19.25]]; Mk 15.40,47; **Mariae Magdalenae** (*d.*) [[Mk 16.9]]; **Magdalene** L 8.2.

maritimus maritimam Mt 4.13; L 4.31.

Martae, *s.v.* **Martha.**

Martha J 11.20,21,24,30,39; 12.2; L 10.38, 40; **Martae** (*g.*) J 11.1; **Martham** J 11.19; **Marthan** J 11.5; **Martha** (*voc.*) L 10.41 *bis.*

martyr martyris A 22.20.

masculinus (*neu.n.*) L 2.23.

masculus masculum (*m.*) Mt 19.4; Mk 10.6.

mater Mt 12.46,47,48,49,50; 13.55; 20.20; 27.56*bis;* [[J 19.25,27]]; L 1.43,60; 2.33,48,51; 8.19,21; 12.53; Mk 3.31,32,33,34,35; 15.40; **materter** L 8.20; **matris** Mt 19.12; [[J 19.25]]; L 1.15; 2.21; A 3.2; 12.12; 14.8; **matri** Mt 14.11; 15.4,5; [[J 19.26]]; L 7.12,15; Mk 6.24, 28; 7.10,11,12; **matrem** Mt 2.13,14,20, [[21]]; 10.35,37; 15.4; 19.5,19,29; J 6.42; [[19.26]]; L 2.34; 8.51; 12.53, 14.26; 18.20; Mk 7.10; 10.7,19,29,30; **matre** Mt 2.11; 14.8; Mk 5.40; A 1.14.

Mathusala L 3.37.

Matthaeum, *s.v.* **Mattheus.**

Matthan Mt 1.15*bis;* L 3.23.

Mattheus Mt 10.3; A 1.13; **Matthaeum** Mt 9.9; L 6.15; **Mattheum col.** Mt; Mk 3.18.

Matthias (A 1.23); **Matthian** A 1.[23],26.

matutinus matutinae (*n.*) L 24.22.

maxilla maxillam Mt 5.39; L 6.29.

Medi A 2.9.

medicus medicum (*m.*) Mk 2.17; **medico** (*m.*) Mt 9.12; L 5.31; **medice** L 4.23; **medicis** (*m.ab.*) Mk 5.26.

mediocriter A 20.12.

meditor meditati sunt A 4.25.

medius J 7.14; A 1.18; **mediam** A 16.25; **medium** Mt 13.25; 14.24; L 4.30; 11.51; 17.11; Mk 3.3; 14.60; **media** Mt 25.6; L 11.5; Mk 13.35; A 20.7; **medio** Mt 10.16; 13.49; 14.6; 18.2,20; J 8.4,9; 20.19,26; L 2.46; 4.35; 5.19; 6.8; 8.7; 10.3; 21.21; 22.27,55; 24.36; Mk 6.47; 9.36; A 1.15; 2.22; 4.7; 6.15; 17.22, 33; **medios** Mk 7.31; **medium** (*adv.*) [[J 19.18]].

mel [[Mt 3.4]]; **mel** (*ac.*) Mk 1.6.

membrum membrorum Mt 5.29.

memini meminit J 16.21; **meministis** Mt 16.9; Mk 8.18; **meminisset** A 7.18; **memento** L 16.25; 23.42; **mementote** J 15.20; L 17.32; 24.6.

memor memores (*m.n.*) J 16.4; A 20.31.

memoria memoriam Mt 26.13; Mk 14.9.

memoror memoratae sunt L 24.8; **memorare** L 1.54; **memorari** L 1.72; **memoratus** A 18.18.

mendacium mendacium (*ac.*) J 8.44.

mendax (*m.*) J 8.44,55.

mendico mendicabat J 9.8; **mendicare** L 16.3; **mendicans** (*m.*) Mk 10.46.

mendicus J 9.8; L 18.35.

mens mentis Mk 5.15; A 10.10; 11.5; **mentem** A 8.9,11; **mente** Mt 22.37; L 2.48; A 10.31.

mensa mensam L 19.23; 22.30; A 16.34; **mensa** L 16.21; 22.21; Mk 7.28; **mensis** A 6.2; **mensas** Mt 21.12; L 19.45; Mk 11.15; **mensis** Mt 15.27.

mensis L 1.36; **mense** L 1.26; **mensis** (*n.*) J 4.35; **menses** (*ac.*) L 1.24,56; A 19.8; 20.3; **mensibus** A 7.20; 18.11; **men** L 4.25.

mensura mensuram Mt 23.32; J 3.34; L 6.37; **mensura** L 6.38; Mk 4.24; **mensuras** Mt 13.33; L 13.21; 16.7.

menta L 11.42; **mentam** Mt 23.23.

mentior es mentitus A 5.4; **mentiri** A 5.3.

mercennarius J 10.12,13; **mercennarii** (*n.*) L 15.17; **mercennariorum** L 15.19,21; **mercennariis** (*ab.*) Mk 1.20.

merces (Mt 5.12); 10.42; L 6.23,35; **mercis** (*n.*) [Mt 5.12]; **mercedem** Mt 5.46; 6.1,2,5;

ministro **ministrat** J 12.26*bis;* L 22.26,27; **ministrabat** J 12.2; Mk 1.31; **ministrabant** Mt 4.11; L 8.3; Mk 1.13; A19.22; **ministrauit** (*fut.*) L 12.37; **ministrauimus** Mt 25.44; **ministraret** L 4.39; **ministrasset** A 13.36; **ministra** L 17.8; **ministrare** Mt 20.28; L 10.40; Mk 10.45; A 6.2; **ministrari** Mt 20.28; Mk 10.45; **ministrans** (*m.*) L 22.27; **ministrantem** (*m.*) A 13.5; **ministrantes** (*f.n*) Mt 27.55.

minuo **minui** Mt 20.28; **minui** (*inf.*) J 3.30.

mirabilis **mirabilis** (*f.*) Mt 21.42; **mirabile** (*n.*) J 9.30; **mirabilia** (*ac.*) Mt 21.15; L 5.26; **mirabilibus** (*neu.*) L 13.17.

miror **miramini** J 7.21; **mirabatur** Mk 6.6; A 7.31; **mirabantur** J 4.27; 7.15; L 1.21; 4.22,32; 8.25; 11.14; Mk 1.27; 5.20; 6.51; 12.17; [A 2.7]; **miratus est** L 7.9; A 13.12; **mirati sunt** Mt 21.20; 22.22; L 1.63; 2.18; **miratae sunt** Mt 9.33; **miremini** J 5.20; **miraretur** Mt 15.31; 27.14; Mk 15.5; **mirarentur** Mt 13.54; **mirari** J 5.28; **mirantes** (*m.*) L 2.33; 20.26; **mirantium** (*m.*) L 9.43; 24.41.

mirus **mirae** (*adv.*) A 15.4.

misceo **miscuit** L 13.1; **mixtum** (*neu.ac.*) Mt 27.34.

misereor Mt 15.32; Mk 8.2; **misertus sum** Mt 18.33; **misertus est** Mt 4.14; (18.27); L 7.13; 10.33; 15.20; Mk 5.19; **misereatur** Mt 16.22; **miserere** Mt 9.27; 15.22; 17.15; 20.30, 31; L 16.24; 17.13; 18.13,38,40; Mk 10.47,48; **misereri** Mt 18.33; **misertus** Mt [18.27]; 20.34; Mk 9.22.

misericordia L 1.50; **misericordiae** (*g.*) L 1.78; **misericordiam** Mt 9.13; 12.7; 23.23; L 1.54,58,72; 10.37; 11.41; **misericordia** Mt 9.36.

misericors **misericordes** (*m.n.*) Mt 5.7.

miseror **miserabuntur** Mt 5.7.

missem, *s.v.* **messis.**

missio **missionem** L 22.41.

mitis (*m.*) Mt 11.29; **mites** (*m.n.*) Mt 5.5.

mitto Mt 10.16; 11.10; 23.34; J 15.26; 20.21; L 7.27; 10.3; 11.49; 24.49; Mk 1.2; **mittit** L 5.37; Mk 2.22; 4.29; 9.22; 11.1; **mittunc** (Mt 9.17); **mittunt** Mt 9.17; [9.17]; 13.42; 22.16; J 15.6; Mk 12.13; **mitteris** Mt 5.25; **mittitur** Mt 3.10; 15.17; L 3.9; 12.28; **mittebat** Mk 4.37; **mittebant** L 21.1; **mittebantur** J 12.6; **mittam** J 16.7; 20.25*bis;* L 13.8; 20.13; A 7.34; **mittet** Mt 13.41; 24.31; J 14.26; Mk 13.27; **mittent** Mt 13.50; L 5.38; 14.35; 19.43; 21.12; **mittetur** J 12.31; **misi** J 4.38; 17.18; L 22.35; [23.15]; A 10.20,33; **missi** (L 23.15); **misisti** J 11.42; 17.3,8,18,21, 23,25; **misit** Mt 10.5,40; 18.30; 20.2; 21.2, 34,36,37; 22.3,4; 27.3,19; J 3.17,34; 4.34; 5.23,24,30,36,37,38; 6.29,38,39,44,57; 7.16,18, 28,29,33,44; 8.16,18,26,29,42; 9.4; 10.36; 12.44,45,49; 13.5,16,20; 14.24; 15.21; 16.5; [[18.24]]; 20.21; 21.7; L 4.18; 7.3,6,20; 9.2,48, 52; 10.1,16; 13.19; 14.17; 15.15; 19.29; 20.10, 11,12; 21.3,4; 22.8; 23.7; Mk 5.13; 6.7,17*bis;* 7.33; 9.37; 12.2,4,5,6,42,43,44; 14.13 A 3.26; 7.12,35; 10.8,36; 12.11; 16.24; 19.22; **misimus** A 15.27; **misistis** J 5.33; **miserunt** Mt 13.48; 14.35; J 7.32; 11.3; [[19.24]]; 21.6; L 19.14; 20.20; 21.4; Mk 3.31; 12.44; A 5.18,21; 8.14; 11.22; 13.15; 16.23,36,37; 21.27; **missus sum** Mt 15.24; J 3.28; L 1.19; 4.43; **missus est** J 15.6; L 1.26; 4.26; **missum est** A 13.26; **miserant** A 15.33; **missus erat** L 16.20; 23.25; **missi erant** L 7.10; A 10.17; 15.38; **missus fuerat** J 3.24; **misere** J 13.20; **mittas** L 16.27; **mittat** J 5.7; 8.7; L 10.2; 12.58; A 3.20; **mitteret** Mk 3.14; **mitterent** J 8.59; Mk 12.41; A 15.22; **mitteretur** Mk 9.42; **misisset** A 7.14; 20.17; **misissent** A 11.30; [19.31]; **mississent** (A 19.31); **mitte** Mt 4.6; 5.29; 8.31; 17.27; 18.8,9; 21.21; J [[18.11]]; 20.27; L 4.9; 16.24; Mk 5.12; A 10.5,32; 11.13; **mittite** Mt 22.13; 25.30; J 21.6; L 5.4; **mittere** (*imv.*) Mk 11.23; **mittere** Mt 10.34*bis;* 15.26; 25.27; 27.6; L 12.5,49; 20.19; Mk 7.27; A 11.29; 15.25; **mitti** Mt 18.8,9; Mk 9.43,45; **mittens** (*m.*) Mt 2.8,16; 11.2; 14.10; 22.7; L 14.32; **mittens** (*f.*) Mt 26.12; **mittentem** (*f.*) L 21.2; **mittentes** (*m.n.*) Mt 27.35; L 5.6; 23.34; Mk 15.24; **mittentes** (*m.ac.*) Mt 4.18; Mk 1.16; **mittentibus** (*m.*) Mk 12.43; **missus** J 9.7; L 23.19; **missae** (*d.*) Mt 13.47; **missum** (*m.*) Mk 7.12; **missum** (*neu.*) Mk 10.28; **missa** Mk 15.37; **missi** A 11.11; **missos** Mt 23.37; L 13.34; **missum** (*inc.*) Mk 8.13; **mis** Mk 6.27.

mittunc, *s.v.* **mitto.**

Mitylene **Mitylenen** A 20.14.

mixtura **mixturam** [[J 19.39]].

mna L 19.16,18,20; **mnas** L 19.13,16,18,24.

mobere, *s.v.* **moueo.**

modicus A 19.23; **modicae** (*g.*) Mt [14.31]; 16.8; **modice** (*g.*) (Mt 14.31); **modicam** A 19.24; **modicum** J 6.7; 7.33; 12.35; A 14.28; **modica** A 15.2; **modico** L 16.10*bis;* 19.17; **modicis** (*neu.ab.*) Mt 25.21,23.

modius **modium** Mt 5.15; L 11.33; **modio** Mk 4.21.

modo Mt 3.15; 9.18; 26.53; J 5.17; 9.19,25;

J 5.46; 9.29,33; Mk 9.5; A 7.44; **Mosen** L 24.27; **Moysen** L 16.29,31; Mk 9.4; A 6.11; 7.35; 21.21; **Moyse** J 7.22.

mulcatio **mulcationem** A 7.34.

mulier Mt 9.20,22; 13.33; 15.22; 22.27; 26.7; J 4.7,9,11,15,17,19,25,28; 8.4,9; 16.21; L 7.37,39; 8.43,47; 10.38; 11.27; 13.11,21; 15.8; 20.32; Mk 5.25,33; 7.25,26; 10.12; 12.22; 14.3; A 16.14; **mulieris** J 4.39; A 16.1; **mulieri** Mt 19.5; 26.10; J 4.42; 8.10; **mulierem** Mt 5.28; J 8.3; L 4.26; 7.44*bis*,50; **muliere** Mt 19.10; J 4.9,27; (8.3); **mulier** Mt 15.28; J 4.21; [[19.26]]; 20.13,15; L 7.50; 13.12; **mulieres** Mt 27.55; L 8.2; 23.27,49,55; 24.22,24; Mk 15.40; A 8.12; 16.13; 17.4; **mulieris** A 17.12; **mulierum** Mt 11.11; L 7.27; A 5.14; **mulieribus** Mt 28.5; **mulieres** L 1.28,42; A 8.3; 13.50; **mulieribus** Mt 14.21; 15.38; A 1.14.

multiloquentia **multiloquentia** (*ab.*) L 11.2.

multiloquium **multiloquio** (*ab.*) Mt 6.7.

multiplico **multiplicabatur** A 6.7; 12.24; **multiplicatus est** A 7.17; **multiplicantibus** (*m.ab.*) A 6.1.

multitudo L 1.10; 2.13; 6.17; 19.37; 23.27; Mk 3.8; A 1.15; 2.6; 5.14,16; 14.1,4,7; 15.12; 17.4; 21.36; **multitudinis** A 4.32; 19.9; **multitudini** A 6.5; **multitudinem** Mt 9.23; L 5.6; A 6.2; 15.30; 17.13; 21.22; **multitudine** J 21.6.

multus Mt 2.18; L 7.12; A 18.10; **multa** Mt 5.12; 9.37; 26.47; J 6.2; 12.12; L 5.29; 6.17,23,35; 7.11; 8.23; 10.2; 22.47; Mk 3.7; 4.1; 5.21,24; 6.35*bis;* 8.1; 12.37; 14.43; A 6.7; 12.5; 15.7; 16.22; **multum** J 6.10; **multum** (*m.*) J 12.24; 15.5,8; A 16.16; **multam** Mt 13.5; 14.14; L 5.6; 9.37; Mk 4.5; 6.34; **multum** Mt 25.19; J 5.6; L 10.40; 11.2; 12.48; A 11.2; 13.44; **multo** L 8.4; A 20.2; **multa** L 21.27; Mk 13.26; **multo** L 16.10*bis;* A 11.2; 18.6; **multi** Mt 9.10; 13.17; 19.30; 20.16; 21.11; 22.14; 24.5,10,11; 26.60; J 4.39; 6.60, 66; 7.31; 8.30; 10.20,41,42; 11.19,45,55; 12.11, 42; [[19.20]]; L 1.1,14; 4.27; 10.24; 13.24; 21.8; Mk 2.2,15*bis;* 3.9; 5.9; 6.2,31,33; 9.26; 10.31,48; 11.8; 13.6; 14.56; A 4.4; 8.7; 13.43; 17.4,12; 18.8; 19.18,19; **multae** Mt 4.25; 12.15; 13.2; 15.30; 19.2; 20.29; 27.55; J 3.23; 6.5; 14.2; L 4.24; 5.15; 8.3; Mk 4.36; 15.41; **multa** Mt 27.52; L 7.47; 8.30; Mk 1.34; A 2.43; 5.12; **multorum** (*m.*) Mt 8.30; 10.31; 24.12; L 2.34; **multorum** (*neu.*) L 2.35; **multis** (*m.*) Mt 27.53; Mk 7.37; **multos** Mt [[3.7]]; 15.30; 24.5,11; J 6.9; L 1.16; 7.21; 14.16; 15.13; Mk 1.34; 3.10; 6.13; 13.6; A 1.5; 10.27; 16.18; **multas** Mt 13.58; 19.22; L 12.47; Mk 10.22; A 14.22; **multa** Mt 13.3; 16.21; 25.21, 23; 27.19; J 8.26; 10.32; 14.30; 16.12; 20.30; L 3.18; 9.22; 12.19; 17.25; 20.9; 22.65; Mk 3.12; 5.26; 6.13,20,23,34; 7.4,8,13; 8.31; 9.12; 15.3; **multis** Mt 20.28; 26.28; L 2.36; 4.41; 12.7; Mk 10.45; 14.24; A 8.7; 11.21; 15.35; 16.39; **multis** L 12.1; Mk 4.2,33; A 16.23; **multis** L 8.27,29; 23.8,9; A 1.3; **plus** (*m.*) Mt 12.41,42; **plus** (*ac.*) Mt 20.10; L 12.43; 21.3; **pleres** (*m.*) A 17.12; **plures** (*m.*) J 4.41; A 19.32; **plura** J 21.25; **plures** (*m.*) Mt 21.36; J 4.1; Mk 12.5; A 14.21; **plura** J 7.31; III J 13; **pluribus** (*m.*) A 2.40; 13.31; **plurima** Mt 21.8; J 12.9; **plurimam** A 19.26; **plurima** Mk 10.46; **plurimo** A 8.11; 14.3; **plurimae** Mt 11.20; **plurimos** A 18.18; **plurimis** (*neu.*) L 11.53; **multum** (*adv.*) Mk 5.10,38; 9.26; 12.27; A 18.27; **multo** J 4.41; Mk 10.48; A 20.1; **multa** Mt 9.14; **plus** Mt 10.37; 26.53; J 21.15; L 7.42,43; 9.13; 11.31; 12.23; Mk 6.51; 12.43; 14.5; **plurimum** A 4.22.

mundo **mundat** L 15.8; **mundatis** Mt 23.25; L 11.39; **mundantur** Mt 11.5; L 7.22; **mundauit** A 10.15; 11.9; **mundatus est** L 4.27; 5.13; 17.15; Mk 1.42; **mundati sunt** L 17.14,17; **munda** Mt 23.26; **mundare** (*imu.*) Mk 1.41; **mundare** L 5.12; Mk 1.40; **mundari** L 5.13; **mundatum** (*m.*) L 11.25; **mundatam** Mt 12.44.

mundus J 3.17; 7.7; 12.19,28; 14.17,19,27; 15.18,19*bis;* 16.20; 17.5,14,21,23,25; **mundi** Mt 4.8; 5.14; 25.34; J 4.42; 6.51; 8.12; 9.5; 11.9; 12.31*bis;* 14.30; 16.11; 17.24; L 4.5; 11.50; 12.30; Mk 4.19; **mundo** Mt 18.7; J 6.33; 7.4; 14.22; [[18.20]]; **mundum** Mt 16.26; J 3.17*bis*,19; 10.36; 11.27; 12.46,47*bis;* 14.31; 16.8,21,28*bis*,33; 17.3,18*bis;* [[18.37]]; 21.25; L 9.25; Mk 14.9; [[16.15]]; A 2.47; 17.24; **mundo** Mt 5.8; 24.14; 26.13; J 8.23*bis*,26; 9.39; 12.25; 13.1*bis;* 15.19*ter;* 16.33; 17.6,9,11 *quater*,13,14,15,16*bis;* [[18.36*bis*]].

mundus (*adi.*) J 13.10; A 18.6; 20.26; **mundum** Mt 23.26; **munda** Mt 27.59; **mundi** J 13.10; **munda** (*n.*) L 11.41.

munio **munierunt** Mt 27.66; **munite** Mt 27.65; **muniri** Mt 27.64.

munus Mt 15.5; **munus** (*ac.*) Mt 5.23,24 *bis;* **munera** (*ac.*) Mt 2.11; L 21.1,4.

murmur J 7.12.

murmuratio A 6.1.

murmuro **murmurant** J 6.61; **murmurabant** J 6.41; L 5.30; 15.2; 19.7; **murmurauerunt** Mt 20.11; **murmurari** J 6.43; **murantes** (*f.ac.*) J 7.32.

27; 5.36,37; 7.27; 8.16,43; 9.62; 10.22; 11.33; 14.24; 15.16; 16.13; 17.18; 18.19,29; 19.30; 23.53; Mk 2.21,22; 3.27; 9.39; 10.18,29; 11.2; 12.34; 13.32; A 4.32; 18.10; **nemini** Mt 16.20; 17.9; J 8.33; L 5.14; 8.56; 9.21; Mk 1.44; 5.43; 8.26,30; [[16.8]]; A 11.19; 16.6; **neminem** Mt 17.8; J 8.15; L 3.14; 4.26; 10.4; Mk 7.24; 9.8; A 5.23; 10.28.

neo **neunt** L 12.27.

Nepthalim **Nephalim** (Mt 4.13); **neptalim** (Mt 4.15); **Nepthalim** [Mt 4.13,15]; **Nephthalim** L 4.31.

nequae, *s.v.* **neque.**

nequam **nequa** A 19.16; **nequam** Mt 20.15; **nequa** (*voc.*) Mt 18.32; 25.26); **nequam** (*voc.*) [Mt 18.32; 25.26]; **nequiores** (*m.ac.*) Mt 12.45; L 11.26.

neque **nequa** L 12.4; **nequae** L 9.3; Mk 13.32; A 2.27; 4.12; 15.10; **neque** Mt 5.34,35 *bis*,36; 10.9*bis*,10*quater;* 11.18*bis;* 12.19*bis*,32 *bis;* 16.9; 22.30*bis*,46; J 4.15,21*bis;* 5.37*bis;* 6.24; 7.5; 8.19*bis;* 9.3*bis;* 11.50; 13.16; 14.27; 16.3; L 3.14; 6.43,44; 7.33*bis;* 9.3*ter;* 11.33; 12.10*bis*,22,24*quater*,27*ter;* 14.12*ter*,35*bis;* 16.26; 17.21,23; 20.35*bis;* 23.28; Mk 5.3; 6.8; 11.26; 12.24,25; 13.19,32; 14.68*bis;* A 2.31*bis;* 4.18; 15.10; 17.25,29; 19.2,37*bis;* 20.24; 21.21; **nec** Mt 5.15; 9.17; 10.14,24; 11.27; 12.4; 16.10; 21.27; 22.29; 23.10,13; 24.20,21,36*bis;* 25.13,45; J 4.11; 5.22; 8.11,42; 12.47; 14.17; 15.4; 21.25; L 8.17; 12.33; 16.31; 18.13; 20.8, 36; 23.15; 24.39; Mk 3.20; 4.22; 5.4,26; 6.11, 31; 7.19; 8.17,18*bis;* 9.30; 11.33; 12.10,21; 13.15; 14.55,59; [[16.13]]; A 4.34; 5.13,39*ter;* 7.5; 15.38; 16.21; **necdum** Mt 24.6; J 6.17; 8.20; 20.9,17.

nequitia Mk 7.22; **nequitiis** (*ab.*) A 3.26.

nescio Mt 25.12; J 8.55; 9.12,25; 20.13; L 13.25; 22.57,60; Mk 14.71; **nescis** [[J 19.10]]; L 6.4; **nescit** Mt 24.50; J 7.49; 12.35; 15.15; Mk 4.27; **nescimus** Mt 21.27; J 9.21,29; 14.5; 16.18; 20.2; Mk 11.33; A 7.40; **nescitis** Mt 20.22; 24.42; 25.13; J 4.22; 8.14; 9.30; 11.50; L 2.49; 9.55; Mk 4.13; 10.38; 13.33,35; **nesciunt** J 10.5; 15.21; L 11.44; **nesciebat** J 5.13; 20.14; **nosciebat** Mk 9.6; **nesciebant** L 18.34; A 19.32; **nescisti** L 24.18; **nescierunt** Mt 24.39; L 2.43; **nesciat** Mt 6.3; **nescire** L 20.7; 22.34; **nesciens** (*m.*) L 9.33; A 20.22; **nesciens** (*f.*) A 5.7; **nescientes** (*m.n.*) Mt 22.29.

nessitas, *s.v.* **necessitas.**

Nicanor **Nicanorem** A 6.5.

Nicholaus **Nicholaum** A 6.5.

Nicodemus J 7.50; [[19.39]].

nidus **nidos** L 2.24.

niger (*adi.*) **nigrum** (*m.*) Mt 5.36.

niger (*nom.*) A 13.1.

nihil Mt 10.26; 17.20; 23.16,18; 27.19,24; L 10.19; 12.2; Mk 7.15; A 20.24; 21.24; **nihil** (*ac.*) Mt 21.19; 26.62; 27.12; J 6.39,63; 7.26; 8.28; 9.33; 11.50; 12.19; 14.30; 16.23,24; [[18.20]]; 21.3; L 3.13; 4.2,35; 5.5,33; 6.35; 9.3; (18.34); 20.40; 23.4,9,14,15,41; Mk 11.13; 14.60,61; 15.5; A 4.14,21; 5.36; 10.20; 15.9, 28; 16.28; 17.21; 19.36; 20.20; 21.25*bis;* **nil** J 8.54; **nihilum** (*ac.*) Mt 5.13; L 19.44; A 19.27; **inihil** [L 18.34].

nimbus L 12.54.

nimis Mt 4.8; 17.1; Mk 9.3; A 6.7.

Nineuitae Mt 12.41; **Nineuitis** (*ab.*) L 11.30.

nisi Mt 5.13; 11.27*bis;* 12.4,24,29,39; 13.57; 14.17; 15.24; 16.4; 17.8,21; 18.35; 21.19; 24.22,36; 26.42; J 3.27; 5.19; 6.22,44, 46,53,56,65; 10.10; 13.10; 14.6; 17.12; [[19.11, 15]]; L 4.26,27; 5.21; 8.51; 9.13; 10.22*bis;* 11.29; 17.18; 18.19; Mk 2.7,26; 3.27; 5.37; 6.4,5,8; 7.3,4; 8.14; 9.8,9,29; 10.18; 13.20,32; A 11.19; 21.25.

nix Mt 17.2; 28.3.

nobellum, nobem, *v.* **nouellus, nouem.**

nobilis (*m.*) L 19.12; **nobiliores** (*m.n.*) A 17.11.

nobit, etc., *s.v.* **nosce.**

nobus, *v.* **nouus.**

noceo **nocebit** L 10.19; [[Mk 16.18]]; **nocui** Mt 20.13; **nocens** (*neu.*) L 4.35.

Noe Mt 24.37,38; L 3.36; 17.26,27.

nolo Mt 15.32; 21.29; Mk 8.3; III J 13; A 18.15; **nolumus** L 19.14; **nolunt** Mt 23.4; **nolebat** L 15.27; 18.4,13; A 15.38; **nolebant** Mt 22.3; **noluit** Mt 2.18; 18.30; 27.34; Mk 6.26; **noluistis** Mt 23.37; L 13.34; **noluerunt** L 19.27; A 7.39; 17.12; **nollet** Mt 1.19; **noli** Mt 6.2; J 5.14; 8.11; 12.15; [[19.21]]; 20.17,27; L 7.6,13; 8.49,50; 11.7; 14.8,12; Mk 5.36; A 10.15; 11.9; **nolite** Mt 5.17; 6.8; 10.19,34; 14.27; 17.7; 23.3,8; 24.6,23,26*bis;* 28.5,10; J 5.28,45; 6.20,43; 7.24; 10.37; L 2.10; 5.10; 6.37,38; 8.52; 9.50; 10.4,7,20; 11.2; 12.11,22, 29,32; 17.21; 18.16; 23.28; Mk 6.50; 9.39; 13.11,21; 16.6; A 20.10.

nomen Mt 27.57; [[J 18.10]]; L 1.5,27*bis*,49, 61,63; 2.21,25; 8.30*bis*,41; 11.2; 24.18; Mk 5.9*bis;* 6.14; 14.32; A 3.16; 4.12; 13.8; 15.17; 19.17; **nominis** A 3.16; **nomini** A 15.14;

noster J 8.39; 9.20; 11.11,14; 21.7; Mk 12.29; A 2.39; **nostra** J 7.51; L 20.14; Mk 12.7; **nostrum** III J 12; **nostri** (*m.*) L 1.78; Mk 1.3; 11.10; A 15.26; 18.8; **nostro** (*m.*) J 12.38; A 7.2; **nostrum** J 11.48; L 1.73; 11.3; 24.32; A 20.21; **nostram** J 10.24; L 7.5; 23.2; A 16.20; 19.37; 21.5; **nostrum** A 7.19; **nostro** J 4.12; **nostra** A 2.8; 3.12; **noster** L 11.2; **nostri** Mt 20.33; J 4.20; 6.31; L 24.20; A 7.4, 11,15,39,45; 15.10; **nostrae** Mt 25.8; **nostra** L 18.28; **nostrorum** (*m.*) Mt 23.30; L 1.71,74; A 3.13; 5.30; 7.45; 22.14; **nostris** (*m.*) L 11.4; A 2.39; 7.38; 13.32; **nostros** Mt 27.25; L 1.55, 75,79; A 3.22,25; 7.12,44; 13.17,32; **nostras** A 17.20; **nostra** L 11.4; **nostris** (*m.*) L 1.72; Mk 12.11; A 15.25; **nostris** (*f.*) L 13.26; A 2.11.

notitia **notitiam** A 4.18.

noto **notauerunt** Mk 15.47; **notum est** A 15.18; **notum sit** A 2.14.

nouellus **nouellum** (*n.*) Mt 9.17; **nobellum** (*neu.ac.*) (Mt 9.17); **nouellum** Mt [9.17]; 9.17; Mk 2.22.

nouem Mt 18.12,13; L 15.4,7; **nobem** L 17.17.

nouis (*pron.*), *s.v.* **ego.**

nouitas A 17.19.

nouus **noua** Mk 1.27; **nouum** [[J 19.41]]; L 5.37; **nobi** (*m.*) (Mt 9.16); **noui** (*m.*) [Mt 9.16]; **noui** (*neu.*) Mt 26.28; **nouum** (*neu.*) J 13.34; L 5.37,38; Mk [2.21]; 14.25; **nouo** (*neu.*) Mt 27.60; **noborum** (*neu.*) A 17.18; **nobos** L 5.38; **nouos** Mt 9.17; **noua** Mt 13.52; A 17.20; **nouis** (*f.*) [[Mk 16.17]]; **nonuum** (*neu.ac.*) (Mk 2.21); **nouius** (*ac.*) A 17.21; **nouissimus** Mt 21.31; 27.64; **nouissimo** (*m.*) Mt 20.14; **nobissimum** (*m.*) (Mt 5.26); **nouissimum** (*m.*) [Mt 5.26]; L 12.59; 14.9,10; **nouissimo** J 6.54; 7.37; **nouissima** J 6.39,40, 44; 11.24; 12.48; **nobissimi** Mt 19.30; **nouissimi** Mt 19.30; 20.12,16*bis;* L 13.30*bis;* Mk 10.31*bis;* **nouissima** (*n.*) Mt 12.45; L 11.27; **nouissimis** (*m.*) Mt 20.8; A 2.17; **nouum** (*adv.*) Mt 26.29; L 22.16; **nouissime** Mt 21.37; 22.27; 25.11; 26.61; L 20.32; [[Mk 16.14]]; **nouissimum** Mk 12.6.

nox J 9.4; 13.30; **noctis** Mt 14.25; L 2.8; Mk 6.48; A 16.33; **noctem** [Mt 2.14]; L 5.5; A 16.9; 17.10; 18.9; **nocte** Mt (2.14); 25.6; 26.31,34; 28.13; J 7.50; 11.10; [[19.39]]; 21.3; L 2.37; 11.5; 12.20; 17.34; 18.7; Mk 4.27; 5.5; 13.35; 14.30; A 5.19; 12.6; 16.25; 20.7, 31; **noctes** (*ac.*) Mt 4.2; 12.40*bis;* **noctibus** A 11.30.

nubes (A 1.9); **nubs** Mt 17.5; L 9.35; Mk 9.7; [A 1.9]; **nubem** L 9.34; 12.54; **nube** Mt 17.5; L 9.35; 21.27; Mk 9.7; **nubes** (*ac.*) Mt 24.30; 26.64; **nubibus** Mk 13.26; 14.62.

nubo **nubit** L 16.18; **nubunt** Mt 22.30; L 20.34,35; Mk 12.25; **nubuntur** Mt 22.30; L 20.34,35; Mk 12.25; **nubebant** L 17.27; **nubebantur** L 17.27; **nubat** Mt 22.24; **nubere** Mt 19.10; **nubens** (*m.*) Mt 22.25; L 16.18; **nubentes** (*m.n.*) Mt 24.38.

nubs, *s.v.* **nubes.**

nuditas **nuditatis** Mk 14.51.

nudo **nudauerunt** Mk 2.4.

nudus Mt 25.36,43; J 21.7; Mk 14.52; **nudum** (*m.*) Mt 25.38,44; **nudi** A 19.16.

nullus **nullius** L 20.21; **nullius** A 19.40; **nullius** L 22.35; **nullam** [[J 18.38; 19.4]]; A 13.28; **nullum** J 10.41; 16.29; **nullo** (*m.*) Mt 22.16; **nullo** (*neu.*) Mk 9.29; **nulli** L 9.36.

numero **numeratae sunt** L 12.7; **numerati** (*n.*) Mt 10.30.

numerus A 4.4; 6.7; **numero** (*ab.*) J 6.10; L 22.3; A 16.5; **numeri** A 5.36; **numeris** (*ab.*) A 11.21.

nummularius **nummulariorum** (*m.*) Mk 11.15; **numulariorum** (*m.*) Mt 21.12; L 19.45; **nummullariis** (*m.d.*) Mt 25.27.

numquam Mt 9.34; 21.16,42; 23.30; 26.33; J 8.33; L 6.3; 7.9; 13.27; 15.29*bis;* Mk 2.25; A 10.14; 11.8; 14.8; **nunquam** Mk 2.12.

numquid Mt 9.15; 12.23; 14.2; 26.22,25; J 4.12,29,33; 6.67; 7.26,31,35,41,46,47,48,51, 52; 8.22,53; 9.27,40; 10.21; [[18.17,25,35]]; 21.5; L 5.34; 6.39; 10.15, 11.11*bis*,12; 17.7,9; Mk 2.19; 4.21; 14.19; A 7.28,42; 10.47; **nunquid** Mk 14.19.

numularius, *v.* **nummularius.**

nunc **nun** J 16.29; **nunc** Mt 18.1; 24.21; 26.65; 27.42,43; 28.19; J 4.18,23; 5.25; 8.5,40, 52; 9.21,41; 11.8,22; 12.27,31*bis;* 13.31,37; 14.29; 15.22,24; 16.5,22,24,30; 17.5,7,13,20; [[18.36]]; 21.11; L 2.29; 6.21,25; 11.39; 16.25; 19.42; 22.36; Mk 10.30; 15.32; A 3.17; 4.29; 5.38; 7.4,34,52; 10.5,33; 12.11; 13.11,31; 15.10; 16.36,37; 17.18,20,30; 18.6; 20.22,25; 22.1,16.

nunciauit, *s.v.* **nuntio.**

nuncupo **nuncupati sunt** A 11.26.

nunquam, nunquid, *v.* **numquam, numquid.**

nuntio **nuntiabat** L 8.39; **nunciauit** [[Mk 16.10]]; **nuntiauit** J 5.15; A 10.25; **nuntiauerunt** J 4.51; L 8.34; 24.9; Mk 5.14; [[16.13]]; **nuntiatum est** L 8.20; A 21.31; **nuntiaret** J

11.57; nuntiate Mt 28.10; nuntians (*f.*) J 20.18; nuntiantes (*m.n.*) A 19.18.

nuntius nuntios L 9.52; nuntiis L 7.24.

nuptiae Mt 22.8,10; nuptias Mt 22.2.3,4,9; 25.10; L 12.36; 14.8; nuptiis Mt 24.38.

nuptialis nuptialem (*f.*) Mt 22.11,12.

nustertianus nustertiana (*ab.*) A 10.30.

nutrico erat nutricatus L 4.16.

nutrio nutrientibus (*f.d.*) Mk 13.17.

nutrix A 13.18.

o Mt 15.28; 17.17; L 9.41; 24.25; Mk 9.19; A 1.1; 13.10; 18.14.

obaudio obaudiunt Mt 8.27; L 8.25; Mk 1.27; 4.41; obaudisset L 17.6.

obdormio obdormiuit L 8.23; obdormiat Mk 4.27.

obduco obduci A 12.19.

Obed L 3.32.

obeo obiabit J 11.20; obisset Mk 15.44.

obes, obet, *s.v.* ouis.

obiurgo obiurgabat L 23.43; obiurgare Mk 8.32.

oblatio A 21.26.

obliuiscor obliti sunt Mt 16.5; Mk 8.14; est oblitum L 12.6.

oboedio oboediebant A 6.7; oboedientes (*m.n.*) A 7.39.

obprobrium (*ac.*) L 1.25.

obrigesco obriguit A 5.5.

obscuro obscurabitur Mt 24.29; obscuratus est L 23.45.

obsecro obsegro A 21.39; obsecrassent A 4.31.

obsegro, *v.* obsecro.

obserb-, *v.* obseru-.

obseruatio obserbatione L 17.20.

obseruo obserbabant L 6.7; Mk 3.2; obseruabi Mk 10.20; obserbate L 12.15; obseruare A 21.25; obseruantes (*m.n.*) L 14.1.

obsiduanus obsiduanos L 20.20.

obstipesco, *v.* obstupesco.

obsto obstitistis A 7.51.

obstupefacio obstupefacti sunt A 10.45.

obstupesco obstupiscebat A 8.13; obstupescebant A 2.7,12; obstupiscebant Mk 1.22; obstipuerunt Mk 5.42; A 12.16.

obtempero obtemperat A 5.32; obtemperabant A 5.36; obtemperare A 5.29.

obteneo obtenebantur A 10.38.

obtentus obtentu Mk 12.40.

obtineo obtinere L 20.35.

obtingo obtinget L 21.13; obtigit A 21.35.

obtusus obtusum (*neu.n.*) Mk 6.52; obtusa (*neu.n.*) Mk 8.17.

obuiam Mt 8.34; 25.6; 27.32; J 12.13. *v.quoq.* inobuiam.

obuio obuiabit L 22.10; obuiauit J 11.30; L 8.27; A 11.2; obuiauerunt J 4.51; 12.18; obuiari L 14.31.

obuius A 10.25; obuiam A 16.16.

obumbro obumbrabat Mt 17.5; obumbrauit (*fut.*) L 1.35; obumbrauit L 9.34; obumbrans (*f.*) Mk 9.7.

occasio occasionem L 11.54; occasione L 20.47.

occido occidis L 13.34; occidunt Mt 10.28; L 12.4; occides Mt 5.21; 19.18; L 18.20; occidetis Mt 23.34; occident Mt 17.23; 24.9; L 18.33; Mk 9.31; occidisti L 15.30; occidit Mt 22.7; L 13.4; 15.27; occidistis Mt 23.35; occiderunt Mt 21.35,39; 22.6; 23.31; L 11.47,48,51; 20.15; Mk 12.5*bis*,8; A 7.52; occisurus est J 8.22; occiderit Mt 5.21; J 16.2; L 12.5; occidas Mk 10.19; occidat J 10.10; occidamus Mt 21.38; L 20.14; Mk 12.7; occidant J 12.10; occiderent Mt 26.4; Mk 14.1; occidisset Mk 1.32; occidi L 9.22; occidite L 15.23; 19.27; occidere Mt 10.28; 14.5; J 5.18; 7.1,19,20,25; 8.37,40; L 12.4; 13.31; Mk 6.19; A 21.31; occidentem (*m.*) L 13.29; occidente (*m.*) L 4.40; occidente (*neu.*) L 12.54; occisa (*neu.n.*) Mt 22.4.

occultus [[J 19.38]]; occultum (*n.*) L 8.17; Mk 4.22; 5.33; occulto (*neu.*) Mt 6.4*bis*,6*bis*; occultae (*adv.*) (Mt 2.7); A 16.37; occulte [Mt 2.7]; occulto (*adv.*), *v.* inocculto.

occupo occupat L 13.7.

occurro occurrit Mt 28.9; occurrerunt Mt 8.29; occurret Mk 14.13.

Ochoziae L 3.23.

octabo, *s.v.* octauus.

octaginta L 2.37; octoginta L 16.7.

octauus octauo (*m.ab.*) L 1.59; octabo (*m.ab.*) A 7.8.

octo J 5.5; 20.26; L 2.21; 9.28; 13.4,11,16.

oculus Mt 5.29; 18.9; 20.15; L 11.34*bis*; Mk 7.22; 9.47; oculum Mt 5.38; oculo Mt 5.38; L 6.41*bis*,42*quater*; Mk 9.47; oculi Mt 9.30; 13.16; 20.33; 26.43; J 9.10; L 2.30; 4.20; 7.22; 10.23; 24.16,31; Mk 14.40; oculos Mt 9.29; 13.15; 17.8; 18.9; 20.34; J 4.35; 9.6,11, 14,15,17,21,26,30,32; 10.21; 11.37,41; 17.1;

L 6.20; 16.23; 18.13; Mk 8.18,23,25; 9.47; **oculis** Mt 13.15; 21.42; J 6.5; 12.40; L 19.42; Mk 12.11; A 1.9; 3.3.

odi **odit** J 3.20; 7.7; 12.25; 15.18,19,23*bis*; 17.14; L 14.26; **odiuit** J 15.18; **oderunt** L 1.71; **odierunt** J 15.24,25; **oderant** L 19.14; **odies** Mt 5.43; **odiet** L 16.13; **odient** Mt 24.10; **odierint** L 6.22; **odisse** J 7.7; **odientibus** (*m.d.*) Mt 5.44; L 6.27.

odibilis **odibiles** (*m.n.*) Mt 24.9; L 21.17.

odium **odio** (*d.*) Mt 10.22; Mk 13.13.

odor **odore** J 12.3.

offendo **offendet** J 11.9,10; **offendas** Mt 4.6; L 4.11.

offero **offeres** Mt 5.23,24; **offerebant** L 18.15; 23.36; **obtuli** Mt 17.16; **obtulisti** A 7.42; **obtulit** Mt 25.20; A 8.18; **obtulerunt** Mt 2.11; 4.24; 9.2; 22.19; A 7.41; **optulerunt** Mt [9.32]; 14.35; [[J 19.29]]; **optulunt** (Mt 9.32); **offertur** L 11.14; **oblatus est** Mt 12.22; 18.24; **oblata est** A 21.26; **oblati sunt** Mt 19.13; **optulissent** A 16.20; **offers** L 5.14; Mk 1.44; **offerre** J 16.2; **offerentibus** (*m.d.*) Mk 10.13.

oleum **olei** L 16.6; **oleum** Mt 25.3,4; L 10.34; **oleo** Mt 25.8; L 7.46; Mk 6.13.

olim Mt 11.21; L 10.13.

oliua **oliuarum** J 8.1; L 19.37.

Oliuetum **Olíueti** Mt 21.1; 24.3; 26.30; L 19.29; 21.37; 22.39; Mk 11.1; 13.3; 14.26; A 1.12.

olocautoma (*inc.*) Mk 12.33.

olus **oleribus** (*ab.*) Mk 4.32.

omitto **omittere** Mt 23.23.

ommutesco **ommutuit** Mt 22.12,34; **ommutesce** L 4.35; Mk 1.25.

omnino Mt 5.34; A 4.18.

omnis **omnes** (*m.s.*) J 12.46; 16.2; L 12.8; 16.16; **omnis** (*m.*) Mt [5.22,28]; 10.32; (11.13); 13.19,52; 19.29; 23.35; 27.25; J 3.16,20; 4.13; 6.40,45; 8.2,34; 11.26; [[18.37; 19.12]]; L 3.5, 21; 6.19,40,47; 7.29; 11.10; 12.10; 13.17; 14.11,33; 16.18; 18.14,43; 19.48; 20.6,18; 21.38; A 2.21; 3.9; 13.39; **omnes** (*f.*) Mk 2.13; **omnis** (*f.*) Mt 3.[[5*bis*]],10; 12.25; 13.2,54; 15.13; 21.10; 24.22; 28.18; L 1.10; 3.5,6,9; 19.37; Mk 1.5; 4.1; 9.15; 11.18; A 2.36; 3.23; 11.14; 14.7; 15.12; 16.15; **omne** Mt 12.25,31, 36; 13.33; 15.11,17; 18.16; J 6.37; 17.2; L 1.37; 2.23; 11.17; Mk 7.18; 9.49; **omnis** (*m.*) L 8.47; 11.53; 24.19; A [13.10]; 13.10; **omnis** (*f.*) J 17.2; L 21.35; A 13.10; 19.26; **omni** (*m.*) L 2.10; 6.30; 12.48; 19.26; A 4.10,31; 10.41; 13.24; 20.28; **omni** (*f.*) [[Mk 16.15]]; A 1.8; 2.43; 6.5; **omnem** Mt 4.23; 9.35; 10.1; L 2.1; 4.37; 9.13; 10.1; A 5.21,34; 10.43; 17.17; **omnem** Mt 3.15; 4.23; 9.35; 10.1; 19.3; 27.45; L 3.3; 4.6,13,14,25; 10.19; 12.44; 23.5,13; Mk 1.28; 5.33; 6.33; A 2.17; 5.15; 7.10,11,14; 13.44,49; 15.36; 16.4; 17.26*bis*; 20.27; 21.27; **omne** Mt 5.11; 18.32; J 5.22; 6.39; 15.2*bis*; L 9.1; 11.42; 21.4; A 10.14; 15.21; 18.4; **omnem** (*neu.ac.*) A 13.27; **omni** L 20.45; A 5.42; **omne** (*f.*) L 6.17; **omni** (*f.*) Mt 18.19; J 16.13; L 6.17; 7.17; 12.15,27; A 2.5; 4.29; 5.23; 6.10; 7.22; 10.35; 12.11; 15.26; 17.11; 20.19; **omne** (*neu.*) A 20.18; **omni** Mt 4.4; 13.47; L 4.4; 5.17; 21.36; A 1.21; **omnes** Mt (5.22,28); 10.30; 11.[13],28; 12.16; 15.37; 19.11; 21.26; 22.28; 23.8; 25.31; 26.27,31,33, 35,52,56; 27.22; J 3.26; 5.23,28; 6.45; 11.48; 13.35; 17.21; [[18.20,40]]; L 1.63,66; 2.3,18,47; 4.22,28,40; 5.26; 8.37,40,52; 9.17,43; 11.14; 12.7; 13.3; 14.18,29; 15.1; 19.7; 20.38; 21.4, 15; 22.70; 23.48,49; Mk 1.27,37; 2.12; 5.20, 42; 6.42,49; 7.3; 11.32; 12.44; 14.23,27,29,31, 50,53,64*bis*; A 1.14; 2.1,12,32,37,44,46; 4.21, 31; 5.17,36; 6.15; 8.1,10; 10.33,43; 11.23; 13.3; 16.3,28,33; 17.7,21,30; 18.17; 19.10; 21.[18],20,24; **omnis** (*m.*) L 13.5; A 3.24; 20.25; **omnes** Mt 1.17; 12.23; 13.56; 24.30; 25.5,7,32; L 1.48; A 15.17; 16.26; **omnis** (*f.*) A 3.25; 8.6; **omnia** Mt 5.18; 11.27; 13.56; 19.26; 22.4; 23.36; 24.8,34; J 10.41; 16.15; 17.7,10; [[19.28]]; L 4.7; 10.22; 11.41; 12.31; 14.17; 15.31; 18.31; 21.22,32; Mk 3.28; 4.11; 7.23; 9.23; 13.4,30; 14.36; A 1.18; 4.32; 10.12; 11.10; **omnium** (*m.*) Mt 22.27; J 10.29; L 1.71; 2.31; 3.15; 4.20; 9.43; 11.50; 24.27; A 1.24; 3.18; 10.36; 16.26; 19.34; 20.26; **omnium** (*neu.*) Mt 13.32; Mk 12.29; A 3.21; 5.32; **omnibus** Mt 5.15; L 2.38; 24.9; Mk 6.41; A 1.19; 2.39,45; 4.10,16; 15.3; 17.25, 31; 19.17; **omnibus** Mt 24.9,14; Mk 11.17; **omnibus** L 1.3; **omnes** Mt 2.4,16; 4.24*bis*; 14.35; 15.30; 21.12; 22.10; 24.39; 26.1; J 3.31; 8.9; L 1.65,75; 4.36; 6.10,19; 7.16; 9.11, 23; 12.18; 13.2,4,28; 17.27,29; Mk 1.32; 6.39, 55; A 4.33; 5.5,11; 10.38,44; 18.2,23; 19.17; 21.28; 22.15; **omnes** Mt 28.19; L 21.24,29; 24.47; Mk 4.13; 7.19; 13.10; A 13.22; 14.16; 20.2; **omnia** Mt 4.8,9; 8.33; 13.34,41,44,51; 17.11; 18.25,26,31; 19.20,27; 21.22; 23.3,5; 24.2,33,47; 28.11,20; J 3.35; 4.25,29,39,45; 5.20; 8.29; 10.4; 12.32; 13.3; 14.26*bis*; 15.15; 16.30; [[18.4]]; 21.17; L 1.65; 2.19,39,51; 4.5; 5.11,28; 7.1; 12.30; 14.21; 15.13,14,30; 18.12, 21,22; 21.12,36; 24.9,44; Mk 5.26; 6.30; 7.37; 8.25; 9.12; 10.20,28; 11.11,24; 12.44; 13.23,

latus fuero Mt 26.48; L 22.47; Mk 14.44; osculans (*f.*) L 7.45.

osculum osculum (*ac.*) L 7.45; osculo L 22.48.

ospitor, *v.* hospitor.

ossana Mt 21.9*bis*,15; J 12.13; ossanna Mk 11.10.

ostendo ostendet (*praes.*) L 22.12; ostendit Mt 4.8; J 5.20*bis;* ostendi J 10.32; ostendit L 3.7; 4.5; 10.1; A 10.28; ostensus est ⟦Mk 16.12⟧; ostendam J 14.21; L 6.47; 12.5; ostenderet Mt 16.1; ostende J 7.4; L 5.14; Mk 1.44; ostendite L 17.14; 20.24; A 2.37; hostendite Mt 22.19; ostendare Mt 16.21; 24.1; J 14.22; ostendens (*m.*) A 18.28.

ostensio ostensionis L 1.80.

osteum J 10.7,9; L 11.7; osteo Mt 27.60; osteum Mt 6.6; J 10.1,2; L 13.25; Mk 15.46; A 14.27; ostium ⟦J 18.16⟧; A 5.9,23; 12.6; osteo J 20.1; Mk 16.3; hosteis (*ab.*) J 20.19, 26; osteis Mk 13.29.

ostiara ⟦J 18.17⟧; ostiariae (*d.*) ⟦J 18.16⟧.

ostiarius J 10.3; ostiario (*d.*) Mk 13.34.

ostium, *s.v.* osteum.

otiosus otiosi (*n.*) Mt 20.6; otiosos Mt 20.3.

ouile ouile (*ac.*) J 10.1.

ouis obet (Mt 12.11); ouem [Mt 12.11]; L 15.6; oue Mt 12.12; obis J 10.3; oues Mt 9.36; 18.12; 26.31; J 10.4,8,12,27; Mk 6.34; 14.27; ouis L 14.5; ouium J 10.1,2,7; ouum (*ac.*) L 11.12; obes (Mt 10.6); J 10.3,12; 21.17; oues Mt 10.[6],16; 15.24; 25.32,33; J 10.16; 21.15,16; L 15.4; 17.7; ouibus J 10.11,13,15,26.

pabor, *v.* pauor.

pacificus pacifici (*n.*) Mt 5.9.

paecunias, *s.v.* pecunia.

paene paenae A 19.26; paene A 13.44; penae L 5.7.

paenitentia A 13.39; paenitentiae (*g.*) Mt 3.8; L 3.3,8; 15.7; Mk 1.4; A 13.24; 19.4; paenitentiam Mt 3.11; 12.41; L 3.16; 5.32; 10.13; 13.3; 15.7; 17.3; 24.47; Mk 6.12; A 2.38; 3.19; 5.31; 11.18; 17.30; 20.21; poenitentiam ⟦Mt 3.2⟧; paenitentia Mt 21.29; 27.3; paenitentia (*inc.*) L 15.10.

paeniteo paenituistis Mt 21.32; paenituerunt Mt 11.20; penitueritis L 13.5; paenituissent Mt 11.21.

paeniteor L 17.4; paenitebuntur L 16.30; paenitemini Mt 4.17; Mk 1.15.

pagus pagi A 17.22; pagum A 17.19.

palam J 7.10,13,26; 8.4; 10.25; 11.14,54; ⟦18.20⟧; L 5.14; Mk 4.22; 8.32; A 19.8; *v.quoq.* inpalam.

palea paleam L 3.17; paleas Mt 3.12.

palleum (*ac.*) L 6.29.

palma palmarum J 12.13.

palpo palpate L 24.39.

Pamphyliam Pamphyliae (*g.*) A 13.13; Pamphyliam A 2.10; 14.24; Pamphylia A 15.38.

panis panes (*n.s.*) J 6.35,48; panis J 6.33, 41,50,51*bis*,58; panis L 24.35; A 2.42; manem L 14.1; panem Mt 15.2,26; 26.26; J 6.23,31, 32*bis*,34,49,56,58; 13.18; 21.9,13; L 9.3; 11.3, 11; 14.15; 22.19; 24.30,31; Mk 3.20; 6.8; 7.2, 3,5,27; 8.14; 14.22; A 20.7,11; pane Mt 4.4; J 6.51; L 4.4; panes Mt 4.3; 15.33; J 6.7; L 4.3; 9.13; panes Mt 12.4; 14.17,19*bis;* 15.34, 36; 16.5,7,8,9,10; J 6.5,9,11; L 6.4; 9.16; 11.5; Mk 2.26; 6.37,38*bis*,41; 8.5,6,14,16,17; A 2.46; panibus Mt 16.11; J 6.13,26; L 15.17; Mk 6.41,52; 8.4,19.

pannus panni (*g.*) Mt 9.16; Mk 2.21; pannis (*ab.*) L 2.7,12.

Paphus Paphum A 13.6; papho A 13.13.

par par (*ac.*) L 2.24.

parabola L 8.9,11; parauola Mk 4.10; parabolam Mt 13.18,24,31,33, [36]; 15.15; 21.33; 24.32; L 4.23; 5.36; 6.39; 8.4; 12.16; 13.6; 14.7; 15.3; 16.19; 19.11; 20.9,19; 21.29; Mk 3.23; 7.17; 13.28; parauolam (Mt 13.36); L 12.41; 18.1; Mk 4.13; 12.12; parabola Mt 13.34; Mk 4.34; parauola Mk 4.30; parabolas Mt 13.53; 21.45; parauolas Mk 4.13; parabolis Mt 13.3,10,13,34,35; [22.1]; L 8.10; Mk 4.11; parauolis (Mt 22.1); Mk 4.2,33; 12.1.

paracletus J 14.26; 15.26; 16.7; paracletum J 14.16.

paradisus paradiso (*ab.*) L 23.43.

paralysis paralysin A 8.7.

paralyticus L 5.18; Mk 2.4; paralytico Mt 9.2,6; L 5.20,24; Mk 2.5,9,10; paralyticum Mt 9.2; Mk 2.3; paralytico L 5.19; paralyticorum J 5.3; paralyticos Mt 4.24.

parapsis parapsidis Mt 23.25; parapside (*ac.*) Mt 26.23; Mk 14.20.

Parasceue ⟦J 19.14,31⟧; Mk 15.42; Parasceuen ⟦J 19.42⟧.

parauola, *v.* parabola.

parbulus, *v.* paruulus.

parco parcentes (*m.n.*) A 20.29.

18.14; pati Mt 16.21; 17.13; L 9.22,25; 17.25; 24.26,46; Mk 8.31; A 3.18; 5.41; 17.3; patiens (*m.*) Mt 18.25; L 18.7; patientes (*m.n.*) A 14.15; passi (*n.*) A 8.7.

patores, *s.v.* peccator.

patria patriam L 2.3; Mk 6.1; patria Mt 13.54,57; J 4.44; L 2.5; 4.23,24; Mk 6.4; A 18.25,26; patriae A 3.25.

patriarcha patriaarcha (*ab.*) (A 2.29); patriarcha [A 2.29]; patriarchae A 7.9; patriarchas A 7.8.

paucus pauci (*n.*) Mt 9.37; 20.16; 22.14; L 10.2; 13.23; pauce (*f.n.*) A 17.4; paucos Mt 15.34; Mk 6.5; 8.7; paucas L 12.48; paucis (*m.*) A 15.30.

paueo pauebant Mk 10.24,32; pauerunt L 24.37; pauere Mk 14.33.

paululum (*adv.*) Mk 14.35.

Paulus A 13.9,16,46; 14.7,11,14; 15.2,35, 36,38,40; 16.3,18,25,28,37; 17.2,22,33; 18.2,5, 6,18; 19.4,6,8,9,13,14,21,26; 20.1,7,10,16; 21.13,18,26,29,39,40; Pauli A 19.11,29; 21.11; Paulo A 15.2; 16.9,29; 17.4; 18.9; 21.4; Paulum A 13.43,44,50; 14.9*bis*,12,19; 15.12; 16.17,19,36; 17.10,14,15,16; 19.15; 20.13; 21.12,30,32,35; Paulo A 13.13,45; 15.2,22,25; 16.14; 17.15; 18.12,14; 19.1,30; 20.9.

pauor pabor L 4.36; pauor [[Mk 16.8]].

pauper L 16.20,22; paupera L 21.3; pauperam L 21.2; pauperes (*m.*) Mt 5.3; 11.5; L 6.20; 7.22; pauperibus (*m.*) Mt 19.21; 26.9; J 12.5; 13.29; L 4.18; 18.22; 19.8; Mk 10.21; 14.5; pauperes (*m.*) Mt 26.11; J 12.6; Mk 14.7.

pax Mt 10.12.13*bis;* J 20.19,21,26; L 2.14; 10.5,6*bis;* 19.38; III J 15; pacis L 1.79; 10.6; pacem Mt 10.34*bis;* J 14.27*bis;* 16.33; L 8.48; 12.51; 14.32; 19.42; Mk 5.34; 9.50; A 7.26; 10.36; 12.20; 14.2; pace L 2.29; 7.50; 11.21; A 15.33.

pecaui, *s.v.* pecco.

peccator J 9.16,24,25; L 5.8; peccatori L 18.13; peccatorem L 19.7; peccatore L 15.7; peccatori L 15.10; patores Mk 2.15; peccatores Mt 9.10; L 6.32,33,34; 13.2, 15.1; peccatorum Mt 11.19; 26.45; J 9.29,31; L 1.77; 7.34; Mk 14.41; peccatoribus L 6.34; peccatores Mt 9.13; L 5.32; 15.2; Mk 2.17; peccatoribus Mt 9.11; Mk 2.16*bis*.

peccatrix L 7.37,39; peccatrice Mk 8.38.

peccatum (*n.*) Mt 12.31; peccatum (*ac.*) J 8.34; 9.41; 15.22,24; [[19.11]]; A 7.60; peccato J 8.3,7,21; 15.22; 16.8,9; peccata Mt 9.2,5; J 9.41; L 5.20,23; 7.48; Mk 2.5,9; 3.28; A 3.19; peccatorum Mt 26.28; L 3.3; 24.47; Mk 1.4; A 2.38; 5.31; 10.43; 13.38; 19.5; peccata [[Mt 3.6]]; 9.6; J 20.23; L 5.21,24; 7.49; Mk 1.5; 2.7,10; 4.12; A 22.16; peccatis Mt 1.21; J 8.24*bis;* 9.34.

pecco pecaui L 15.18; peccaui Mt 27.4; L 15.21; peccauit J 9.2,3; peccauerit Mt 18.15,21; L 17.3,4; peccare J 5.14; 8.11.

pectus pectus (*ac.*) J 13.25; 21.20; L 18.13; pectora (*ac.*) L 23.48.

pecunia pecuniam Mt 27.6; 28.12; L 9.3; 19.15,23; 22.5; Mk 14.11; A 4.37; pecunia Mt 28.15; paecunias A 8.18; pecunias L 18.24; Mk 10.22,23,24.

pecus pecus (*ac.*) L 10.34; pecora (*n.*) J 4.12.

pedester pedestri (*inc.*) Mt 14.13; pedestre (*inc.*) Mk 6.33.

pehibuit, *s.v.* perhibeo.

peiuro peiurabis Mt 5.33.

pelagus pelago (*ab.*) Mt 18.6.

pellicius pelliciam [[Mt 3.4]].

pellio pellionis A 10.32; pellionem A 10.6.

peluis peluem J 13.5.

penae, *v.* paene.

pendo pendebat L 19.48; pendet Mt 22.40.

penes (*c.ac.*) A 7.44; 15.36; 18.11.

peniteo, *v.* paeniteo.

Pentecoste Pentecostes (*g.*) A 2.1; 20.16; Pentecosten A 1.5.

penuria penuria (*ab.*) Mk 12.44.

per (*c.ab.*) Mt 2.14; 28.13; A 5.19; 11.2; 16.16; 20.18; per (*c.ac.*) Mt 1.20,22; 2.5,12*bis*, 15,17,[[23; 3.3]]; 4.14; 8.28,32; 11.2; 12.1,17, 43; 13.35; 18.7; 19.3,24; 21.4; 24.7,15; 26.24, 63; 27.9,15,18,19; J 3.17; 4.4; 10.1,2,9; 11.4; 14.6; 17.20; [[19.23]]; 21.8; L 1.70; 2.39; 4.14, 30; 5.5; 6.1; 8.33; 9.37; 10.31; 11.24; 13.22,24; 15.14; 17.1,11; 18.25,31; 21.11,37; 22.22; 23.5,17; Mk 2.23; 5.7, [13]; 6.2,7; 7.13,31; 10.25; 11.16; 13.8; 14.21; 15.6,10,33; III J 13; A 1.2,16; 2.16,22,23,43,46; 3.16,17,18,21; 4.16,25*bis*,30; 5.12; 6.8; 7.25,36; 8.1,3,18; 10.36,37,43; 11.2,4,28,30; 12.1,9; 13.27,38,44, 49; 14.3,22,23; 15.7,11,12,21*bis*,23*bis*,36; 16.9, 18,19; 17.2,10,17,22; 18.4,8,9*bis*,28; 19.8,11, 13,21; 20.3,20,23,28; 21.4,19*bis;* 22.19; sper (Mk 5.13); per (*c.adv.*) A 10.16; 11.10; per (*c.indec.*) Mk 6.40*bis*.

pera peram Mt 10.10; L 9.3; 10.4; 22.36; Mk 6.8; pera L 22.35.

peruersus **peruersa** (*voc.*) Mt 17.17; L 9.41; **peruersa** (*neu.ac.*) A 20.30.

pes Mt 18.8; Mk 9.45; **pedis** A 7.5; **pedem** Mt 4.6; L 4.11; **pedes** A 5.9; **pedum** Mt 5.35; 10.14; L 9.5; Mk 6.11; 12.36; A 2.35; 7.33,49; 13.25; **pedes** Mt 18.8; 22.44; 28.9; J 11.2,32,44; 12.3*bis;* 13.5,6,8,9,10,12,14*bis;* 20.12; L 1.79; 5.8; 7.38*ter*,44*bis*,45; 8.35,41; 10.39; 15.22; 17.16; 24.39; Mk 5.22; 7.25; 9.45; A 4.35,37; 5.2,10; 7.58; 10.25; 14.10; 16.24,29; 21.11; **pedibus** Mt 15.30; 22.13; L 10.11; 20.43; A 13.51; 14.8.

petitio **petitionem** L 23.24.

peto **petis** J 4.9; **petit** Mt 5.42; 27.58; L 11.10,11; **petitis** Mk 11.24; **petunt** L 12.20; **petebant** L 23.25; **petam** Mk 6.24; **petetis** J 16.26; **petiit** A 7.46; **petit** Mk 15.43; **petiuit** L 23.52; **petistis** J 16.24; **petierunt** A 13.21, 29; **petieris** J 11.22; Mk 6.23; **petierit** L 11.11; **petieritis** Mt 21.22; J 14.13,14; 15.16; 16.23; **petierint** Mt 18.19; **petieremus** Mk 10.35; **petatis** Mt 20.22; Mk 10.38; **peteres** J 4.10; **peteret** A 3.2; **peterent** Mt 27.20; **petierit** Mt 14.7; L 11.12; **petisset** L 1.63; **petissent** Mk 15.6; **pete** Mk 6.22; **petite** J 15.7; 16.24; L 11.9; **petens** (*m.*) A 16.29; **petens** (*f.*) Mt 20.20; **petenti** (*m.d.*) L 6.30; **petentes** (*m.n.*) L 23.23; **petentibus** (*m.d.*) L 11.13.

petra **petram** Mt 16.18; L 6.48*bis;* 8.6,13; **petra** Mt 27.60; Mk 15.46; **petrae** Mt 27.51.

petrosus **petrosa** (*neu.ac.*) Mt 13.5,20; Mk 4.5,16.

Petrus Mt 4.18; 10.2; 14.28,29; 15.15; 16.18,22; 17.4; 18.21; 19.27; 26.33,35,58; J 13.8,9; ⟦18.16,18,26,27⟧; 20.3; 21.17,20,21; L 8.45; 9.20,32,33; 12.41; 18.28; 22.54,55,60; Mk 3.16; 8.29,32; 9.5; 10.28; 11.21; 13.3; 14.29,54,66,72; A 1.13,15; 2.14,38; 3.1,4,6, 12; 4.8,19; 5.3,8,9,29; 8.20; 10.5,9,17,18,21, 23,25,26,32,34,46; 11.2,4,13; 12.5,6,11,18; 15.7; **Petri** A 4.13; 5.15; 12.7,14; **Petro** Mt 16.23; 17.24; 26.40; ⟦J 18.11,17⟧; 21.7; Mk 8.33; 14.37; ⟦16.7⟧; A 12.7; **Petrum** Mt 17.1; 26.37; ⟦J 18.16⟧ 20.4; L 6.14; 8.51; 9.28; 22.8,61; Mk 5.37; 9.2; 14.33,67; A 2.37; 3.3, 11; 8.14; 12.3,14; **Petro** A 10.19,44,45; 15.11; **Petre** L 22.34; A 10.13; 11.7; **Simon Petrus** Mt 16.16; J 6.68; 13.24,36; ⟦18.10,15,25⟧; 20.6; 21.2,3,7,11; **Simonis Petri** J 6.8; **Simoni Petro** J 21.15; **Petrum Simonem** J 13.6; **Simonem Petrum** J 20.2; **Simon** Mt 10.2; L 5.5,8; 22.31*bis;* Mk 1.36; A 10.18; **Simonis** L 4.38*bis;* 5.3; Mk 1.29,30; **Simoni** L 24.34; Mk 3.16; **Simonem** Mt 4.18; L 5.4; 6.14; Mk 1.16; A 10.5,32; 11.13; **Simon** (*voc.*) Mt 17.25; J 21.15,16,17; Mk 14.37; **Simon Bariona** Mt 16.17.

pexiuit, *s.v.* **exeo.**

Phalec L 3.35.

phantasma **fantasma** (*n.*) Mt 14.26; **fantasma** (*ac.*) L 24.37; Mk 6.49.

Pharao **Farao** A 7.10; **Pharao** A 7.13,21.

pharisaeus L 7.39; 11.38; 18.10,11; A 5.34; **pharisaei** L 7.36,37; **pharisaeum** L 18.14; **phariseae** (*voc.*) Mt 23.26; **farisaei** J 4.1; 11.47,57; **pharisaei** Mt 9.11,14; 12.2,14, 24; 15.1,12; 16.1; 19.3; 21.45; 22.15,34; 23.2; 27.62; J 7.32*bis*,47; 8.3,13; 9.15; 12.19; L 5.21,30; 6.7; 7.30; 11.53; 15.2; 16.14; Mk 2.16,18,24; 3.6; 7.1,3,5; 8.11; 12.14; **farisaeorum** Mt 16.6,11; **pharisaeorum** Mt ⟦3.7⟧; 12.38; 16.12; L 5.33; 7.36; 12.1; 13.31; 14.1; Mk 2.18; 8.15; 12.13; A 15.5; **pharisaeum** L 11.37; **pharisaeis** L 11.42; **farisaeos** J 7.45; 12.42; **pharisaeos** J 9.13; 11.46; L 5.17; 14.3; **farisaeis** J 9.40; L 6.2; **pharisaeis** Mt 22.41; 27.41; J 7.48; 9.16; ⟦18.3⟧; L 17.20; 19.39; **farisaei** Mt 23.23; **pharisaei** Mt 23.13,15,25, 27,29; L 11.43,44; **farisae** L 11.39.

Philippi **Philippis** (*ab.*) A 16.12; 20.6.

Philippus Mt 10.3; J 6.7; 12.22*bis;* 14.8; A 1.13; 8.5; **Philippi** Mk 6.17; **Philippo** A 8.12,13; **Filippum** Mk 3.18; **Philippum** J 6.5; 12.21; L 6.14; A 6.5; **Philippo** A 8.6; **Philippe** J 14.9; *v.quoq.* **Caesaria Philippi.**

philosophus **philosophorum** A 17.18.

Phoenice **Phoenicem** A 15.3; **Phoenicen** A 11.19.

Phrygia **Frygiam** A 2.10; **Phrygiam** A 18.23; **Phygiam** A 16.6.

phylacterium **phylacteria** (*ac.*) Mt 23.5.

phyto **phytonem** A 16.16.

pietas **pietate** A 3.12.

piger **piger** (*voc.*) Mt 25.26.

pila **pilis** (*ab.*) ⟦Mt 3.4⟧.

Pilatus Mt 27.13,17,22,24,58,65; ⟦J 18.29, 31,33,35,37,38; 19.1,4,6,8,10,12,13,15,19,22, 38⟧; L 13.1; 23.3,4,6,12,13,20,24; Mk 15.2, 4,5,9,12,14,15,44; **Pilati** A 3.13; **Pilato** ⟦J 19.21⟧; L 23.11; Mk 15.1; A 13.28; **Pilatum** Mt 27.58,62; ⟦J 19.31,38⟧; L 23.1,52; Mk 15.43; A 13.29; **Pontius Pilatus** A 4.27; **Pontio Pilato** (*d.*) Mt 27.2; **Pontio Pilato** (*ab.*) L 3.1.

pilus **pilos** Mk 1.6.

pinna **pinnam** Mt 4.5; L 4.9.

piscator **piscatores** (*n.*) Mt 4.18; L 5.2,10;

11.42; L 3.18; 9.13; 20.1,19; 22.2; 23.5; A 4.1,2,17,21; 5.25,26,34,37; 6.12; 13.15,17,31; 15.14; 17.5; 21.28,39; **populo** Mt 4.23; 26.5; 27.24; [[J 18.14]]; L 3.15; 8.4; 12.13; 20.45; A 3.23; 5.12; 6.8; **populi** L 3.7,10; 23.48; A 4.25; **populorum** L 2.31; **populos** A 5.13; **populis** A 4.27.

porcus **porci** (*pl.*) L 15.16; **porcorum** Mt 8.30,31; L 8.32; Mk 5.11; **porcos** Mt 8.32; L 8.32,33; 15.15; Mk 5.12,13*bis;* **porcis** Mk 5.16.

porrigo **porrexit** J 13.26; **porrexerunt** L 24.42; **porrexero** J 13.26; **porrectus est** L 4.17.

porta **porte** (*d.*) L 7.12; **portam** A 12.10; 16.13; **porta** A 3.10; **portae** Mt 16.18.

portentum **portenta** (*neu.n.*) A 2.43;4.30; 5.12; **portenta** (*neu.ac.*) A 6.8; 7.36; 14.3.

porticus **porticum** J 10.23; A 3.11; 5.12; **porticos** J 5.2.

porto **portabant** L 7.14; **portabatur** Mk 2.3; **portauimus** Mt 20.12; **portare** Mt 3.11; **portari** L 11.46; **portans** (*m.*) [[J 19.5]]; Mk 14.13.

portuis, *s.v.* **morior.**

pos, *v.* **post.**

positus **posita** (*f.n.*) Mt 5.14; **positum** (*m.*) L 2.16; **positum** (*neu.ac.*) J 20.7; **positos** J 21.9; **posita** J 20.5,6.

posquam, *v.* **postquam.**

possessio **possessionem** A 7.5*bis*,45; 13.33; **possessione** A 5.1; **possessiones** (*ac.*) Mt 19.22; A 2.45.

possessor **possessores** (*n.*) A 4.34.

possibilis **possibile** (*neu.n.*) Mt 24.24; 26.39; Mk 10.27; A 2.24; **possibilia** (*neu.n.*) Mt 19.26; L 18.27; Mk 9.23; 14.36.

possideo **possidebant** A 4.32; **possideritis** (*coni.*) Mt 10.9; **possidete** Mt 25.34; **possidere** A 13.19; **possidens** (*m.*) A 14.9.

possido **possedit** [A 1.18]; **possidit** (A 1.18).

possum Mt 9.28; 26.53,61; J 5.30; 13.37; L 11.7; 14.19,20; **potes** Mt 5.36; J 13.36; L 5.12; 6.42; 16.2; Mk 1.40; 9.22,23; 15.31; **potest** Mt 3.9; 5.14; 10.28; 19.12,25; 26.42; 27.42; J 3.27; 5.19; 6.44,52,60,65; 7.7; 9.4,16; 10.21,29,35; 14.17; L 5.21; 6.39; 11.15; 12.25; 14.26,27,33; 16.13; 18.26; Mk 2.7; 3.23,24,25, 26,27; 7.18; 9.3,29; 13.22; 14.35; (A 1.5); 10.47; **possumus** Mk 10.39; A 4.16,20; 17.19; 19.40; **potestes** Mt 12.34; J 7.34; A 15.1; **potestis** Mt 16.3; 20.22; J 5.44; 7.36; 8.21,22, 43; 13.33; 15.5; 16.12; L 16.13; Mk 10.38; 14.7; **possunt** Mt 9.15; 10.28; L 5.34; 11.46; 12.4; 20.36; Mk 2.19; **potebat** L 19.3; **potuit** L 6.48; 14.30; Mk 6.5; 7.24; **potuimus** Mt 17.19; Mk 9.28; A 15.10; **potuistis** Mk 14.37; A 13.39; **potuerunt** Mt 13.17; 17.16; L 9.40; 20,26; Mk 9.18; **poterat** Mt 22.46; 26.9; J 9.33; 11.37; L 1.22; 8.43; 13.11; Mk 5.3; 6.19; **potuerat** Mk 14.5; **poterant** J 12.39; 21.6; L 8.19; Mk 4.33; A 6.10; **poterit** Mt 12.29; Mk 9.39; 10.26; **poteritis** A 5.39; **poterint** L 21.15; **possim** A 11.17; **possit** Mk 1.45; 7.15; 8.4; A 21.34; **possimus** Mt 20.22; **possint** Mk 4.32; **posset** Mt 8.28; Mk 2.2; 5.4; **possent** L 16.26; Mk 2.4; 3.20; **potuerit** L 14.29; **posse** L 5.14; **potens** (*m.*) L 1.20,49; 3.8; 14.31; 24.19; A 7.22; 18.24; **potens** (*f.*) A 19.20; **potentes** (*m.n.*) L 24.20; A 6.10; **potentes** (*m.ac.*) L 1.52.

post (*c.ab.*) A 20.7; **post** (*c.ac.*) **pos** A 20.29; **post** Mt 1.12; 4.10,19; 10.38; 15.22,23; 16.21, 23,24; 17.1,23; 24.29; 25.19; 26.2,61; 27.53, 63; J 3.22; 4.43; 5.1,14; 6.1; 7.1; 11.7,11; 12.19; [[19.38]]; 20.26; 21.1; L 1.24; 2.46; 9.22,23,28; 15.13; 17.8; 18.4; 19.14; 21.8; 22.58; Mk 1.7,17; 2.1; 8.34; 9.2; 10.34; 13.2, 19,24; 14.1,58,70; [[16.12]]; A 1.3,[5]; 5.37*bis;* 7.4,5,30; 10.37,40; 13.15,25; 15.16,36; 17.19; 19.4; 20.6,30; 21.15; **post** (*c.adv.*) Mt 26.32; L 12.5; **post** (*c.indec.*) A 12.4; **post** (*c.ab. et ac.*) Mt 27.62.

postea Mt 21.29,32; J 13.7; [[19.28]]; A 7.2,7.

posteaquam Mk 14.28.

posterus **postero** (*m.ab.*) A 10.24; **postera** (*ab.*) J 12.12; A 10.9,23; **postero** (*adv.*) J 13.36; **postera** (*adv.*) Mt 4.2.

postquam **posquam** Mk 15.20; A 20.1; **postquam** Mk 1.14; [[16.19]]; A 1.3; 10.41; 15.13.

postulo **postulabant** A 12.20; **postulastis** A 3.14; **postulasset** A 13.16; **postula** A 13.33.

potestas Mt 28.18; L 22.53; Mk 1.27; **potestatem** Mt 9.6,8; 10.1; 21.23; J 5.27; 10.18*bis;* 17.2; [[19.10*bis*,11]]; L 4.6; 5.24; 9.1; 10.19; 12.5; 19.17; 20.2; 22.25; Mk 1.22; 2.10; 3.15; 6.7; 10.42; A 8.19; **potestate** Mt 21.23,24,27; L 4.32,36; 7.8; 20.2,8; 23.7; Mk 11.28,29,33; 13.34; A 1.7; 5.4; **potestates** (*ac.*) L 12.11.

potius Mt 25.9.

poto **potabat** Mt 27.48; **potauimus** Mt 25.37; **potastis** Mt 25.35,42; **potauerit** Mt 10.42.

terire L 16.17; **praeteriens** (*m.*) Mk 1.16; **praetereuntem** (*f.*) L 18.36; **praetereuntes** (*m.n.*) Mk 15.29; **praeteritis** (*neu.ab.*) A 14.16.

praeternauigo **praeternauigare** A 20.16.

praetiosi, *s.v.* **pretiosus.**

praetium Mt 27.6; **praetium** (*ac.*) Mt 27.9; A 5.3; **praetio** A 5.2; 7.16; **praetia** (*ac.*) A 4.34; **praetiis** A 19.19.

praetor A 5.24,26; **praetores** A 16.36; **praetoribus** A 16.20,38; **praetores** A 16.38.

praetorium **praetorii** Mk 15.16; **praetorium** Mt 27.27; [[J 18.33; 19.9]]; **pretorium** [[J 18.28*bis*]].

praeualeo **praeualebunt** Mt 16.18.

praeuaricor **praeuaricatis** (*f.ab.*) A 10.46.

praeuenio **praeuenit** (*perf.*) Mt 12.28; 17.25; Mk 14.8.

prandeo **prandeam** (*coni.*) L 15.29; **pranderet** L 11.37,38; **prandissent** J 21.15; **prandete** J 21.12.

prandium **prandium** (*ac.*) Mt 22.4; L 14.12.

prauus **prauua** (*ab.*) A 2.40; **prauua** (*neu.n.*) L 3.5.

prendo **prendederunt** J 21.3.

presbyter **praesbyteri** (*n.*) A 15.6; 21.18; **presbyteri** A 15.23; **presbyterorum** A 15.41; 16.4; **presbyteris** A 15.22; **praesbyteros** A 15.4; **presbyteros** A 11.30; 14.23; 15.2,11; 20.17; **praesbyteris** L 20.1; **presbyteris** J 8.9; L 9.22; A 15.4.

prestabat, *s.v.* **praesto.**

pretiosus **praetiosi** (*m.g.*) Mk 14.3; **praetiosi** (*neu.g.*) Mt 26.7; **pretiosi** J 12.3; **praetiosam** Mt 13.46.

pretorium, *v.* **praetorium.**

pridie A 20.15.

primogenitus **primogenitum** (*m.*) Mt 1.25; L 2.7.

primus Mt 10.2; 20.27; 22.25; L 14.18; 19.16; 20.29; Mk 10.44; 12.20; A 2.14; **prima** L 2.2; **primum** Mt 22.38; Mk 12.28,29,30; **primi** (*m.*) [[J 19.32]]; **primo** (*m.*) L 16.5; **primum** L 6.14; 14.8; A 1.1; **primam** L 15.22; A 12.10; **primo** L 6.1; A 13.33; **prima** Mk 14.12; [[16.9]]; A 20.18; **primi** Mt 19.30*bis;* 20.10 16*bis;* L 13.30*bis;* 19.47; Mk 10.31*bis;* **primis** (*m.*) Mk 6.21; **primos** Mt 20.8; 23.6; L 11.43; 14.7; 20.46; Mk 12.39; **primas** Mt 23.6; L 11.43; 20.46; Mk 12.39; **primo** (*adv.*) Mk 7.3; [[16.9]]; **primum** (*adv.*) Mt 12.29; 13.30; 17.10,27; 23.26; J 10.40; 12.16; 15.18; [[18.13; 19.39]]; L 6.42; 9.59,61; 11.38; 12.1; 14.28,31; 17.25; 21.9; Mk 4.28; 9.11,12; 13.10; A 3.26; 7.12; 11.26; 13.46; 15.14.

princeps Mt 9.18; 26.62,63,65; J 11.49,51; 14.30; 16.11; L 8.41; 18.18; 19.2; A 14.12; **princprinceps** J 12.31; **principes** (*g.*) Mt 26.51; **principis** Mt 9.23; 26.3,58; L 22.50,54; Mk 14.47; **principem** Mt 12.24; 26.57; L 12.58; Mk 3.22; A 3.15; 7.27,35*bis;* **principe** L 3.2; 11.15; **principes** Mt 21.15,23,45; 26.3, 59; 27.6,20,41,62; J 7.26,32; 11.57; 12.10; L 19.47; 20.1,19; 22.2,66; 23.10; 24.20; Mk 15.11; A 3.17; 4.5,26; 13.27; 14.2; **principum** L 14.1; 23.23; **principibus** Mt 20.18; 27.3; 28.11; L 22.4; Mk 6.21; **principes** Mt 2.4,6; 26.14; J 7.45; L 22.52; 23.4,13*bis;* A5.35; 13.50; 17.6,8; **principibus** Mt 16.21; 26.47; 27.12; J 7.48; 12.42; L 9.22; A 11.5; **principes** (*voc.*) A 4.8.

principalis **principales** (*m.ac.*) A 15.22.

principatus **principatus** (*ac.*) L 12.11.

principium **principium** (*ac.*) A 11.15; **principiis** (*ab.*) A 10.11.

principor **principantur** Mt 20.25; **principari** Mk 10.42.

prior **prior** (*m.*) J 8.7; 20.4,8; **priori** (*m.d.*) Mt 21.28; 27.64; **prioribus** (*neu.ab.*) Mt 21.36,45; L 11.26.

Priscilla A 18.18,26; **Priscillam** A 18.2.

prius (*adv.*) Mt 5.24; J 9.8; Mk 3.27; 7.27; A 13.24.

priusquam J 4.49; L 2.26; 22.15,61; Mk 14.30; A 2.20.

pro (*c.ab.*) Mt [[2.22]]; 5.38*bis*,44; 9.36; 12.36; 17.27*bis;* 20.28; 26.28; 27.19; J 6.51; 10.11,15; 11.50,51,52; 13.37,38; 15.13; 17.9 *bis*,19,20; [[18.14; 19.13]]; L 5.14; 6.28; 9.50; 11.11; Mk 1.44; 8.37; 9.40; 10.45; 14.24; A 2.36; 5.41; 12.5,21,23; 21.26.

probo **probatis** L 12.56; **probatur** A 6.10; **probare** L 12.56; 14.19; **probatum** (*m.*) A 2.22.

procedo **procedunt** Mk 7.15,21,23; **procedebant** Mk 3.11; **procedent** J 5.29; **processit** [[J 18.4]]; Mk 1.28; 2.13; **processerunt** A 12.10; **processerat** L 2.36; **processisset** Mk 14.35; **procedens** (*m.*) Mk 1.29; **procedente** (*m.ab.*) Mk 13.1.

procella L 8.23; Mk 4.37.

Prochorus **Prochorum** A 6.5.

procido **procidit** L 5.8; Mk 5.33; 7.25; A 16.29; **procidens** (*m.*) Mk 5.22; A 10.25; **procidens** (*f.*) L 8.47.

[8]Order of verses in MS.

8. [2],3; 10.28; 11.12,21; 12.13,17; 13.1,19,35; 15.12,36; 16.23, [26]; 17.19; 18.6,12,20; 19.3, 10,18,29; 20.3,7,11,18; 21.40.

quemadmodum, quemadmodmodum (A 1.11); quemadmodum L 13.34; Mk 4.26; [A 1.11]; 7.28; 12.17; 15.11,14; 20.18.

quero, questio, *etc., v.* **quaero, quaestio,** *etc.*

questus questos A 19.36.

qui (*inter.*) qui Mt 12.11; quae Mt 12.48; L 6.32,33,34; 15.8; Mk 3.33; 4.10; 6.2; A 10.17,21; quod Mt 22.36; 24.3; L 21.7; Mk 5.9; 12.28; 13.4; quem Mt 16.13,15; quam Mt 5.46; quod Mt 26.50; J 6.30; 10.32; L 2.49; 17.8; quo Mt 12.27; qua Mt 21.23,24,27; 24.43; L 20.2,8; Mk 4.30; 11.28,29,33; A 4.7; 10.29; quo A 4.7,9; qui Mt 12.48; A 19.15; quae (*neu.n.*) L 24.17; quae (*neu.ac.*) Mt 19.18; L 18.20; 24.19; qui (*rel.*) que (*m.n.s.*) ⟦J 19.13⟧; qui Mt 2.2,6,14,⟦21; 3.3⟧, 11,14; 4.3,16,18; 5.16,22*ter*,28,39,40,41,42,45; 6.1,4,6; 9.8,12,22; 10.2,4,20,22,28,32*bis*,33,37, 38,39*bis*,40*ter*,41; 11.3,10,11,14,15; 12.3,11 *bis*,30*bis*,39,48,50; 13.9,11,12*bis*,19*bis*,20*bis*, 22*bis*,23*bis*,28,37*bis*,39,43,52; 14.16,18,29; 15.3,4,13,16,23,24,26; 16.2,17,23,25*bis;* 17.11, 20,27; 18.6,10,14,19,23,28,30; 19.4,11,12,17; 20.1,13,21,26,27; 21.9,29,30,33; 22.2,12; 23.9, 16,17,18*bis*,20,21,22*bis*,39; 24.2*bis*,4,13,15,16, 17,18,30; 25.12,16,17,18,20,22,24; 26.3,14,18, 23,25,28,36,46,66; 27.3,16,17,22,33,40,57; J 3.16,18*bis*,20,21,26,29*bis*,31*ter*,33,36*bis;* 4.10, 12,13,14,25,26,29,34,36*ter*,37*bis;* 5.10,11,12, 15,23*bis*,24*bis*,25,30,32,37,45; 6.9,14,33,35*bis*, 37, 38, 39, 40, 41, 44, 45, 46, 47, 50, 51, 54, 56, 57, 58*bis*,63,64; 7.15,16,18*ter*,28,33,38,50; 8.12,16, 18*bis*,26,29,34,40,47,50,54; 9.4,8,11,13,18,25, 37; 10.2,12,29; 11.16,25,26,27,37,42,44; 12.1, 4, 13, 17, 21, 25*bis*, 35, 44*bis*, 45*bis*, 46, 48*bis*, 49; 13.10,11,16,18,20*ter;* 14.5,9,10,12,21*ter*,22,24 *bis;* 15.5,21,23,26; 16.2,5; ⟦18.2,5,13,14,16,37; 19.11,12,17,32,35,39⟧; 20.8,24; 21.2*bis*,20*bis*, 24*bis;* L 1.19,49,61,(65); 2.11; 3.11*bis*,16,23 *tricies*, 31, 32*quinquiens*, 33*quinquiens*, 34*quinquiens*,35*quinquiens*,36*quater*,37*quinquiens*,38 *quater;* 5.18,27; 6.8,15*bis*,16,29*bis*,30,47,48,49; 7.2,19*bis*,20,23,27,28,49; 8.8,18*bis*,27*bis*,35; 9.24*bis*,26,48*bis*,50; 10.11,16*quater*,22,36,37; 11.2,10*bis*,23*bis*,27,40; 12.8,9,10,28,47,48; 13.35; 14.9,10,11*bis*,12,15,27,31,33,35; 15.4, 30; 16.1,10*bis*,18*bis;* 17.7,18,24,30,31*bis*,33 *bis;* 18.14*bis*,29; 19.3,24,26,29,30,38; 20.2,18; 21.6,37; 22.1,3*bis*,21,23,26*quater*,27,36*bis*,47, 64; 23.19,25,33,43,51; 24.19,21; Mk 1.2; 2.3; 3.19,35; 4.9,14,25*bis;* 5.3,15,16,18; 7.10; 8.35 *bis*,38; 9.33,37,38,39,40; 10.29,30*bis;* 11.2,9, 25,26; 12.28; 13.2,13,14,15,16; 14.18,20,24 *bis*,42; 15.7*bis*,29,39,43; ⟦16.16*bis*⟧; III J 11; A 1.11,12*bis*,16,17,20,23*bis*,24; 2.10,45; 3.10, 11; 4.11*bis*,24,25,35; 5.32,36; 7.18,20,24,27, 34,35,37,38*ter*,40,44,46; 10.5,7,18,32*bis*,35,42, 43; 11.13,14,17,23; 12.12,20,25; 13.1,6,7,9,22, 27,31,39; 14.3,8,15,16; 15.8,22,37; 16.24,35; 17.24*bis;* 18.27; 19.4,24,35; 21.28,32,38; 22.15; quae Mt ⟦2.23⟧; 14.8; 15.25,27; 18.12; 23.37; 27.62; J 4.5; 5.2; 6.27*bis;* 7.49; 11.2,54; 12.12; L 1.36,45; 2.4,10,36,37; 5.3; 7.11,39; 8.2,9,26,43,44; 10.39,42; 12.1; 13.34; 15.6; Mk 5.26,30,32; 6.2,24; 15.41,42; A 3.2, [16]; 5.17; 6.9,10; 8.1,10; 11.19,22,28; 12.10*bis;* 13.32; 16.12,16; 18.15; que (*n.*) A (3.16); 17.19; quo (*neu.n.*) Mt 12.17; quod Mt 1.20, 22,23; 2.15,17,⟦23⟧; 4.14; 5.37; 10.26*bis;* 12.2, 4; 13.19,32,35; 15.5,11*bis*,17,37; 18.11,30; 20.4; 21.2,4; 22.31; 23.18,19,25,26*bis*,35; 24.15; 25.25,27; 27.9,33; J 9.7; 12.38; 15.2*bis*, 25; 20.7,16; L 1.35; 2.15,17,21,24; 3.13; 6.2, 14; 8.14,15,17,34,56; 9.10,17; 11.35,39,40*bis*, 50; 12.2*bis;* 15.12; 16.11,15; 19.10; 20.17; 21.2; 22.37,49; Mk 3.17; 4.15,31; 5.41; 7.11, 15,34; 8.8; 11.10; 12.42,44; 13.11; 15.16,22, 34,42,46; A 2.12,16; 3.10; 4.12,21,36; 5.7; 10.11; 12.9; 13.12,40; 15.16; 17.27,29; 21.34; cuius Mt 3.11,12; J 4.46; 6.42; 10.12; ⟦18.26; 19.24⟧; L 3.16,17; 9.55; Mk 1.7; A 7.52; 10.6; 13.25; 17.31; 18.7; cus (*m.*) A 21.11; cuius J 11.2; Mk 7.25; A 16.14; 19.40; cuius A 2.32; cui Mt 1.16; 11.27; 27.57; J 3.26; 13.26; L 1.27; 2.25; 4.6; 6.47; 7.4,43; 8.41; 10.22; 12.48*bis;* 24.18; A 5.36; 7.39; 8.10; 13.22; 16.2; cui L 10.39; A 7.7; cui Mk 14.32; qem J 5.38; quem Mt 12.18; 13.44; 14.2; 18.7; 21.42; 23.35; 24.45,46; 26.24,48; 27.9,15; J 3.34; 4.18; 5.45; 6.27,29,51; 7.25,28,36,39; 8.54; 9.19; 10.36; 11.3; 12.1,9; 13.23; 14.17, 26; 15.26; 17.3; 18.1,⟦9,11,32; 19.26,37⟧; 20.2; 21.7,20; L 6.14; 7.39; 8.43; 9.31; 11.51; 12.5*bis*,42,43; 17.1; 20.17; 22.22,47; 23.25,53; Mk 1.11; 6.16; 8.14,32; 9.36; 10.38,39; 11.2; 12.10; 14.21,44,71; A 1.2,24; 2.24,36; 3.2,13, 15,16,21; 4.10*bis*,22,27; 5.15,30,32; 7.35; 10.21,38,39; 13.1,30,37; 14.23; 16.19; 17.3; 19.13,14; 21.16,29; quam Mt 2.9; 15.13; J 4.14*bis*,32; 6.22; 8.40; 12.28; 17.5,22,24,26; ⟦18.29⟧; L 8.47; 13.16; 15.9; 19.20; 21.15; Mk 7.13; A 1.4,16; 3.25; 7.17,44; 10.17,21; 16.21; 20.28; quod Mt 2.16; 10.27*bis;* 12.36; 13.5,12,31,33; 16.19; 19.6; 20.15,22; 25.29,41; 26.13; 27.8,60; J 3.32; 4.5,22*bis*,50; 5.32; 6.14, 37,39; 11.45,46; 12.48,50; 13.7,27; 14.24; 16.17; 17.2,4,11,24; ⟦19.22⟧; L 1.35,73; 2.5, 15,31,50; 4.18; 6.3,4; 7.40,47; 8.6,18; 9.7; 11.6,8; 12.3; 13.21; 14.19,20,22; 15.4; 16.8; 17.10; 18.5; 19.11,21*bis*,22*bis*,26,44; 20.3;

quicumque Mt 5.19,21,31,32; 10.14,33,42; 11.6; 12.32*bis*,50; 15.5; 18.4,5; 19.9,29; 23.12 *bis*,16; J 8.51; L 9.48; 18.17; Mk 9.37; 10.11, 43,44; 11.23; A 2.21; **quaecumque** A 3.23; **quodcumque** Mk 7.11; **cuicumque** (*m.*) A 8.19; **quecumque** L 9.5; **quemcumquae** Mk 15.6; **quemcumque** J 13.20; L 9.4; A 5.15; **quamcumque** Mt 18.19; L 10.5,8; A 7.3; **quodcumque** Mt 14.7; 16.19; J 14.13; 15.7; Mk 10.35; 11.23; **quacumque** Mt 10.11; L 10.10; **quicumque** Mk 6.11; **quaecumque** (*neu.ac.*) Mt 18.18; [18.18]; 21.22; J 4.39; 5.19,20; 11.22; 14.26; 16.13; L 4.23; Mk 3.28; 9.13; 10.21; 11.24; A 3.22; 4.28; 15.29.

quid (*adv.*) Mt 9.4; 17.10; 19.7,17; 20.6; 22.18; 26.8,10; 27.46; J 6.62; 7.19; 10.20; 14.22; ⟦18.21,23⟧; 20.13,15; 21.21,22,23; L 2.48,49; 5.21,22; 6.41,46; 12.26; 13.7; 16.2; 18.19; 20.23; 24.5,38; Mk 2.7,8,24; 4.40; 5.35,39*bis;* 8.12,17; 9.16; 10.18; 11.3; 12.15; 14.4,6,63; 15.34; A [1.11]; 3.12*bis;* 5.4,9; 7.26; 14.15; 15.10; 22.16.

quidam Mt 12.47; 13.44; J 4.46; 11.1,49; L 1.5; 7.36; 9.57; 10.25,30,31,33; 11.1,37,45; 12.13; 13.6,23; 14.16; 15.11; 16.1,19,20; 18.2, 18; 19.12; Mk 5.22; 14.51; A 3.2; 5.1,25,34; 8.9; 14.8; 16.1,9; 18.24; 19.24,26; 20.9; 22.12; **quaedam** L 11.27; 22.56; A 16.14; **quodam** Mt 13.23; A 11.5; **cuiusdam** (*m.*) L 7.2; 12.16; 14.1; A 7.58; 18.7; 19.9,14; **cuidam** (*m.*) Mt 25.15*ter;* L 7.41; **quemdam** Mk 9.38; A 18.2; **quendam** Mt 26.18; L 6.4; 9.49; 17.12; 23.26; A 5.36; 7.24; 8.9; 13.6; 19.38; 21.16; **quandam** L 21.2; 23.19; A 5.2; **quendam** (*f.*) A 16.16; 21.16; **quodam** A 10.11; 18.23; **quoddam** L 10.38; **quodam** (*m.ab.*) L 11.1; [A 4.12]; **quidam** Mt 9.3; 12.38; 13.8*ter;* 16.28; 22.5*bis;* 27.47; 28.11,17; J 7.25,44; 9.16; 11.37; 12.20; 13.29; L 6.2; 9.27; 11.2,15; 13.1,31; 19.39; 20.27,39; 24.1,24; Mk 2.6; 7.1; 8.3; 9.1; 14.65; 15.35; A 2.37; 6.9; 10.23; 11.20; 15.1,5,24; 17.4,12,18*bis*,28,34; 18.26; 19.2,9,13,31; 21.4; **quaedam** L 8.2; 24.22; **quaedam** Mt 13.4,5; **quorundam** (*m.*) L 21.5; **quosdam** L 18.9; Mk 7.2; 12.5,13; A 12.1; 15.2; 17.5,6; 19.2; **quaedam** A 17.20; **quibusdam** (*m.ab.*) L 9.7; **quendam** (*inc.*) Mk 5.25.

quidem Mt 3.11; 9.37; 13.32; 16.3; 17.11; 20.23; 21.35; 22.8; 23.28; 25.15; 26.24,41; J 10.41; 11.6; 16.9,22; ⟦19.24,32⟧; 20.30; L 1.1; 3.17,18; 6.4; 8.5; 11.48; 12.56; 13.9; 18.35; 22.22; 23.41,56; Mk 1.7; 10.39; 14.21, 38; ⟦16.19⟧; A 1.1,5; 3.17,21,22; 4.16; 8.4; 11.2,16,19; 14.4,17; 15.3,30; 17.27; 18.14; 19.38; 21.39.

quiesco **quieuit** Mt 14.32; **quieuimus** A 21.14.

quinam L 12.42; **quaenam** (*f.s.*) Mk 1.27.

quindecim J 11.18.

quingenti **quingentos** L 7.41.

quinquageni **quinquagenos** L 9.14.

quinquaginta J 8.57; 21.11; L 7.41; 16.6; Mk 6.40; A 13.20.

quinque Mt 14.17,19,21; 16.9*bis;* 25.2*bis*, 15,16*bis*,20*quater*,28; J 4.18; 5.2; 6.9,10,13,19; L 1.24; 9.13,14,16; 12.6,52; 14.19; 16.28; 19.18,19; Mk 6.38,41*bis*,44; 8.19*bis;* A 4.4; 7.14.

quintanus **quintani** (*inc.*) A 20.6.

quintus **quinta** (*ab.*) A 19.9.

quintusdecimus **quintodecimo** (*m.ab.*) L 3.1.

quis (*pron.inter.*) Mt ⟦3.7⟧; 10.11; 18 1; 19.25; 21.10,23,31; 23.17; 24.45; J 4.10; 5.12, 13; 6.60,64; 7.20,36; 8.25; 9.2,21,36; 12.34,38; 13.24,25; 21.12,20; L 3.7; 4.34,36; 5.21; 7.42, 49; 8.45*bis;* 9.9; 10.22,29; 11.5,11; 12.14,25; 14.28,31; 15.4; 16.11,12; 17.7; 18.26; 20.2; 22.23,64; 24.1; Mk 1.24; 2.7; 5.30,31; 9.34; 10.26; 16.3; A 7.27,35,49; 11.17; 19.35; 21.33; **quis** (*f.*) L 7.39; **quid** Mt 8.29; 9.5,13; 12.7; 16.26; 17.25; 18.12; 19.20,27; 21.28; 22.17, 42; 23.19; 26.66; 27.4; J 6.9; 16.17,18; ⟦18.38⟧; L 1.66; 4.34; 5.23; 8.28,30; 9.25; 10.26; 15.26; 20.17; 23.31; Mk 1.24; 2.9; 5.7, 14,33; 8.36; 9.10; 14.64; A 2.12; 5.3; 6.3; 7.40; 10.4,37; 12.18; 21.22; **cuius** (*m.*) Mt 22.20,28,42; L 12.20; 14.5; 20.24,33; Mk 12.16,23; **cuius** (*f.*) A 19.32; **cui** (*m.*) J 12.38; **cui** (*neu.*) Mt 11.16; L 7.31*bis;* 13.18*bis*,20 *bis;* Mk 4.30; **quem** Mt 27.17; J 6.68; 8.53; ⟦18.4,7⟧; 20.13,15; L 9.18,20; 10.36; Mk 8.27,29; A 7.52; 13.25; **quid** Mt 5.47; 6.3; 10.19; 11.7,8,9; 12.3; 15.32; 16.8,26; 19.16; 20.21,22,32; 21.3,16,40; 26.15,62,65; 27.22, 23; J 4.27*bis;* 6.6,28,30; 7.51; 8.5; 9.17,26,27; 11.47,56; 12.27,49*bis;* 13.12,28; 15.15; 16.18; ⟦18.21,35⟧; L 1.62; 3.10,12,14; 6.2; 7.24,25, 26; 9.33; 10.25; 12.4,11,17,22*bis*,29*bis*,49; 16.3,4; 18.6,18,41; 19.15,48; 20.13,15; 22.60, 71; 23.22; Mk 2.25; 4.24; 6.24; 8.37; 9.6,33; 10.3,17,38,51; 11.5,31; 12.9; 13.11; 14.40,60, 68; 15.12,14; A 2.37; 4.16; 7.26; 10.21,26; 16.30; 17.18,20; 19.3; 21.13,33; **quo** L 11.19; **qua** L 12.39,40; **quo** Mt 5.13; L 14.34; Mk 9.50; **quae** (*neu.n.*) J 10.6; **quibus** (*m.ab.*) Mt 17.25; **quis** (*inc.*) A 20.16.

quis (*pron.indef.*) Mt 12.19,29; 16.24; 21.3; 22.24; 24.23; J 6.50,51; 7.17,37; 8.7,52; 9.22,

ratio rationem Mt 12.36; 18.23; 25.19; L 16.2; A 19.33,40; 22.1; ratione Mt 5.32; (19.9); A 10.29; 18.14.

recedo recedunt L 8.13; recedebat L 2.37; recedet L 9.39; recedent A 19.12; recessit L 1.38; 4.13; 9.10; 22.41; A 19.9; recessisset A 18.7; recedite L 13.27; recedentes (*m.n.*) L 20.20; recedentibus (*m.ab.*) Mt 2.13.

recens (*m.*) A 18.2.

recipio recipit Mt 10.40*quater*,41; 18.5; Mk 9.37; recipimus L 23.41; recipient A 22.18; recepisti L 16.25; recepit L 15.27; Mk 10.15; receperit Mt 10.14; Mk 9.37; receperint Mk 6.11; recipiant L 6.34; recipere L 6.34; A 16.21; recepturi (*n.*) A 20.13.

reclino reclinauit (*fut.*) L 12.37; reclinauit L 2.7; reclinet L 9.58; reclinate L 9.14.

recognosco recognitus est A 7.13.

reconcilio reconciliauit A 7.26; reconciliare [Mt 5.24]; reconciliari (Mt 5.24).

recordatio recordatione A 10.4.

recordor recordatus sum A 11.16; recordatus Mk 11.21.

rectus A 14.10; rectas ⟦Mt 3.3⟧; L 3.4; Mk 1.3; A 13.10; recte L 7.43; 10.28; 20.21.

recumbo recumbit L 22.26,27; recumbunt L 14.10; recumbebat L 7.39; recumbebant L 7.49; 14.15; Mk 2.15; recumbet L 7.37; recumbent L 13.29; recubuit J 21.20; L 7.36; 11.37; 22.14; recubuerunt J 6.10; recubuisset L 24.30; recumbe L 14.10; 17.7; recumbere J 6.10; L 14.8; recumbens (*m.*) J 13.12,23; recumbente (*m.*) Mk 14.3; recumbentium (*m.*) L 5.29; recumbentibus (*m.d.*) J 6.11; Mk 6.22; ⟦16.14⟧; recumbentibus (*m.ab.*) J 13.28; Mk 2.15; 6.26.

redargutio redargutionem A 19.27.

reddo A 22.1; redditis J 3.28; reddebant A 4.33; reddam Mt 18.29; reddes Mt 5.33; reddet Mt 6.4,6; (12.36); 16.27; reddent Mt [12.36]; 21.41; reddidisti J 3.26; reddidit L 9.42; reddas Mt 5.26; L 12.59; redderet Mt 18.25,30,34; redderent L 7.42; redde Mt 18.28; 20.8; L 16.2; reddite Mt 22.21; L 20.25; Mk 12.17; reddere A 19.33,40; reddi Mt 27.58; reddens (*m.*) L 4.20; reddentis (*f.*) J 4.39.

redemptio Mt 24.31; redemptionem Mt 20.28; Mk 10.45.

redemptor redemptorem A 7.35.

redeo rediebant Mk 6.31; redie A 18.21; redeunte (*m.*) A 18.27; rediturum (*m.*) A 13.34.

redigo redigent A 7.6.

reditus A 16.19; reditum A 16.16.

refectio Mk 14.14.

refero referit A 7.46.

reficio reficiam Mt 11.28; refecimus A 21.15.

refrigerium refrigerii A 3.19.

refrigero refrigeret L 16.24.

refrigesco refrigescet Mt 24.12.

refulgeo refulgens (*f.*) A 12.7.

regeneratio regeneratione Mt 19.28.

regia Mk 3.24.

regina Mt 12.42; L 11.31.

regio ⟦Mt 3.5⟧; L 8.37; 12.16; Mk 1.5; regionis L 3.1; 4.37; regioni (*g.*) L 15.15; regionem Mt 2.12; 14.35; J 11.54; L 3.3; 4.14; 8.26; 15.13,14; 19.12; Mk 1.28; 5.1,10; 6.55; A 13.49; 14.6; 16.6; 18.23; regione J 11.55; L 2.8; 7.17; A 10.39; regiones (*n.*) A 12.20; regiones (*ac.*) J 4.35; A 8.1; regionibus L 21.21; Mk 5.17.

regius regio (*m.ab.*) A 12.21.

regno regnauit (*fut.*) L 1.33; regnaret ⟦Mt 2.22⟧; regnare L 19.14,27.

regnum Mt ⟦3.2⟧; 4.17; 5.3,10; 10.7; 11.12; 12.25,26,28; 13.24,31,33,44,45,47; 18.23; 19.14; 20.1; 21.43; 22.2; 24.7; 25.1,34; ⟦J 18.36*ter*⟧; L 6.20; 10.9,11; 11.2,17,18,20; 13.18,20; 16.16; 17.20*bis*,21; 18.16; 19.11; 21.10,31; 22.18; Mk 1.15; 3.24,26; 4.26; 10.14; 11.10; 13.8; regni Mt 4.23; 9.35; 13.11, 19,38; 16.19; 24.14; L 1.33; 8.10; Mk 1.14; 4.11; 6.23; regnum Mt 19.12,23 24; 23.13; 24.7; L 4.43; 8.1; 9.2,60,62; 12.31,32; 18.17, 24,25,29; 19.12,15; 21.10; 22.29; 23.51; Mk 4.30; 9.1,47; 10.15,23,24,25; 13.8; 15.43; A 1.6; 8.12; 14.22; 20.25; regno Mt 5.19; 11.11; 13.41,43,52; 16.28; 18.1,3,4; 20.21; 21.31; 26.29; L 7.28; 9.11,26; 10.12; 13.28,29; 14.15; 22.16,30; Mk 12.34; 14.25; A 1.3; 12.20; 19.8; regna (*ac.*) Mt 4.8; L 4.5.

rego regat Mt 2.6; regere A 20.28.

regredior regrediebantur A 15.3; regressus A 18.1; regressi (*n.*) A 14.24.

regulus J 4.49.

reinuito reinuitent L 14.12.

relaxo relaxata sunt A 16.26

relinquo relinquet Mt 18.12; 19.5; Mk 10.7; relinquetur Mt 24.2,40,41*bis*; L 17.34; 21.6; Mk 13.2; reliquisti Mt 27.46; reliquid Mt 19.29; J 4.3; 8.29; Mk 12.20,21; A 14.17; reliquimus L 18.28; reliquistis Mt 23.23;

24.22]; **salba** J 12.27; **salbare** (Mt 18.11; 27.42); L 19.10; **saluare** Mt 16.25; [18.11; 27.42]; L 6.9; 9.24; 24.21; **saluari** Mt 19.25; L 6.17; 18.26.

salus J 4.22; L 19.9; **salutis** L 1.69,77; A 13.26; 16.17; **salutem** L 1.68,71; A 7.25; 13.47; 15.23.

salutaris **salutarem** (*m.*) L 3.6.

salutatio L 1.29; **salutationis** L 1.44; **salutationem** L 1.41; **salutationes** (*ac.*) Mt 23.7; L 11.43; 20.46; Mk 12.38.

saluto **salutant** III J 15; **salutauit** (*fut.*) Mt 1.21; **salutabit** (*perf.*) L 1.40; **salutauimus** A 21.7; **salutauerunt** Mk 9.15; **salutaueritis** Mt 5.47; L 10.4; **salutasset** A 18.21, 22; 21.19; **salutassemus** A 21.6; **saluta** III J 15; **salutate** Mt 10.12; **salutare** L 2.30; Mk 15.18; **salutans** (*m.*) A 20.1; **salutantes** (*m.n.*) A 20.12.

saluus **salbus** J 10.9; 11.12; **saluus** Mt 10.22; Mk 10.26; 13.13; ⟦16.16⟧; A 2.21; 4.9; 11.14; 14.9; 16.30,31; **salba** (Mt 12.13); Mk 5.23; **salua** [Mt 12.13]; Mk 5.28; 13.20; **salbum** L 15.27; 18.42; 23.35; Mk 15.30; **saluum** Mk 10.52; 15.31; **salbam** L 7.50; 8.48; Mk 3.4; **saluam** Mk 5.34; 8.35*bis;* **salbi** J 5.34; L 3.10,12,14; A 15.11; **salui** L 5.31; 8.12; Mk 6.56; A 2.40,47; 15.1; **salbos** Mk 15.31; (A 4.12); **saluos** Mt 27.42; L 23.35; [A 4.12].

Samaria A 8.14; **Samariae** (*g.*) J 4.5; L 17.11; A 8.1,5,9; **Samariam** A 15.3; **Samaria** J 4.7; A 1.8; **Sama** J 4.4.

Samaritanus J 8.48; L 10.33; 17.16; **Samaritana** J 4.9; **Samaritanae** (*g.*) J 4.9; **Samaritani** J 4.40; **Samaritanorum** Mt 10.5; J 4.39; L 9.52.

Samotrachia **Samotrachiam** A 16.11.

Samuel A 3.24; 13.20.

Samus **Samum** A 20.15.

Sanan, *s.v.* **Satanas.**

sanctifico J 17.19; **sanctificat** Mt 23.19; **sanctificauit** Mt 23.17; J 10.36; **sanctificetur** L 11.2; **sanctifica** J 17.17; **sanctificati** (*m.n.*) J 17.19.

sanctitas **sanctitate** L 1.75.

sanctus J 6.69; 14.26; L 1.35; 2.25; 4.34; 12.12; Mk 1.12; 13.11; A 1.16; 8.18; 10.44; 11.15; 13.2; 19.6; 20.28; 21.11; **santus** J 7.39; Mk 1.24; A 1.8; **santa** A 7.33; **sanctum** L 1.49; 2.23; **sancti** (*m.*) Mt 28.19; A 2.33; 6.5; 10.45; **santi** A 4.30; **sancti** (*neu.*) L 1.72; **sancto** (*m.d.*) A 5.3; 6.10; 7.51; 15.28; **sanctum** Mt 12.32; J 20.22; L 1.35; 3.22; 12.10; Mk 3.29; 6.20; A 1.2; 2.27,38; 3.14; 4.25,27; 5.32; 6.13; 8.15,17,19; 10.47; 11.17; 13.35; 15.8; 19.2*bis;* 20.23; 21.28; **sanctam** Mt 4.5; 27.53; **sancto** (*m.*) Mt 1.18,20; 3.11; 24.15; L 1.41,67; 2.26; 3.16; 4.1; 10.21; Mk 1.8; 12.36; A 1.5,15; 2.4; 4.8,31; 7.55; 10.22,38; 11.16, 24; 13.4,9,52; 15.32; 16.6; **santo** A 15.29; **sancte** J 17.11,25; **sanctorum** (*m.*) Mt 27.52; L 1.70; 9.26; A 3.21; **sancta** A 13.34; **sanctis** (*m.*) Mt 16.27; Mk 8.38.

sandalium **sandalia** (*ac.*) Mk 6.9.

sanguem, *s.v.* **sanguis.**

sanguis Mt 16.17; 23.35; 26.28; 27.25; ⟦J 19.34⟧; Mk 14.24; A 22.20; **sanquis** L 11.50; **sanguinis** Mt 9.20; 27.6,8; L 8.43,47; 22.44; Mk 5.25,29; A 1.19; **sanguem** J 6.53, 54,56; **sanguinem** Mt 23.35; 27.4,(24); L 13.1; A 5.28; 15.20; 18.6; **sanquinem** A 20.28; **sanguine** Mt 23.30,35; [27.24]; L 11.51*bis;* A 2.20; 15.29; 17.26; 20.26; 21.25.

sanitas **sanitatis** L 9.11; A 4.22; **sanitates** (*ac.*) L 13.32.

sano **sanabat** L 4.40; 6.19; **sanabo** Mt 13.15; **sanauit** Mk 3.10; A 14.16; **sanauerunt** Mk 6.13; **sanatus est** Mt 17.18; **sanata est** Mt 15.28; L 8.47; **sanatus erat** J 5.10; **sanem** J 12.40; **sanaret** J 4.47; **sana esset** Mk 5.29; **sanare** L 9.2; **sanans** (*m.*) L 14.4; A 10.38.

sanquis, *v.* **sanguis.**

santus, *v.* **sanctus.**

sanus J 5.6,9,14; [A 4.10]; **sana** Mk 5.34; **sanum** (*m.*) J 5.11,15; 7.23; L 7.10; (A 4.10); **sanem** (*m.*) Mk 5.15; **sani** Mk 2.17.

Sapfurim J 11.54.

sapientia Mt 11.19; 13.54; L 7.35; Mk 6.2; **sapientiae** (*d.*) A 6.10; **sapientiam** Mt 12.42; L 11.31; 21.15; A 7.10; **sapientia** L 1.17; 2.40,52; A 6.3; 7.22.

sapio **sapiens** (*m.*) Mt 24.45; L 12.42; **sapientes** (*m.n.*) Mt 10.16; **sapientes** (*f.n.*) Mt 25.2,4,9; **sapientibus** (*f.d.*) Mt 25.8; **sapientes** (*m.ac.*) Mt 23.34; **sapientibus** (*m.ab.*) Mt 11.25; L 10.21; **sapientiores** (*m.n.*) L 16.8; **sapienter** L 16.8; Mk 12.34.

sapio **sapis** Mt 16.23; Mk 8.33.

Sapphira **Sapphira** (*ab.*) A 5.1.

Sarepta L 4.26.

sarmentum J 15.6; **sarmentum** (*ac.*) J 15.2; **sarmenta** (*n.*) J 15.5.

sartofagus (**sarcophagus**) **sartofagum** L 7.14.

Satanas Mt 12.26; J 13.27; L 11.15,18; 13.16; 22.3,31; Mk 3.23,26; 4.15; A 5.3; **Sanan** L 10.18; **Satanam** Mt 12.26; **Satanan**

Mk 12.10; A 1.16; scripturae Mt 26.54,56; Mk 14.49; scripturas Mt 22.29; J 5.39; 7.52; L 24.32,45; Mk 12.24; A 13.27; 17.11; 18.28; scripturis (*ab.*) Mt 21.42; L 24.27; A 17.2; 18.6,24.

scrutino scrutina J 7.52.

scruto scrutate J 5.39.

sculpo sculpto (*neu.ab.*) L 23.53.

sculptio sculptioni A 17.29.

secedo secessit Mt 2.14,[[22]]; 4.12; 12.15; 14.13; 15.21; J 6.15; Mk 3.7.

secerno secernite A 13.2.

secessus secessum Mt 15.17; Mk 7.19.

secretus secreto (*adv.*) Mk 9.28.

secta A 5.17.

secundum (*praep.c.ac.*) saecundum Mt 9.29; secundum Mt 2.16; 16.27; 23.3; 25.15; col. *bis;* J 7.24; 8.15; 12.50; [[18.31; 19.7]]; col. *bis;* L 1.9,38; 2.22,24,27,29,39,41,42; 4.16; 6.26; 17.30; 22.22,39; 23.41; col. *bis;* Mk 6.39; 7.5; [[col.]]; A 2.45; 3.22; 13.22,23; 16.13; 17.2,28; 18.15; 19.1; 22.12; secundum (*ab.*) A 2.30; (*inc.*) A 4.35.

secundus Mt 22.26; L 20.30; Mk 12.21; secundum (*neu.n.*) Mt 22.39; Mk 12.31; secundam A 12.10; secundum (*neu.ac.*) J 4.54; secundo (*m.ab.*) L 6.1; secunda (*f.ab.*) L 12.38; secundo (*neu.ab.*) Mt 26.42; Mk 14.72; A 7.13.

Secundus (*nomen*) A 20.4.

secuntur, *v.* sequor.

securis Mt 3.10; L 3.9; securem L 13.7.

securus securos Mt 28.14.

secus (*c.ac.*) Mt 4.18; 13.1,4,19; 15.29; 20.30; L 18.35; Mk 1.16; A 7.21.

sed Mt 4.4; 5.15,17,39; 9.12,13,18,24; 10.20,30,34; 11.8,9; 13.21; 15.11; 16.12,17,23; 17.12; 18.22,30; 19.6,11; 20.26,28; 21.21; 22.30,32; 24.6; 26.39; 27.24; J 3.16,17,28,36; 4.2,14,23; 5.18,22,24,30,34,42; 6.9,19,22,26, 27,32,36,38,39,64; 7.10,12,16,22,24,27,28,44, 49; 8.12,16,17,26,28,37,42,49,55; 9.3,31; 10.1, 5,8,26,33; 11.4,11,15,22,30,42,51,52,54; 12.6, 9,16,27,30,42,44,47,49; 13.9,10,18; 14.24,31; 15.16,19,21,25; 16.2,6,7,12,20,25,33; 17.9,15, 20; [[18.28,40; 19.21,24,34]]; 20.7,27; 21.8,23; L 1.60; 4.4; 5.14,31,32,38; 6.27; 7.7,25,26; 8.16,17,27,52; 11.2,4,33,42; 12.7,51; 13.3; 14.10,13; 16.21,30; 17.8; 18.13,34; 20.21,38; 21.9; 22.26,27,36,42,53; 23.15,28; 24.21,22; Mk 1.14,44,45; 2.17*bis;* 3.26,29; 4.17,22*bis;* 5.26,39; 6.9,27; 7.5,15,19,28; 8.33; 9.13,22,37; 10.8,43,45; 11.23; 12.14,25,27; 13.7,11*bis*,20, 24; 14.28,29,36,49; [[16.7]]; III J 13; A 1.4,8; 2.16; 4.17,32; 5.4,13; 7.5,39,48; 10.20,35,41; 12.23; 13.25,46; 15.11,20; 16.37; 18.4,9,21; 19.2,26,27*bis;* 20.24; 21.13,24.

sedeo sedet Mt 23.22; sedebam Mt 26.55; saedebat Mk 10.46; sedebat Mt 4.16; 13.1; 15.29; 21.7; 26.58; 28.2; J 4.6; 6.3; 9.8; 11.20; L 18.35; 22.55; Mk 3.32; 11.7; A 3.10; 14.8; sedebant Mt 4.16; Mk 3.34; A 6.15; sedebit Mt 25.31; sedebitis Mt 19.28; L 22.30; sedit J 12.14; [[19.13]]; L 4.20; 19.30; Mk 11.2; [[16.19]]; A 2.3; sederunt Mt 23.2; A 13.14; sederit Mt 19.28; sedeamus Mk 10.37; sedeant Mt 20.21; sederet Mt 13.2; sedissemus A. 16.13; sede Mt 22.44; L 20.42; Mk 12.36; A 2.34; sedete Mt 26.36; L 24.49; Mk 14.32; sedere Mt 20.23; Mk 4.1; 10.40; sedens (*m.*) J 12.15; L 5.3; 14.28,31; 22.69; Mk 12.41; 14.54; A 20.9; sedentem (*m.*) Mt 9.9; 26.64; J 9.1; L 2.46; 5.27; 8.35*bis;* 22.56; Mk 2.14; 5.15; 14.62; 16.5; sedente (*m.*) Mt 5.1; 24.3; 27.19; Mk 13.3; saedentes (*m.n.*) (Mt 20.30); sedentes (*m.n.*) Mt 13.43; [20.30]; 27.36; Mk 2.6; A 2.2; sedentes (*f.n.*) Mt 27.61; sedentibus (*d.m.*) Mt 11.16; L 1.79; 7.32; sedentes (*m.ac.*) J 20.12; L 21.35; sedi A 12.21.

sedes sedis (*n.s.*) Mt 5.34; sedem Mt 19.28; 25.31; sede Mt 23.22; sedes (*ac.*) Mt 19.28; L 22.30; A 7.46; sedibus (*ab.*) L 1.52.

seditio seditionis A 19.40; seditione Mk 15.7; A 15.2.

seditiosus seditiosis (*m.ab.*) Mk 15.7.

seduco seducit J 7.12; L 23.5; seducent Mt 24.5,11; Mk 13.6; seduxerunt L 24.22; seducti estis J 7.47; seducat Mt 24.4; Mk 13.5; seducantur Mt 24.24; seducendos Mk 13.22.

seductio Mt 13.22.

seductor Mt 27.63.

seges segetes (*ac.*) L 6.1.

segrego segregat Mt 25.32*bis;* segregabunt Mt 13.49; segregauit A 19.9.

Seleucia Seleuciam A 13.4.

Sem L 3.36.

semen Mt 13.38; J 8.33; L 8.11; Mk 4.27; A 7.6; semini L 1.55; A 7.5; semen (*ac.*) Mt 13.24,27,37; 22.[24],25; L 8.5; 20.28; Mk 4.26; 12.19,20,21,22; semine J 7.42; A 3.25; 13.23; semena (*n.*) J 8.37; seminum Mt 13.32; seminibus (*ab.*) Mk 4.31; sem (Mt 22.24).

semicinctium semicintia (*n.*) A 19.12.

Seruc L 3.35.

seruio L 15.29; **seruies** Mt 4.10; **seruiuimus** J 8.33; **seruierint** A 7.7; **seruire** L 1.74; 16.13*bis;* **seruiens** (*m.*) A 20.19; **seruiens** (*f.*) L 2.37.

seruitas **seruitute** A 7.6.

seruo J 8.55; **serbat** J 9.16; 14.21; **seruantur** Mt 9.17; L 5.38; **serbabam** J 17.11; **serbabant** (Mt 27.54); **seruabant** Mt 27.36, [54]; **serbabit** J 14.24; **seruabit** J 14.23; **seruabi** J 15.10; **serbaberunt** J 17.6; **seruauerit** J 8.52; **seruaueritis** J 15.10; **serues** J 17.15; **seruet** J 12.7; **serba** J 17.11; **serua** Mt 19.17; **serbate** J 14.15; **seruare** Mt 28.20; Mk 7.4; **serbari** A 15.5; **seruari** A 16.23.

serus **sero** (*neu.ab.*) Mt 14.15,23; 16.2; 20.8; 26.20; 27.57.

seruus **serbus** (Mt 24.46); **seruus** Mt 10.24,25; 18.26,28; 20.27; 24.45,[46],48; J 8.34,35; 13.16; 15.15,20; L 12.43,45,47; 14.21, 22; 16.13; Mk 10.44; **serui** Mt 18.27; 24.50; **seruo** ⟦J 18.10⟧; L 7.8; 14.21; 17.9; **serbum** L 2.29; 14.23; 19.27; **seruum** Mt 25.30; 26.51; ⟦J 18.10⟧; L 7.3; 14.17; 17.7; 20.10,11; 22.50; Mk 12.2,4,5; 14.47; **serue** Mt 18.32; 25.21, 23,26; L 19.17,22; **serui** Mt 13.27,28; 22.10; J 4.51; ⟦18.18⟧; L 7.10; 12.37; 17.10; A 16.17; **seruorum** Mt 25.19; **seruis** Mt 22.8; Mk 13.34; A 4.29; **seruos** Mt 21.34,35,36; 22.3,4, 6; 25.14; J 15.15; L 15.22; 19.13,15; A 2.18; **seruis** Mt 18.23; ⟦J 18.26⟧; A 10.25.

sessio **sessiones** (*ac.*) L 11.43.

sestertium **sestertia** (*ac.*) A 19.19.

Seth L 3.38.

sex Mt 17.1; J 12.1; L 13.14; A 11.12; 18.11; **sexs** Mk 9.2.

sexaginta Mt 13.8,23; L 24.13; Mk 4.8,20.

sexs, *v.* **sex.**

sextus L 1.36; **sexta** J 4.6; ⟦19.14⟧; L 23.44; Mk 15.33; **sextam** Mt 20.5; **sexto** L 1.26; **sexta** (*ab.*) Mt 27.45; A 10.9.

si (*c.ind.*) Mt 4.3,6,9; 5.13,23,29,46,47; 8.31; 9.21; 10.13,23,25; 11.14; 12.10,26,27,28; 14.28; 16.24; 17.4,20; 18.8,9,12,13,15*bis*,16, 17*bis*,19; 19.3,10,17,21; 21.3,21*bis*,24,25,26; 22.24,45; 24.23,24,26; 26.33,39,42,63; 27.40, 43*bis*,49; 28.14; J 4.48; 5.31,43,46,47; 6.51,62; 7.4,17,23,37; 8.16,24,31,36,39,42,52,54,55; 9.19,25,31; 10.9,24,35,37,38; 11.9,10,12,25, 40,48; 12.26*bis*,32,47; 13.8,14,17*bis;* 14.3,7, 14,15,23; 15.7,10,14,18,20*bis*,24; 16.7*bis*,23; ⟦18.8,23*bis;* 19.12⟧; 20.15,23*bis*,25; 21.22,23; L 4.3,7,9; 5.12,36,37; 6.4*bis*,9,32,33,34; 9.23; 10.6*bis;* 11.12,13,18,19,20,22,35; 12.28,38*bis*, 45,49; 13.3,9*bis*,23; 14.26,28,31,32; 15.8; 16.11, 12,31; 17.3*bis*,4; 18.4,30; 19.8,31,40; 20.5,6, 28; 22.42,49,67,68; 23.6,31,35*bis;* Mk 1.40; 3.26,29; 4.23; 5.28; 7.11,16; 8.12,34; 9.12,22, 23,43,45,47,50; 10.2,12; 11.3,22,25,26,31,32; 12.14,19; 13.21,22; 14.35,36; 15.36; ⟦16.18⟧; A 1.6; 4.9,19; 5.8,39; 10.18; 11.17; 13.15,18, 41; 16.15; 18.15; 19.2,38,39; 21.37; **si** (*c.coni.*) Mt 11.21,23; 12.7; 15.14; 16.26; 18.3; 20.28; 21.40; 23.30; 24.43,48; 26.24; J 4.10; 6.50; 7.51; 8.19; 9.22,33,41; 11.21,32,57; 12.24*bis;* 13.35; 14.2,28; 15.4*bis*,6,19,22; ⟦18.30,36⟧; 21.25; L 6.7; 7.39; 10.13; 12.39; 16.30,31; 17.2,6; 19.42; Mk 3.2,24,25; 4.26; 8.23,36; 9.42; 11.13; 14.21; 15.44*bis;* A 17.11,27; 18.14; **si** (*inc.*) L 6.4.

sic Mt 1.18; 2.5; 3.15; 5.16,46; 9.34; 12.40; 13.49; 17.13; 18.14; 19.8,10,12; 20.16; 26.40, 54; J 4.6; 5.21,26; 7.46; 11.48; 12.50; 14.31; 15.4; ⟦18.22⟧; 21.1,22; L 1.25; 2.48; 6.23; 9.15; 10.21; 11.30*bis;* 12.28,38,43,54; 14.33; 15.7,10; 17.24,26; 19.31,32; 21.31; 22.26; 24.24,46; Mk 2.7,8; 4.26; 7.18; 8.17; 13.29; 14.59; 15.39; A 1.11; 3.18; 5.38; 7.1*bis*,6,8; 12.8,23; 13.8; 14.1; 15.2,15; 17.33; 19.20,21; 20.11,13; 21.11.

sicarius **sicariorum** (*m.*) A 21.38.

sicco **siccatus est** Mk 5.29.

sicera **sicera** (*ac.*) L 1.15.

siclus **siclos** L 16.6.

sicut Mt 1.24; 3.16; 5.48; 6.2,5,7; 9.36; 10.16*ter*,25*bis;* 12.13,40; 13.40,43; 14.5; 15.28; 17.2*bis*,20; 18.3,4,17*bis*,33; 19.19; 20.14,28; 21.6,26,46; 22.30,39; 23.37; 24.27,37,38; 25.14, 32; 26.19,24,39*bis;* 27.10,65; 28.3*bis*,6,15; J 5.21,23,26,30; 6.31,56*bis*,57,58; 7.38; 8.28; 10.15,27; 11.33; 12.14; 13.15,33,34; 14.27,31; 15.6,9,10,12; 17.2,11,16,18,21,22,23; ⟦19.40⟧; 20.21; 21.8; L 1.2,55,70; 2.20,23,39; 3.4; 4.25; 5.14; 6.10,22,31,36,40; 9.14,54; 10.3,18, 27; 11.1,2*bis*,4,30*bis;* 12.27; 15.19,21; 17.6, 24,26,28; 18.11*bis*,17; 21.35; 22.13,26*bis*,27 *ter*,29,31,44,52,61; 23.14,44; 24.20,24,32,39; Mk 1.2; 6.34; 9.13,26; 10.1; 11.6; 12.25,31; 13.34; 14.16,21,36*bis;* 15.8; ⟦16.7⟧; A 2.4,15, 22; 3.17; 7.42,44,48,51; 10.47; 11.15,16,17,29; 13.33; 15.2,8,15; 17.28.

sideror **sideratum** (*m.*) Mt 18.8; **sideratos** Mt 15.30,31.

Sidon **Sidoni** Mt 11.22; L 10.14; **Sidonem** Mk 3.8; 7.31; **Sidona** Mt 11.21; **Sidone** L 10.13; **Sidoni** L 10.13.

Sidona **Sidonae** (*g.*) Mt 15.21.

sol Mt 13.43; 17.2; 24.29; L 23.45; Mk 1.32; 4.6; 13.24; A 2.20; solem Mt 5.45; A 13.11; sole Mt 13.6; L 4.40; 21.25; Mk 16.2.

solbo, *v.* soluo.

solemnis, *v.* sollemnis.

soleo solebat Mk 15.6.

solitudo solitudinem Mk 8.4; solitudine A 7.30,36,38,42,44; 13.18.

sollemnis solemnis (*m.*) J 6.4; sollemnem (*m.*) A 18.21.

sollicito sollicitasti A 21.38.

sollicitudo Mt 13.22; sollicitudinem Mk 4.19; sollicitudinibus (*ab.*) L 8.14.

sollicitus solliciti (*n.*) L 12.11,22,26.

Solomon L 3.23; 11.31; 12.27; A 7.47; Solomonis Mt 12.42; J 10.23; L 11.31; A 3.11; 5.12; Solomone Mt 12.42.

soluo soluet (*praes.*) L 13.15; soluitis Mk 11.3; soluit A 16.33; soluerunt Mk 11.4; solueris Mt 16.19; soluerit Mt 5.19; solbatur J 7.23; solueret J 5.18; soluta est L 1.63; solutum est Mk 7.35; solue A 7.33; soluite J 11.44; Mk 11.2; solbere L 3.16; Mk 1.7; soluere A 13.25; solui J 10.35; L 13.16; solbentes (*m.n.*) (Mt 21.2); soluentes (*m.n.*) [Mt 21.2]; L 19.30; Mk 11.5; solutum (*neu.n.*) Mt 16.19; soluta (*ac.*) Mt 18.18; solutis (*m.*) A 2.24.

solus Mt 14.23; 24.36; J 6.15; 8.9,16; 16.32; L 5.21; 9.36; 24.18; Mk 2.7; 6.47; 9.2; 10.18; A 15.34; solum J 12.24; soli (*m.*) Mt 4.10; L 4.8; solum (*m.*) Mt 17.8; 18.15; J 8.29; 16.32; 17.3; solam L 10.40; solo (*m.*) Mt 4.4; L 4.4; soli L 9.18; solis (*m.*) Mt 12.4; L 6.4; A 11.19; solos A 18.4; solum (*adv.*) Mt 21.21; J 5.18; 11.52; 17.20; A 18.25; 19.26,27; 21.13.

somnio somniabunt A 2.17.

somnium somnia (*ac.*) A 2.17.

somnus somnus (*g.*) J 11.13; somnum Mt 2.12; somno Mt 1.24; L 9.32; Mk 14.40; A 20.9*bis;* somnis (*ab.*) Mt 2.19,[[22]]; A 16.27.

sonia soniis (*ab.*) L 21.34.

sono sonante (*neu.ab.*) L 21.25.

Sopater A 20.4.

sopor soporem A 22.17.

soror Mt 12.50; J 11.39; [[19.25]]; L 10.39, 40; Mk 3.35; sororis J 11.1; sororem J 11.5,28; sorores (*n.*) Mt 13.56; J 11.3; Mk 3.32; 6.3; sorores (*ac.*) Mt 19.29; L 14.26; 18.29; Mk 10.29,30.

sors A 1.26; sortem Mt 27.35; [[J 19.24]]; L 23.34; Mk 15.24; A 1.17; sortes (*ac.*) A 1.26.

sortior sorciamur [[J 19.24]]; sortitus fuit A 1.17.

Sosthenes Sosthenen A 18.17.

spargo sparsisti Mt 25.24.

spatium A 5.7; spatium (*ac.*) Mk 6.31.

species L 9.29; speciem J 5.37; specie L 11.44.

spectaculum spectaculum (*ac.*) L 23.48.

specto spectabant L 2.38.

speculator speculatore Mk 6.27.

spelucam speluncham, *s.v.* spelunca.

spelunca J 11.38; spelucam (Mt 21.13); speluncam L 19.46; Mk 11.17; speluncham [Mt 21.13].

sper, *s.v.* per.

spermologus A 17.18.

sperno spernit J 12.48; L 10.16*bis;* spernent L 18.9.

spero III J 14; sperat Mt 24.50; speratis Mt 24.44; J 5.45; 8.49; L 6.34; sperabat L 23.8; sperabunt Mt 12.21; sperauimus L 24.21; sperauerunt Mt 20.10.

spes ispes (A 16.19); spes [A 16.19]; spem [A 2.26]; spsem (A 2.26).

spica spicam Mk 4.28*bis;* spicas Mt 12.1; L 6.1; Mk 2.23.

spina spinae (*n.*) Mt 13.7; L 8.7; Mk 4.7; spinarum L 8.7; spinas L 8.14; Mk 4.7; spinis Mt 13.7,22; 27.29; [[J 19.2]]; L 6.44; 23.37; Mk 4.18; 15.17.

spineus spineam [[J 19.5]].

spiramentum spiramentum (*ac.*) A 17.25.

spiritus Mt 10.20; 12.43; 26.41; J 4.24; 6.63*bis;* 7.39; 14.17,26; 16.13; L 1.35,47; 2.25; 4.18; 8.55; 9.39; 11.24; 12.12; 24.39; Mk 1.12,26; 9.20; 13.11; 14.38; A 1.8,16; 2.2,4; 8.18; 10.19,44; 11.12,15; 13.2; 16.7; 17.16; 19.1,6,12,15,16; 20.3,28; 21.11; spiritui (*g.*) L 9.55; spiritus Mt 12.31; 28.19; L 4.14; 13.11; A 2.33; 10.45; spirito A 6.10; 7.51; spiritui L 9.42; Mk 9.25; A 5.3; 15.28; spiritum Mt 3.16; 12.18,32; 27.50; J 3.34; 15.26; [[19.30]]; 20.22; L 3.22; 12.10; 23.46; Mk 1.10; 3.29,30; 7.25; 9.17; A 1.2; 2.17,18,38; 4.25; 5.9,32; 7.59; 8.7,15,17,19; 10.47; 11.17,28; 15.8; 16.16; 19.2*bis;* 20.23; 21.4; spirito Mt 1.20; L 1.67; 2.27; 3.16; Mk 12.36; A 1.5; 4.8,31; 10.38; 11.16,24; 13.4,9; 15.7,29,32; 16.6; 19.21; 20.22; spiritu Mt 1.18; 3.11; 4.1;

suauitas suabitati (*ab.*) L 8.14.

sub (*ac.*) Mt 15.30; L 3.2; 4.27; 7.8; 20.43; Mk 4.21,32; 12.40; A 2.5; [4.12]; 11.19,28; suc (A 4.12); sub (*c.ac.*) Mt 5.15; 23.37; L 7.6,8; 8.41; 11.33; 13.19,34; Mk 4.21; subante A 5.21; *v.quoque* desub.

subdo subdita sunt L 10.17,20; subditus L 2.51.

subdolus subdolum (*n.*) A 18.14; subdoles (*m.ac.*) A 17.5.

subeo subierunt J 11.55.

subitanus L 21.34.

subito Mt 21.19,20; A 5.5; 14.10; *v.quoq.* desubito.

subiugalis subiugalem (*m.*) Mt 21.5.

subleuo subleuate L 21.28.

subpedaneum Mt 5.35.

subsanno subsannabant L 16.14; 23.35.

subsisto substitit A 19.22.

substantia L 11.21; substantiae (*g.*) L 15.12; substantiae (*d.*) L 14.33; substantiam Mt 19.21; 25.14; L 12.33,44; 15.12,13; 16.1; 21.4; substantia L 8.3; 12.15; 19.8.

substerno substernebant L 19.36.

substraxi, *s.v.* subtraho.

subtraho substraxi A 20.27; subtraxit A 5.2; substraxerim A 20.20; subtrahens (*m.*) L 5.16.

subtus (*c.ab.*) Mk 7.28; suptus (*c.ac.*) Mt 22.44; L 8.16.

subuenio subueni (*imv.*) Mk 9.22.

subuerto subuertentem (*m.*) L 23.2.

suc, *s.v.* sub.

succingo succinget L 12.37.

sudarium sudarium (*ac.*) J 20.7; sudario J 11.44; L 19.20; sudaria (*n.*) A 19.12.

sudor L 22.44.

sufferentia sufferentia (*ab.*) L 8.15; 21.19.

suffero sustulisti J 20.15; sustulit J 5.9; A 7.21; sustulistis Mk 8.19; sustulerunt Mk 6.43; 8.8; sublatus est A 20.9; sublatum est L 9.17; sublata sunt A 11.10; sublatus fuerit L 5.35; sublatum (*m.*) J 20.1; sublato (*m.*) Mk 2.12; sublatis (*f.ab.*) A 13.19.

sufficio sufficit Mt 10.25; J 14.8; L 22.38; Mk 14.41; sufficiunt J 6.7; sufficiat Mt 25.9; sufficientes (*m.n.*) L 3.14.

suffoco suffocat Mt 13.22; suffocant Mk 4.19; suffocantur L 8.14; subfocabat Mt 18.28; suffocabant L 8.42; suffocauerunt Mt 13.7; L 8.7; Mk 4.7; suffocata est L 8.33; suffocati sunt Mk 5.13; esuffocarent (L 12.1); suffocarent [L 12.1].

suggillo suggillet L 18.5.

sugo suxisti L 11.27.

sui sibi Mt 12.48; ⟦J 19.17⟧; Mk 3.9; 5.20; A 7.21; 17.20; 19.22; 20.28; se Mt 9.21, 23; 12.25*bis*,26; 16.24; 18.4; 19.1; 23.12*bis;* 27.5,42; J 5.18,26; 6.42; 8.7,10,22,59; 12.36; 16.2; ⟦18.18,25; 19.7,12⟧; 21.1,7*bis;* L 1.24; 5.16; 7.39; 8.18; 9.47; 10.29; 11.17,18; 12.17, 37; 13.11; 14.11*bis;* 16.3; 18.4,9,14*bis*,16; 22.55; 23.2; 24.28; Mk 3.13,24,26; 5.5,10,37; 8.34; 14.67; 15.31; A 1.3; 5.37; 14.17; 16.27; 19.31; semet J 5.26; 11.38; 13.4; L 9.23,25; 15.17; Mk 3.25; se (*ab.*) Mt 12.45; 13.21; J 5.19; 7.18; 11.51; 15.4; L 11.26; Mk 5.28; A 10.17; 12.11; secum Mt 12.45; 15.30; 25.3; L 5.34; 8.51; Mk 14.33; A 16.3; semet J 9.21; 13.32; 16.13; L 1.29; 11.38; sibi (*pl.*) Mt 14.15; 27.32,35; J 6.24; ⟦19.24⟧; Mk 6.36; A 13.42; 14.18; 15.20; se Mt 9.3; 16.7; 19.12; 21.25,38; 27.7; J 6.61; 7.35; 20.10; L 7.49; 14.18; 20.7,20; 24.1; Mk 1.27; 2.8; 9.10,34; 14.54; A 19.38; 20.30; 21.23,25; semet J 11.55,56; L 20.5; 22.23; 24.14,32; Mk 10.26; 11.31; A 18.12; se (*ab.*) J 20.4; Mk 4.17; 6.51; secum Mk 8.14; 9.8; A 15.38; semet L 3.8.

sulfur L 17.29.

sum Mt 3.11; 11.29; 14.27; 20.15; 22.32; 24.5; 26.22,25; 27.24,43; 28.20; J 3.28; 4.26; 6.20,35,41,48,51; 7.29,33,36; 8.12,16, 18,23*bis*,24,28,58; 9.5*bis*,9; 10.7,9,11,14,36; 11.25; 12.26; 13.13,19,33; 14.3,6,9; 15.1,5; 16.32; 17.11*ter*,14,16,24; ⟦18.5,6,8,17,25,35, 37; 19.21⟧; L 1.18,19; 3.16; 5.8; 7.6; 15.19, 21; 18.11; 19.22; 21.8; 22.27,58,70; 24.39; Mk 1.7; 6.50; 13.6; 14.62; A 7.32; 10.21,26; 13.25*bis;* 18.10; 20.26; 21.39; es Mt 2.6; 3.17; 4.3,6; 5.25; 11.3; 14.28,34; 16.16,17,18, 23; 22.16; 25.24; 26.63; 27.11,40; J 4.12,19; 6.69; 7.52; 8.25,48,53; 9.28; 10.24; 11.27; ⟦18.17,25,33,37; 19.9,12⟧; 21.12; L 3.22; 4.3, 9,34,41; 6.4; 7.19,20; 9.50; 11.2; 12.58; 15.31; 19.21; 20.38; 22.67,70; 23.3,35*bis;* 24.18; Mk 1.11; 3.11; 8.29; 12.14,34; 14.61,70*bis;* 15.2; A 4.24; 13.33; 21.38; is Mk 1.24; est Mt 1.20,23; 2.2; 3.⟦3⟧,11,15; 5.3,16,34,35*bis*, 37,45,48; 6.1; 8.27; 9.5,15; 10.10,11,24,26,32, 33,37,38; 11.6,10,11*bis*,14,16,30; 12.6,8,11,23, 30*bis*,48,50*bis;* 13.19,20,21,22,23,24,31,32*bis*, 33,37,38,39*bis*,44,45,47,52,55,57; 14.2,15,26; 15.8,28; 16.2,17,20; 17.4,5,15; 18.1,7,8,9,10, 14*bis*,19,23; 19.10,14,17,24,26; 20.1,15,23,26; 21.10,11,25,38,42; 22.2,32,38,42; 23.8,9,10,16

[9] Order of verses in MS.

supplementum **supplementum** (*ac.*) Mk 2.21.

supra (*c.ab.*) Mt 14.11; **supra** (*c.ac.*) Mt 2.9; 4.5; 5.15; 13.2; 15.35; 23.22; 24.7; J 3.31; 4.6; Mk 7.30; A 14.10; **supra** (*adv.*) L 11.44; **superius** Mt 20.28; L 14.10.

suptus, *v.* **subtus.**

surdus Mt 9.33; 12.22; L 1.22; 11.14; **surdum** (*m.*) Mt 9.32; Mk 7.32; **surde** (*m.*) Mk 9.25; **surdi** Mt 11.5; L 7.22; **surdis** (*m.*) Mk 7.37; **surdos** Mt 15.31.

surgo **surgit** J 7.52; **surgunt** Mt 25.7; **surrexi** [A 22.11]; **surrexit** Mt 9.25; 11.11; 14.2; 27.64; 28.6,7; J 11.29,31; 13.4; L 4.16; 7.16; 8.55; 9.7,8; 10.25; Mk 2.12; 6.16; 9.27; ⟦16.6⟧; A 5.36,37; 10.41; 15.7; (22.11); **surrexerunt** Mt 27.52; A 6.9; 15.5; **surrexero** Mt 26.32; Mk 14.28; **surrexerit** L 16.31; **surrexisset** Mk 9.10; A 1.15; 5.17,34; 10.23; 13.16; 14.20; **surrexissent** A 5.6; **surge** Mt 9.5,6; J 5.8; L 5.23,24; 6.8; 7.14; 8.54; Mk 2.9,11; 3.3; 5.41; 10.49; A 10.13,20; 12.7; 14.10; 22.16; **surgite** Mt 17.7; 26.46; J 14.31; Mk 14.42; **surgens** (*m.*) Mt 2.13,20 ⟦21⟧; 9.7,9,19; 26.62; J 5.9; 21.14; L 4.38; 5.25,28; 6.8; 8.24; 11.7,8*bis;* 15.18,20; 17.19; 22.45; Mk 2.14; ⟦16.9⟧; A 11.7; 15.13; **surgens** (*f.*) L 1.39; **surgentem** (*f.*) L 4.39; **surgentes** (*m.n.*) L 4.29; 22.46; 24.33; Mk 14.57.

sursum, *v.* **desursum.**

Susanna L 8.3.

suscipio **suscipit** Mt 12.45; Mk 9.37; **suscipiunt** Mk 4.20; **suscepisti** A 16.35; **suscepit** Mt 1.24; 4.5,8; 17.1; 20.17; L 10.38; 19.6; A 1.9; 15.40; 17.7; **susceperunt** ⟦J 19.17⟧; L 9.53; A 21.17; **susceptus est** A 1.2; **susceperit** Mt 18.5; Mk 9.37; **suscipe** Mt 2.13; **suscipere** Mt 1.20; **suscipiens** (*m.*) Mt 16.22; 26.37; 27.59; L 9.11; 10.30; Mk 7.33; **suscipientes** (*m.n.*) Mt 27.27.

suscito **suscitat** J 5.21; **suscitabo** Mk 14.58; **suscitauit** (*fut.*) A 7.37; **suscitabit** (*perf.*) J 12.1; (A 3.7); [3.22]; **suscitauit** J 12.9,17; A 2.24; 3.[7],15,(22,26); 4.10; 5.30; 10.40; 12.7; 13.32,34,37; **suscitauerunt** A 13.50; **suscitate** Mt 10.8; **suscitare** Mt 3.9; L 3.8; A 2.30; **suscitans** (*m.*) [A 3.26].

suspendo **suspendit** Mt 27.5; **suspendatur** Mt 18.6; **suspensum** (*m.*) A 5.30; 10.39.

suspicor L 7.43; **suspicamini** A 2.15; 13.25.

sustineo **sustinent** Mt 15.32; **sustinebit** Mt 10.22; **sustinuit** A 10.24; **substinuit** A 17.14; **sustinuerit** Mt 24.13; Mk 13.13; **sustinete** Mt 26.38; Mk 14.34; **sustinere** A 15.34.

susu, *s.v.* **seorsum.**

susum J 11.41; A 2.19.

suus Mt 25.21,23; **sui** Mt 13.43; 14.3; 16.27; 25.18; J 12.41; L 1.54,59,69; 3.19; 9.26; 12.47; 16.5,24; Mk 6.17; 8.38; A 7.4; **suae** Mt 13.26*bis;* 19.28; 25.31; L 1.15,48; Mk 8.36; A 1.18; 3.2; 14.8; **sui** L 1.8; 6.45; 7.38; **suo** Mt 5.22*bis;* 8.31,35; 20.8; 22.2,24 *bis*,25; J 4.5; L 1.68; 9.42; 14.21*bis;* 15.29; 20.28; Mk 7.11; 12.19; **suae** Mt 14.11; 19.5; ⟦J 19.26⟧; L 7.12,15; 14.33; Mk 6.24,28; **suo** A 15.14; **suum** Mt 1.21; 4.22; 5.45; 10.24,35; 15.5; 21.37; 22.5,7; 26.51,52; J 3.16,17; 5.9, 18; 8.27; L 2.7; 9.51; 11.11; 12.36,53; 13.15, 19; 14.17,23,26; 15.20; 21.30; Mk 12.44; 13.24; A 1.25; 3.13,18,26; 5.10; 7.14; 12.11; 20.28; **suam** Mt 1.24; 2.12; 3.12; 5.31,32; 6.2, 5; 9.1,7,38; 10.35*bis*,38,39*bis;* 16.24,25*bis;* 17.6; 19.3,9; 20.1,2,28; 22.5,25; 24.18,43,45; 25.14,15; 26.39; J 4.28; 7.18,53; 10.11; 11.28; 12.25*bis;* 15.13; L 1.23,56,58; 2.3,39; 5.25; 7.16; 9.24*bis*,52,62; 10.1,2,7,38; 11.21; 12.25, 44,53; 14.26*bis*,27; 15.13; 16.8,18; 17.33; 21.4; 22.36; Mk 1.41; 6.1; 8.26,34,35; 9.41; 10.7*bis*,11,45; 13.16,34; A 2.14; 7.10; 10.22; 14.11; 15.26; 16.34; **suum** Mt 3. ⟦7⟧,12; 5.2; 24.29; 27.39; J 13.18; 15.19; L 8.5; 10.34; 18.13; 22.66; A 4.32; 10.36; 19.1; **suo** Mt ⟦2.22⟧; 13.24,31; 23.4; J 8.6,8; 13.16; 15.20; L 6.44; 23.11; Mk 1.20; 6.21; **sua** Mt 2.11; 10.10; 13.54,57; 14.8; 25.31; J 4.44; 5.5; L 1.36; 2.36; 4.24; 5.29; 8.3; 9.27; 11.2; 12.27; 13.6; 21.4; Mk 4.2; 6.4*bis;* 8.37; 12.44; 13.15; A 1.7; 2.6; 5.1,2,31; 11.13; 12.10; 13.36; 16.34; 18.8; **suo** Mt 5.28; 6.7; 16.28; 24.48; 27.60; J 5.43; 8.44; L 1.20,51; 2.19,51; 9.26; 12.45; 21.4; Mk 6.4; 10.50; 11.23; A 7.24; **sui** J 7.3; Mk 8.4; **suorum** Mt 15.27; J 13.5; 20.30; L 7.19; 18.7; Mk 7.2; A 3.21; **suarum** A 7.41; **suis** (*m.*) Mt 4.6; 9.11,37; 11.1; 14.2; 16.21,24; 19.23; 22.8; 23.1; 26.36; J 6.12; 11.7,16; 14.1; 21.1,14; L 4.10; Mk 3.9; 4.34; 8.6; 10.23; 13.34; A 16.16; **suos** Mt 2.11,18; ⟦3.4⟧; 10.1; 11.2; 12.49; 13.15,41; 15.32; 17.8; 21.2,34*bis*,43; 22.3,16; 23.37; 24.31,49; 25.14; 26.40,45; J 11.41; 13.1; 17.1; L 6.13,20; 9.14, 43,60; 10.23; 11.1; 12.22; 13.34; 15.5,22; 16.23; 17.1; 18.13; 19.13,15; 24.5; Mk 6.45; 7.33; 8.27,33; 9.31; 12.43; 13.20; A 4.23; 7.23, 25; 13.36; 19.18; 21.11; **suas** Mt 4.21; 15.2; 23.37; 25.1,3,7; 27.24; J 10.3; L 2.28; 13.34; 16.4; 19.35; 21.12; A 1.26; 12.1; 14.16; 15.23; **sua** Mt ⟦3.6⟧; 16.27; 23.5*bis;* 24.47; 26.65; 27.31; J 10.4; 13.4; 14.10; 16.32; ⟦19.27⟧; L 2.8; 19.36; 21.1; Mk 1.5; 5.26; 11.7,8; 14.63; A 7.58; 14.14; 18.6; 21.6; **suis** Mt 11.19;

Thessalia Thessaliam A 17.15.

Thessalonica Thessalonicae (*g.*) A 17.11; Thessalonicam A 17.1; Thessalonica A 17.13.

Thessalonicensis Thessalonicensium (*m.*) A 20.4.

Theudas A 5.36.

Thomas Mt 10.3; J 11.16; 14.5; 20.24,26, 28; 21.2; A 1.13; Thoman J 20.27; L 6.15; Mk 3.18.

thronus A 7.49; thronum L 1.32; A 2.30.

thus thus (*ac.*) Mt 2.11.

Thyatira Thyatirum (*g.*) A 16.14.

Tiberias Tiberiadis J 6.1; 21.1; Tiberiade J 6.23.

Tiberius, *s.v.* Caesar.

Timeas Timeae (*g.*) Mk 10.46.

timeo L 18.4; times L 23.40; timet J 9.31; A 10.35; timemus Mt 21.26; Mk 11.32; timetis A 13.16; timebam L 19.21; timebant J 9.22; L 9.45; 22.2; Mk 9.32; 11.18; [[16.8]]; A 5.26; timuit Mt [[22.22]]; 14.5,30; [[J 19.8]]; timuerunt Mt 9.8; 17.6; 19.25; 21.46; 27.54; J 6.19; L 2.9; 8.35; 9.34; 20.19; Mk 4.41; 5.15; 12.12; A 16.35,38; timueritis L 12.7; timeas Mt 1.20; L 1.30; A 18.9; timeatis L 12.5; timueris L 1.13; timueritis Mt 10.26,28, 31; L 21.9; Mk 13.7; timete Mt 10.28; L 12.5; timere Mt 14.27; 17.7; 28.5,10; J 6.20; 12.15; L 2.10; 8.50; 12.4,32; Mk 5.36; 6.50; 16.6; timens (*m.*) Mt 25.25; L 18.2; A 10.22; timens (*f.*) Mk 5.33; timentes (*m.n.*) L 8.25; A 13.26; timentibus (*m.d.*) L 1.50.

timidus timidi (*n.*) Mk 4.40.

Timon Timonem A 6.5.

timor L 1.12,65; 5.9; 7.16; A 2.43; 5.5,11; 19.17; timorem J 7.13; 20.19; L 2.9; timore Mt 14.26; 28.4,8; L 1.74; 5.26; 8.37; 21.26; 24.5,37; Mk 4.41; 9.6; A 14.9; timores (*n.*) L 21.11.

timoratus A 22.12; timorati (*n.*) A 2.5; 8.2.

Timotheus A 16.1; 17.14; 18.5; 20.4; Timotheum A 17.15; 19.22.

tinea L 12.33.

titulus titulum [[J 19.19,20]].

tolerabilis tolerabilius (*n.*) Mt 10.15; 11.22,24; L 10.12,14.

tollo tollis J 10.24; tollit Mt 9.16; 25.19; J 10.18; 15.2; L 6.29; 8.12; 11.22; tollam J 20.15; tollet J 16.22; L 6.30; 22.36; tollent Mt 4.6; J 11.48; L 4.11; [[Mk 16.18]]; tolletur Mt 13.12; 25.29; L 8.18; 19.26; tollas J 17.15; tollat Mt 16.24; Mk 8.34; tollatur Mt 9.15; tolleret Mt 27.32; [[J 19.38]]; Mk 15.21; tollerent Mk 6.8; tollerentur [[J 19.31]]; tolle Mt 9.6; 17.27; 20.14; J 5.8,11,12; [[19.15*bis*]]; L 5.24; 19.22; 23.18*bis;* Mk 2.9,11; tollite Mt 22.13; 25.28; J 11.39; L 19.24; A 21.36; tollere (*imv.*) Mt 21.21; Mk 11.23; tollere (*inf.*) Mt 18.23,24; 24.17,18; J 5.10; 10.18; L 17.31; Mk 13.15,16; tollens (*m.*) L 5.25; tolles (*part.m.*) L 19.21.

tondeo tonso (*neu.ab.*) A 18.18.

tonitruum J 12.29; tonitrui L 6.14; Mk 3.17.

torcular torcular (*ac.*) Mt 21.33.

tormentum tormenti L 16.28; tormentis (*ab.*) Mt 4.24; L 16.23.

torqueo torqueas L 8.28; Mk 5.7; torquere Mt 8.29; torquentes (*m.n.*) Mt 27.29.

torrens torrentem J 18.1.

tortor tortoribus (*d.*) Mt 18.34.

tot L 15.29.

totus Mt 8.32; J 9.34; 12.19; 13.10; tota Mt 8.34; J 4.53; 11.50; Mk 1.33; 15.8; A 13.44; 19.27,29; 21.30,31; totum Mt 1.22; 5.29; 22.40; 26.56,59; L 11.34; 13.21; totius (*f.*) Mt 23.27; totum Mt 16.26; J 7.23; L 9.25; Mk 12.44; A 2.47; 11.26; totam Mt 4.23,24; 9.26; L 5.5; 7.17; 23.44; Mk 1.39; 6.55; 15.16,33; A 2.2; 5.11; 10.37; 13.6; 14.6; totum [[J 19.23]]; L 13.11; toto Mt 20.6; 24.14; 26.13; A 11.28; tota Mt 9.31; 22.37*bis;* L 1.65; 10.27*bis;* 19.44; Mk 12.30*bis*,33*bis;* A 10.22; 15.22; 16.34; 18.8; toto Mt 22.37; L 10.27; Mk 12.30,33; toti J 13.10.

trabaricator L 6.4.

trabs trabis (*n.s.*) L 6.42; trauem L 6.41, 42.

Trachonitis Trachonitidis L 3.1.

tracto tractabatis Mk 9.33; tractabunt A 7.6; tractauit A 7.19; tractent A 17.27.

traditio traditionem Mt 15.2,3,6; Mk 7.3, 5,9,13; traditiones (*ac.*) Mk 7.8.

traditor Mk 14.44.

trado Mt 26.15; tradis L 22.48; traditur Mt 26.24; L 22.22; Mk 14.41; tradebat Mt 26.25,48; [[J 18.2,5]]; A 8.3; tradebant A 16.4; tradet Mt 10.21; 26.21,23; J 13.21; L 12.58; 22.21; Mk 13.12; 14.18,42; tradent Mt 10.17; 20.19; 24.9,10; L 21.16; Mk 10.33; 13.9; A 21.11; tradetur Mt 20.18; 26.2,45; Mk 9.31; 10.33; 14.21*bis;* L 18.32; trademini L 21.16; tradidisti Mt 25.20,22; tradidit Mt 10.4; 18.34; 25.14; 27.3,26; J [[19.11,16,30]]; 21.20; L 6.16; 20.9; 23.25; Mk 3.19; 12.1; 15.15; A

tristitia J 16.6,20; **tristitae** (*g.*) J 16.21; **tristitiam** J 16.20, 21,22; **tristitia** L 22.45.

triticum **tritici** Mt 13.25; J 12.24; L 16.7; **triticum** Mt 3.12; 13.29,30; L 3.17; 22.31.

Troas **Troadae** (*g.*) A 16.11; **Troada** A 16.8; **Troadam** A 20.6; **Troade** A 20.5.

Trogylium **Trogylio** (*ab.*) A 20.15.

Trophimus A 20.4; **Trophimum** A 21.29.

tu Mt 2.6; 3.14,17; 6.6; 11.3,23; 14.28,34; 16.16,18; 26.25,39,63,64; 27.4,11*bis;* J 3.26; 4.9,10,12; 6.30,69; 7.52; 8.5,13,25,33,48, 52,53; 9.17,28,34*bis*,35; 10.24; 11.27,42; 12.34; 13.6,7,36; 14.9; 17.8,21*bis*,23*ter*,25; ⟦18.17,25,33,37*bis;* 19.9⟧; 20.15; 21.12,15,16, 17*bis*,18; L 1.28,42; 3.22; 4.7,41; 5.33; 7.19, 20; 15.31; 16.25; 17.8; 19.19,42; 22.67,70; 23.3*bis*,40; 24.18; Mk 1.11; 3.11; 8.29; 14.36, 61,67; 15.2*bis;* A 4.24; 10.26,33; 13.33; 16.31; 21.38; **tui** Mt 18.33; Mk 5.19; **tibi** Mt 2.13; 4.9; 5.26,29; 6.4,6; 8.29; 9.2,5; 11.21,25; 12.47; 14.4; 15.5,28; 16.17,18,19,22*bis*; 17.4, 25; 18.8,9,17,22,29,32; 20.[13],14,28*ter;* 21.5, 23; 22.17; 25.44; 26.17,34; 27.19; J 4.10*bis;* 5.10,12,14; 6.30; 9.10,27,26*bis;* 11.22,40,41; 13.38; ⟦18.30,34; 19.11*bis*⟧; 21.18; L 1.3,13, 14,19; 4.6,34; 5.20,23,24; 7.14,40,47,48; 8.28, 30,39; 9.33; 10.13,21,40; 11.7; 12.59; 14.9,10 *bis*,12,14*bis;* 15.29; 18.11,22,41; 19.42; 20.2; 22.9,34; Mk 1.24; 2.5,9,11; 5.7,9,19,41; 6.18, 22,23; 7.11; 9.5,25,43,45,47; 10.21,51; 14.12, 30,36,60; III J 13*bis;* A 3.6; 5.4; 7.3; 10.32,33; 13.33; 14.10; 16.18,28; 18.10; 19.14; 21.23; **te** Mt 4.6*bis;* 5.23,25*bis*,29,39,41,42; 6.2; 9.22; 11.10,26; 14.28; 18.8,9,15*ter*,33; 19.19, 27; (20.13); 21.21; 22.16,39; 23.37; 25.21, 23, 27,37,38,39*bis*,44; 26.18,35,63; 27.40; J 6.69; 7.4,20; 8.10,11,53; 10.33*bis;* 11.8,28; 12.28; 13.8,37; 14.22; 16.30; 17.1,3,4,5*bis*,11,13,25 *bis;* ⟦18.26,35; 19.10*bis*⟧; 21.15,16,17,18*ter*, 20,22,23; L 1.19,35*bis;* 2.48; 3.22; 4.9,10,11, 23,34; 5.14; 6.29,30; 7.6,20,50; 8.20,28,45,48; 9.38,57,61; 10.27,41; 11.27; 12.58*ter;* 13.31, 34; 14.9,10,12,18; 16.27; 17.3,4*bis*,8,19; 18.28, 42; 19.21,22,43*bis*,44; 22.64; 23.35; Mk 1.37, 44; 3.32; 4.38; 5.7,31,34; 9.17,43,45,47; 10.28, 35,49,52; 12.31,33; 14.31; 15.4,30; III J 14,15; A 5.3*bis*,9; 7.27,34,35; 10.19,22,33*bis;* 11.14; 12.8*bis;* 13.11,33,47; 17.32; 18.10; 21.25,37; 22.10,14,19; **te** Mt 2.6; 3.14; 4.6; 5.29; 6.3; 11.23; 12.38; 17.27; 18.8,9; 20.28 *bis;* 21.19; 26.33,62; 27.13; J 8.13; 13.37; 17.7,8,21; L 4.10; 11.35; 12.20; 14.8; 16.2; 19.44; 22.32; Mk 11.14; A 10.22,33; 17.19; 21.21,24; **tecum** Mt 18.16; 26.35; J 3.26; 4.26; 9.37; 21.3; L 1.28; 22.33; III J 15; A 18.10; **temet** J 17.13; ⟦18.34⟧; **tu** J 17.5; 21.22; L 1.76; 9.60; 10.15,37; 16.7; 22.32; A 10.15; 11.9; **uos** Mt 5.13,14; 10.20; 15.3,5,16; 16.15; 19.28*bis;* 20.28; 21.13,32; 23.8,13,28, 32; 26.31; 27.24; J 3.28; 4.20,22,32,35,38*bis;* 5.20,33,34,35,38,39,44,45; 6.67; 7.21,28,34,36, 47; 8.14,15,21,22,23*bis*,31,38,41,44,45,47,49, 54; 9.19,27,30; 10.26,36; 11.50; 13.10,13,14, 15,33,34; 14.3,17,19*bis*,20*bis;* 15.4,5,14,16*bis*, 27; 16.20*bis*,22,27; ⟦19.35⟧; L 9.20; 10.24*bis;* 11.13,39,48; 12.7,24,36; 16.15; 19.46; 22.26, 27,70; 24.48; Mk 7.11,18; 8.29; 11.17,26; 12.27; 13.11; 14.27; A 1.5; 2.15,36; 3.14,17, 25; 4.7,10; 5.30,39; 7.4,51*bis*,52; 10.28,37; 11.16; 15.7; 19.15; 20.18,25; **uestri** Mt 10.30; A 4.19; **uestrum** J 8.7; L 11.39; 13.15; 22.27; Mk 10.44; A 1.7; 2.22,38; **uobis** Mt 3. ⟦7⟧,9; 5.18,22,28,32,34,39,44; 6.2,5; 9.29; 10.15,23, 27,42; 11.9,11,17,22*bis*,24*bis*; 12.6,31,36; 13.11,17; 16.28; 17.12,20*bis;* 18.3,10,12,13,18, 19,35; 19.8,9,23,24,28; 20.4,32; 21.3,21,24,27, 28,31,43; 22.31,42; 23.3,9,13,15,16,23,25,27, 29,31,36,38,39; 24.2,23,25,26,34,47; 25.9*bis*, 12,34,40,45; 26.13,21,29,64; 27.17,21; 28.7, 20; J 4.35; 5.19,24,25; 6.26,27,32*ter*,36,47,53, 56,63,65; 7.19,22; 8.24,25,34,40,51,55,58; 9.27; 10.1,7,25,27,32; 11.50; 12.24; 13.12,15 *bis*,16,19,20,21,33,34; 14.2*bis*,3,10,12,16,25, 26,27*ter*,28,29,30; 15.[7],11,14,15,16,17,20, 26; 16.1,3,4*ter*,6,7*bis*,12,13,14,15,20,23*bis*,25 *ter*,26,33; ⟦18.8,39*ter;* 19.4⟧; 20.19,21,26; L 2.10,11,12; 3.7,8,13; 4.24,25; 5.14; 6 24,25*bis*, 26*bis*,27,31,32,33*bis*,34,37,38,47; 7.9,26,28,32; 8.10; 9.27; 10.8,11,12,14,19,20,24; 11.8,9 *ter*,41,42,43,44,46,47,51,52; 12.1,4,5*bis*,8,22, 27,31,32,33,37,44,51; 13.3,5,24,25,27,35*bis;* 14.24; 15.7,10; 16.8,9*bis*,11,12; 17.3,6,23,34; 18.8,14,17,29; 19.26,31,40; 20.8; 21.3,13,15 *bis*,32,34; 22.10,12,16,17,18,29,67; 24.6; Mk 2.27; 3.28; 4.11,24; 8.12; 9.1,13,41*bis;* 10.3, 15,29,36; 11.3,23,24*bis*,25,26,29,33; 12.43; 13.2,11,21,23,30,37; 14.9,13,15,18,25,64; ⟦16.7⟧; A 2.14,33; 3.14,20,22,26; 4.10; 5.9,28, 35,38; 13.34,38*bis*,41,46; 14.15*bis*,17; 15.28, 29; 16.17; 17.3,23; 20.20,27; **uouis** A 7.37; **bos** (Mt 21.24); **uos** Mt 3.9,11*bis;* 4.19; 5.11 *bis*,12,44*ter*,46; 10.13,14,16,17*bis*,19,23*bis*,31, 40; 11.28,29; 12.28; 16.8; 17.17; 21.2,[24],31, 32; 23.15,35; 24.4,9*bis;* 25.12; 26.32,55; 28.7, 14; J 4.38; 5.42,45*bis;* 6.43,61,70; 7.7; 8.32, 36; 11.15; 12.30,35; 13.34; 14.3,17,18*bis*,25, 26*bis*,28; 15.9,12,15*bis*,16*bis*,18,19*bis*,20,21; 16.2*ter*,7*bis*,13,22,27; 20.21; L 3.16*bis;* 5.10; 6.9,22,27,28*bis*,32; 9.5,41*bis*,50; 10.3,6,8,9,10, 16*bis*,20; 11.20; 12.11,12,14,28,29; 13.25,27,28; 16.9,15,26*bis;* 17.14,21; 20.3; 21.12; 22.31,35;

2.35; 14.10; **tuas** J 21.18; L 16.6,7; 23.46; **tua** Mt 5.33; J 17.8; L 6.30; 16.25; A 12.8; 22.16; **tuis** L 19.42; 20.43, **tuis** Mt 20.21; Mk 5.23; **tuis** Mt 12.37*bis;* **tur** (Mt 6.4).

Tyrannus **Tyranni** (*g.*) A 19.9.

Tyrius **Tyrios** A 12.19,21.

Tyrus **Tyri** Mt 15.21; Mk 7.24,31; **Tyro** Mt 11.22; L 10.14; **Tyrum** Mk 3.8; **Tyro** Mt 11.21; A 21.3,7; **Tyru** L 10.13.

ua Mt 27.40.

uaco **uacabant** A 17.21; **uacantem** (*f.*) Mt 12.44.

uacuus **uacum** (*n.*) (Mt 12.36); **uacuum** (*n.*) [Mt 12.36]; **uacuum** (*m.*) L 20.10,11,12; Mk 12.3.

uado J 7.33,34; 8.14*bis*,21*bis*,22; 13.33,36; 14.4,12,28*bis;* 16.5,10,17,28; 21.3; L 18.5; A 18.6; 20.22; **badis** J 13.36; 14.5; **uadis** J 11.8; 16.5; L 12.58; **uadit** Mt 12.45; 13.44; 26.24; J 11.31; 12.35; 13.3; L 7.8; 11.24,26; 15.4; 22.22; **uadunt** Mt 25.10; **uadet** J 10.4; **uadat** J 11.44; **bade** Mk 1.44; **uadae** (Mt 13.14); **uade** Mt 4.10; 5.24,41; 9.6; [13.14]; 16.23; 18.15; 19.21; 20.14; 21.28; J 4.16,50; 7.3; 8.11; 9.7,11; 20.17; L 5.14,24; 7.8,50; 8.39,48; 9.60; 10.37; 13.31; 17.19; Mk 2.9,11; 5.19,34; 7.29; 8.26,33; 10.21,52; A 10.20; **uadens** (*m.*) L 8.39; **uadens** (*f.*) [[Mk 16.10]].

uae Mt 11.21; 18.7*bis;* 23.13,15,16,23,25, 27,29; 24.19; 26.24; L 6.24,25*bis*,26; 10.13; 11.42,43,44,46,47,52; 17.1; 21.23; 22.22; Mk 13.17; 14.21.

uagina **uaginam** [[J 18.11]].

ualde Mt 2.10,16; 8.28; 17.6,23; 18.31; 19.25; 26.22; 27.14,54; L 4.5; 18.23; 23.8; Mk 16.3.

ualefacio **ualefecit** A 18.18.

ualeo L 16.3; **ualet** Mt 5.13; **ualuit** A 19.16; **ualuistis** Mt 26.40; **ualete** A 15.29.

ualetudo **ualetudinem** A 5.15; **ualetudinems** (Mt 3.15); **ualetudines** (*ac.*) [Mk 3.15].

ualidus **ualidum** (*m.*) Mt 14.30.

uallis L 3.5.

uanus **uanum** (*neu.ac.*) Mk 7.7; **uana** (*ac.*) Mt 6.7; **uanis** (*neu.*) A 14.15.

uapulo **bapulabit** L 12.47; **bapulauit** L 12.48; **uapulabitis** Mk 13.9.

uarius **bariis** (*m.ab.*) L 4.40; **uariis** (*m.*) Mk 1.32,34; **uariis** (*f.*) Mt 4.24.

uas [[J 19.29]]; A 10.16; 11.5; **uas** (*ac.*) Mk 11.16; A 10.11.

uases, *s.v.* **basis.**

uasum **uaso** (*ab.*) L 8.16; **uasa** (*n.*) L 17.31; **uasa** (*ac.*) Mt 12.29; Mk 3.27; **uasis** Mt 13.48; 25.3,4.

ubam, *s.v.* **uua.**

uber **uberam** L 8.8; **ubera** (*n.*) L 23.29; **uberes** (*m.*) L 12.16.

ubi Mt 2.2,4; 13.5; 25.24*bis*,26*bis;* 26.17, 57; 28.6,16; J 4.20,46; 6.23,62; 7.11,34,35,36, 42; 8.10,14*bis*,19,21,22; 9.12; 10.40; 11.30,32, 34,57; 12.1,35; 13.33,36*bis;* 14.3,4,5; 16.5; 17.24; 18.1; [[19.18,20,41]]; 20.2,12,13,15,19; 21.18*bis;* L 4.16,17,29; 5.19; 8.25; 9.58; 10.1; 12.17,33,34; 17.12,17,37*bis;* 22.9,10,11*bis;* 23.53; 24.28; Mk 2.4; 5.40; 9.43,44,46,48; 13.14; 14.14*bis;* 15.47; [[16.6]]; A 1.13; 2.2; 7.23,29; 12.12; 16.13; 17.1; 20.8,18.

ubicumque **ubicumquae** Mk 14.9; **ubicumque** Mt 24.28; 26.13; J 12.26; Mk 6.55; 9.18.

ubique L 9.6; [[Mk 16.20]]; A 17.30; 21.28.

ueatus, *v.* **beatus.**

uectigal **uectigal** (*ac.*) Mt 17.25.

uehementer **uehementius** L 22.44.

uel Mt 12.25; 18.16; J 6.19; 14.11; L 12.38; Mk 6.56*bis;* 10.40; A 5.15.

uello **bellere** (Mt 12.1); **uellere** L 6.1; Mk 2.23.

uelum Mt 27.51; L 23.45; Mk 15.38.

uelut Mk 8.24; 10.15; A 11.5.

uendo **uendit** Mt 13.44; **uendebant** L 17.28; **uendedit** [Mt 13.46]; **uendedit** A 5.1; **uindedit** (Mt 13.46); **uendedistis** A 5.8; **uendat** L 22.36; **uende** Mt 19.21; L 18.22; Mk 10.21; **uendite** L 12.33; **uendentes** (*m.*) A 4.34; **uendentium** (*m.*) Mt 21.12; L 19.45; **uendentes** (*m.*) Mt 21.12; 25.9; L 19.45; Mk 11.15.

ueneo **ueniunt** Mt 10.29; L 12.6; **ueniebant** A 4.34; **uenitum est** J 12.5; **ueniri** Mk 14.5.

uenio J 5.7; 8.14; 14.3,18,28; 17.11,13; 21.22,23; L 13.7; 19.13; **uenis** Mt 3.14; 11.3; **benit** Mt 21.9; **uenit** Mt 3[[1]],11; 13.19; 17.11; 18.7; 21.5; 23.39; 25.19; 26.36,40,45; 27.49; J 3.20,21,31*bis;* 4.5,7,21,23,25,35; 5.24,25,28; 6.35,37*bis*,45; 7.6,41,42; 9.4; 10.10; 11.20,27,28,29,38; 12.12,13,15,22; 13.6; 14.6,30; 16.2,25,32; [[18.3; 20.1]],18,26; 21.13; L 3.16; 5.27; 6.47; 7.8; 8.12,17; 12.39,40,46, 54; 13.35; 14.26,27,31; 17.20*bis;* 19.38; Mk 1.40; 3.31; 4.15; 5.22; 6.48; 9.12; 10.1,46; 11.9,10,27; 14.17,37,41,43; 15.36; A 19.1 **ueniunt** J 3.(26),26; 6.5; L 8.49; 17.1; Mk

12.47; **uerborum** J 7.40; L 1.4; 3.4; 20.20; Mk 14.72; A 5.32; **ueruorum** L 24.8; **uerbis** J 5.47; L 1.20; A 2.14; **berba** L 6.47; A 10.44; **uerba** J 3.34; 6.68; 8.20,47; 10.19; 12.48; 14.10,24; 17.8; L 1.65; 2.19,51; 7.1; 9.28,44; Mk 8.38; A 4.1; 5.20; 6.11,13; 10.22; 11.14; 13.42; 16.38; 19.10; **uerbis** Mt 12.37*bis;* L 4.22; 23.9; Mk 10.24; A 15.24.

uere Mt 14.34; 27.54; J 4.42; 6.55; 7.26,40; 8.31,36; 17.8; L 9.27; 21.3; 23.47; 24.34; Mk 11.32; 14.70; 15.39; A 12.11.

uereor **uerebuntur** Mk 12.6.

ueritas J 8.32,44; 14.6; 17.17; ⟦18.38⟧; **ueritatis** J 4.37; 14.17; 15.26; 16.13; **ueritati** J 5.33; ⟦18.37⟧; A 6.10; **ueritatem** J 3.21; 8.32,40,45; 16.7; L 1.4; Mk 5.33; 12.14; **ueritate** Mt 22.16; J 4.23,24; 8.44; 16.13; 17.17,19; ⟦18.37⟧; L 4.25; 20.21; 22.59; Mk 12.32; III J 12; A 10.34.

uermis **mermis** Mk 9.44; **uermis** Mk 9.46,48; **bermibus** (*ab.*) A 12.23.

uersus A 17.14.

uersutia **uersutiam** Mk 12.15.

uerto **uertere** A 13.8.

uerus J 7.18,28; **uera** J 15.1; **uerum** J 5.31, 32; 8.13,14,16,17; ⟦19.35⟧; 21.24; L 16.11; III J 12; A 12.9; **uerum** (*m.*) J 6.32; 17.3; **uera** A 4.27; **ueri** J 4.23; **uera** J 10.42; **uera** (*ac.*) ⟦J 19.35⟧; **uero** (*adv.*) Mt 21.8,35,36; Mk 10.27; 12.44; 14.29,55,62; 15.11,14; III J 12; A 2.13; 3.15; 4.4,13,27,35; 5.9,12,16,19, 22,24,29,41; 6.8; 7.12,17,21,49; 8.1,5,12,14; 10.10,24,26; 11.1,9,22,26; 12.1,5*bis*,6,15,16, 18,22,25; 13.4*bis*,5,9,13,15,31,42,46,52; 14.4, 12,28; 15.35,37,39; 16.25,29; 17.5,6,10,12,15, 16,21,32; 18.1,5,8,18,19; 19.1,2,9,22,31,32; 20.4,6,13; 21.6,12,25; **uerum** (*adv.*) Mt 11.22, 24; 18.7; 26.39,64; J 4.18; L 6.24,35; 10.11,14, 20; 11.41; 12.3,56; 13.33; 17.1; 18.8; 19.27; 22.21,22.

ueruum, *s.v.* **uerbum.**

uesper **uespere** Mk 1.32; 14.17; **uespere** (*adv.*) Mk 11.19.

uespera A 4.3.

uespertinus **uespertina** (*ab.*) L 12.38.

uesperus **uespera** (*f.n.*) Mk 11.11; **uesperum** (*neu.ac.*) L 24.29; A 3.1.

uester Mt 5.37,48; 9.11; 17.24; 20.26,27; 23.8,9,10,11*bis;* 24.42; J 8.42,54,56; 9.19; 15.16; ⟦19.14⟧; L 6.36; 12.30,34,35; Mk 10.43, 44; 11.25,26; A 3.22; **uestra** Mt 5.12; 10.13 *bis;* 23.38; 24.20,31; J 16.20; L 6.23,35; 8.25; 10.6*bis;* 21.28; 22.53; **uestrum** Mt 5.16; J 7.6; 14.1,27; 15.11; 16.22,24; L 6.20; 12.34; **uestri** (*m.*) Mt 5.45; [10.20]; J 8.41,44; **uestri** (*neu.*) Mk 10.5; **uestro** L 12.32; **uestrum** Mt 5.16; 6.1; J 8.38; ⟦19.15⟧; 20.17*bis;* A 18.6; **uestram** Mt 6.1; 9.29; 15.3,6; 17.20; ⟦J 18.31⟧; L 6.24; 12.33; Mk 7.9,13; A 19.35; **uestrum** Mt 19.8; J 15.20; 16.6,22; L 6.22; 16.12; 24.38; A 18.6; **uestro** Mt 10.29; 18.14; L 23.14; A 4.10; **uestra** J 8.17; L 10.11; 21.19; A 5.28; **uestro** Mt 25.8; J 8.21; L 21.18; **uestri** Mt 12.27*bis;* 13.16; J 6.49,58; L 7.22; 11.19*bis*,47; 12.7; A 3.17; 7.51; **uestrae** Mt 13.16; **uestre** (*f.*) L 7.22; **uestra** J 9.41; L 10.20; 21.34; Mk 8.17; A 3.19; **uestrorum** (*m.*) Mt 10.14; 23.32; L 9.5; 11.46,48; Mk 6.11; **uestris** (*m.*) L 11.13; **uestris** (*f.*) Mt 11.29; **uestros** Mt 5.44,47; 10.14; J 4.35; 13.14; L 6.27,35,38; 23.28; **uestras** Mt 19.8; L 5.4; 9.44; 21.19; A 15.24; **uestra** Mt 5.16; 24.31; L 16.15; Mk 11.25,26; A 14.17; **uestris** Mt 21.42; J 13.21; L 17.7; A 3.22; 7.37; 13.41; **uestris** Mt 10.9; L 4.21; **uestris** Mt 9.4; 18.35; J 8.24*bis;* L 3.14; 5.22; 21.14; Mk 2.8; 8.17; **uestris** (*inc.*) (Mt 10.20); **ues** L 13.35.

uestia, *v.* **bestia.**

uestigium **uestigio** (*ab.*) A 10.33.

uestimentum **uestimenti** Mt 9.20,21; 14.36; Mk 6.56; **uestimento** Mk 2.21; **uestimentum** Mt ⟦3.4⟧; 5.40; ⟦J 19.5⟧; Mk 5.27, 28; A 12.8; **uestimento** Mt 9.16*bis;* L 12.23; Mk 10.50; **uestimenta** (*n.*) Mt 17.2; L 9.29; Mk 9.3; **uestimenta** (*ac.*) Mt 21.7,8; 26.65; 27.31,35; J 13.4,12; ⟦19.23,24⟧; L 19.36; 23.34; Mk 5.30; 11.7,8; 14.63; 15.24; A 7.58; 14.14; 18.6; **uestimentis** L 7.25*bis;* Mk 15.20; A 16.22.

uestio **uestit** L 12.28; **uestierunt** Mt 27.31; **uestientes** (*m.n.*) Mt 27.28; **uestitus** Mt 28.3; Mk 1.6; **uestitum** (*m.*) L 7.25; 8.35; Mk 5.15.

uestis **uestem** Mt 22.11,12; ⟦J 19.24⟧; **ueste** ⟦J 19.2⟧; A 1.10; 10.30.

ueteresco **ueterescentes** (*m.ac.*) L 12.33.

uethania, uethleem, *v.* **bethania, bethleem.**

ueto **uetuit** A 16.7; **uetastis** L 11.52; **uetatus est** A 17.15; **uetueris** L 6.29; **uetare** L 18.16; **uetantem** (*m.*) L 23.2.

uetus **ueteri** (*f.d.*) L 5.36; **ueteri** (*neu.*) Mk 2.21; **ueterem** (*f.*) L 5.36; **ueteri** (*neu.*) Mt 9.16; Mk 2.21; **ueteres** (*m.ac.*) Mt 9.17; L 5.37*bis;* Mk 2.22; **ueteria** Mt 13.52.

uexo **uexas** Mk 5.35; **uexabatur** Mt 14.24; Mk 5.18; **uexauabatur** Mk 5.15; **uexauatur**

uigilo **uigilabat** L 21.38; **uigilaret** Mt 24.43; Mk 13.34; **uigilate** Mt 24.42; 25.13; 26.38,41; L 22.36; Mk 13.33,35,37; 14.34,38; A 20.31; **uigilare** Mt 26.40; Mk 14.37; **uigilantes** (*m.ac.*) L 12.37.

uiginti J 6.19; L 14.31; 23.53; A 1.15.

uilicatio **uilicationis** L 16.2; **uilicationem** L 16.3; **uilicatione** L 16.4.

uilico **uilicare** L 16.2.

uilicus L 12.42; L 16.3; **uilicum** L 16.8.

uilla **uillam** [[Mk 16.12]]; **uilla** L 15.25; Mk 15.21; **uillas** L 9.12; Mk 6.36,56.

uincio **uinctus** Mk 15.7; **uinctum** (*m.*) Mt 27.15,16; Mk 15.1; **uincti** A 16.25; **uinctis** (*m.ab.*) Mk 15.6.

uinco **uici** J 16.33.

uincticta, *v.* **uindicta.**

uinculum Mk 7.35; **uinculo** (*ab.*) L 13.16; **uincula** (*n.*) A 16.26; 20.23; **uincula** (*ac.*) L 8.29.

uindemio **uindemiant** L 6.44.

uindico **uindicauit** A 7.24.

uindicta **uincticta**e (*g.*) L 21.22; **uindictam** L 18.7,8; A 7.24.

uinea **uineae** (*g.*) Mt 20.8; 21.40; L 13.6; 20.10,13,15; 22.18; Mk 12.9; **uineam** Mt 20.1,2,4,7; 21.28,29,33,39,41; L 20.9,15,16; Mk 12.1,8,9; **uinea** L 13.6; Mk 12.2.

uini, *v.* **bini.**

uinipotator Mt 11.19; L 7.34.

uinum Mt 9.17*bis;* L 5.37; Mk 2.22*bis;* **uinum** Mt 9.17*bis;* 27.34; J 4.46; L 1.15; 5.37,38; 10.34; Mk 2.22; **uino** Mk 15.23.

uiolentus A 2.2.

uiolo **uiolant** Mt 12.5.

uipera **uiperarum** Mt [[3.7]]; 12.34; 23.33; L 3.7.

uir Mt 1.19; J 4.18; L 5.8,12; 8.27,38,41; 9.38; 19.2; 23.50; 24.19; A 3.2; 5.1; [8.9]; 10.22,30; 11.24; 14.8; 16.9; 18.24; 22.12; **uiri** Mt 19.10; A 11.12; **uiro** L 1.27; Mk 10.2; A 10.28; **uirum** J 4.16,17*bis;* L 1.34; Mk 6.20; A 2.22; 3.14; 5.9,10; 6.5; 13.6,21,22; 18.27; 21.11; **uiro** L 2.36; Mk 10.12; A 13.7; 17.31; **uiri** Mt 12.41; 14.21,35; 15.38; J 6.10; L 5.18; 7.20; 9.14,30; 17.12; 22.63; 24.4; A 1.10; 2.5; 5.25; 8.2,(9),12; 10.17,19; 11.11,20; 16.39; 17.12,34; 19.7; 20.30; 21.23; **uirorum** Mk 6.44; A (1.21); 4.4; 5.14,36; 21.38; **uiros** J 4.18; L 9.32; A 6.3,11; 8.3; 10.5,21; 11.3; 15.22*bis*,25; 17.5; 19.37; 21.26; **uiris** L 11.31; [A 1.21]; **uiri** A 1.11,16; 2.14,22,29,37; 3.12, 17; 5.35; 7.2,26; 13.15,16,26,38; 14.15; 15.7, 13; 17.22; 18.14; 19.25,35; 21.28; 22.1.

uirga **uirgam** Mt 10.10; L 9.3; Mk 6.8; **uirgis** (*ab.*) A 16.22.

uirginitas **uirginitate** L 2.36.

uirgo Mt 1.16,23; **uirginis** L 1.27; **uirginem** L 1.27; **uirgines** (*n.*) Mt 25.7,11; **uirginibus** (*d.*) Mt 25.1.

uiridis **uiridem** (*m.*) Mk 6.39.

uirrus **uirri** A 20.4.

uirtus L 1.35; 8.44; A 8.10; **uirtutis** Mt 26.64; L 22.59; Mk 14.62; **uirtutem** Mt 22.29; 25.15; L 1.51; L 8.46; 9.1; 10.19; 24.49; Mk 5.30; 6.5; 9.1; 12.24; A 1.8; 4.24; **uiruirtutem** Mk 9.39; **uirtute** Mt 24.30; L 1.17; 4.14,36; 10.27; 21.27; Mk 12.30,33; 13.26; A 3.12; 4.7,33; 6.8; 10.38; **uirtutes** (*n.*) Mt 11.20,21, 23; 13.54; 14.2; 24.29; L 10.13; 21.26; Mk 6.2,14; 13.25; **uirtutes** (*ac.*) Mt 13.58; A 8.13; 19.11; **uirtutibus** A 2.22; **uir** L 6.19.

uis **uim** A 5.26; 21.35.

uiscus **uiscera** (*n.*) A 1.18; **uiscera** (*ac.*) L 1.78.

uisio A 10.17; **uisionem** L 1.22; 24.23; **uisione** A 10.19; **uisiones** (*ac.*) A 2.17.

uisitatio **uisitationis** L 19.44.

uisito **uisitauit** L 1.68,78; 7.16; **uisitastis** Mt 25.36,43; **uisitemus** A 15.36; **uisitare** A 7.23.

uisum (*n.*) A 16.9; **uisum** (*ac.*) A 16.10; 18.9.

uisus **uisum** Mt 1.20; 17.9; 27.19; J 9.18; L 4.18; A 7.31; 10.8; 11.5; 12.9; **uisu** Mt 2.13.

uita J 6.63; 11.25; 12.50; 14.6; 17.3; L 12.15; **uitae** (*g.*) J 5.29; 6.35,48,56,58; 8.12; A 2.28; 3.15; 5.20; **uitam** Mt 18.8,9; 19.16,17, 29; 25.46; J 3.16,36*bis;* 4.14,36; 5.24*bis*,26*bis*, 39,40; 6.27,33,40,47,53,54,56; 10.10,28; 12.25; 17.2; 20.31; L 10.25; 18.18,30; Mk 9.43,45; 10.17,30; A 11.18; 13.46,48; 17.25; **uita** J 6.51; L 16.25.

uitis **uites** (*n.s.*) J 15.1; **uitis** J 15.5; **uitis** (*g.*) Mt 26.29; Mk 14.25; **uite** J 15.4.

uitulus **uitulum** L 15.23,27,30; A 7.41.

uitupero **uituperauerunt** Mk 7.2.

uiuifico **uiuificat** J 5.21*bis;* 6.63; **uiuificauit** (*fut.*) L 17.33; **biuicare** L 17.33.

uiuo J 6.57; 14.19; **uibit** J 4.51; **uiuit** J 4.50,53; 11.26; **uiuimus** A 17.28; **uiues** L 10.28; **uiuet** Mt 4.4; 9.18; J 6.51,57,58; 11.25; L 4.4; **uiuetis** J 14.19; **uiuent** J 5.25; L 20.38; **uixit** L 2.36; **uibat** Mk 5.23; **uiueret** [[Mk

2.17; uocari Mt 23.7,8; L 1.62; 15.19,21; 19.15; Mk 10.49; uocans (*m.*) Mt 2.7; L 16.2; 19.13; Mk 15.44; uocantes (*m.n.*) Mk 3.31; A 4.18; uocati (*n.*) Mt 20.16; 22.14; uocatis (*m.ab.*) A 10.7.

uolatilis uolatilia (*n.*) L 8.5; 9.58; 13.19; A 10.12; uolatilia (*ac.*) L 12.24; A 11.6; uolatilibus (*neu.*) L 12.24.

uolo Mt 9.13; 12.7; 20.14,15; 26.39; J 17.24; 21.22,23; L 4.6; 5.13; 12.49; Mk 1.41; 14.36; A 21.13; bis (Mt 17.4); L 22.9; Mk 14.36; uis Mt 13.28; 15.28; [17.4]; 19.17,21; 20.21; 26.17; J 5.6; 21.18; L 5.12; 9.33,54; 18.41; 22.42; Mk 6.22; 9.5; 10.51; 14.12; A 7.28; uult Mt 16.24; 27.43; J 5.21; L 1.62; 9.23; Mk 8.34; A 2.12; uolumus Mt 12.38; J 12.21; Mk 10.35; A 10.33; 17.20; uultis Mt 11.14; 20.32; 26.15; 27.17,21; J 5.40; 6.67; 8.44; 9.27*bis;* 10.38; 15.7; [[18.39]]; L 6.31; Mk 15.9,12; A 5.28; 10.21; 15.29; uolunt L 16.26; 20.46; Mk 12.38; A 15.20; uolebas J 21.18; bolebat A 10.10; uolebat J 7.1; Mk 6.48; 9.30; A 15.37; 19.33; uolebant Mt 27.15; J 6.11,21; 7.44; 16.19; A 16.7; uolui Mt 23.37; L 13.34; uoluit Mt 1.19; 18.23; Mk 3.13; 7.24; A (3.13); 11.2; 13.7; 16.3; 20.3; uoluistis J 5.35; uoluerunt Mt 17.12; L 10.24; Mk 9.13; A 19.14; uolueris Mk 1.40; uoluerit Mt 5.40; 11.27; 16.25; 20.26,27; J 7.17; L 9.24; 10.22; 17.33; Mk 8.35; 10.43,44; uolueritis Mk 14.7; uellit A 17.18; uellint A 17.20; uellet L 15.26; uolens (*m.*) Mt 14.5; L 10.29; 14.28; 23.8,20; A 12.4; uolenti (*m.*) Mt 5.42; A 4.31; uolente (*m.*) A 18.21; 19.1,30; 20.4; bolentes A 14.13.

uolucris uolucres (*m.n.*) Mt 13.4; uolucres (*f.n.*) Mk 4.4.

uoluntas Mt 11.26; 18.14; 26.42; J 6.39,40; L 11.2; 22.42; A 4.28; 21.14; uoluntati L 23.25; uoluntatem Mt 12.50; 21.31; J 5.30 *bis;* 6.38*bis;* 7.17; 9.31; L 12.47*bis;* Mk 3.35; A 22.14; uoluntate A 13.36; uoluntates (*ac.*) A 13.22.

uoluo uoluens (*m.*) L 4.20.

uoluptas uolumptatem A 20.27; uoluptatem J 4.34.

uoluto uolutabatur Mk 9.20.

uonus, *s.v.* bonus.

uorax Mt 11.19.

uotum uotum (*ac.*) A 21.23.

uouis, *s.v.* tu.

uox Mt 2.18; 3.[[3]],17; 17.5; J 12.28,30; L 1.44; 3.4; 9.35,36; Mk 1.3,11; 9.7; A 2.6; 7.33; 10.13,15; 11.9; 19.34; uocis J 10.3,16,27; uocem Mt 12.19; J 3.29; 5.25,28,37; 10.4,5; [[18.37]]; L 3.22; 11.27; A 2.14; 4.24; 11.7; 12.14; 14.11; 22.14; uoce Mt 24.31; 27.46,50; J 11.43; L 1.42; 4.33; 8.28; 17.13,15; 23.46; Mk 1.26; 5.7; 15.34,37; A 7.57,60; 8.7; 14.10; 16.28; uoces (*n.*) L 23.23; A 12.22; uocibus (*ab.*) L 23.23.

upra, *s.v.* supra.

urbs urbem A 18.2.

urguo urguor L 12.50.

urnatis, *s.v.* orno.

usquae dum (*c.coni.*) L 21.32; usque dum J 21.22,23; L 15.4; 20.43; 24.49.

usque usquae A 13.31; usque Mt 11.12; 18.21; 24.21; 27.51; J 5.17; 16.24; L 2.15; 9.27; 12.50; 23.5; Mk 13.19; 15.38; usque (*c.ac.*) Mt 27.45; L 22.51; A 11.19,22; usque (*c.ab.*) L 23.44; A 17.15; 19.9; usquae ad (*c.ab.*) L11.51; usque ad Mk 14.34; usquae ad (*c.ac.*) Mt 11.23; 23.35; L 11.50; A 13.6,47; 20.4,11; usque ad Mt 1.17*bis;* 2.15; 11.13,23; 13.30; 20.8; 24.31; 26.29,38,58; 27.64; L 4.13, 29,42; 7.18; 10.15*bis;* 16.16; Mk 2.2; 13.27; A 1.5,8; 3.21; 7.45; 8.10; 11.5; 13.11,20; usque ad (*c.indec.*) Mt 1.17; 22.26; usquae in (*c.ac.*) (A 1.22); usque in Mt 11.23; 24.27,38; 27.8; 28.15,20; L 1.20,80; 17.27; Mk 14.25,54; 15.33; A 1.2,[22]; 2.29; 10.30; usque in (*c.ab.*) A 20.7.

usque quo (*c.ind.*) J 9.18; 10.24; 13.38; L 9.41; 13.8,21; 22.34; usque quo (*c.coni.*) L 12.59; 15.8; 17.8; 21.24; 22.16,18.

ustio ustione L 16.24.

usura usura (*ab.*) Mt 25.27; L 19.23.

ut (*c.ind.*) J 3.16; 6.61; 11.29,32,33; 14.3; 16.2; [[18.6,39; 19.33]]; L 1.23,41,44; 2.15; 3.23; 17.7; Mk 4.36; 6.49; 7.25; A 1.10; 5.24; 7.17; 10.7; 14.5; 16.15; 17.13; 18.5; 20.14; 22.11; ut (*c.coni.*) Mt 1.22; 2.8,13,15,[[23]]; 3.13; 4.1,3,14; 5.13,15,16,29,45; 6.1,2,4,5; 8.28,34; 9.6,38; 10.1,25; 12.10,14,16,17,22; 13.2,13,32,35,54; 14.15,29,36; 15.31,33; 16.20; 17.27; 18.6,13,14,16; 19.13,16; 20.21,31,32, 33; 21.1,4,32; 22.24; 23.5,15,26,35; 24.20,24; 26.2,4,5,41,56,63; 27.14,20,26,31,32; 28.10; J 3.16,17*bis*,20,21,36; 4.8,15,34,36,40,47; 5.7, 20,23,34,36,40; 6.5,7,12,15,28,29,30,38,39*bis*, 40,50; 7.3,23,32; 8.4,56,59; 9.2,3,22,36,39; 10.10*bis*,17,31,38; 11.4,11,15,16,19,31,37,42, 44,50,52,53,55,57*bis;* 12.7,9,10,20,23,35,36,40, 42,46,47*bis;* 13.1,2,15,18,19,29,34*bis;* 14.13, 16,29,31; 15.2,8,11,12,13,16*bis*,25; 16.2,4,7, 24,30,32,33; 17.1,2,3,4,11,12,13,15*bis*,19,21 *ter*,22,23*bis*,24*bis*,26; [[18.9,28,32,36,37; 19.4, 16,24,28,31*bis*,35,36,38]]; 20.31*bis;* L 1.43,57,